Contemporary Artificial Intelligence

Contemporary Artificial Intelligence

Edited by **Mitch Hoppe**

LANRYE
INTERNATIONAL

New Jersey

Published by Clanrye International,
55 Van Reypen Street,
Jersey City, NJ 07306, USA
www.clanryeinternational.com

Contemporary Artificial Intelligence
Edited by Mitch Hoppe

International Standard Book Number: 978-1-63240-549-4 (Hardback)

Contents

Preface

Artificial intelligence is the field of computer science that is concerned with creation and design of software and machines exhibiting intelligence as in case of human beings. Intelligence means that the machines must be capable of adapting to changing environments and changing goals. It is an interdisciplinary field that includes mathematics, computer science, philosophy, neuroscience, linguistics, and psychology. There are certain varieties of tools that are employed in this field for example methods based on economics and probability, logic, mathematical optimization and many others. This book brings forth some of the most innovative concepts and elucidates the unexplored aspects related to this area of study. As this field is emerging at a fast pace, this book will help the readers to better understand the concepts of artificial intelligence. It is a compilation of chapters that discuss the most vital concepts and emerging trends in this discipline. It is a ripe text for computer engineers, software developers, researchers and students associated with artificial intelligence.

After months of intensive research and writing, this book is the end result of all who devoted their time and efforts in the initiation and progress of this book. It will surely be a source of reference in enhancing the required knowledge of the new developments in the area. During the course of developing this book, certain measures such as accuracy, authenticity and research focused analytical studies were given preference in order to produce a comprehensive book in the area of study.

This book would not have been possible without the efforts of the authors and the publisher. I extend my sincere thanks to them. Secondly, I express my gratitude to my family and well-wishers. And most importantly, I thank my students for constantly expressing their willingness and curiosity in enhancing their knowledge in the field, which encourages me to take up further research projects for the advancement of the area.

Editor

The Expected Value of a Fuzzy Number

Mohamed Shenify, Fokrul Alom Mazarbhuiya

College of Computer Science, Albaha University, Albaha, Saudi Arabia
Email: mshenify@yahoo.com, fokrul_2005@yahoo.com

Academic Editor: Zhongzhi Shi, Institute of Computing Technology, CAS, China

Abstract

Conjunction of two probability laws can give rise to a possibility law. Using two probability densities over two disjoint ranges, we can define the fuzzy mean of a fuzzy variable with the help of means two random variables in two disjoint spaces.

Keywords

Probability Density Function, Probability Distribution, Fuzzy Measure, Fuzzy Expected Value, Fuzzy Mean, Fuzzy Membership Function, Dubois-Prade Reference Functions

1. Introduction

Zadeh [1] introduced the concept of fuzziness into the realm of mathematics. Accordingly, various authors have studied the mathematics related to the fuzzy measure and the associated fuzzy expected value [2]-[7] studied the fuzzy expected value and its associated results by defining the fuzzy expected value in terms of fuzzy measure. In their definition they tried to find the fuzzy expected value of a possibility distribution. In [8], authors developed a new method of analysis of possibilistic portfolio that associates a probabilistic portfolio. Similar works were done in associating possibility and probability [9] [10]. In [11] [12], the author tries to establish a link between possibility law and probability law using a concept discussed in the paper called set superimposition [13]. In [14], the author tries to establish a link between and randomness.

In this article, using the superimposition of sets, we have attempted to define the expected value of a fuzzy variable in term of expected values of two random variables in two disjoint spaces. It can be seen that the expected value of a fuzzy number is again a fuzzy set.

2. Definitions and Notations

Let X be a continuos random variable in the interval $[a,b]$ with probability density function $f(x)$ and probability distribution function $F(x)$. Then

$$\text{Prob}(a \le X \le b) = \int_a^b f(y)\,dy = F(b) - F(a)$$

Further, the expected value of X would be

$$E(X) = \int_{-\infty}^{\infty} x\,dF(x) \tag{1}$$

where the integral is absolutely convergent.

Let E be a set and $x \in X$ then we can define a fuzzy subset A of E as

$$A = \{x, \chi_A(x); x \in E\}$$

where $\chi_A(x) \in [0,1]$ is the fuzzy membership function of the fuzzy set A for an ordinary set, $\chi_A(x) = 0$ or 1. A fuzzy set A is called normal if $\chi_A(x) = 1$ for at least one $x \in E$.

A α-cut A_α for a fuzzy set A is an ordinary set of elements such that $\chi_A(x) \ge \alpha$ for $0 \le \alpha \le 1$, i.e. $A_\alpha = \{x \in E, \chi_A(x) \ge \alpha\}$.

The membership function of a fuzzy set is known as a possibility distribution [15]. We usually denote a fuzzy number by a triad $[a,b,c]$ such that $\chi_A(a) = 0 = \chi_A(c)$ and $\chi_A(b) = 1$. $\chi_A(x)$, for $x \in [a,b]$, is the left reference function and for $x \in [b,c]$ is the right reference function. The left reference function is right continuous, monotone and non-decreasing, while the right reference function is left continuous, monotone and non-increasing. The above definition of a fuzzy number is known as an L-R fuzzy number.

Kandel's Definition of a Fuzzy Measure

Kandel [5] [16] has defined a fuzzy measure as follows: Let B be a Borel field (σ-algebra) of subset of the real line Ω. A set function $\mu(.)$ defined on B is called fuzzy measure if it has the following properties:

(1) $\mu(\phi) = 0$ (ϕ is the empty set);

(2) $\mu(\Omega) = 1$;

(3) If $A, B \in B$ with $A \subset B$, then $\mu(A) \le \mu(B)$;

(4) If $\{A_i; 1 \le i \le \infty\}$ is a monotonic sequence, then $\underset{i \to \infty}{\text{Lim}}[\mu(A_i)] = \mu\left[\underset{i \to \infty}{\text{Lim}}(A_i)\right]$ Clearly, $\phi, \Omega \in B$. Also, if $A_i \in B$, then $\underset{i \to \infty}{\text{Lim}}(A_i) \in B$. (Ω, B, μ) is called a fuzzy measure space. $\mu(.)$ is the fuzzy measure of (Ω, B).

Let $\chi_A : \Omega \to [0,1]$ and $A_\alpha = \{x; \chi_A(x) \ge \alpha\}$. The function χ_A is called a B-measurable function, if $A_\alpha \in B$ for all $\alpha \in [0,1]$. In their notations, fuzzy expected value is defined as follows: Let χ_A be a B-measurable function such that $\chi_A \in [0,1]$. The fuzzy expected value (FEV) of χ_A over a set A with respect to the measure $\mu(.)$ is defined as $\underset{\alpha \in [0,1]}{\text{Sup}}\{\min[\alpha.\mu(A_\alpha)]\}$.

Now $\mu\{x; \chi_A(x.) \ge \alpha\} = f_A(\alpha)$ is a function of the threshold α. The calculation of FEV (χ_A) then consists of finding the intersection of the curves of $\alpha = f_A(\alpha)$. The intersection of the curves will be at a value $\alpha = H$ so that FEV $(\chi_A) = H \in [0,1]$ as in the diagram.

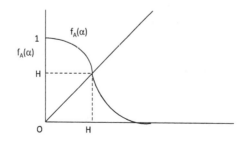

3. Definition of an Expected Value of Fuzzy Number

Kandel's definition of a fuzzy expected value is based on the definition of the fuzzy measure. However, the fuzzy measure being non-additive is not really a measure.

Baruah [13] has shown that instead of expressing a fuzzy measure in $[a,b,c]$, if we express the possibility distribution first as a probability distribution function in $[a,b]$ and then as a complementary probability distribution function in $[b,c]$, the mathematics can be seen to be governed by the product measure on $[a,b]$ and $[b,c]$. As such, the question of non-additivity of the fuzzy measure does not come into picture.

We propose to define the fuzzy expected value or the possibilistic mean based on the idea that two probability measures can give rise to a possibility distribution. In other words, the concerned possibilistic measure need not be fuzzy at all.

Accordingly, we propose to define a possibilistic mean as follows: Let X be a fuzzy variable in the fuzzy set $A = [a,b,c]$. We divide A into two intervals $A_1 = [a,b]$ and $A_2 = [b,c]$ such that $A_1 \cup A_2 = A$ and $A_1 \cap A_2 = \phi$. Let X be a random variable on A_1. Then from (1), the mean of X would be

$$E_1(X) = \int_a^b xf(x)\,dx \tag{2}$$

where $f(x)$ is the concerned probability density function defined on $[a,b]$. Let the mean of the random variable an A_2 be

$$E_2(X) = \int_b^c xg(x)\,dx \tag{3}$$

where $g(x)$ is the concerned probability density function defined on $[b,c]$.

Thus, from (2) and (3), we get the possibilistic mean of $X \in [a,b,c]$ as

$$M = \left[\int_a^b xf(x)\,dx, b, \int_b^c xg(x)\,dx \right] = \{x, \chi_M(x) \in [r,1], x \in E\} \tag{4}$$

where $r = \min\left\{ \chi_M\left(\int_a^b xf(x)\,dx\right), \chi_M\left(\int_b^c xg(x)\,dx\right) \right\}$.

Equation (4) is our required result that shows that poissibilistic mean of a fuzzy variable is again a fuzzy set.

To illustrate the result (4), we take $A = [a,b,c]$, a triangular number such that $\chi_A(a) = 0 = \chi_A(c)$ and $\chi_A(b) = 1$. The probability distribution function is given by

$$F(x) = \begin{bmatrix} 0 & x \leq a \\ \dfrac{(x-a)}{(b-a)} & a \prec x \prec b \\ 1 & x \geq b \end{bmatrix} \tag{5}$$

where

$$f(x) = \frac{1}{(b-a)} \tag{6}$$

is the probability density function in $a \leq x \leq b$.

The complementary probability distribution or the survival function is given by

$$G(x) = \begin{bmatrix} 1 & x \leq b \\ 1 - \dfrac{(x-b)}{(c-b)} & b < x < c \\ 0 & x \geq c \end{bmatrix} \tag{7}$$

where $F(x) = 1 - G(x)$ and the probability density function in $b \leq x \leq c$ is

$$g(x) = \frac{1}{(c-b)} \tag{8}$$

Therefore, the expected value of a uniform random variable X on $[a,b]$ is

$$E_1(x) = \frac{(a+b)}{2} \tag{9}$$

and similarly, the expected value of another uniform random variable X on $[b,c]$ is

$$E_2(x) = \frac{(b+c)}{2} \tag{10}$$

Equations (9) and (10) together give the expected value of a triangular fuzzy variable in $[a,b,c]$ as

$$M' = \left[\frac{(a+b)}{2}, b, \frac{(b+c)}{2} \right] = \left\{ x, \chi_{M'}(x) \in [p.1], x \in E \right\} \tag{11}$$

where $p = \min \left\{ \chi_{M'}\left(\frac{(a+b)}{2} \right), \chi_{M'}\left(\frac{(b+c)}{2} \right) \right\} = 1/2$.

Equations (4) and (11) show that the expected value of a fuzzy number is again a fuzzy set.

4. Conclusion

The very definition of a fuzzy expected value as given by Kandel is based on the understanding that the so called fuzzy measure is not really a measure in the strict sense. The possibility distribution function is viewed as two reference functions. Using left reference function as probability distribution function and right reference function as survival function, in this article we redefine the expected value of a fuzzy number which is again a fuzzy set.

References

[1]   Zadeh, L.A. (1965) Fuzzy Sets as Basis of Theory of Possibility. *Fuzzy Sets and Systems*, **1**, 3-28. http://dx.doi.org/10.1016/0165-0114(78)90029-5

[2]   Aczel, M.J. and Ptanzagl, J. (1966) Remarks on the Measurement of Subjective Probability and Information. *Metrica*, **5**, 91-105.

[3]   Asai, K., Tanaka, K. and Okuda, T. (1977) On the Discrimination of Fuzzy States in Probability Space. *Kybernetes*, **6**, 185-192. http://dx.doi.org/10.1108/eb005451

[4]   Baldwin, J.F. and Pilsworth, B.W. (1979) Fuzzy Truth Definition of Possibility Measure for Decision Classification. *International Journal of Man-Machine Studies*, **11**, 447-463.

[5]   Kandel, A. (1979) On Fuzzy Statistics. In: Gupta, M.M., Ragade, R.K. and Yager, R.R., Eds., *Advances in Fuzzy Set Theory and Application*, North Holland, Amsterdam.

[6]   Kandel, A. and Byatt, W.J. (1978) Fuzzy Sets, Fuzzy Algebra and Fuzzy Statistics. *Proceedings of the IEEE* 66, USA, January 1978, 1619-1639.

[7]   Teran, P. (2014) Law of Large Numbers for Possibilistic Mean Value. *Fuzzy Sets and Systems*, **245**, 116-124. http://dx.doi.org/10.1016/j.fss.2013.10.011

[8]   Georgescu, I. and Kinnunen, J. (2011) Credibility Measures in Portfolio Analysis: From Possibilistic to Probabilistic Models. *Journal of Applied Operational Research*, **3**, 91-102.

[9]   Sam, P. and Chakraborty, S. (2013) The Possibilistic Safety Assessment of Hybrid Uncertain Systems. *International Journal of Reliability, Quality and Safety Engineering*, **20**, 191-197.

[10]   Zaman, K., Rangavajhala, S., Mc Donald, M. and Mahadevan, S. (2011) A Probabilistic Approach for Representation of Interval Uncertainty. *Reliability Engineering and System Safety*, **96**, 117-130. http://dx.doi.org/10.1016/j.ress.2010.07.012

[11]   Baruah, H.K. (2010) The Randomness-Fuzziness Consistency Principle. *International Journal of Energy, Information and Communications*, **1**, 37-48.

[12]   Baruah, H.K. (2012) An Introduction to the Theory of Imprecise Sets: The Mathematics of Partial Presence. *Journal of*

Mathematical and Computational Science, **2**, 110-124.

[13] Baruah, H.K. (1999) Set Superimposition and Its Application to the Theory of Fuzzy Sets. *Journal of Assam Science Society*, **40**, 25-31.

[14] Mazarbhuiya, F.A. (2014) Finding a Link between Randomness and Fuzziness. *Applied Mathematics*, **5**, 1369-1374.

[15] Prade, H. (1983) Fuzzy Programming Why and How? Some Hints and Examples. In: Wang, P.P., Ed., *Advances in Fuzzy Sets, Possibility Theory and Applications*, Plenum Press, New York, 237-251.
http://dx.doi.org/10.1007/978-1-4613-3754-6_16

[16] Kandel, A. (1982) Fuzzy Techniques in Pattern Recognition. Wiley Interscience Publication, New York.

2

Discovering Monthly Fuzzy Patterns

M. Shenify, F. A. Mazarbhuiya

College of Computer Science and IT, Albaha University, Albaha, Saudi Arabia
Email: mshenify@yahoo.com, fokrul_2005@yahoo.com

Academic Editor: Zhongzhi Shi, Institute of Computing Technology, CAS, China

Abstract

Discovering patterns that are fuzzy in nature from temporal datasets is an interesting data mining problems. One of such patterns is monthly fuzzy pattern where the patterns exist in a certain fuzzy time interval of every month. It involves finding frequent sets and then association rules that holds in certain fuzzy time intervals, viz. beginning of every months or middle of every months, etc. In most of the earlier works, the fuzziness was user-specified. However, in some applications, users may not have enough prior knowledge about the datasets under consideration and may miss some fuzziness associated with the problem. It may be the case that the user is unable to specify the same due to limitation of natural language. In this article, we propose a method of finding patterns that holds in certain fuzzy time intervals of every month where fuzziness is generated by the method itself. The efficacy of the method is demonstrated with experimental results.

Keywords

Frequent Item Sets, Superimposition of Time Intervals, Fuzzy Time Intervals, Right Reference Functions, Left Reference Functions, Membership Functions

1. Introduction

Analysis of transactional data has been considered as an important data mining problem. Market basket data is an example of such transactional data. In a market-basket data set, each transaction is a collection of items bought by a customer at one time. The concept proposed in [1] is to find the co-occurrence of items in transactions, given minimum support and minimum confidence thresholds. Temporal Association rule mining is an important extension of above-mentioned problem. When an item from super-market is bought by a customer, this is called transaction and its time is automatically recorded. Ale *et al.* [2] have proposed a method of extracting association rules that hold within the life-span of the corresponding item set.

Mahanta *et al.* [3] have introduced concept of locally frequent item sets as item sets that are frequent in certain time intervals and may or may not be frequent throughout the life-span of the item set. An efficient algorithm is developed by them which is used find such item sets along with a list of sequences of time intervals. Considering the time-stamp as calendar dates, a method is discussed in [4] which can extract yearly, monthly and daily periodic or partially periodic patterns. If the periods are kept in a compact manner using the method discussed in [4], it turns out to be a fuzzy time interval. In this paper, we discuss such patterns and device algorithms for extracting such patterns. Although our algorithm works for extracting monthly fuzzy patterns, it can be modified for daily fuzzy periodic patterns. The paper is organized as follows. In Section 2, we discuss related works. In Section 3, we discuss terms, definitions and notations used in the algorithm. In Section 4, the proposed algorithm is discussed. In Section 5, we discuss about results and analysis. Finally a summary and lines for future works are discussed in Section 6.

2. Related Works

Agrawal *et al.* [1] first formulated association rules mining problems. One important extension of this problem is Temporal Data Mining [5] by taking into account the time aspect, more interesting patterns that are time dependent can be extracted. The problems associated are to find valid time periods during which association rules hold and the discovery of possible periodicities that association rules have. In [2], an algorithm for finding temporal rules is described. There each rule has associated with it a time frame. In [3], the works done in [2] has been extended by considering time gap between two consecutive transactions containing an item set into account.

Considering the periodic nature of patterns, Ozden *et al.* [6] proposed a method, which is able to find patterns having periodic nature where the period has to be specified by the user. In [7], Li *et al.* discuss about a method of extracting temporal association rules with respect to fuzzy match, *i.e.* association rule holding during "enough" number of intervals given by the corresponding calendar pattern. Similar works were done in [8] incorporating multiple granularities of time intervals (e.g. first working day of every month) from which both cyclic and user defined calendar patterns can be achieved.

Mining fuzzy patterns from datasets have been studied by different authors. In [9], the authors present an algorithm for mining fuzzy temporal patterns from a given process instance. Similar work is done in [10]. In [11] method of extracting fuzzy periodic association rules is discussed.

3. Terms, Definitions and Notations Used

Let us review some definitions and notations used in this paper.

A fuzzy number is a convex normalized fuzzy set A defined on the real line R such that
1) there exists an $x_0 \in R$ such that $A(x_0) = 1$, and
2) $A(x)$ is piecewise continuous.

Thus a fuzzy number can be thought of as containing the real numbers within some interval to varying degrees. Fuzzy intervals are special fuzzy numbers satisfying the followings:
1) There exists an interval $[a,b] \subset R$ such that $A(x_0) = 1$ for all $x_0 \in [a,b]$, and
2) $A(x)$ is piecewise continuous.

A fuzzy interval can be thought of as a fuzzy number with a flat region. A fuzzy interval A is denoted by $A = [a,b,c,d]$ with $a < b < c < d$ where $A(a) = A(d) = 0$ and $A(x) = 1$ for all $x \in [b,c]$. $A(x)$ for all $x \in [a,b]$ is known as left reference function and $A(x)$ for $x \in [c,d]$ is known as the right reference function. The left reference function is non-decreasing and the right reference function is non-increasing [12].

The support of a fuzzy set A within a universal set E is the crisp set that contains all the elements of E that have non-zero membership grades in A and is denoted by $S(A)$. Thus

$$S(A) = \{x \in E; A(x) > 0\}$$

The core of a fuzzy set A within a universal set E is the crisp set that contains all the elements of E having membership grades 1 in A.

Set Superimposition

When we overwrite, the overwritten portion looks darker for obvious reason. The set operation union does not explain this phenomenon. After all

$$A \cup B = (A - B) \cup (A \cap B) \cup (B - A)$$

and in $(A \cap B)$ the elements are represented once only.

In [13] an operation called superimposition denoted by (S) was proposed. If A is superimposed over B or B is superimposed over A, we have

$$A(S)B = (A - B)(+)(A \cap B)^{(2)}(+)(B - A) \tag{1}$$

where $(A \cap B)^{(2)}$ are the elements of $(A \cap B)$ represented twice, and $(+)$ represents union of disjoint sets.

To explain this, an example has been taken.

If $A = [a_1, b_1]$ and $B = [a_2, b_2]$ are two real intervals such that $A \cap B \neq \varnothing$, we would get a superimposed portion. It can be seen from (1)

$$[a_1, b_1](S)[a_2, b_2] = \left[a_{(1)}, a_{(2)}\right)(+)\left[a_{(2)}, b_{(1)}\right]^{(2)}(+)\left(b_{(1)}, b_{(2)}\right] \tag{2}$$

where
$$a_{(1)} = \min(a_1, a_2) \quad a_{(2)} = \max(a_1, a_2)$$
$$b_{(1)} = \min(b_1, b_2) \quad \text{and} \quad b_{(2)} = \max(b_1, b_2).$$

(2) explains why if two line segments are superimposed, the common portion looks doubly dark [5]. The identity (2) is called fundamental identity *of* superimposition of intervals.

Let now, $[a_1, b_1]^{(1/2)}$ and $[a_2, b_2]^{(1/2)}$ be two fuzzy sets with constant membership value $\frac{1}{2}$ everywhere (*i.e.* equi-fuzzy intervals with membership value $\frac{1}{2}$). If $[a_1, b_1] \cap [a_2, b_2] \neq \varnothing$ then applying (2) on the two equi-fuzzy intervals we can write

$$[a_1, b_1]^{(1/2)}(S)[a_2, b_2]^{(1/2)} = \left[a_{(1)}, a_{(2)}\right)^{(1/2)}(+)\left[a_{(2)}, b_{(1)}\right]^{(1)}(+)\left(b_{(1)}, b_{(2)}\right]^{(1/2)} \tag{3}$$

To explain this we take the fuzzy intervals $[1, 5]^{(1/2)}$ and $[3, 7]^{(1/2)}$ with constant membership value $(1/2)$ given in **Figure 1** and **Figure 2**. Here $[1, 5] \cap [3, 7] = [3, 5] \neq \varnothing$.

If we apply *superimposition* on the intervals then the *superimposed* interval will be consisting of $[1, 3)^{(1/2)}$, $[3, 5]^{(1)}$ and $(5, 7]^{(1/2)}$. Here the membership of $[3, 5]$ is (1) due to double representation and it is shown in **Figure 3**.

Figure 1. Equi-fuzzy Interval $[1, 5]^{(1/2)}$.

Figure 2. Equi-fuzzy interval $[3, 7]^{(1/2)}$.

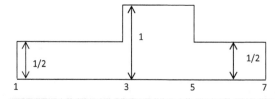

Figure 3. Superimposed interval.

Let $[x_i, y_i]$, $i = 1, 2, \cdots, n$, be n real intervals such that $\bigcap_{i=1}^{n} [x_i, y_i] \neq \varnothing$. Generalizing (3) we get

$$
\begin{aligned}
& [x_1, y_1]^{(1/n)} (S) [x_2, y_2]^{(1/n)} (S) \cdots (S) [x_n, y_n]^{(1/n)} \\
& = \left[x_{(1)}, x_{(2)} \right)^{(1/n)} (+) \left[x_{(2)}, x_{(3)} \right)^{(2/n)} (+) \cdots (+) \left[x_{(r)}, x_{(r+1)} \right)^{(r/n)} (+) \cdots \\
& \quad (+) \left[x_{(n)}, y_{(1)} \right]^{(1)} (+) \left(y_{(1)} y_{(2)} \right]^{((n-1)/n)} \\
& \quad (+) \cdots (+) \left(y_{(n-r)}, y_{(n-r+1)} \right]^{(r/n)} (+) \cdots (+) \left(y_{(n-2)}, y_{(n-1)} \right]^{(2/n)} (+) \left(y_{(n-1)}, y_{(n)} \right]^{(1/n)}.
\end{aligned}
\tag{4}
$$

In (4), the sequence $\{x_{(i)}\}$ is formed by sorting the sequence $\{x_i\}$ in ascending order of magnitude for $i = 1, 2, \cdots, n$ and similarly $\{y_{(i)}\}$ is formed by sorting the sequence $\{y_i\}$ in ascending order.

Although the set superimposition is operated on the closed intervals, it can be extended to operate on the open and the half-open intervals in the trivial way.

Lemma 1. The Glivenko-Cantelli Lemma of Order Statistics

Let $X = (X_1, X_2, \cdots, X_n)$ and $Y = (Y_1, Y_2, \cdots, Y_n)$ be two random vectors, and $(x_1, x_2, \cdots, x_n)$ and $(y_1, y_2, \cdots, y_n)$ be two particular realizations of X and Y respectively. Assume that the sub-σ fields induced by X_k, $k = 1, 2, \cdots, n$ are identical and independent. Similarly assume that the sub-σ fields induced by Y_k, $k = 1, 2, \cdots, n$ are also identical and independent. Let $x_{(1)}, x_{(2)}, \cdots, x_{(n)}$ be the values of $x_1, x_2, \cdots, x_n$, and $y_{(1)}, y_{(2)}, \cdots, y_{(n)}$ be the values of $y_1, y_2, \cdots, y_n$ arranged in ascending order.

For X and Y if the empirical probability distribution functions $\phi_1(x)$ and $\phi_2(x)$ are defined as in (5) and (6) respectively. Then, the Glivenko-Cantelli Lemma of order statistics states that the mathematical expectation of the empirical probability distributions would be given by the respective theoretical probability distributions.

$$
\phi_1(x) = \begin{cases} 0 & x < x_{(1)} \\ (r-1)/n & x_{(r-1)} \leq x \leq x_{(r)} \\ 1 & x \geq x_{(n)} \end{cases}
\tag{5}
$$

$$
\phi_2(x) = \begin{cases} 0 & y < y_{(1)} \\ (r-1)/n & y_{(r-1)} \leq y \leq y_{(r)} \\ 1 & y \geq y_{(n)} \end{cases}
\tag{6}
$$

Now, let X_k is random in the interval $[a, b]$ and Y_k is random in the interval $[b, c]$ so that $P_1(a, x)$ and $P_2(b, y)$ are the probability distribution functions followed by X_k and Y_k respectively. Then in this case Glivenko-Cantelli Lemma gives

$$
\left. \begin{aligned}
& E\left[\phi_1(x) \right] = P_1(a, x), \quad a \leq x \leq b \\
& \text{and} \\
& E\left[\phi_2(y) \right] = P_1(b, y), \quad b \leq y \leq c
\end{aligned} \right\}
\tag{7}
$$

It can be observed that in Equation (4) the membership values of $\left[x_{(r)}, x_{(r+1)} \right]^{(r/n)}$, $r = 1, 2, \cdots, n-1$ look like empirical probability distribution function $\phi_1(x)$ and the membership values of $\left[y_{(n-r)}, y_{(n-r+1)} \right]^{(r/n)}$, $r = 1, 2, \cdots, n-1$ look like the values of empirical complementary probability distribution function or empirical survival function $\left[1-\phi_2(y)\right]$.

Therefore, if $A(x)$ is the membership function of an L-R fuzzy number $A=[a,b,c]$. We get from (ix)

$$A(x)=\begin{cases} P_1(a,x), & a\le x\le b \\ 1-P_2(b,x), & b\le x\le c \end{cases} \tag{8}$$

Thus it can be seen that $P_1(x)$ can indeed be the Dubois-Prade left reference function and $\left(1-P_2(x)\right)$ can be the Dubois-Prade right reference function [13]. Baruah [14] has shown that if a possibility distribution is viewed in this way, two probability laws can, indeed, give rise to a possibility law.

4. Algorithm Proposed

If the time-stamps stored in the transactions of temporal data are the time hierarchy of the type *hour_day_ month_year*, then we do not consider *month_year* in time hierarchy and only consider day. We extract frequent item sets using method discussed in [3]. Each frequent item set will have a sequence of time intervals of the type (day 1, day 2) associated with it where it is frequent. Using the sequence of time intervals we can find the set of superimposed intervals (Definition of superimposed intervals is given in Section 3) and each superimposed intervals will be a fuzzy intervals. The method is as follows: for a frequent item set the set of superimposed intervals is initially empty, algorithm visits each intervals associated with the frequent item set sequentially, if an interval is intersecting with the core of any existing superimposed intervals (Definition of core is given in Section 3) in the set it will be superimposed on it and membership values will be adjusted else a new superimposed intervals will be started with the this interval. This process will be continued till the end of the sequence of time intervals. The process will be repeated for all the frequent item sets. Finally each frequent item sets will have one or more superimposed time intervals. As the superimposed time intervals are used to generate fuzzy intervals, each frequent item set will be associated with one or more fuzzy time intervals where it is frequent. Each superimposed intervals is represented in a compact manner discussed in Section 3.

For representing each *superimposed* interval of the form

$$\left[t^{(1)},t^{(2)}\right]^{1/n}\left[t^{(2)},t^{(3)}\right]^{2/n}\left[t^{(3)},t^{(4)}\right]^{3/n}\cdots\left[t^{(r)},t^{(r+1)}\right]^{r/n}\cdots$$

$$\left[t^{(n)},t'^{(1)}\right]^{1}\left[t'^{(1)},t'^{(2)}\right]^{(n-1)/n}\cdots\left[t'^{(n-2)},t'^{(n-1)}\right]^{2/n}\left[t'^{(n-1)},t'^{(n)}\right]^{1/n}$$

we keep two arrays of real numbers, one for storing the values $t^{(1)},t^{(2)},t^{(3)},\cdots,t^{(n)}$ and the other for storing the values $t'^{(1)},t'^{(2)},t'^{(3)},\cdots,t'^{(n)}$ each of which is a sorted array. Now if a new interval $[t,t']$ is to be superimposed on this interval we add t to the first array by finding its position (using binary search) in the first array so that it remains sorted. Similarly t' is added to the second array.

Data structure used for representing a *superimposed* interval is
struct superinterval
{ *int arsize, count;*
short *l, *r;
}

Here *arsize* represents the maximum size of the array used, *count* represents the number of intervals *superimposed*, and *l* and *r* are two pointer pointing to the two associated arrays.

Algorithm 4.1
for each locally frequent item sets do
{L ← sequence of time intervals associated with s
Ls ← set of superimposed intervals initially set to null
lt = L. get ();
// lt is now pointing to the first interval in L
Ls. append (lt);
while ((lt = L.get ()) != null)

```
{flag = 0;
                    while ((lst = Ls.get ()) ! = null)
      if (compsuperimp (lt, lst))
        flag = 1;
        if (flag == 0) Ls. append (lt);
              }
   }

Compsuperimp (lt, lst)
{ if (| intersect (lst, lt) | != null)
{ superimp(lt, lst);
    return 1;
}
    return 0;
}
```

The function *compsuperimp* (*lt, lst*) first computes the intersection of *lt* with the core of *lst*. If the intersection non-empty it superimposes *lt* by calling the function *superimp* (*lt, lst*) which actually carries on the superimposition process by updating the two lists associated as described earlier. The function returns 1 if *lt* has been superimposed on the *lst* otherwise returns 0. *get* and *append* are functions operating on lists to get a pointer to the next element in a list and to append an element into a list.

5. Results Obtained

For experimentation purpose we have used retail market basket dataset from an anonymous Belgian retail store. The dataset contains 88,162 transactions and 17,000 items. This dataset does not have attribute, so time was incorporated on it. The domain of the time attribute was set to the calendar dates from 1-1-2001 to 30-2-2003. For the said purpose, a program was written using C++ which takes as input a starting date and two values for the minimum and maximum number of transactions per day. A number between these two limits are selected at random and that many consecutive transactions are marked with the same date so that many transactions have taken place on that day. This process starts from the first transaction to the end by marking the transactions with consecutive dates (assuming that the market remains open on all week days). This means that the transactions in the dataset are happened in between the specified dates. A partial view of the generated monthly fuzzy frequent item sets from retail dataset is shown in **Table 1**.

6. Conclusions and Lines for Future Work

An algorithm for finding monthly fuzzy patterns is discussed in this paper. The method takes input as a list of time intervals associated with a frequent item set. The frequent item set is generated using a method similar to the method discussed [4]. However, in our work we do not consider the *month_year* in the time hierarchy and only consider day. So each frequent item set will be associated with a sequence of time intervals of the form (day 1, day 2) where it is frequent. The algorithm visits each interval in the sequence one by one and stores the intervals in the superimposed form. This way each frequent item set is associated with one or more superimposed time intervals. Each superimposed interval will generate a fuzzy time interval. In this way each frequent item set is associated with one or more fuzzy time intervals. The nicety about the method is that the algorithm is less user-dependent, *i.e.* fuzzy time intervals are extracted by algorithm automatically.

Future work may be possible in the following ways.
• Daily patterns can be extracted.

Table 1. Monthly fuzzy frequent item sets for different set of transactions.

Data Size (No. of Transactions)	10000	20000	30000	40000	50000	60000	70000	Whole Dataset
No. fuzzy time intervals	1	2	2	3	3	4	4	4

- Clustering of patterns can be done based on their fuzzy time interval associated with yearly patterns using some statistical measure.

References

[1]   Agrawal, R., Imielinski, T. and Swami, A.N. (1993) Mining Association Rules between Sets of Items in Large Data-bases. *Proceedings of the 1993 ACM SIGMOD International Conference on Management of Data*, **22**, 207-216. http://dx.doi.org/10.1145/170035.170072

[2]   Ale, J.M. and Rossi, G.H. (2000) An Approach to Discovering Temporal Association Rules. *Proceedings of 2000 ACM Symposium on Applied Computing*, Como, 19-21 March 2000, 294-300.

[3]   Mahanta, A.K., Mazarbhuiya, F.A. and Baruah, H.K. (2005) Finding Locally and Periodically Frequent Sets and Periodic Association Rules. *Pattern Recognition and Machine Intelligence*, **3776**, 576-582.

[4]   Mahanta, A.K., Mazarbhuiya, F.A. and Baruah, H.K. (2008) Finding Calendar-Based Periodic Patterns. *Pattern Recognition Letters*, **29**, 1274-1284.

[5]   Antunes, C.M. and Oliviera, A.L. (2001) Temporal Data Mining: An Overview. *Workshop on Temporal Data Mining—7th ACM SIGKDD International Conference on Knowledge Discovery and Data Mining*, San Francisco, 26-29 August 2001, 1-13.

[6]   Ozden, B., Ramaswamy, S. and Silberschatz, A. (1998) Cyclic Association Rules. *Proceedings of the 14th International Conference on Data Engineering*, Orlando, 23-27 February 1998, 412-421. http://dx.doi.org/10.1109/ICDE.1998.655804

[7]   Li, Y., Ning, P., Wang, X.S. and Jajodia, S. (2001) Discovering Calendar-Based Temporal Association Rules. Elsevier Science, Amsterdam.

[8]   Zimbrado, G., de Souza, J.M., de Almeida, V.T. and de Silva, W.A. (2002) An Algorithm to Discover Calendar-Based Temporal Association Rules with Item's Lifespan Restriction. *Proceedings of the 8th ACM SIGKDD*, Alberta, 23 July 2002.

[9]   Subramanyam, R.B.V., Goswami, A. and Prasad, B. (2008) Mining Fuzzy Temporal Patterns from Process Instances with Weighted Temporal Graphs. *International Journal of Data Analysis Techniques and Strategies*, **1**, 60-77. http://dx.doi.org/10.1504/IJDATS.2008.020023

[10] Jain, S., Jain, S. and Jain, A. (2013) An assessment of Fuzzy Temporal Rule Mining. *International Journal of Application or Innovation in Engineering and Management (IJAIEM)*, **2**, 42-45.

[11] Lee, W.-J., Jiang, J.-Y. and Lee, S.-J. (2008) Mining Fuzzy Periodic Association Rules. *Data & Knowledge Engineering*, **65**, 442-462.

[12] Klir, J. and Yuan, B. (2002) Fuzzy Sets and Logic Theory and Application. Prentice Hill Pvt. Ltd., Upper Saddle River.

[13] Dubois, D. and Prade, H. (1983) Ranking Fuzzy Numbers in the Setting of Possibility Theory. *Information Sciences*, **30**, 183-224. http://dx.doi.org/10.1016/0020-0255(83)90025-7

[14] Baruah, H.K. (1999) Set Superimposition and Its Application to the Theory of Fuzzy Sets. *Journal of Assam Science Society*, **10**, 25-31.

3

An Experiment in Use of Brain Computer Interfaces for Cognitive Researches

Necmettin Firat Ozkan, Emin Kahya

Department of Industrial Engineering, Eskisehir Osmangazi University, Eskisehir, Turkey
Email: ozkanfirat@gmail.com

Abstract

Brain-Computer Interfaces (BCIs) are systems that are primarily developed for use of paralyzed people. Although their main aim of use has a medical point of view, they can also be used for different aims such as entertainment and cognitive researches. Since BCI systems have specific brain potentials (P300, steady state evoked potential) and ERD/ERS (Motor Imagery), they are also flexible tools for cognitive science. In this study, an experiment was conducted with 30 participants. Each participant completed two tasks through a BCI and filled NASA-TLX forms. The results were analyzed using paired t-tests to see whether BCI tasks are significantly different in terms of creating cognitive load. The results showed that NASA-TLX scores of the BCI tasks were significantly different and these systems can be considered for estimating cognitive states studies.

Keywords

Cognitive Load, BCI, NASA-TLX

1. Introduction

Human error can be defined as some undesired behaviors caused by some improprieties such as lack of knowledge, lack of communication, lack of attention, excessive stress, mental fatigue, and environmental factors. Monitoring cognitive state is a useful tool to reduce these errors. Therefore, many studies about cognitive load have been conducting in several research areas.

According to cognitive load theory, two persons may complete the same task under the same conditions, at the same time and with the same level of success. However, it doesn't guarantee that both people have the same level of cognitive load. It depends on many different factors, such as personal qualifications, attributes, cognitive load, and cognitive state. Although it is important to define the level of cognitive load, there is no available certain metrics to measure. The current methods to measure cognitive load in the literature just try to give some efficient indicators to estimate cognitive load.

Tracy and Albers [1] state that when the cognitive load increases, the ability to perform effectively decreases slowly until the person reaches a point of cognitive overload. According to Hussain *et al.* [2], monitoring cognitive load is crucial for developing adaptive systems aware of the user's mental workload. Because such systems can reduce error related risks during task-critical operations. Cain [3] states that a commonly accepted definition of workload does not exist. However, it is possible to characterize workload as a mental structure that reflects the mental strain caused by performing a task under specific environmental and operational conditions, besides the capability of the operator to respond to demands of the task.

Methods for measuring cognitive load can be grouped under three titles: subjective methods, behavioral methods, and physiological methods. Subjective methods are based on self-evaluations of people who completed the relevant tasks. Behavioral methods deal with task completion time and task completion success. These methods usually include secondary task implementations that require completing two tasks concurrently. Physiological methods are used via monitoring some indications from autonomic nerve system and brain activities. Pupil responses, galvanic skin response, and heart rate variability are some of the most common indicators used to estimate cognitive load. EEG and fMRI systems are preferred in studies based on brain activities to estimate cognitive load by monitoring cognitive state.

Antonenko *et al.* [4] study on comparing NASA-TLX and EEG data and state using EEG is a more objective approach to estimate cognitive load. Haapalainen *et al.* [5] explain using more than one physical symptom makes the cognitive load estimation more reliable. The study has an experimental part that considers 20 participants. The parameters below were collected from the participants during the experiment:

- Changes on pupil sizes,
- Eye movements,
- Number and duration of eye blinking,
- Heart rate variability,
- Respiration, and
- Monitoring brainwaves.

Walczyk *et al.* [6] explain that when somebody is telling a lie, his/her pupil sized shows some changes. They conducted a scenario based experiment with 145 participants to identify pupil size differences between telling truth and lie.

BCIs mainly have medical aims but they also have huge potential to be used in different areas of life. Since they are being activated via specific brain activities brain based cognitive researches. They usually offer three kinds of applications that are activated through P300 potential, steady state visual evoked potential, and event related desynchronization/synchronization. In this study, one of the recently developed BCI system's letter matrix applications was utilized. Different difficulty levels and cognitive load of participants was measured via a well-known subjective method: NASA-TLX.

1.1. NASA-TLX

Since subjective methods are easy to use, low cost and provide simple quantitative results, they still keep their popularity. One of the widely used subjective methods is NASA-TLX. This method was developed in Hart and Staveland [7] and its application areas were investigated by Hart [8] after 20 years development. There are many other numbers of studies that used NASA-TLX in the relevant literature. Rubio *et al.* [9] conducted a comparison with NASA-TLX and another subjective method SWAT. Noyes and Bruneau [10] searched differences between use of pencil and computer versions of NASA-TLX. Alm and Nilsson [11] investigated negative effects of using mobile telephone during driving via NASA-TLX method. Yurko *et al.* [12] stated that higher mental workload caused poorer laparoscopic performance. A paper published by Miyake [13] offered a combined workload estimating method including physiological and subjective methods.

NASA-TLX has six sub-scales which reflect participant's feelings and opinions about the task. The sub-scales are listed below:

- Mental demand,
- Physical demand,
- Temporal demand,
- Performance,

- Effort,
- Frustration.

Participants evaluate the task with these scales from 0 to 100. It is also possible to decide weights of the scales with participants' evaluations. Fifteen paired comparisons are available and the participant decides more considerable scales for each comparison. Finally it provides an overall score between 0 and 100 to evaluate the difficulty level of the task.

1.2. Brain Computer Interfaces

BCIs are technological systems including a computer, relevant software, EEG components (bonnet, electrodes, etc.), and an amplifier. The system works based on EEG and simply brain activities by converting them to comments for the computer using interfaces [14]. **Figure 1** illustrates working steps of BCI systems. The main goal of BCI research for the last thirty years is to help paralyzed people for their daily life. However, it is also possible to use these interfaces for other cognitive researches related with ERD and other brain activities.

Karagoz *et al.* [15] state that BCI systems utilize three main neurophysiological facts. One of them is P300 potential that appears when a problem is solved, a decision is made, or an fogginess disappears in 300 ms. Alkaç [16] stated that P300 doesn't appear with the standard stimulates. It requires specific target stimulates. That's why this potential is used in the studies about gathering attention and focusing. The relevant interface of P300 is usually a letter matrix that columns and rows flash and the participant tries to focus on his/her target letter to type it on the screen.

Since P300 potential has a close relationship with decision making, problem solving and focusing on target stimulus, it is also an attractive brain fact for cognitive load researchers. Schultheis and Jameson [17] designed an experiment with a task including reading written materials with various level of difficulty. They used an EEG, remote eye tracker, and subjective scale to measure the cognitive load. Based on the results, it can be satated that more difficult texts led to lower reading speed, higher subjective load ratings, and a reduced P300 amplitude.

SSVEP is an another fact that is being used by BCI systems. BCIs generate this potential with flashing controls. The direction indicators flash with various frequencies and the participant tries to focus on the target indicator to give the comment. This application makes possible to control some electronic systems [18]. Also, It requires a high level of attention and concentration to be able to catch quick flickers. Further, SSVEP is an useful fact for cognitive load researchers. Perego *et al.* [19] conducted an experimental study and they stated that the test showed SSVEP based BCI can be used for psychometric test.

The third neurophysiologic fact used by BCIs is changes on motor zones of the brain when participant focuses on thinking amovement to a specific direction [18]. When we think to move our right hand, an activity appears on the left side of our brain. BCI system converts it to a comment for the computer to move cursor on the screen.

2. Method

In this study, an experiment was designed using a BCI system developed by G-TEC Company. The system includes a letter matrix (**Figure 2**) to type letters via P300 potential. Thirty 18 - 27 aged participants (15 female,

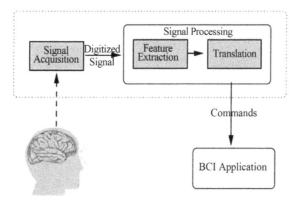

Figure 1. Operation Diagram of BCI [20].

15 male) were recruited for this experiment. Each participant completed two tasks using the letter matrix. All the experiments were conducted in the same silent room with same climatic, illumination conditions. For running BCI, the same computer (Core i5, 8 GB Ram, 15.6 inch screen) was used.

Before executing the task EEG, electrodes were mounted. **Figure 3** illustrates the locations for electrode placement for using the matrix.

Task 1: The first task was defined as typing "ABCDE" on the screen. Letter matrix's rows and columns started flashing and participants must have focused on the target letters one by one starting from the first letter. Each target letter flashed 15 times for 75 ms. Besides each target letter had flashed for a second right before the rows and columns' flashes started to make the participant realize its position on the matrix.

Task 2: After Task 1 had been completed, participants filled a paper version NASA-TLX form and took a rest for 5 minutes. For Task 2, participants were asked to type "ESOGU2014" on the screen. For this task, consecutive target letters were not assigned side to side. There was no flashing to show letter's initial position. Therefore, participants had to find the letter's location by themselves during 2 seconds that is a constant time period between typing a letter and starting flashing for the next one. In this task, each target letter flashed 5 times for 50 ms. After completing Task 2, participants filled NASA-TLX form again. It was expected that Task 2's performances would be lower and mental workload score would be higher.

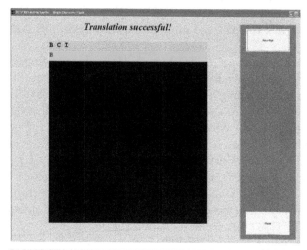

Figure 2. P300 Letter Matrix.

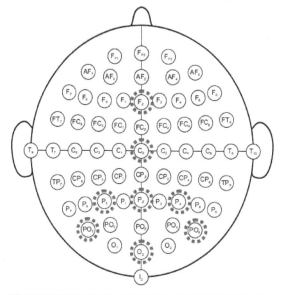

Figure 3. P300 Electrode Placement Locations.

3. Results

All participants' task performances were recorded (number of correct letters/total number of letters) and NASA-TLX scores were calculated for both tasks. Since Task 2 was more difficult, it was expected that NASA-TLX scores for Task 2 would be dramatically lower. **Appendix A** and **Appendix B** illustrate scale weights and overall NASA-TLX scores and **Figure 4** summarizes task performances of all participants.

Due to longer word, no help for finding letter on the matrix, quicker, and shorter flashings a huge decrease is recorded in Task 2 performances. Average success levels are 64.00 and 34, 81 for task 1 and task 2 respectively.

As seen in **Appendices A and B**, better overall NASA-TLX scores was obtained for task 1. Difference between difficulty levels of the tasks can be seen from the average values. The most dramatic change was provided for mental demand in terms of raw scores. When the weight of the scales is investigated, the largest change belongs to weight of temporal demand due to quicker flashings and trying to find the next target letter during Task 2.

4. Analysis

A paired t-test was conducted to assess whether the difference between overall NASA-TLX scores is significant or not. Before conducting paired t-test, normality of the overall scores was checked with Anderson-Darling test in Minitab 16. Both tasks' NASA-TLX scores distributed normally (**Figure 5** and **Figure 6**).

Result of paired t-test is presented below. Since P-value is less than 0.05, we can say that mental workload levels of the tasks are statistically significant (**Table 1**).

5. Conclusion and Future Work

In this study, it aims to see how possible it is to use BCI systems for cognitive load measurement and cognitive state monitoring. Results show that it is possible to use these systems with at least one brain potential including

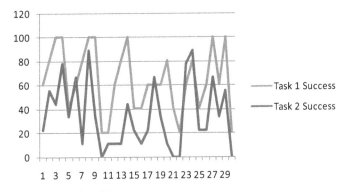

Figure 4. Task Performances.

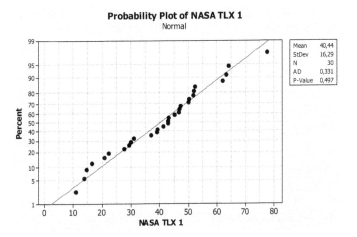

Figure 5. Normality Test of Overall NASA-TLX Score for Task 1.

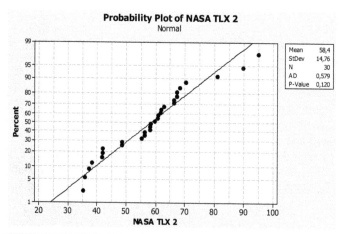

Figure 6. Normality Test of Overall NASA-TLX Score for Task 2.

Table 1. Paired t-test result for overall NASA-TLX scores.

	N	Mean	StDev	SE Mean
NASA-TLX 1	30	40.44	16.29	2.97
NASA-TLX 2	30	58.40	14.76	2.69
Difference	30	−17.96	19.87	3.63

95% CI for mean difference: (−25, 38; −10, 54); t-test of mean difference = 0
(vs not = 0); T-value = −4.95; P-value = 0.000.

well-determined task parameters. Obtaining significant differences in terms of subjective mental load assessment indicates that these systems can be used as a member of combined methods of estimating cognitive state or measuring cognitive load. With the support of some physiological parameters, these systems can become a wide task designing and application platforms. In the future studies, this BCI system will be combined with a remote eye tracker and Galvanic Skin Response device and a new experiment can be designed with more participants.

Acknowledgements

This Study is a part of the project (No. 201315A208) which is supported by Eskisehir Osmangazi University Scientific Research Projects Office.

References

[1]   Tracy, J.P. and Albers, M.J. (2006) Measuring Cognitive Load to Test the Usability of Web Sites. *Society for Technical Communication 53rd Annual Conference*, Las Vegas, 7-10 May 2006, 256-260.

[2]   Hussain, S., Chen, S.Y., Calvo, R.A. and Chen, F. (2011) Classification of Cognitive Load from Task Performance & Multichannel Physiology during Affective Changes. *MMCogEmS: Inferring Cognitive and Emotional States from Multimodal Measures, ICMI* 2011 *Workshop*, 17 November 2011, Alicante.

[3]   Cain, B. (2007) A Review of the Mental Workload Literature. Defence Research and Development Canada, Toronto.

[4]   Antonenko, P., Paas, F., Grabner, R. and van Gog, T. (2010) Using Electroencephalography to Measure Cognitive Load. *Educational Psychology Review*, **22**, 425-438. http://dx.doi.org/10.1007/s10648-010-9130-y

[5]   Haapalainen, E., Kim, S., Forlizzi, J.F. and Dey, A.K. (2010) Psycho-Physiological Measures for Assessing Cognitive Load. *Proceedings of the 12th ACM International Conference on Ubiquitous Computing*, Copenhagen, 26-29 September 2010, 301-310. http://www.ubicomp.org/ubicomp2010/

[6]   Walczyk, J.J., Griffith, D.A., Yates, R., Visconte, S.R., Simoneaux, B. and Harris, L.L. (2012) Lie Detection by Inducing Cognitive Load Eye Movements and Other Cues to the False Answers of "Witnesses" to Crimes. *Criminal Justice and Behavior*, **39**, 887-909. http://dx.doi.org/10.1177/0093854812437014

[7]   Hart, S.G. and Staveland, L.E. (1988) Development of NASA-TLX (Task Load Index): Results of Empirical and Theoretical Research. *Advances in Psychology*, **52**, 139-183. http://dx.doi.org/10.1016/S0166-4115(08)62386-9

[8] Hart, S.G. (2006) NASA-Task Load Index (NASA-TLX); 20 Years Later. *Proceedings of the Human Factors and Ergonomics Society Annual Meeting*, **50**, 904-908.

[9] Rubio, S., Díaz, E., Martín, J. and Puente, J.M. (2004) Evaluation of Subjective Mental Workload: A Comparison of SWAT, NASA-TLX, and Workload Profile Methods. *Applied Psychology*, **53**, 61-86. http://dx.doi.org/10.1111/j.1464-0597.2004.00161.x

[10] Noyes, J.M. and Bruneau, D.P. (2007) A Self-Analysis of the NASA-TLX Workload Measure. *Ergonomics*, **50**, 514-519. http://dx.doi.org/10.1080/00140130701235232

[11] Alm, H. and Nilsson, L. (1995) The Effects of a Mobile Telephone Task on Driver Behaviour in a Car Following Situation. *Accident Analysis & Prevention*, **27**, 707-715. http://dx.doi.org/10.1016/0001-4575(95)00026-V

[12] Yurko, Y.Y., Scerbo, M.W., Prabhu, A.S., Acker, C.E. and Stefanidis, D. (2010) Higher Mental Workload Is Associated with Poorer Laparoscopic Performance as Measured by the NASA-TLX Tool. *Simulation in Healthcare*, **5**, 267-271. http://dx.doi.org/10.1097/SIH.0b013e3181e3f329

[13] Miyake, S. (2001) Multivariate Workload Evaluation Combining Physiological and Subjective Measures. *International Journal of Psychophysiology*, **40**, 233-238. http://dx.doi.org/10.1016/S0167-8760(00)00191-4

[14] Ozkan, N.F. and Kahya, E. (2014) Measurement of Cognitive Workload by Use of Combined Methods Including Brain-Computer Interfaces. *Advances in Social and Organizational Factors*, **12**, 458-468.

[15] Karagöz, M., Alkaç, U., Ergen, N., Erdamlar, N. and Alpkan, L. (2005) Psikiyatrik Hastaliklarda Elektrofizyolojik (P300) Yöntemler. *Düşünen Adam*, **18**, 210-216.

[16] Alkaç, U. (2009) Beyin Araştirmalari Tarihinde Bir Gezinti: Elektronörofizyoloji. *Klinik Gelişim*, **3**, 14-19

[17] Schultheis, H. and Jameson, A. (2004) Assessing Cognitive Load in Adaptive Hypermedia Systems: Physiological and Behavioral Methods. In: De Bra, P.M.E. and Nejdl, W., Eds., *Adaptive Hypermedia and Adaptive Web-Based Systems*, Springer Berlin, Heidelberg, 225-234. http://dx.doi.org/10.1007/978-3-540-27780-4_26

[18] Gencer, N., Usakli, A.B., Erdogan, H.B., Akinci, B. and Acar, E. (2010) ODTÜ Beyin Araştirmalari Laboratuvari: Beyin-Bilgisayar Arayüzü çalişmalari. *ODTÜLÜ*, **45**, 20-21

[19] Perego, P., Turconi, A.C., Andreoni, G., Maggi, L., Beretta, E., Parini, S. and Gagliardi, C. (2011) Cognitive Ability Assessment by Brain-Computer Interface: Validation of a New Assessment Method for Cognitive Abilities. *Journal of Neuroscience Methods*, **201**, 239-250. http://dx.doi.org/10.1016/j.jneumeth.2011.06.025

[20] www.wired.com.

Appendix A: NASA-TLX Results of Task 1

	Mental Demand	Physical Demand	Temporal Demand	Performance	Effort	Frustration	Mental D. Weight	Physical D. Weight	Temporal D. Weight	Performance Weight	Effort Weight	Frustration Weight	Weighted Overall Score
1	45	70	35	30	55	35	5	0	1	2	4	3	43.00
2	25	10	25	40	45	30	2	2	2	3	3	3	31.00
3	25	20	50	5	85	35	3	0	3	4	4	1	41.33
4	20	5	60	80	50	15	3	0	3	4	4	1	51.67
5	30	5	5	65	15	5	3	1	2	4	5	0	29.33
6	40	40	65	50	50	35	5	0	2	3	3	2	46.67
7	10	10	10	20	15	20	2	0	2	5	2	4	16.67
8	15	10	15	40	55	45	4	0	1	2	4	4	37.00
9	10	10	15	20	5	10	3	3	0	3	3	3	11.00
10	40	5	40	80	55	15	4	0	1	2	5	3	45.33
11	15	5	25	80	60	20	5	1	2	4	2	1	39.33
12	15	5	10	25	15	5	3	0	1	3	5	3	14.67
13	20	15	25	25	30	10	4	1	0	4	4	2	22.33
14	10	20	5	20	10	5	3	2	1	5	3	1	14.00
15	50	50	50	50	50	50	3	0	5	2	2	3	50.00
16	55	5	85	55	70	30	2	1	0	3	4	5	47.33
17	50	25	30	70	85	55	3	1	1	3	5	2	63.33
18	30	5	35	75	80	65	2	1	1	4	5	2	62.00
19	25	30	70	40	55	50	4	1	1	2	3	4	43.00
20	20	55	60	30	55	65	3	0	2	1	4	5	50.33
21	10	5	25	70	40	10	5	1	4	3	1	1	27.67
22	40	15	25	55	50	50	4	0	1	4	3	3	47.00
23	60	20	40	50	65	10	3	2	1	4	5	0	52.33
24	15	5	65	30	60	20	4	1	3	5	0	2	30.00
25	65	15	45	50	75	100	3	1	0	5	4	2	64.00
26	60	20	45	60	45	60	4	0	4	2	4	1	52.00
27	15	20	80	85	70	25	5	2	3	1	1	3	39.00
28	40	30	65	55	55	30	4	2	1	2	3	3	43.33
29	35	35	20	20	25	5	1	2	1	5	3	3	21.00
30	80	90	65	90	65	80	4	3	3	1	2	2	77.67
AVG	32.33	21.83	39.67	48.83	49.67	33.00	3.43	0.93	1.73	3.17	3.33	2.40	40.44

Appendix B: NASA-TLX Results of Task 2

	Mental Demand	Physical Demand	Temporal Demand	Performance	Effort	Frustration	Mental D. Weight	Physical D. Weight	Temporal D. Weight	Performance Weight	Effort Weight	Frustration Weight	Weighted Overall Score
1	60	70	40	35	65	65	5	1	2	2	2	3	56.33
2	55	25	45	20	45	55	5	0	4	1	2	3	48.67
3	90	15	90	85	90	90	3	0	2	1	5	4	89.67
4	45	10	60	35	45	25	2	1	1	4	5	2	38.33
5	65	20	70	65	65	15	3	0	1	3	5	3	55.33
6	45	30	45	45	30	20	2	0	3	3	3	4	35.33
7	80	10	15	85	55	55	4	0	2	1	3	5	58.33
8	25	15	30	45	50	40	2	0	1	4	5	3	42.00
9	70	20	70	70	75	50	4	0	2	2	4	3	67.33
10	65	15	45	85	65	20	3	1	0	4	5	2	61.00
11	35	35	50	100	60	15	5	0	2	4	3	1	58.00
12	50	5	20	60	30	5	2	0	2	4	5	2	36.00
13	65	55	75	45	65	35	4	1	5	2	2	1	63.00
14	40	50	70	45	65	45	2	0	5	1	4	3	58.00
15	55	55	55	55	55	5	3	0	5	1	2	4	41.67
16	80	15	75	70	75	45	2	1	0	3	4	5	60.67
17	75	25	75	55	75	60	2	1	2	1	5	4	66.33
18	55	5	75	65	65	55	3	1	5	3	2	1	61.67
19	90	35	55	75	80	50	4	2	0	1	3	5	66.33
20	100	65	100	100	100	90	4	1	4	0	2	4	95.00
21	35	5	40	60	55	5	3	2	3	2	5	0	42.00
22	60	45	70	70	70	65	3	0	3	3	4	2	67.33
23	40	10	30	35	55	10	4	1	4	3	3	0	37.33
24	50	25	75	25	40	30	2	1	5	2	3	2	48.67
25	75	15	65	25	80	75	4	0	1	4	3	3	62.00
26	75	45	85	15	70	55	3	0	4	1	4	3	68.33
27	85	30	90	95	80	65	3	1	2	4	3	2	81.00
28	60	55	55	30	70	50	2	0	3	1	4	5	56.33
29	75	75	85	75	65	15	0	1	4	3	3	4	59.67
30	85	40	70	90	65	90	2	3	3	2	3	2	70.33
AVG	62.83	30.67	60.83	58.67	63.50	43.33	3.00	0.63	2.67	2.33	3.53	2.83	58.40

4

Hyperscale Puts the *Sapiens* into *Homo*

Ron Cottam[1], Willy Ranson[2], Roger Vounckx[1]

[1]The Living Systems Project, Department of Electronics and Informatics, Vrije Universiteit Brussel (VUB), Brussels, Belgium
[2]IMEC vzw, Leuven, Belgium
Email: life@etro.vub.ac.be

Academic Editor: Zhongzhi Shi, Institute of Computing Technology, CAS, China

Abstract

The human mind's evolution owes much to its companion phenomena of intelligence, sapience, wisdom, awareness and consciousness. In this paper we take the concepts of intelligence and sapience as the starting point of a route towards elucidation of the conscious mind. There is much disagreement and confusion associated with the word intelligence. A lot of this results from its use in diverse contexts, where it is called upon to represent different ideas and to justify different arguments. Addition of the word sapience to the mix merely complicates matters, unless we can relate both of these words to different concepts in a way which acceptably crosses contextual boundaries. We have established a connection between information processing and processor "architecture" which provides just such a linguistic separation, and which is applicable in either a computational or conceptual form to any context. This paper reports the argumentation leading up to a distinction between intelligence and sapience, and relates this distinction to human "cognitive" activities. Information is always contextual. Information processing in a system always takes place between "architectural" scales: intelligence is the "tool" which permits an "overview" of the relevance of individual items of information. System unity presumes a degree of coherence across all the scales of a system: sapience is the "tool" which permits an evaluation of the relevance of both individual items and individual scales of information to a common purpose. This hyperscalar coherence is created through mutual inter-scalar observation, whose recursive nature generates the independence of high-level consciousness, making humans human. We conclude that intelligence and sapience are distinct and necessary properties of all information processing systems, and that the degree of their availability controls a system's or a human's cognitive capacity, if not its application. This establishes intelligence and sapience as prime ancestors of the conscious mind. However, to our knowledge, there is no current mathematical approach which can satisfactorily deal with the native irrationalities of information integration across multiple scales, and therefore of formally modeling the mind.

Keywords

Hyperscale, Hierarchy, Intelligence, Sapience, Consciousness

---

1. Introduction

There is much disagreement and confusion associated with the word intelligence. A lot of this results from its use in diverse contexts, where it is called upon to represent different ideas and to justify different arguments. James Albus [1] has defined intelligence as

"... *the ability to act appropriately in an uncertain environment; appropriate action is that which maximizes the probability of success; success is the achievement or maintenance of behavioral goals; behavioral goals are desired states of the environment that a behavior is designed to achieve or maintain*".

Although many will find this definition insufficient, we will provisionally accept it, in that it is the most concise and complete description we are aware of which is amenable to use within a computational paradigm. We can extract from it the simplified message that intelligence promotes survival-related information-reductive decision-making in complex contexts (see also [2]). So far so good, but if intelligence is a tool for survival, what is sapience: merely more of the same thing? If such were the case, it would be difficult to justify the addition of yet another technical term to the cognitive domain, which is already saturated with contextually-ambiguous terminology. Addition of the word "sapience" to the linguistic mix merely complicates matters, unless we can relate both of these words to different concepts in a way which acceptably crosses contextual boundaries.

The authors have earlier published [3] the identification of mind with the continuously evolving anticipatory capability of a complex networked information-processing system. In the work leading up to this, following paper we have established a connection between information processing and processor "architecture", which provides linguistic separation between intelligence and sapience, and which is applicable in either a computational or a conceptual form to any context. The paper reports the argumentation leading up to this distinction between intelligence and sapience, relates the distinction to human "cognitive" activities, and establishes their relevance to the evolutionary appearance of the human conscious mind. The story is more than a little recursive, as will later become clear. Maybe, therefore, the best approach will be to adopt the communication principles laid down by Jean-Luc Doumont[1] and begin by stating our final conclusion.

We live within hyperscale: intelligence is how we get there; sapience is how we remain there.

On its own, this statement will convey little, but our task now in this introduction is clear: it is to explain what this short conclusion means before delving into the technical arguments which lead up to it. There are two main areas of human concern which we must first address those of scale and presence.

1.1. Scale

Arguably, human technical evolution has progressed from initially "dealing with things at our own scale", whether of size, hardness, time... towards progressively both larger and smaller scales—considerations of size, for example, have expanded outwards from the meter to Ångstroms, to light years, and even beyond. We now unthinkingly relate to numerous different scales of parameters or phenomena, but the critical distinction is not simply one of size, but how we access different scalar magnitudes. Our own eyes, for example, enable us to access reasonably and directly sizes down to about one micrometer, but not smaller. All observation or measurement devices suffer from similar limitations, which often relate the "size" of a device's operational parameters (e.g. wavelength) to the "size" of the entity or effect which is to be observed. Waves on the sea, for example, only penetrate a harbor's entrance in a diffracted manner for a restricted range of distance (or time) between their crests—their wavelength.

Unfortunately, therefore, we cannot access all scales directly, but are forced to rely on technically developed instruments to assist us, for example on electron microscopes, or on electronic signal integrators. Our belief in the "correctness" of the information these devices provide depends on our belief in the "correctness" of the modeling chains outwards from our own scale which we use to build them, to understand their operation and to

---

[1]Principiæ, Belgium.

derive meaningful information from them. These modeling chains similarly invoke sequences of scale—a particular scientific model may only be accurate within a certain parametric range, for example. It is worth pointing out here that there is no easily available single model which "works" well right across the meter, Ångstrom, and galactic range of scales[2]. Consequently, whether we are basing our considerations on "real" parametric sizes or "abstract" (model) parametric sizes, the same restriction holds—we can't escape the implications of perceptional scale in any simplistic mechanical manner.

1.2. Presence

A current "hot topic" of research is that of presence: how should we formulate technical multimedia systems to enhance the impression that we are "somewhere else". Interestingly, this question has already exercised the directors of theatre and film for many decades in terms of the "suspension of disbelief"[3] they require of their audiences; we will return to the meaning of "suspension of disbelief" later. Surprisingly, technical presence research, with its emphasis on "being there", appears to avoid a central aspect of philosophical presence research which could greatly inform it—namely "being here"! Psychology has long been interested in yet another aspect of presence, which is germane to the argument we will present—namely the capability of a human to effectively place him or herself at the location of a tool's operation. Metzinger [5] has presented the hypothesis that we are unable to distinguish between the objects of our attention and the internal representations of them which we "observe":

"That is why we 'look through' those representational structures, as if we were in direct and immediate contact with their content, with what they represent for us." [5]

When we use a screwdriver, we are at the screw; when we drive a car, we become the car[4]. This transfer of presence is singular in character—we can only be present in one location at a time. In this, it is closely related to the concept of consciousness, which abides by a similar constraint.

The most astounding characteristic of this transfer of presence is the way in which we can effortlessly skip between different scales of an overall picture. Nowhere is this more evident than when riding a motorcycle at speed[5], where safety demands a mental "backing off" from direct visual contact with the surroundings to a holistic "place" where any scalar aspect of the scene's totality can be equivalently and speedily accessed whenever needed. It is tempting to associate this "place" with "the zone" referred to by professional athletes as the "state" within which they perform their best, and to identify the different "locations" to which we transfer our presence with the multiple differentiated conscious states of Tononi and Edelmans' [6] Dynamic Core Hypothesis.

1.3. Hyperscale and the Present Argument

A central part of our argumentation in this paper will involve the combination of these two ideas of scale and presence, where there is an immediately noticeable dissimilarity of pluralism. Many of our day-to-day actions, if not all, are simultaneously associated with multiple scales of representation of a single context. How on earth do we manage to relate to a multiplicity of mutually-exclusive scales of our environment through the singular focus of consciousness? Presumably there must be some kind of interface between the two which implements coding/decoding—either of which may be integral or dis-integral in character. In any unified system the unification of multiple scales by their interaction is itself a recognizable system property: this is hyperscale.

---

[2]The only model we are aware which does appear to remain valid across this extreme range of scales of is that of Quantum Holography, developed by Walter Schempp [4]—which far from coincidentally corresponds in many ways to the architectural scheme underlying the argumentation of this paper—most particularly in its exploitation of birationality. *"Quantum holography is a non-local information processing technique* [4], *the range of which includes the superluminal expansion of light echoes created by the explosion of the supernova 1987A within the Large Magellanic Cloud at a distance of 170,000 light years, and the excitation patterns of neuronal cooperativity in the cerebral cortex generated by external and internal stimuli and visualized by the modality of functional magnetic resonance imaging (fMRI), as well as the holographic tweezer for the non-invasive handling of chromosomes by means of optical micromachines"* (Walter Schempp, private communication).

[3]A term originally used by Samuel Taylor Coleridge in *Biographia Literaria* (1817).

[4]A fascinating example of this is that we can "automatically" drive an automobile through a narrow gap without hitting one side or the other, even though we are not sitting centrally in the automobile (*i.e.* we are sitting on the right hand side of the automobile's cabin, or, of course, in countries where citizens drive on the wrong side of the road, on the left hand side).

[5]N.B. this is very different from driving an automobile, as any surviving motorcyclist will confirm: it is no longer acceptable that other drivers control the generation of events requiring reaction—everything must be anticipated, from a global picture of current and future vehicle positions, through expectations of feasible individual vehicular deviations, to the detail of road surfaces and the restrictions it places on maneuvers.

The quality and realization of system unification is by far the most complex and difficult aspect of our environment to understand; so much so that its implications are virtually absent from conventional science, which until the "birth" of chaos in the nineteen-sixties habitually restricted itself to situations where information content changed little across scales, as in the case of inorganic crystals, for example [7]. Consistent with a view of nature which accepts that evolution cannibalizes old capabilities for new purposes[6] [9], the cognitive resolution of this problem has been to adopt the architecture of the stimulus in formulating a response: we relate to hyperscalar systems from within our own assiduously-constructed hyperscalar mental environment!

In this paper we will describe not only how hyperscale can fulfill the function of integral/dis-integral coding/decoding between the multiple scales and the singular forms of mental consciousness of an organism, but also how it is a natural and necessary part of any unified multiscalar system. We believe that the "spotlight of consciousness"[7] in humans is momentarily focused at a single "location" within a spatio-temporal hyperscalar "phase space" which we construct from the entire history of our individual and social existences, including the "facts" of our believed "reality", numerous apparently consistent but insufficiently investigated "logical" suppositions, and as yet untested or normally-abandoned hypothetical models which serve to fill in otherwise inconvenient or glaringly obvious omissions in its landscape[8]. Again, in reference to evolution's cannibalism, this resembles the way our visual system "fills in" missing or occluded parts of an object or a visual scene with the most likely shapes, colors or objects.

Our major task here is to make sense of the relationship between these three technical terms: intelligence, sapience and hyperscale. Information is always contextual. The term "data" presupposes an externally predefined context within which it has a meaning. Those of us whose blood pressure has been measured will probably recognize the way the results were quoted as something like "sixteen, eight" (if they were lucky)—whatever that might mean! Information, however, cannot be dissociated from its context in a similar way. In this it is semiotic in nature, rather than simply semantic. Most people would almost certainly have no idea in what units the numbers of a blood-pressure measurement make sense as data, but are probably well aware that "twenty, eighteen" is worth worrying about; the context within which the numbers have a meaning is far wider and more diffuse than "in mm of mercury" (e.g. "... *the doctor told my auntie she had 'twenty, eighteen', and she had to go into hospital...*").

Information processing in a system always takes place between different "architectural" scales of a processing entity: simplistically, we can view intelligence as the "tool" which permits an "overview" of the relevance of individual items of information and the means by which all available information is taken account of in generating or updating a new, higher-level, simplified representation of the information system. As such it functions as a complex mix of context-translator, interpreter and comparator. The reason why "normal" rationality loses track of this is that the translations, interpretations and comparisons it makes cannot be simply reduced to a combination of one-to-one, one-to-many and many-to-one relationships. Following Robert Rosen (see, for example, [10] [11]) categorize complexity by

"... *If there is no way to completely model all aspects of any given system, it is considered 'non-computable' and is, therefore, 'complex' in this unique sense*".

Intelligence not only resembles this categorization, but also depends on it in the way it operates. The authors are not aware of any single analytic or synthetic form capable of completely mirroring the properties and operation of intelligence, nor does it seem likely that there could be. Similarly referring to Rosen's description of complexity, this time through the words of Mikulecky [12]:

"*Complexity is the property of a real world system that is manifest in the inability of any formalism being adequate to capture all its properties. It requires that we find distinctly different ways of interacting with systems. Distinctly different in the sense that when we make successful models, the formal systems needed to describe each distinct aspect are not derivable from each other*".

As we indicated above, the translations, interpretations and comparisons intelligence makes cannot be simply reduced to a combination of one-to-one, one-to-many and many-to-one relationships. This, then, is the most inconvenient characteristic of intelligence: we cannot make conventionally simple models of it. We have commented earlier [13] that

[6]"*What serves for thermoregulation is re-adapted for gliding; what was part of the jaw becomes a sound receiver; guts are used as lungs and fins turn into shovels. Whatever happens to be at hand is made use of.*" [8]
[7]An expression derived for use in our context from Bernie Baars' metaphor of a "'*spotlight' on the theater of consciousness*".
[8]For example, the "flat earth" hypothesis is a very convenient one, whose manipulation makes the sale of two-dimensional maps of our quasi-spherical earth extremely lucrative.

"the primary quality of any recognizable entity is its unification. It is easy to bypass this aspect and concentrate on more observable characteristics, but an entity's unification cannot be ignored if we are to come to any understanding of its nature and operation. A viable characterization of 'unification' is provided by comparison between intra-entity correlative organization and entity-environment inter-correlative organization—between cohesion and adhesion [14]. Although the difference between these two for a crystal is substantial, that for a living organism is far higher".

System unity presumes a degree of coherence across all the scales of a system, where all of these are derived from others through intelligence. Sapience is the "tool" which permits evaluation of the relevance to a common purpose not only of individual items of information—as does intelligence—but also of the multiple system scales themselves as individual informational "entities". In this its usefulness, value or meaning is reminiscent of the overarching Aristotelian concept of final cause, rather than his other more local concepts of material, formal and efficient cause. We will return to Aristotle's [15] causes later—not only to final cause, but most especially to Rosen's [16] consideration of the importance of internalization of efficient cause in organisms.

When quantum mechanics forced itself onto the scientific stage at the beginning of the twentieth century it brought with it a major illumination of the way nominally independent entities relate to each other through measurement. No longer was it sufficient to presume that we could stand outside an experiment and remain extraneous to its results. Matsuno [17] and Salthe [18] have pointed out that measurement in its most general form may be likened to a mutual observation between experimental "subject" and "object"—both contribute to the experiment's conclusion, and neither remains untouched. This describes perfectly the dynamic relationship between different scales in a unified system: their mutual observation promotes an unending mutual adaptation.

Rosen [16] has proposed in great mathematical detail a formal self-referencing cycle of constructive causes which could be capable of maintaining the temporal viability of living systems. However, although his work includes a single but important reference to the mathematical possibility of "*a hierarchy of (different) informational levels*" [19], to the best of the authors' knowledge he never explicitly referred to the importance of scale in organisms, let alone the generation of hyperscale. Arguably, the most significant aspect of hyperscale is that it permits an organism to simultaneously operate, or appear to operate, as both a mono-scalar and a multiscalar entity [13]. The individual scales of a natural system are partially isolated from each other (through enclosure) but also partially in communication (through process-closure). The balance between these two through mutual observation takes the form of an autonomy negotiation [13]. Hyperscalar coherence is created through this mutual inter-scalar observation, whose recursive nature ultimately generates the independence of high-level consciousness, making humans human. Consciousness acts both as the servant of intelligence and sapience and their master in promoting an entity's coherence, cohesion and survival. We conclude that intelligence and sapience are distinct and necessary properties of all information processing systems, and that the degree of their availability controls a system's or a human's cognitive capacity, if not directly its application. This establishes intelligence and sapience as prime ancestors of the conscious mind.

To our knowledge there is as yet no mathematical approach which can satisfactorily deal with the native irrationalities of information integration across multiple scales, although one promising suggestion has been published [20]. The principle difficulty lies, however, not in the mechanics of developing a self-consistent mathematics, but in escaping from the 'blindness to viewpoint' which is a natural consequence of our stated final conclusion that

we live within hyperscale.

The central hypothesis is that we mentally integrate all observational scales into a hyperscalar "phase space" within which we are free to roam without taking any account of the "reality" of the "location" from which we make our observations. Considerations of internalism, externalism and even the "existence" of our viewpoint itself are ephemeral within hyperscale: we are the lords of our own creation, of our own "scale-free selves", and we can fly anywhere, view anything. Powerful though this may be, it dangerously conceals any distinction between "what really is"[9] and "what we make use of"—as we pointed out earlier, we can expect the landscape of our spatio-temporal hyperscalar "phase space" to include not only "facts", but also suppositions and conveniences.

2. Intelligence Sees Scale

Our first concrete task will be to address a long-standing problem related to sensory integration which most ob-

---

[9]The reader should note that we are expressing this "in common parlance", and not as a fundamental philosophy. The authors would lean towards a view that reality is what is left after we have modeled as far as we can be bothered to!

viously raises its head in the way we habitually think about combining a number of elements into a whole. We are used to presuming that we can be simultaneously and accurately aware of both an entity and its constituent elements. Unfortunately, this presumption creates an apparently esoteric but intellectually-catastrophic problem, especially in the cognitive domain, which we must address before going any further. Whilst being a necessary part of our argument, this also provides an excellent example of both the logical power and the logical risk of relying on hyperscalar-located transferable presence in constructing a world view of presumed accuracy.

Let us first propose a simplistic provisional difference between natural and artificial contexts. As their name suggests, we will define natural contexts as those which come to pass without human intervention, and following the usual meaning of artificial we will define artificial contexts as those resulting from human intervention. Continuing our simplistic progress, we note that the stability of natural systems depends on naturally occurring constraints, while that of artificial systems depends primarily on imposed constraints, either directly or indirectly exercised by human intervention. Simplistic though this proposition may be, it leads us to an important conclusion about the possibility of simultaneous and accurate awareness of both an entity and its constituents. **Figure 1** illustrates different forms of this relationship. **Figure 1(a)** shows what we will refer to as a collection of elements or observations, each of which is labeled as a kind of **a**. It is rather like "a bag" containing a black hole—we can put things in, but never see any relationship between those things—only the local exists, and there is no consequent global representation. **Figure 1(b)** shows a classical mathematical set[10], where we can manipulate both elements and their global representation within one and the same rational environment. **Figure 1(c)** shows the usual implication of "self-organization", where "the whole" **b** is not equivalent to "the sum of the parts" a_1, a_2, a_3... *i.e.* the global representation cannot be directly obtained from knowledge of the elements from which it is generated–there is no complete direct local-to-global correlation.

Figure 2 illustrates the *collection* a_1, a_2, a_3 ... we have referred to, presented as if we could "see everything" —a dangerous operation, because if we are not careful the *collection* will mutate into a *set*, whether we want it to or not! This *collection* of a_1, a_2, a_3 ... can be represented from "a single viewpoint" in a number of different ways b_1, b_2, b_3... There is an implied 'quod homines, tot sententiae', in that in general the collection can appear to have as many different implications or meanings as we attribute points-of-view b_1, b_2, b_3...

We can define (*i.e.* conveniently refer to) the collection a_1, a_2, a_3... as **A**, but we cannot derive **A** from a_1, a_2, a_3... as it is outside their individual contexts (we would have to be able to see into "the bag", and know all of their current inter-relationships). **A** is the single-point-of-view collection of **a1**, a_2, a_3... (N.B. there is only one **A**—so far as we are aware), and from a single collection **A** we get a one-to-many relationship with a multiplicity of b_1, b_2, b_3... This is radically different from the more familiar construction of a set **A** of a_1, a_2, a_3... (**Figure 1(b)**), where we can not only derive **A** from a_1, a_2, a_3, ... , but we usually presuppose that the two are equivalent.

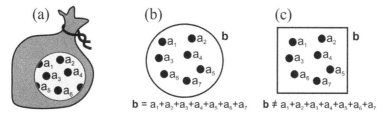

Figure 1. (a) A collection of elements **a**, where there is no global representation; (b) a mathematical set of elements, where **b** equals the sum of the **a**'s; (c) "self-organization", where **b** is not easily related to the sum of the **a**'s.

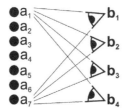

Figure 2. The collection of elements **a**, presupposing that we could "see everything", and showing a number of different global representations **b** as seen from different points of view.

---

[10]Our references to "mathematical sets" correspond to "naïve" or "intuitive" set theory.

Whereas the collection of **Figure 2** exemplifies an isolated natural context, the (mathematical) set of **Figure 1(b)** is an example of an artificial context, where stability is maintained by intentionally/externally imposed constraints (in this case the axioms which delineate the domain of applicability of the context's logic system). These two—the collection and the set—provide limiting extremes of the more familiar context shown in **Figure 3**, where there is a greater degree of predictability in the derivation of a "more globally applicable" global form **b** from a set of elements or observations a_1, a_2, a_3.... Any specific **b** is given by all of a_1, a_2, a_3... mutually aligning themselves within some kind of stability—an infinite process if carried out to perfection. Here again, however, it is easy to fool ourselves. Any collection is a purely externalist description—**A** is externalist from the point of view of an externalist formal model of the viewpoint of a chosen **b**. This raises all sorts of problems!

To try and accurately describe the character of a specific **b**, *either* you have to do this from its own single point-of-view, in which case you can't directly relate to **A** but **b** equals some kind of recursive integral of a_1, a_2, a_3..., or you have to adopt another different (single) viewpoint. In this latter case you are then using an external model of **b** (*i.e.* you have to formalize—simplify—to say anything at all!). So either you only "see" a single **b**—a rather Newtonian conclusion, depending on intentionally imposed constraints—and **b** equals **A** or is derivable from **A** or you presume it is derivable from **A** (*i.e.* there is a causal relationship), or you "see" multiple **b**'s and you have no idea where they come from or how they are derived!

All of this implies that a collection is "defined" without "observer intelligence"; definition of a mathematical set presumes that there is "observer intelligence"—when in fact there is no intelligence involved; recognition of real scale requires "observer intelligence". And it all seemed so simple to start with!

A small linguistic example should help at this point. If we think of each a as an individual's pronounced word, then **A** is the hypothetically (and probably inaccessible) complete established set of meanings attributed to that pronounced word by the complete community of pronouncing individuals. Any specific **b** is then the community-negotiated agreement as to the sense of **a** within a specific meaningful context, where the entire collection of understood meanings is **B** (N.B. the sound we would make in English from the syllable "ma" can mean at least either "mother" or "horse" in Chinese by dint of its pronounced intonation—a somewhat risky confusion, which English-speakers would not usually be aware of). Note that a completely uniform language would exhibit[11] **b** = **a**; a somewhat egotistical individual would presume **b** = **a**; a successful "living" language would exhibit **a** ≈ **b** by cultural agreement: only a completely controlled language (e.g. the "Newspeak" portrayed in George Orwell's book "1984") would make **A** equal to a controller-decided **b**—clearly an intentionally-constrained context!

The central conclusion we can draw from this account is that the incredible successfulness of our reliance on hyperscalar-based transferable presence effectively blinds us to whether we can reasonably presuppose equivalent access to different scales of a system or not. We would argue that in general we do not have equivalent access to different perceptional scales, and that the "scales" we apparently access are our internal models of them, which may be very different from "reality". Scanning electron microscopes are now capable of providing photographs of single atoms, but whether the spherical images they produce prove that atoms are indeed spherical is somewhat debatable![12]

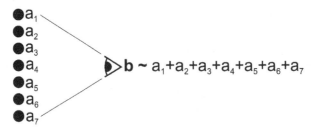

Figure 3. A more "normal" situation intermediate between the collection of **Figure 1(a)** and the set of **Figure 1(b)**, where there is a reasonably predictable emergent global representation **b**.

---

[11]Note that in these few quoted relationships, as is usual in mathematical representation, the left hand side of the "equation" is derived from the right hand side.

[12]At this, the reader may bridle, and point out that the proposition for "reality" the authors provided in Footnote 9 would embrace the *real* atomic nature portrayed by such photographs. We would agree. The critical point here is whether we keep an open mind in the face of apparently conclusive evidence and remain ready to accept that "we may have been wrong all the time!" A part of this problem is that the resulting photographs—or screen displays—are static, or at least effectively so in comparison to the timescales of intra-atomic change.

So, the idea we would wish the reader to hold on to at this point is that of the fallibility of our observation and understanding of scale. It may come as no surprise that our next action will be to apparently contradict this notion! Apparently yes–but in fact no! We merely wish to use this reminder as a device to emphasize that intelligence is not the logically self-consistent mechanism our transferable-presence intelligence tells us it is. We may not "correctly" view scale, but intelligence does! Logical rules are a crutch to rely on in the absence of intelligence. Intelligence is capable of far more than that.

We now appear to be suggesting something thoroughly idiotic: that although our human intelligence—of which we are so proud—is capable of transparently manipulating inter-scalar information conversions, we "ourselves" with our "all-powerful" conscious minds are incapable of maintaining a similar transparency without relying on the artificially constructed logical completeness of simple inter-scalar models. However, not only is the suggestion valid, but it could be no other way. We have already planted the seeds of this conundrum in previous sections of the paper.

Intelligence operates locally between system scales, and as such it is just as directly inaccessible from a "global" point of view as are the individual scales themselves: the wonderful integration of multiply-scaled phenomena through hyperscale precludes our direct and accurate access to local phenomena. Intelligence is an isolated component of our thought processes; a tool which operates within the confines of an ephemeral cage we construct momentarily to provoke its function. This idea that although we may be aware of the astounding capacity of intelligence we are unable to "reproduce" it within our conscious actions recalls Metzinger's [5] "naïve realism" hypothesis concerning the emergence of a "first-person perspective" in consciousness, that

"the representational vehicles employed by the system are transparent in the sense that they do not contain the information that they are models on the level of their content... 'Phenomenal transparency' means that we are systems which are not able to recognize their own representational instruments as representational instruments... A simple functional hypothesis might say that the respective data structures are activated in such a fast and reliable way that the system itself is not able to recognize them as such any more (e.g. because of a lower temporal resolution of met are presentational processes making earlier processing stages unavailable for introspective attention)... For biological systems like ourselves—who always had to minimize computational load and find simple but viable solutions—naïve realism was a functionally adequate 'background assumption' to achieve reproductive success".

In the strict sense we earlier gave to the word artificial, intelligence operates within an artificially constrained environment, or at least that is how it must locally appear to be, as the constraints are applied from scales other than local ones. In a natural context, however, there is a local-to-and-from-global consistency across the system-wide gamut of constraints, which corresponds to the unification of hyperscale. Local information processing is then mediated through natural intelligence, characterized as we describe above. In an artificial system, although there may be an attempt at consistency of constraints, this will never be complete[13], and local information processing will be mediated through artificial intelligence (which linguistic usage corresponds exactly to that of Artificial Intelligence—AI). This situation corresponds to **Figure 1(b)**.

Figure 2 illustrates the typical form of an inter-scalar information processing scenario. The multiple outcomes b_1, b_2, b_3... correspond to different processing constraints, either on different occasions or at different points in time within a single occasion[14]. It is easy to see from this why it is tempting to be scathing about the commonly addressed "phenomenon" of "self-organization". In anything other than a radically simple system different external system constraints result in different outcomes—organization is essentially externally driven and not internally: it would be more accurate to invoke as a description "environmental-organization", rather than "self-organization"! It is important to note that "external" here only means "external to an entire system" if we are talking about system-wide processing. It may also mean only "external to a sub-system"—in which case the drive can still be internal to the system as a whole. This is an important point in systems exhibiting cyclic process- closure, for example in the organisms analyzed by Robert Rosen [16], where the internalization of efficient cause depends on this duplicity of appearance.

If we rely on our "typical form of an inter-scalar information processing scenario" (see **Figure 3**) to represent a manifestation of intelligence, then in a multiscalar system it appears in a number of locally isolated processes, as illustrated by (**pre-a → a**), (**a → b**) and (**b → c**) in **Figure 4**. This diagram, however, presupposes that there

---

[13]Because if it were complete, the system would be alive—and the intelligence natural!

[14]There are clearly other possible processing scenarios, but these result from a combination of that presented here and the extended description of multiscalar systems given in the Appendix to this paper.

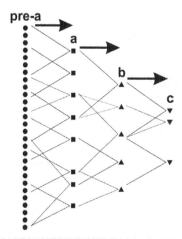

Figure 4. The manifestation of intelligence at a series of different levels in a multiscalar "system" where there is no global consistency between the various locally-applicable rationalities.

is no single cross-scalar rationality (e.g. as in a digital computer—which is therefore scale-less) and no hyper-scalar correlation which couples together all the individual scales. The local processing constraints, therefore, are in all cases just that—purely local and individual—and the "system" is in fact not a system at all, but a completely fragmented assembly of multiply-scaled sub-components. In the absence of a global unifying "mechanism", the individual scales correspond to the concept of a collection we proposed earlier. Global coherence would demand the presence of

1) a single globally consistent cross-scalar rationality (in which case it is an artificially constrained system, and is therefore in reality scale-less), or

2) a set of inter-scalar rationalities which conforms to some consistent global pattern (*i.e.* it is again a scale-less artificial system), or

3) a hyperscalar correlation (*i.e.* it is a natural system exhibiting real perceptional scale).

We conclude that in a naturally cohering multiscalar system there are two independent information processing "tools". One of these operates between pairs of scalar levels to establish local scalar coherences; the other operates across the entire assembly of scalar levels to establish global scalar coherence. We associate the former tool with intelligence and the latter with sapience. Neither tool is independent, nor in a natural system does each of them rely on the other to provide its indispensable constraints. There is, however, a clear difference between the two relative to the emergence of a system and its stabilization. Intelligence is primarily a system-building tool; it can promote the creation of new scales and local stabilization. Sapience, however, is more concerned with the viability of an already-built scalar assembly: it has no function in a minimally-scaled entity, but comes into its own with increasing system size as the central generator of system-wide coherence and stability:

intelligence is how we get there; sapience is how we remain there.

In distinguishing between intelligence and sapience we have located the two precisely within different contexts, which provides a precise separation in meaning. Although within this paper we can establish an exact context for intelligence, outside the pages of this journal we completely lose control, and in this as in every other categorization the result becomes less than entirely clear[15].

Across the complete spectrum of possibilities, a categorical separation of intelligence and sapience from an external viewpoint is implausible, most especially in that at a higher level they are both complementary components of wisdom. However, the primary distinction remains: intelligence sees scale; sapience sees all scales.

3. Sapience Sees All Scales

What happens when a multi-cellular network starts to expand? Rather than answering the question immediately we will back-track a little, to ask "how is it that a collection of cells constitutes 'a network' in the first place?" A simple description would be to suggest that inter-cellular cohesion must be greater than adhesion between the cells and parts of their environment. One possibility would be that a primitive force is responsible for the cohe-

---

[15] … as in the linguistic example of Chinese pronunciation we provided earlier.

sion: gravity holds our planet Earth together, for example. A more advanced possibility is that it may be in the interest of a given cell to associate with others; often small fish remain in large shoals, apparently to increase their individual chance of survival in the presence of a predator. This "self-interest" proposal is of a cohesion based on communication[16]. Unfortunately, however, the basic nature of our surroundings is that of a restriction on communication, which makes it possible to differentiate between here and there; between this and that. A consequence is that communication is never instantaneous between different spatial locations; which leaves a spatially-large network vulnerable to stimuli which drive its various parts out of synchronization. Our answer to the initial question, therefore, must be that when a network of cells expands it will risk fragmenting if it cannot find a way to overcome the energetic needs of its progressively massively-scaled inter-cellular communication.

It is a basic tenet of information theory that communication requires energy. Ultimately, if a network expands beyond a certain point, the energy required to maintain communication-based cohesion will rise beyond the collection's available resources. The only interesting strategy—interesting from our own point of view, that is—is for the network to generate a new global representation of itself, which both communicates internally in a simplified less energetic manner and permits economical external relations to be exercised. Intra-network communication energy can be saved by formalizing the nature of inter-cellular communication—by slaving [21]-[23] all the cells to one communication-model. Extra-network energy can be saved by only communicating information which is externally relevant[17]. Biological cells operate in precisely this manner. By first enclosing themselves in an "impenetrable" lipid membrane they are free to open up only those specific communication channels they wish to, and can portray themselves to their surroundings in whatever manner is "convenient" or "successful".

This expansion scheme is a classical emergent scenario, where a new simplified architectural level emerges from an underlying population, and the new level exerts "downward causation", or slaving, on the population individuals. It is important to notice that this creates a temporally infinite feedback loop:

1) (upward) emergence causes(downward) slaving,
2) which modifies (upward) emergence,
3) thus realigning(downward) slaving,
4) modifying (upward) emergence, and so on.

We will return to this vitally important aspect of infinity in the next section of the paper.

What has happened once can reoccur: a network which has managed to generate a new survival-promoting architectural level can do the same again and again... Arguably, and surprisingly, it will be easier to generate further new levels than it was to create the first one [24]. If we follow through with the logic of this argument, we can relatively easily end up with a naturally constrained system which is multiscalar and still unified. Let us stop for a moment at this critical point: what does it mean to say that the system is both multiscalar and unified? The entire architecture must be quasi-stable; each of the many scalar representations must be quasi-stable; each of the many inter-scalar interfaces must be quasi-stable. But notice, as in the skeletal representation of **Figure 5**, that this is only possible if there is a degree of correlation across the entire architecture, across all representations, across all interfaces. Not, however, complete correlation, which would imply that the scales are not real, but a partial correlation which is local to both individual representations and individual interfaces.

The relationship between any scale and its direct neighbors is fundamentally local in nature: the meaning or function of a biological cell when seen from a biological organ is very different from the meaning or function of an organ when seen from the organism. Inter-scalar relationships are very much a "you scratch my back and I'll

---

[16]It is a moot point whether there is a fundamental difference between the two kinds of cohesion we refer to here: our own view would be that they are both aspects of a single network-dependent property, but that is too large a question to be addressed within the confines of this paper.

[17]There is a rather nice parallel between this "survival" strategy and that of Internet IP addressing. An individual Internet node, or computer, is recognized by its IP address, which is commonly represented as four sequential decimal numbers, each in the range 0 - 255. If communication from a specific computer were to be broadcast to the entire network, the Internet would be completely swamped. To avoid this, a subnet mask, also consisting of four sequential decimal numbers, is used to limit the part of the network which is addressed. An attempt to communicate to a node at (192.168.2.1) with subnet mask (255.255.255.0), for example, will only be transmitted to those nodes whose address begins with (192.168.2.): the zero at the fourth location of the subnet mask implies that any valid number (*i.e.* any number between 0 and 255) is acceptable there, and consequently the transmission will be sent to all of the nodes (192.168.2.0), (192.168.2.1), (192.168.2.2)..., right up to (192.168.2.255), but nothing will be sent to any other node, for example to (192.168.3.1), (113.66.1.254), etc. This not only restricts the capacity requirement ("bandwidth") of the system, it also in general reduces the energy required to transmit the signal (*i.e.* it reduces the fan-out of the network electronics). Effectively, the Internet then consists of a number of different "scales", from "the whole World" down through "a given Country" and an "Internet Service Provider" to a domestic Local Area Network. The critical difference between this scheme and a naturally hierarchical system, however, is that all "scales" of the Internet are accessible using the same rationality: it is an artificially constrained system, and not a natural one, and consequently the apparent "scales" are not real.

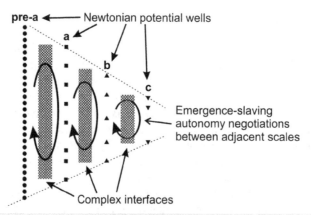

Figure 5. An archetypal multiscalar natural system, displaying quasi-stability across the entire gamut of its features, evidencing a degree of correlation across the entire architecture, across all representations, across all interfaces.

scratch yours" kind of thing—but the different scales' "backs" are poles apart! Adjacent scales are at liberty to negotiate away some uninteresting aspect of their autonomy in return for the receipt from their neighbors of a more valuable autonomy. Collier [14] has proposed as a plausible example of this autonomy negotiation that the brain has in the past ceded its biological support function to the body in return for greater freedom of information processing.

The global "integration" of this multiplicity of local negotiations serves to optimize as many aspects of a system's operation as possible. A major result is the ejection into the scalar-interface regions of the majority of the intractable complexity which would otherwise reside at the scalar levels [13], converting them into approximate Newtonian potential wells[18] and raising the efficiency of the system's computational response to external stimuli.

So, we now have a picture of a unified large system as a set of different quasi-stable scalar levels which are all quasi-correlated through hyperscale[19]. Centuries of philosophical effort, decades of neurological investigation and years of accurate imaging of the brain's operation culminate in the supposition that we construct models in our "mind's eye" which mirror the objects of our thoughts. The authors believe that we relate to hyperscalar systems from within our own assiduously-constructed hyperscalar mental environment! More than this, even— we believe that this is our "mind's eye"!

We live within hyperscale.

There is a great similarity between this suggestion and Metzinger's [5] proposition of naïve realism through phenomenal transparency:

"The phenomenal self is a virtual agent perceiving virtual agents in a virtual world. This agent doesn't know that it possesses a visual cortex, and it does not know what electromagnetic radiation is: It just sees 'with its own eyes'—by, as it were, effortlessly directing its visual attention. This virtual agent does not know that it possesses a motor system which, for instance, needs an internal emulator for fast, goal-driven reaching movements. It just acts 'with its own hands'. It doesn't know what a sensorimotor loop is—it just effortlessly enjoys what researchers in the field of virtual reality call 'full immersion', which for them is still a distant goal." [5]

Figure 6 illustrates how we imagine this environment to be built and used. Inter-scalar constructional integration (though intelligence) adds all of the individual scales into the "virtual"[20] scale-space of hyperscale. Within this space there is freedom of movement of the "spotlight of consciousness", as we are now only dealing with

---

[18]The success of a Newtonian scenario is that it reduces differences between local events and their global consequences in a relativistic environment [25], making it possible to respond rapidly to local stimuli without having to wait and see if a chosen response has large-scale unforeseen or unpleasant effects!

[19]Note, following our comments above on relativity, that in "normal" space, nonlocality would imply the disappearance of spatial differentiation: all different locations are "correlated". In our present context, if we picture our multiscalar system residing in scale-space, then hyperscale performs the same function as nonlocality: all different scales are correlated.

[20]Although, here and also indirectly in Metzinger's arguments, it is not at all clear whether this scale-space is really "virtual", or whether it is virtually "real", or even "the most real that there is"! Following on from the comment in Footnote 19, if "unvizualizable nonlocality" is "real", as the most advanced formulations of quantum mechanics would most likely presume, then there is no apparent reason why "unvizualizable" nonlocality of hyperscale should not be.

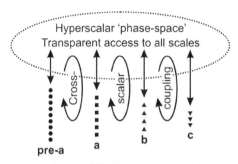

Figure 6. The construction of a hyperscalar environment from its constituent collection of "mutually inaccessible" individual scales, and its use in transparently accessing them.

models of a particular system scale, and not that scale itself in all its characteristics, and the "conscious observer" can access everything and everywhere in a transparent manner—with or without knowledge that "it is all only models".

Sapience permits the "observer" to visit all scales, all points of view, and to "see" clearly whether they are in correlation with each other, or what changes need to be made. As such, sapience is the main "synergetic[21] tool" permitting stabilization of the overall architecture of a system or, in our representation, of the "mind" itself.

We are now in a position from which we can provide an example of how this scheme works. All of the information, propositions, models and figures we have discussed in this paper appear within the hyperscalar scale-space of you, the attentive reader. This text itself is a hyperscalar device! **Figure 6** presents a hyperscalar viewpoint; so, most particularly, does **Figure 1(a)**, where we have transcended the impenetrable nature of our imagined "bag containing a black hole" in drawing the figure! The authors suggest that at this point the reader should "think about his or her complete environment" (a hyperscalar term, if ever there was one!), and notice that there is apparently no barrier to imagining, nay visiting all scales of all contexts [26].

The greatest difference between naïve realism through phenomenal transparency and hyperscalar scale-space is that while Metzinger's [5] proposition is derived from philosophical considerations in a top-down manner, our own argument is constructed bottom-up from system architecture.

We must now turn our attention to the "conscious observer" who we somewhat inexcusably slipped into the discussion in the manner of the author in Fowles' [27] novel *The French Lieutenant's Woman*.

4. Consciousness Makes It All Happen

Consciousness is a tricky phenomenon to get hold of. The reader will already have noticed that we, the authors, do not treat consciousness as being the sovereign of cognition, but as both the servant and master of intelligence and sapience. Consciousness only gains credibility in the context of mind; and vice versa! The emergence of consciousness depends primarily on the presence of real scale in a system—for this reason it is most likely that artificial systems could never exhibit consciousness. To see how we can justify attributing the emergence of consciousness to scale we must first follow through the arguments presented by Robert Rosen [16] for the success of Newtonian physics and the independent sustainability of living organisms.

The key to stability lies in the convergence or truncation of temporally infinite feedback loops such as that we described in the previous section, where up-scaling causes down-scaling, which causes up-scaling, which causes down-scaling, and so on.

A nice example of a convergent loop can be found in electronics in the guise of an operational amplifier (an "op-amp"). **Figure 7(a)** shows the symbolic representation of an op-amp with a "complementary" pair of inputs (labeled "+ve" and "−ve" in the figure) whose output V_{out} is fed back after a short delay τ to the negative input, −ve. Positive input voltage V_{in} applied to the +ve input will drive the output positively; positive input to the −ve one drives the output negatively. However, the op-amp itself pushes its output up to a large multiple of the dif-

---

[21]Synergy, or synergism stems from the 1657 theological doctrine that humans will cooperate with the divine grace in regeneration. The term is often attributed, however, to early 20th century cybernetics, where it came to refer to the dubious concept of a process in which two or more discrete influences or agents act together to create an effect which is greater than that predicted from their individual properties—"the whole being greater than the sum of the parts". In common with the concept of emergence, its citation most often indicates the shortcomings of a formal, and therefore simplified integration of a number of formalized, and therefore simplified models of different real influences.

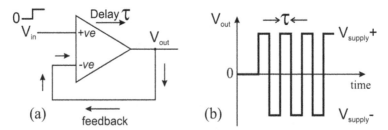

Figure 7. (a) An operational amplifier without internal energy dissipation; (b) the resulting sequence of output voltages V_{in}.

ference between the two input voltages at +ve and −ve. For practical op-amps this amplification would be probably by a factor of more than one million. It is not difficult to see that having once been started up by a voltage at the +ve input, the op-amp output will cycle negative, positive, negative, positive... without stopping, as shown in **Figure 7(b)**. However, that is not what electronics textbooks tell us—and on the contrary, if we measure the output, within certain constraints it will be equal to the input. The model we have presented left out "imperfections" in the op-amp which cause the cycling signal to lose energy, and the output converges towards a final state. In general terms this would correspond to the emergence of a new system character through the dissipation of energy. More often than not, however, dissipation leads to the eradication of structure, and to the phenomenon usually referred to as "heat death"[22]. In the case of our op-amp, internal dissipation does indeed lead to the decay of signals which are above the op-amp's characteristic cutoff frequency, leaving only a quasi-static (low-frequency) output. Truncated infinite looping is infinitely more interesting than convergence through dissipation, as it does not preclude rapid changes in cycling information.

Rosen's argument in relation to Newton's Laws [16] is (very sketchily) as follows. We split the Universe into self and ambience, then ambience into system and environment, and begin with the identification of a "particle" as a formal structureless object which encodes 'something' in the "real" world. The first relevant question is where is it? The answers form a "chronicle"—a list of positions, but no way to derive any one of them from any other one. A second feasible question is of the derivative of the particle's position: What is its velocity? The answers again form a chronicle–a list now of velocities; but of prime importance is that there is no way to derive the entries in one chronicle from those in the other! This questioning can be continued indefinitely, through what is the derivative of its velocity, what is the derivative of its acceleration, and so on, to infinity.

We now have, unhelpfully, an infinite collection[23] of chronicles containing apparently unrelated entries! Newton's First Law then specifies that in an empty environment the particle cannot accelerate: this truncates the infinite collection of chronicles, leaving just those of position and velocity. The key to performing a similar truncation for a non-empty environment lies in Taylor's Theorem. The infinite set of chronicles expresses everything there is to know about the particle—they determine its state-and Taylor's Theorem tells us that present state entails subsequent state: the state is recursive.

Newton's Second Law collapses the state down to two variables by first representing the environment entirely by its effect as a force on the particle, then by reflecting this force in a single chronicle of acceleration, and finally by expressing the force as an explicit function of only position and velocity:

$$F\{x(t), x'(t)\} = m \cdot x''(t) \tag{1}$$

where F is the environmental force, x the particle position, x' its velocity, x'' its acceleration, m its mass and t the time; or more familiarly

$$\text{Force} = \text{mass times acceleration.} \tag{2}$$

Rosen has used the curtailment of infinity in Newtonian physics as an introduction to his own formulation in *Life Itself* [16]. His general argument is that both Newtonian and living systems require an apparently infinite sequence of conditions to be valid, but also that both are stabilized by cutting off that infinite sequence. More accurately, his argument in respect of living organisms does not refer to simple truncation–by just cutting off a

---

[22] ... the traditionally expected ultimate future state of the Universe which follows from the second law of thermodynamics—but only if we presume that classical thermodynamics can be blindly applied to open rather than closed systems: *i.e.* in the absence of life!

[23] Our emphasis (c.f. **Figure 1(a)**)—to make clear in the terms of our own argument, in addition to that of Rosen, that there is no way that we can legally "pull out of the hat" a global consequence of the collection.

sequence—but to truncation of the form of the sequence by replacing the cut off member by one which was already encountered, earlier in the sequence. The result resembles the form of the op-amp circuit shown in **Figure 7**: the "output" is connected back to the "input", creating a loop. As for the op-amp circuit; once the circuit has been started up, it will continue on its own—assuming, of course, as we initially did, that there is no dissipation. The original input is now no longer necessary, and it can be removed, leaving a self-sufficient system to oscillate into eternity. There are two important points here:

1) this self-sufficiency was Rosen's main concern—to explain how life can be self-perpetuating once started, and

2) in fact, infinity is not removed from the picture: the infinity of one kind of sequence is merely replaced by the infinity of another. Connecting the output of an op-amp back to its input creates a temporal infinity through feedback, as we pointed out above[24].

Rosen [16] defines an organism in relation to Aristotle's [15] efficient cause[25]:

"a material system is an organism if, and only if, it is closed to efficient cause".

Life, when described this way, is similar to fire from the point of view of a primitive people who cannot light fires on their own. Once started it can continue on its own, transfer from one substrate to another, split up, sire new offspring, populate large areas, and all this with just the input of some environmental material. But if it dies out, then that is the end of it. By "closed", Rosen means that the answer to "Who or what constructed this part of the organism?"—*i.e.* its efficient cause—can always be found inside the organism itself.

Rosen's argument leading to the self-sufficiency of organisms [16] is (again sketchily) as follows. The initial step is to draw in relational form the metabolic conversion of a collection of "environmental chemicals" A to a collection of "enzymes" B (**Figure 8(a)**) by a biological component f[26].

The hollow-headed arrow indicates a flow from an "input" to an "output"; the solid-headed arrow denotes the induction of this flow by a component (or "processor")[27]. If efficient cause is to be internalized, we must now ask "what makes f?" We can resolve this problem by adding in a new processor Φ, which "makes" f (Rosen calls this function repair) from its internally available supply of ingredients B (**Figure 8(b)**).

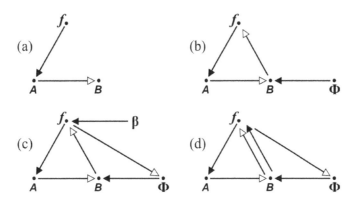

Figure 8. Rosen's constructional sequence to internalize efficient cause in organisms: (a) the first step—establishing the relational form of a metabolic process; (b) adding a repair function based on internally available metabolic products; (c) adding a replication function as a separate component; (d) deriving replication from metabolism and repair, which merges replication into the system, rather than imposing it as an external cause.

---

[24]The authors believe that somewhere in this "resolving one infinity by imposing another" is the generation of time itself, as a convenient "means to an end"; but to what "end" they have no idea!

[25]The following provides an example of Aristotle's four causes and their place within a unified environment. On the specific occasion of building a particular house: material cause would be the bricks and the cement; formal cause is the architect's plan; efficient cause is the builder; final cause is the reason for the house—to live in, maybe? It should be carefully noted that, depending on the final cause, the exact delineation of the other causes may alter. The one of Aristotle's causes which exercises Rosen the most is efficient cause: in the context of *Life Itself*, it is the answer to the question "who or what constructed this".

[26]Note that in the version of **Figure 8(c)** which appears in Rosen's *Life Itself* as **Figure 10(c)** [14] the hollow- and solid-headed arrows have been unfortunately exchanged, owing to an editorial error.

[27]The relationships Rosen uses between inputs and outputs are formal mathematical mappings—where "one-to-one" and "many-to-one" are valid relationships, but "one-to-many" is not. Our use of the italicized words "collection" here are intended to remind the reader that there may be more than "meets the hyperscalar eye" in this story.

This relational diagram represents any one of Rosen's category of "(M, R)-systems"[28]. Unfortunately, of course, we must now ask "what makes Φ" Easy! We throw in another processor β which "makes" Φ (Rosen calls this function replication) from its internally available supply of components f (**Figure 8(c)**). Guess what comes next... "What makes β?" However, and it is a very big "however", it is now possible to resolve the problem in quite a different way.

Rosen points out that under certain, not unduly restrictive, formal constraints on the mapping from A to B, this replication component β can be derived from the already-present mappings of metabolism (induced by f) and repair (induced by Φ). The replication "component" β can then be replaced by the addition of one new solid-headed arrow of induction to the diagram (**Figure 8(d)**) between Φ and f, which represents the new assumption that an element b of B is in fact a processor (a not too unrealistic proposition if b is an enzyme). Efficient cause is now completely internalized: Rosen states that

"*as far as entailment is concerned, the environment is out of the picture completely, except for the initial input A.*" [16]

The "not unduly restrictive" constraint this imposes on the mapping A to B is that it must be invertible (*i.e.* mapping B back to A must also be valid). This formally requires that the metabolic mapping A to B be one-to-one, and not many-to-one[29].

Let us look at what has happened here. If we take A to be a package of hand-written code, and f to be a compiler ("metabolism"), then the output B can be a functional program[30]. Given suitable inputs Φ to B, we can arrange that the program (re)generates the compiler f ("repair"), but now we must justify the appearance of Φ (**Figure 9(a)**). If we continue the generative sequence, then we can spawn Φ, and therefore everything up to this point (except the initial "environmental supply" of written code A) from yet another program which is external to f, B and Φ.

To finalize this project, we are now well on the way to constructing an infinite set of nested computational environments, each of which creates everything which is inside itself, but each of which must be created from outside (**Figure 9(b)**)[31]. This is the ineffective scenario which Rosen avoids by referring his new replicating processor β back to the already-included processors f, B and Φ. In doing so he truncates the otherwise necessarily infinite series of "efficient cause" processors. **Figure 9(c)** illustrates this process within our nested-environ-

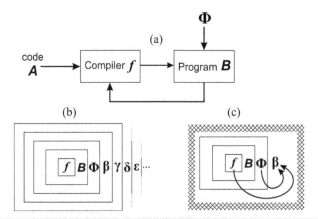

Figure 9. (a) Representing Rosen's metabolism and repair as a program and its compiler; (b) redrawing the system as an infinite series of nested environments; (c) truncating the infinite nesting series by referring back to an earlier stage.

[28] "M" for metabolism; "R" for repair.

[29] As A. H. Louie has pointed out (in a private communication), the constraint on the mapping A to B corresponds to an "abstract version of the one-gene-one-enzyme hypothesis". Rosen's book *Life Itself* was published in 1991. Given more recent post-Genome-Project discoveries of the importance of previously "discarded" junk-DNA and the critical nature of non-protein-creating reactions inside regions closely surrounding the DNA double helix, the sufficiency of this hypothesis must be called into doubt—and along with it the sufficiency of this constraint in Rosen's model, and of his reliance on formal mappings which preclude one-to-many relationships. This is critical in transplanting "infinity-truncation" to our own context of a naturally multiscaled system, where it is impossible to maintain externally-formal constraints on inter-scalar relationships—Rosen is effectively describing the occurrence of natural events in a formally-artificial system.

[30] Note that this formulation corresponds to Rosen's final proposition that b may be a processor.

[31] Note that it is also possible to construct the nesting using Rosen's (M, R) system as the "initial element", in which case the central box would contain both f and B, but that the truncation argument then still holds.

ment formulation, where the constituents of β are assembled from levels which are inside β, thus truncating the infinite environmental nesting. The reader should be aware that Rosen's "relational argument" and our own "nesting of computational environments" are mathematically equivalent, in that prior to truncation they share the same relational sequence in Rosen's graph-theoretic formulation [16]:

$$A \rightarrow B \rightarrow H(A,B) \rightarrow H(B,H(A,B)) \rightarrow \tag{3}$$

where

$$A \rightarrow B = f \tag{4}$$

$$B \rightarrow H(A,B) = \Phi \tag{5}$$

$$H(A,B) \rightarrow H(B,H(A,B)) = \beta \tag{6}$$

The computational nesting is nominally multiscalar, but it is in fact a scale-less artificial system[32], as can be concluded from examination of the graph-theoretic formulation, where it is possible to travel along the entire relational sequence by recourse to a single formal rationality (*i.e.* that within which Rosen constructed his arguments). This confirms our earlier conjecture that Rosen's approach takes no account of scale. Even if that were not the case, if we now attempt to derive by truncation an enclosing environment (or scale) from only a single enclosed environment (or "smaller" scale), then the result is again an artificial system, whose operations indeed apparently "converge"—but not to anything of any particular interest! Much more interesting is that by truncating the infinite series of computational environments we move from global system control to some kind of local control, corresponding to Rosen's [16] requirement for the internalization of efficient cause in living systems.

Our interest in Rosen's approach to internalizing efficient cause is probably now becoming clear. Can we use it to see how the conscious mind appears "as if from nothing" in an organism, and in doing so can we relate the mind to intelligence and sapience?

Let us assemble the elements we need for this argument.

1) The quasi-stability of very large natural systems demands that they are multiscalar.

2) Inter-scalar transit in a natural system is counter-rational, in that we cannot rely on the rationality of any specific scale when crossing between scales[33].

3) Individual scales are partially en-closed, and communicate with their neighbors through autonomy negotiation.

4) Intelligence is a tool which permits inter-scalar transit, in that it facilitates derivation of the "sub-global" representations of scale from collections of individual elements.

5) Sapience is a "higher-level" tool, in that it facilitates the derivation of "global" hyperscalar representations from collections of individual scales.

6) Intelligence and sapience depend for their success on mutual observation between the subjects of their "integrations".

7) From within hyperscale we can "transparently" observe all scales, all elements which go to make up that hyperscalar environment—even those scales or elements which are fundamentally perceptionally invisible to us, for example the inside of a black hole!

Figure 6 illustrates the construction and use of a hyperscalar environment. This could never be a static construction, or its "owner"[34] would no longer evolve, and would certainly fall victim to environmental change. The perpetual updating of all its inter-scalar and hyperscalar-scalar relationships, however, requires perpetual re-negotiation of all of its subsumed partial autonomies—there is a permanent mutual observation taking place. Now, is it possible that all of this takes place at a single scale? No, clearly not. So we again have a nested collec-

---

[32]Note the generality that if all parts and scales of a nominally multiscalar system can be accessed through a single rationality, then it will collapse into a scale-less system [28].

[33]1 + 1 = 2 is itself counter-rational: the only conclusion we can draw from 1 + 1 is that it equals 1 + 1: any other conclusion is an externally imposed constraint on the system! The equation itself represents a multiscalar system (as do all equations), where apparently "2" emerges from "1 + 1"! There is no generally applicable natural manner in which the reduction of two parameters to one can be carried out unambiguously. It is worth noting that inter-scalar transit in the other direction—from one parameter to two—is even worse: this is the very nature of inter-scalar transit.

[34]Note that through transparency, hyperscale and its owner ultimately become each other, and there is no longer any distinction between subject and object. Metzinger states at the conclusion of his paper [5], "... the conscious self is an illusion which is no one's illusion": it would more reasonably follow from our propositions that the conscious self is its own illusion.

tion of environments similar to our re-formulation of Rosen's proposition. To cut a (very) long story short[35], we believe that the internalization of material replication in Rosen's organisms is mirrored by the internalization of observational replication in natural multiscalar systems. How could this take place?

Rosen depends on the formalized partial isolation of the mappings induced by f, Φ and b to permit the equivalence between the "replicator" β and a combination of the "metabolizer" f and the "repairer" Φ. The development of consciousness from mutual observation in a multiscalar natural system would depend on the partial isolation of individual scales from each other, and most particularly on the negotiated isolation of hyperscale from the collection of individual scales. In Metzinger's [5] words:

"We are systems that are not able to recognize their subsymbolic self-model as a model. For this reason we are permanently operating under the conditions of a 'naïve-realistic misunderstanding': we experience ourselves as being in direct and immediate epistemic contact with ourselves. What we have in the past simply called 'self' is not a non-physical individual, but only the content of an ongoing, dynamical process—the process of transparent self-modeling".

And where does this dynamical "process of transparent self-modeling" take place?

Within the confines of an ongoing partially transparent hyperscale-to-and-from-multi-individual-scalar negotiation.

And how does observation from within hyperscale become stabilized to observation within hyperscal—how does the efficient cause of observation become internalized?

By the natural convergence of inter-scalar and hyperscale-to-and-from-multi-individual-scalar autonomy negotiations, which leads to coherent quasi-stabilized unity of the system and effectively to truncation of the infinite mutuality of observation of observation of observation of observation of observation...

We believe that *observation* becomes progressively restricted to within the hyperscalar "phase-space", where it can more easily access "everything it needs" through phenomenal transparency. It should by now be evident that we are not limiting ourselves to a proposition that "consciousness is the ultimate emergence of networked intelligent processing", but that "consciousness" is more or less a property of all information processing: Tononi [29] [30] maintains that consciousness is equivalent to the integration of information. This does not preclude the generation of a degree of consciousness within the confines of a real neural network which is impossible at lower information-processing densities [24]—only that this kind of "high-level" consciousness is only ever generated within a hyperscalar environment. Nor does this suggest that we should be able to be aware of different levels of our own mind's consciousness: all of these would be subsumed into the transparency of hyperscale, where the only "different levels" we observe are ones that we internally "permit to exist": ego naturally resolves the problem, by insisting that there is "me and only me"! Even so, intelligence requires an observational capacity at its own level; sapience does too; even the interactions of apparently "Newtonian" particles (controversially) do: "unconscious" cognitive processing is maybe not so unconscious after all!

5. The Computational Implementation of Sapience

It will be evident from the preceding discussion that computational implementation of sapience is not only an exceedingly complex affair, but that it also depends on prior computational implementation of intelligence. Herein lies the problem. Is it currently feasible to artificially implement intelligence? Clearly not. The constraints which are imposed on computational machines to validate their performance eliminate any possibility of non-preprogrammed operations. Computers are blind servants of their designers and users. More specifically, the primary function of the system clock in a digital computer, for example, is to eliminate any unforeseen[36] global-to-local influences: computer gates are completely isolated from each other, except for the inter-gate pathways laid down during the diffusion, poly-Si and metallization stages of their chips' manufacture. This aspect of a computer cannot be overstated. Much is made of the emergence of global properties in digital-computational simulations of multi-agent systems. There is no such emergence. The output of a digital computer is solely the result of its design, programming and data input: nothing is created that could not be done, albeit much more slowly, by personally following the process manually. The expression artificial intelligence is an oxymoron: intelligence is real, or it is not at all!

So, is all lost? Is a search for computational sapience worthless? No, not at all. Computers are in their infancy.

---

[35]In fact, to truncate an infinite sequence of considerations!
[36]... or even foreseen!

The first, unreliably accurate analog ones were replaced by their digital counterparts, where the somewhat forgiving nature of analog manipulations was replaced by the theoretically (and approximately practically) absolute precision of binary arithmetic, in return for the ever-present risk of catastrophic "system crash". Alleviation of this risk entailed the categorical elimination of anything which lies outside their designers' specifications[37]. Inside a modern digital processor, extensive if not complete design testing has virtually eliminated catastrophic failure, but the risk is still unavoidably present in the combination of processor design with insufficiently tested application software. Current Air Traffic Control systems are demonstrably close to the limit of error-free design complication, but they are still nowhere near the complexity of even the simplest biological information processors.

So where do we go next? How do we solve the dual computational problems of overbearing operational formality and design error? And, more relevant to this paper, is it sufficient or even of value to decide within a digitally-computational scenario which techniques and mechanisms are required to build computational intelligent or sapient systems? Is it enough, for example, to assume that James Albus' description of intelligence is sufficient for our general purpose, and to confidently say, therefore, that all that intelligent systems need to be able to do is to reason about actions, to generate plans, to compute the consequences of plans and compare them, to execute plans, etc.? Given the mismatch between current digital computation techniques and the nature of intelligence we have described in this paper, this would be very shortsighted. If we are to rely on the at least dual specification of intelligence and sapience, we must first attempt to decide which of them does what, even if we are not yet able to say how. Our exercise in terms of reasoning, actions, plans, decisions, and executions should then be used to inform ourselves where we should go next in what will be a very long search for implementation.

One thing is clear. All of the examples of intelligence we meet in nature are at the very least multi-scalar. We will not be able to implement intelligence without attention to scale, to inter-scalar complexity, to scalar isolation and to its attendant partial autonomies [7] [20]. None of these properties have any meaning in a purely digital context. Nature relies on digital-to-analog-to-digital codings in all its dealings. If we are to implement intelligence, we must do likewise. Sapience is an even more esoteric "property", in its reliance on all of the scales of a processing entity. Sapience does not reside "here" or "there": it has, for an individual entity, something of the character of "language" across a quasi-unified society, with all its attendant multiplicities of definition, of meaning, of implication. An important facet of both inter-scalar-(intelligent) and multi-scalar-(sapient) correlations is that any presumed orthogonality between systemic properties collapses [20]. Consequently, even the philosophically basic modes of analogic, inductive, deductive, abductive and subductive reasoning merge into a generalized contextually variable birational process [31]. Where could we "implement" these extreme systemic characteristics in a scheme which relies on absolute localization of its processing elements, as does a digital computer? Nowhere! We must first deal with the relatively simple intelligence of inter-scalar correlation, cooperation and conflict before we can even contemplate "integrating" a multiplicity of inter-scalar "systems" into a unified sapience.

6. Wisdom Is Everything

Homo sapiens (Latin) means "wise" or "clever" human—further classified into the subspecies of *homo sapiens neanderthalensis* (Neanderthals) and *homo sapiens sapiens* (Cro-Magnons and present-day humans).

Again following Jean-Luc Doumont's criteria, we should first state the major conclusion which we will draw from this section of the paper. This will be that

wisdom subsumes intelligence, sapience and consciousness.

So what does wisdom consist of?

"To Socrates, Plato, and Aristotle, philosophy is about wisdom. The word 'philosophy', philosophia, to 'love' (phileîn) 'wisdom' (sophía), supposedly coined by Pythagoras, reflects this. Just what wisdom would involve, however, became a matter of dispute"[38].

One of our major contentions in this paper is that if we equate the term sapience directly to wisdom we risk missing out a critical aspect of cognitive processing. Problematically, however, a substantive "architecture" of

---

[37]A very early problem with digital circuitry, for example, was the unpredictable result of applying simultaneous "ones" to both inputs of an (R-S) flip-flop. This indeterminacy was eliminated by adding circuitry which ensures that the subsequent state of a (J-K) flip-flop is well defined (always assuming, of course, that the power supply and system clock are operating as we expect them to!).

[38]Proceedings of the Friesian School: http://www.friesian.com/wisdom.htm

wisdom has never been articulated, and we find ourselves lacking a name for the specific attribute of wisdom which in "architectural" terms provides an intermediate faculty between the apparent simplicity and comprehensibility of intelligence and the "godlike" state of wisdom:

"The truth is this: no one of the gods loves wisdom {philosopheîn} or desires to become wise {sophós}, for he is wise already. Nor does anyone else who is wise love wisdom. Neither do the ignorant love wisdom or desire to become wise, for this is the harshest thing about ignorance, that those who are neither good {agathós} nor beautiful {kalós} nor sensible {phrónimos} think that they are good enough, and do not desire that which they do not think they are lacking." [32]

We propose using the word sapience uniquely to describe this faculty of intermediacy between intelligence and wisdom. In doing so we do not presuppose that "this is the end of the matter"—but hope that by locating intelligence, sapience and wisdom realistically with respect to each other we may stimulate further, more detailed analysis of the extreme complexity of cognitive processing.

It is tempting to think in terms of a comparative scale. Wisdom stands far above the other individual elements of our conclusion, but we cannot establish an immutable order for intelligence, sapience and consciousness. Wisdom collapses in the absence of any one of these, and there is no state or performance of "partial wisdom" corresponding to the presence of only one or two of these three dramatis personae. Wisdom emerges from intelligence, sapience and consciousness, and this in the context of mind.

It is relatively easy to distinguish between intelligence, sapience and wisdom if we check to which domains of a hyperscalar system each is relevant. Intelligence is local with respect to scale (and operates primarily in a "bottom-up" manner); sapience is local with respect to hyperscale (and operates primarily in a "top-down" manner); wisdom is global with respect to both scale and hyperscale, and it is consequently "outside rationality" (and takes account of not only "bottom-up" and "top-down" considerations, but also scalar and hyperscalar aspects of all the relationships between a system and its environment[39]).

It is essential to notice that in a multiscalar system Aristotle's [15] final cause is not unique: interscalar communicational difficulties preclude complete transfer of knowledge from one scale to another, and consequently in a naturally-correlated hyperscalar system there are at least as many versions of final cause as there are recognizable representations of the system, and there will be a sense of hierarchy in the degree to which a specific "local final cause" may be relevant from the "point of view" of a more global one.

A fine example of the relationship between intelligence, sapience and wisdom can be found in the hypothetical reactions of a soldier, threatened along with his[40] comrades by an enemy machine gun. Intelligence may tell him amongst other things that if he wants to see what is happening he should put his head up; his sapient instinct to survive may moderate his choice of action and use his intelligence to keep his head down; his wisdom may well initially support his sapient conclusion, but his societal mind may cause him to rush forwards to disable the gun and thus save his comrades—even though he will be aware that in doing so he may lose his own life. Cognitive processing may well remain purely internal up to and including the level of sapience, but to arrive at a state of wisdom, society must necessarily enter into consideration.

Although wisdom is often equated to goodness[41], the authors do not accept that this is necessarily the case. It seems more likely that the wisdom we have been describing in this paper is that pertaining to an individual (human) organism—even though that individual may well act in the knowledge and consideration of the society in which he or she is embedded, as in our "hypothetical example". It seems more likely that a yet "higher form of wisdom" could be established, which resides in the abstraction of "society", and which establishes its own code of auto-defined good and evil through globally-correlated peer pressure. Such a phenomenon would be a socially-hyperscalar construction of individual-hyperscalar elements. Could this equate to ethics?

---

[39]The inclusion of environmental or ecosystemic influences at this point in our argument would be both superfluous and confusing—we have left discussion these aspects to the later Annex to this paper.

[40]Our use of the masculine form here is intentionally sexist—if possible we should prefer to remove any person from this hypothetical context, but if we cannot do so we would prefer to eliminate at least those whose survival is most important in the medium term to the continuation of both species and society. It is worth remembering that the hypothetical example we refer to here is reflected in the real wartime actions of many soldiers, and in the peacetime actions of many individuals who find themselves caught up with others in large-scale disasters (for example in the sinking of the *Herald of Free Enterprise*: http://en.wikipedia.org/wiki/MS_Herald_of_Free_Enterprise: "*A number of the disaster's heroes received awards, including a George Medal for ex-policeman Andrew Parker. He became known as 'the human bridge' when he saved his wife, his 12-year-old daughter and about 20 other passengers who walked over his body to safety*": http://www.edp24.co.uk/norfolk-life/the_memories_live_on_1_695035

[41]Aristotle's view of good is that "mankinds always act in order to obtain that which they think good" [15].

7. Intelligence, Sapience and Semiotics

The argumentation we have presented is not in itself strange—it is an empirical construction, not an intellectual one. Apparent strangeness appears purely as a result of our insistence on accurately locating the viewpoints we adopt in our observations.

There is no obvious reason why nature should obey the presupposition that rationality be homogeneous across different scales; "reason" leads us to exactly the opposite conclusion. Information is always contextual. Information processing in a system always takes place between "architectural" scales, rather than at a single scale. Intelligence is the "tool" which permits an "overview" of the relevance of individual items of information to their assembly for a scale-specific purpose. The overall scalar and hyperscalar characters of informational architectures are most striking, however, in the way they mirror Peirce's [33] semiosic categories [34]. We can do no better than to quote the following three passages from Edwina Taborsky [35].

"There are three basic Peircean modalities of codal organization. They are a Firstness of possibility, a Secondness of individuality and a Thirdness of normative habits of the community... Firstness is an internal codification that measures matter without references to gradients of space and time, and 'involves no analysis, comparison or any process whatsoever, nor consists in whole or in part of any act by which one stretch of consciousness is distinguished from another' [33]. Matter encoded within firstness... is unable to activate recording or descriptive systems, which are secondary referential codes that provide the stability of memory".

Which excellently describes the collection at a single scale whose distinctiveness we have proposed earlier (see **Figure 1(a)**, for example).

"Secondness as a measurement collapses the expansive symmetrical capacities of firstness, by providing spatial gradients and temporal parameters that act as proximate referential values to inhibit and constrain the energy encoded in firstness. Secondness refers to 'such facts as another, relation, compulsion, effect, dependence, independence, negation, occurrence, reality, result' [33]. Matter encoded within secondness is oriented and intimately linked to this local context, and we can assign a definite quantitative and qualitative description to its identity".

Which corresponds to both the emergent scenario illustrated in **Figure 1(c)** and **Figure 3** and its resultant downward elemental slaving and, as we have made clear, requires intelligence for its accomplishment.

"Thirdness is a process of distributive codification, operative both externally and internally, that transforms the multiplicity of diverse sensory-motor data into universal diagrammes. '... there is some essentially and irreducibly other element in the universe than pure dynamism or pure chance (and this is) the principle of the growth of principles, a tendency to generalization' [33], or more simply, the tendency to 'take habits'. Thirdness sets up a general model that works to glue, to bind, to relate, to establish relationships and connected interactions. It extracts descriptions from the diverse instantiations of experiences and 'translates' them into a syncretic diagramme such that subsequent local instantiations can emerge as versions or representations of these general morphologies. Thirdness is a 'matter of law, and law is a matter of thought and meaning' [33]".

Which mirrors our description of hyperscalar form and character, and the resultant operational function of sapience.

8. Conclusions

It is comparatively easy to state our final conclusion—the reader has been aware of it throughout this text—that we live within hyperscale: intelligence is how we get there; sapience is how we remain there.[42]

The section headings we have used in the paper make up the next most detailed level of conclusion: intelligence sees scale; sapience sees all scales; consciousness makes it all happen; wisdom is everything.

Biological cells can portray themselves to their surroundings in whatever manner they "wish", by enclosing themselves in an "impenetrable" lipid membrane and then opening up the communication channels they require. A hyperscalar sapient environment provides the means of managing such a selectively-communicative survival strategy, by delivering an apparently multiscalar view of surrounding phenomena without the computational

---

[42]The authors wish to thank one of their internal reviewers of this paper for suggesting that they answer the following question: "Is a cockroach intelligent and sapient because (through its capacity to survive) it fulfills the argumentation: 'intelligence is how we get there; sapience is how we remain there'". As an answer we propose the following. Yes, of course it is... but also, of course, only to the limits of its inherent (neural...) capabilities. Although sapience is a (~the) "high-level" characteristic, its "presence" or "absence" is not defined by the neural capacities of its possessor, but by the degree of unification of its entire information-processing assembly, including motor/sensor relationships with its environment.

complexities of inter-scalar transit. In a complex, multiscalar, ever-changing environment there is much to be said for the construction of a strategic interface between the simplicity of our thinking and the complexity "out there". System unity presumes a degree of coherence across all the scales of a system: sapience is the "tool" which permits an evaluation of the relevance of both individual items and individual scales of information to a common purpose. We have proposed using the word sapience uniquely to describe the faculty of intermediacy between intelligence and wisdom.

Hyperscalar coherence is created through mutual inter-scalar observation, whose recursive nature generates the independence of high-level consciousness, making humans human. We conclude, however, that intelligence and sapience are distinct and necessary properties of all information processing systems, and that the degree of their availability controls a system's or a human's cognitive capacity, if not its application. This establishes intelligence and sapience as prime ancestors of the conscious mind.

We have presented in this paper an argument which associates intelligence and sapience with the specific characteristics of a natural multiscalar hierarchy (for an introduction to hierarchy, see [36]). It would be most useful if the generation of hyperscale from an assembly of individual scales could be formally represented. To our knowledge, however, there is no currently available mathematical approach which can satisfactorily deal with the native irrationalities of information integration across multiple scales.

And finally, with respect specifically to sapience: sapience goes much further than does intelligence, in its wide ranging considerations, and its cross-scale harmonizing and resolution of conflicting goals, causes and effects. We conclude that sapience is a fundamental system property, but one which only manifests itself within systems whose hierarchical structure is sufficiently complex for hyperscalar interactions to be able to dominate the crude automatisms of inter-scalar slaving [21], namely within the high-level mental capacities of living systems, and most particularly of humans:

hyperscale puts the sapiens into homo.

References

[1]   Albus, J.S. (1991) Outline for a Theory of Intelligence. *IEEE Trans Systems, Man and Cybernetics*, **21**, 473-509. http://dx.doi.org/10.1109/21.97471

[2]   Albus, J.S. and Meystel, A.M. (2001) Engineering of Mind: An Introduction to the Science of Intelligent Systems. Wiley, Hoboken.

[3]   Cottam, R., Ranson, W. and Vounckx, R. (2008) The Mind as an Evolving Anticipative Capability. *Journal of Mind Theory*, 39-97.

[4]   Schempp, W. (1992) Quantum Holography and Neurocomputer Architectures. *Journal of Mathematical Imaging and Vision*, **2**, 279-326. http://dx.doi.org/10.1007/BF00121876

[5]   Metzinger, T. (2004) The Subjectivity of Subjective Experience: A Representationalist Analysis of the First-Person Perspective. *Networks*, **3-4**, 33-64.

[6]   Tononi, G. and Edelman, G.M. (1998) Consciousness and Complexity. *Science*, **282**, 1846-1851. http://dx.doi.org/10.1126/science.282.5395.1846

[7]   Cottam, R., Ranson, W. and Vounckx, R. (2004) Autocreative Hierarchy I: Structure-Ecosystemic Dependence and Autonomy. *SEED Journal*, **4**, 24-41.

[8]   Sigmund, K. (1993) Games of Life: Explorations in Ecology, Evolution, and Behavior. Oxford University Press, New York.

[9]   Cottam, R., Ranson, W. and Vounckx, R. (2000) A Diffuse Biosemiotic Model for Cell-to-Tissue Computational Closure. *Biosystems*, **55**, 159-171. http://dx.doi.org/10.1016/S0303-2647(99)00094-5

[10]   Rosen, R. (1997) Transcript of a Videotaped Interview of Dr. Robert Rosen, Recorded in July 1997 in Rochester, New York, USA by Judith Rosen. http://www.people.vcu.edu/~mikuleck/rsntpe.html

[11]   Rosen, J. and Kineman, J. (2005) Anticipatory Systems and Time: A New Look at Rosennean Complexity. *Systems Research and Behavioral Science*, **22**, 399-412. http://dx.doi.org/10.1002/sres.715

[12]   Mikulecky, D.C. (2009) Definition of Complexity. http://www.people.vcu.edu/~mikuleck/ON%20COMPLEXITY.html

[13]   Cottam, R., Ranson, W. and Vounckx, R. (2005) Life and Simple Systems. *Systems Research and Behavioral Science*, **22**, 413-430. http://dx.doi.org/10.1002/sres.716

[14]   Collier, J.D. (1999) Autonomy in Anticipatory Systems: Significance for Functionality, Intentionality and Meaning. In:

Dubois, D.M., Ed., *Proceedings of Computing Anticipatory Systems*: *CASYS*'98-2*nd International Conference, AIP Conference Proceedings*, **465**, 75-81.

[15] Aristotle (2000) Politics 1 (1), 1. Translated by Jowett, B. Dover Publications Inc., New York.

[16] Rosen, R. (1991) Life Itself: A Comprehensive Enquiry into the Nature, Origin, and Fabrication of Life. Columbia University Press, New York.

[17] Matsuno, K. (1996) Internalist Stance and the Physics of Information. *BioSystems*, **38**, 111-118. http://dx.doi.org/10.1016/0303-2647(95)01580-9

[18] Salthe, S.N. (2001) Theoretical Biology as an Anticipatory Text: The Relevance of Uexküll to Current Issues in Evolutionary Systems. *Semiotica*, **134**, 359-380.

[19] Rosen, R. (1985) Anticipatory Systems: Philosophical, Mathematical and Methodological Foundations. Pergamon, New York, 423.

[20] Cottam, R., Ranson, W. and Vounckx, R. (2003) Autocreative Hierarchy II: Dynamics—Self-Organization, Emergence and Level-Changing. *International Conference on Integration of Knowledge Intensive Multi-Agent Systems*, Piscataway, IEEE, 30 September-4 October 2003, 766-773.

[21] Haken, H. (1984) The Science of Structure: Synergetics. Prentice Hall, New York.

[22] Tschacher, W. and Haken, H. (2007) Intentionality in Non-Equilibrium Systems? The Functional Aspects of Self-Organized Pattern Formation. *New Ideas in Psychology*, **25**, 1-15. http://dx.doi.org/10.1016/j.newideapsych.2006.09.002

[23] Salthe, S.N. (2012) Information and the Regulation of a Lower Hierarchical Level by a Higher One. *Information*, **3**, 595-600. http://dx.doi.org/10.3390/info3040595

[24] Cottam, R., Ranson, W. and Vounckx, R. (1998) Emergence: Half a Quantum Jump? *Acta Polytechnica Scandinavica*, **91**, 12-19.

[25] Cottam, R., Ranson, W. and Vounckx, R. (1999) A Biologically Consistent Hierarchical Framework for Self-Referencing Survivalist Computation. In: Dubois, D.M., Ed., *Proceedings of Computing Anticipatory Systems*: *CASYS*'99-2*nd International Conference, AIP Conference Proceedings*, **517**, 252-262.

[26] Cottam, R., Ranson, W. and Vounckx, R. (2006) Living in Hyperscale: Internalization as a Search for Reunification. 15*th Annual Conference of the International Society for the System Sciences Proceedings*, #06-382, ISSS, Sonoma, 9-14 July 2006, 1-11.

[27] Fowles, J. (1969) The French Lieutenant's Woman. Little, Brown & Co., Boston.

[28] Cottam, R., Ranson, W. and Vounckx, R. (2008) Bi-Sapient Structures for Intelligent Control. In: Mayorga, R.V. and Perlovsky, L., Eds., *Toward Artificial Sapience*, Springer, New York, 175-200. http://dx.doi.org/10.1007/978-1-84628-999-6_11

[29] Tononi, G. (2004) An Information Integration Theory of Consciousness. *BMC Neuroscience*, **5**, 1-22.

[30] Tononi, G. (2008) Consciousness as Integrated Information: A Provisional Manifesto. *Biological Bulletin*, **215**, 216-242. http://dx.doi.org/10.2307/25470707

[31] Cottam, R., Ranson, W. and Vounckx, R. (2013) A Framework for Computing Like Nature. In: Dodig-Crnkovich, G. and Giovagnoli, R., Eds., *Computing Nature*, in the SAPERE Series, Springer, Heidelberg, 23-60.

[32] Plato (2001) Symposium, a Translation by Benardete, S. with Commentaries by Bloom, A. and Benardete, S., 203E-204A. University of Chicago Press, Chicago.

[33] Peirce, C.S. (1958-1966) Collected Papers. In: Hartshorne, C., Weiss, P. and Burks, A., Eds., *The Collected Papers of Charles Sanders Peirce*, Vol. 1, Harvard University Press, Cambridge, III, 2, A6; III, 2, B3; III, 2, C3.

[34] Cottam, R. and Ranson, W. (2013) A Biosemiotic View on Consciousness Derived from System Hierarchy. In: Pereira Jr., A. and Lehmann, D., Eds., *The Unity of Mind, Brain and World: Current Perspectives on a Science of Consciousness*, Cambridge University Press, Cambridge, 77-112. http://dx.doi.org/10.1017/CBO9781139207065.004

[35] Taborsky, E. (2004) Dynamics of the Informational Interface. *Journal of Computing Anticipatory Systems*, **16**, 169-185.

[36] Salthe, S.N. (1985) Evolving Hierarchical Systems. Columbia University Press, New York.

[37] Cottam, R., Ranson, W. and Vounckx, R. (2001) Artificial Minds? 45*th Annual Conference of the International Society for the System Sciences Proceedings*, #01-114, ISSS, Asilomar, 8-13 July 2001, 1-19.

Appendix: Environment and Birationality

In the aftermath of argumentation, we should now "come clean" and admit that we have judiciously cheated a little. As the astute reader will have noticed, we have not until now followed up on the comment which concluded Footnote 2 above—namely that

"(*Quantum Holography*) *corresponds in many ways to the architectural scheme underlying the argumentation of this paper—most particularly in its exploitation of birationality*".

Birationality has been conspicuously absent from the bulk of the paper, and consequently there are a good many details of the architectural scheme which have necessarily been left rather "hanging in the air". An extensive treatment of birationality can be found in [7] [20]; we will here present a skeletal outline of its implications for intelligence, sapience and wisdom.

The key aspect of birationality popped up at the start of Section 1 of this paper, in James Albus' definition of intelligence, which is phrased entirely in terms of the relationship between an entity and its environment. The upsurge in environmentalism during the last few decades of the twentieth century, and its concentration on the importance of ecosystem to the perpetuation of species, provides a powerful analogue for the relationship between any entity and the domain within which it resides. This can be conveniently extended to... no, that is not at all correct... we should not be categorizing our synthesis as an extension of ecosystemics to other domains: ecosystemics is the primeval nature of all domains, from the birth of the universe down to the smallest action—it is simply our shortness of vision which has led us in general to presume until now the viability of systems which are divorced from ecosystemic influence. The crucial point here is that we cannot model entity-ecosystemic interactions using a single rationality [37]—we require a rationality which is at least as comprehensive as the subject of our modeling. Consequently, if we are to coherently model not only complex living organisms, but also the way they are embedded in their environment or ecosystem, we require a rationality which as the bare minimum can deal with a pair of complementary points of view—we need at least birationality.

Figure 10(a) shows the bare bones of a birational multiscalar natural hierarchy. Each vertical line represents a different scale of the same entity, as indicated. As we have pointed out, inter-scalar transit is not at all easy, and adjacent scales of the entity are separated by regions of complexity. Techniques for inter-scalar "transit" in a birational system appear to be related to a generalized form of quantum error correction [20], but much further research is needed to verify this assumption and apply it to cross-scalar integration in practical contexts. The surprising feature of a natural hierarchy is that these complex regions are differently scaled representations of the entity's ecosystem; and most surprising is that the collection of complex regions forms a second complementary hierarchy, interleaved with the first one (**Figure 10(b)**).

We suggested earlier that intelligence operates primarily in a bottom-up mode. **Figure 10(c)** indicates how the top-to-and-from-bottom loop is closed by operation of the ecosystemic companion process to intelligence, which also operates in a bottom-up manner, but now within the complementary hierarchy. There is similarly a complementary association of the collection of ecosystemic scales, so now we have two hyperscalar correlations, one for the entity and the other for its ecosystem, and consequently two formulations of sapience (**Figure 11**). We have proposed elsewhere [7] that these two hyperscalar constructions provide the groundings for reason and emotion in the human psyche, and that they are associated with conscious and unconscious aspects of cognition.

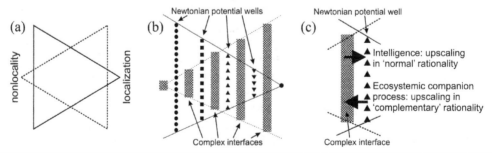

Figure 10. (a) The simplified representation of a birational hierarchy: the "normal" rationality (solid line) is reductive towards localization; the "complementary rationality" (dashed line) is reductive towards nonlocality; (b) the two interleaved complementary-rational hierarchies of a natural hierarchy; the simplest entity-scale (solid line) is associated with the most complex ecosystem-scale (cross-hatching), and vice versa; (c) closing of the bottom-up-top-down loop of intelligence by its companion ecosystemic process.

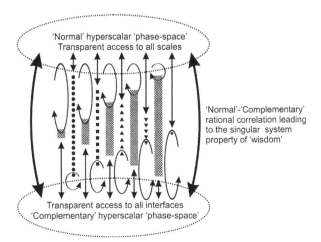

Figure 11. Interactions between the two hyperscalar "phase-spaces" of a birational natural hierarchy, providing an environment within which relationships between "reason" and "emotion" may develop.

It is notable that all the way up the "tree of emergence" in an entity, from the smallest detail up to hyperscalar integration, there is a bifurcation of scalar character between entity and ecosystem. At the highest cognitive level, however, the interplay between these two hyperscalar integrations culminates in the generation of a single unified property—that of wisdom. It is for this reason that we distinguish in this paper between sapience—as the property of only one of the pair of hyperscalar integrations in a natural system—and wisdom, which is the merged property of both hyperscalar integrations. Wisdom is the sole singular systemic property and the ultimate overarching consequence of cognition that drives action.

5

A Data-Placement Strategy Based on Genetic Algorithm in Cloud Computing

Qiang Xu*, Zhengquan Xu, Tao Wang

State Key Laboratory of Information Engineering in Surveying, Mapping and Remote Sensing, Wuhan University, Wuhan, China
Email: *xuqiangwhu@163.com

Abstract

With the development of Computerized Business Application, the amount of data is increasing exponentially. Cloud computing provides high performance computing resources and mass storage resources for massive data processing. In distributed cloud computing systems, data intensive computing can lead to data scheduling between data centers. Reasonable data placement can reduce data scheduling between the data centers effectively, and improve the data acquisition efficiency of users. In this paper, the mathematical model of data scheduling between data centers is built. By means of the global optimization ability of the genetic algorithm, generational evolution produces better approximate solution, and gets the best approximation of the data placement at last. The experimental results show that genetic algorithm can effectively work out the approximate optimal data placement, and minimize data scheduling between data centers.

Keywords

Cloud Computing, Data Placement, Genetic Algorithm, Data Scheduling

1. Introduction

With the increase of network equipment as well as the development of the Internet, data generation and storage capacity are growing explosively; data centers will face unpredictable visitor volume [1]. The large amount of data and the complex data structures make traditional database management unable to meet the requirements of big data storage and management. The distributed architecture of cloud computing can provide high-performance computing resources and mass storage resources [2] [3]. However, in distributed cloud computing system, data-intensive computing needs to deal with large amounts of data; in multi-data center environment, some data

---

*Corresponding author.

must be placed in a specified data center and cannot be moved. A computation may process datasets from different data centers, then data scheduling between data centers will occur inevitably. Because of the huge size of data and limited network bandwidth, data scheduling between data centers has become a huge problem. The datasets processed simultaneously by a computation should be placed in the same data center, then almost all data processing is completed locally; that is the basic idea of the paper.

Much work has been developed about the data placement in distributed system and they can be divided into two types in general: static data placement and dynamic data placement. Most static data placement algorithms require complete knowledge of the workload statistics such as service times and access rates of all the files. Dynamic data placement algorithms [4] [5], generate file-disk allocation schemes on-line to adapt to varying workload patterns without a prior knowledge of the files to be assigned in the future. Dynamic data placement strategies update the placement strategy potentially upon every request. Obviously, they are effective when the data size is relatively small such as the case in web proxy caching. However, in applications like distributed video servers, dynamic schemes become less useful [6] [7]. In data-intensive computing, if multiple computations jointly process multiple datasets in a frequent way, these datasets are supposed to be correlative with each other. Some researches on data placement are based on data correlation [8]-[12]; however, the definitions of data correlation are not reasonable, and no effective method is proposed to reduce the data scheduling between the data centers. Replica strategy [13] is an effective measure to reduce the data scheduling and has earned widespread research interests, and it is also based on data placement.

This paper presents a genetic algorithm-based data placement strategy. First, a mathematical model of data scheduling between the data centers in cloud computing is built, and the fitness function based on the objective function is defined to evaluate the fitness of each individual in a population. After the initial population generated in accordance with the principle of survival of the fittest, the evolution of each generation produces better approximate solution. In every generation, roulette-wheel selection is used to choose the appropriate individuals with high fitness value and the individuals with low fitness value are eliminated. With the crossover and mutation operations, we change the placement location of datasets. Under the principle of survival of the fittest, the optimal individual can be found during the evolution.

2. Data Placement Strategy in Cloud Computing

In cloud computing systems, data storage typically achieves petabytes magnitude scale, complex and diverse data structures, high requirements of data service type and level have brought great pressure to data management [14]. Cloud systems have the characteristics of data-intensive and compute-intensive, and the concurrent executions of large-scale computations in the systems require massive data and generate amass intermediate data. This paper attempts to establish a model of data scheduling between data centers that provides an accurate mathematical theoretical basis for data placement.

2.1. The Model of Data Scheduling between Data Centers in Cloud Computing

Assuming that a cloud computing system is composed by l data centers, and data are divided into n different datasets based on their inherent properties. When user request for data resources, we assign their different operations into m computations. If performing a computation needs to process datasets in different data centers, data scheduling between data center happen. The physical model of data scheduling between data center is showed in **Figure 1**.

Assuming that the collection of datasets stored in a distributed cloud computing system is:

$$D = \{d_1, d_2, \cdots, d_n\} \tag{1}$$

where n is the number of datasets and the size of dataset d_i is ε_i , $i = 1, 2, \cdots, n$.

The l data centers in the system are denoted as:

$$S = \{S_1, S_2, \cdots, S_l\} \tag{2}$$

The basic capacity of data center S_k is S_k.

The m computations in the system are denoted as:

$$C = \{c_1, c_2, \cdots, c_m\} \tag{3}$$

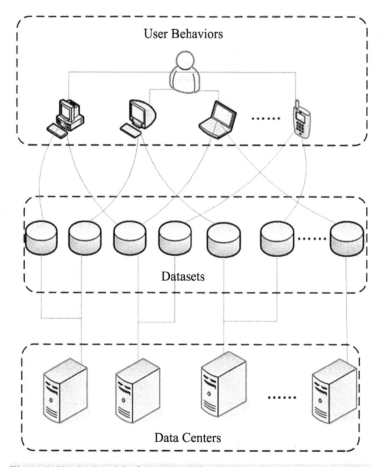

Figure 1. Physical model of data scheduling between data center.

The execution frequencies of each computation can be denoted as:

$$U = \{\mu_1, \mu_2, \cdots, \mu_m\} \tag{4}$$

where μ_1 is the execution frequency of computation c_i in unit interval.

We define a processing factor α_{ij}, where

$$\alpha_{ij} = \begin{cases} 1 & \text{dataset } d_j \text{ is needed to process during the execution of the computation } c_i \\ 0 & \text{dataset } d_j \text{ is not needed to process during the execution of the computation } c_i \end{cases} \tag{5}$$

Thus we can get the association matrix of the computation set C and the datasets D, which is denoted as:

$$A = \left[\alpha_{ij}\right]_{m \times n} \tag{6}$$

Data placement is to distribute datasets into each data center. In this paper, data replica is out of consideration. Similarly, we define a placement factor β_{jk}, where

$$\beta_{jk} = \begin{cases} 1 & \text{when dataset } d_j \text{ is placed in data center } S_k \\ 0 & \text{when dataset } d_j \text{ is not placed in data center } S_k \end{cases} \tag{7}$$

Thus we can get the association matrix (placement matrix) of the datasets D and the data center S, denoted as:

$$B = \left[\beta_{jk}\right]_{n \times l} \tag{8}$$

Matrix B reflects the status of the datasets D stored in the data centers S. We can easily find that the sum of the elements of each row in matrix B is 1,

$$\sum_{k=1}^{l} \beta_{ik} = 1 \tag{9}$$

The sum of the elements of the kth column in matrix B is the number of datasets stored in the data center S_k, when we place datasets into data center S_k, the stored data size should not exceed the basic capacity of S_k, thus

$$\sum_{j=1}^{n} \beta_{jk} \times \varepsilon_j \leq s_k \tag{10}$$

Define a matrix Z, denoted as

$$Z = A * B = \left[\sum_{j=1}^{n} \left(\alpha_{ij} \times \beta_{jk} \right) \right]_{m \times l} \tag{11}$$

Suppose

$$z_{ik} = \sum_{j=1}^{n} \left(\alpha_{ij} \times \beta_{jk} \right) \tag{12}$$

then matrix $Z = [z_{ik}]_{m \times l}$, z_{ik} is the number of datasets processed when the computation c_i is performed one time in data center. The sum of elements in each row in matrix Z, denoted as $\sum_{k=1}^{l} z_{ik}$, is the total number of times of accessing all data centers during the execution of the computation c_i, also is the number of datasets processed during the execution of the computation c_i. The sum of elements in each column, denoted as $\sum_{i=1}^{m} z_{ik}$, is the number of the datasets processed in data center S_k when all the computations are performed one time. Define a function $u(z_{ik})$ denoted as,

$$u(z_{ik}) = \begin{cases} 1 & z_{ik} \neq 0 \\ 0 & z_{ik} = 0 \end{cases} \tag{13}$$

Then the number of data centers accessed during the execution of computation c_i is $\sum_{k=1}^{l} u(z_{ik})$, the number of data scheduling is $\left(\sum_{k=1}^{l} u(z_{ik}) - 1 \right)$ when computation c_i is executed one time. When the placement matrix is B, the total number of data scheduling during the execution of all computations in the system in unit interval can be expressed as:

$$\Gamma(B) = \sum_{i=1}^{m} \left(\sum_{k=1}^{l} u(z_{ik}) - 1 \right) \times \mu_i \tag{14}$$

Our objective is to find the optimal data placement solution B^* that minimize $\Gamma(B)$. When placing datasets to data centers, we should meet the requirements of data center capacity and no duplication of datasets placement.

$$B^* = \arg\min_{B} \left\{ \Gamma(B) \right\} \tag{15}$$

2.2. Genetic Algorithm

In the issue of big data placement, the solution space is very huge, and B matrices are sparsely distributed in it. There are a lot of traditional optimization algorithms, such as the exhaustive search algorithm, Monte Carlo algorithm, Genetic algorithm, Simulated Annealing algorithm and so on. In this paper, different algorithms are compared to find the optimal data placement solution B^*.

Exhaustive search algorithm is a direct way to search the optimal placement matrix. It works out all possible data placement B matrices, then traverses to find the smallest $\Gamma(B)$, at this point the placement matrix is the optimal solution. However, the computation complexity of exhaustive search algorithm is very high which approximates (l^n). In a distributed cloud computing system, the number of datasets n is so great that the computation complexity is unbearable to system. What is more, some constraint conditions, such as storage capacity limitation $\sum_{j=1}^{n} \beta_{jk} \times \varepsilon_j \leq s_k$ and no replicas $\sum_{k=1}^{l} \beta_{jk} = 1$, make solving the placement problem being a NP-hard problem. So the exhaustive search algorithm is only available when the number of datasets is small.

Monte Carlo algorithm is based on probability theory and statistics methods. In big data placement based on Mont Carlo algorithm, we randomly generate a certain number of B matrices as a sample, then calculate data scheduling between data centers on each sample matrix B, and find out the placement matrix with the minimum data scheduling. Compared with the exhaustive search algorithm, the computation complexity of Monte Carlo algorithm is improved, however, B matrices are sparsely distributed in the solution space, the search efficiency of Monte Carlo algorithm is still not high. It has a strong regularity as well as constraint conditions to generate placement matrices, genetic algorithm uses a strategy of a directed search through a problem state space from a variety of points in that space [15], it is more efficient and robust than the random search, enumerative or calculus based techniques [16]. Therefore, the use of genetic algorithm can deal with this problem.

Genetic algorithm is an adaptive search and optimization algorithm based on the mechanics of natural selection and natural genetics [17] [18]. A population of candidate solutions (called individuals) to an optimization problem is evolved toward better solutions [19] [20]. In genetic algorithm, the degree of adaptation of each individual to the environment is represented by fitness. Individual with high fitness has a greater chance to survive. In each generation, the fitness value of each individual in the population is evaluated, individuals with higher fitness value are stochastically selected from the current population, then crossover and mutation operator are manipulated to form a new generation. The new generation of candidate solutions is then used in the next iteration of the algorithm.

1) Encoding

In the issue of genetic algorithm-based data placement, the placement of datasets in data centers is represented by matrix B, because of the string structure of matrix, the placement matrix is directly manipulated as genotype in genetic algorithm.

2) Individual and population

An individual is a point in the searching space, the collection of placement matrices is the searching space of the data placement.

A population consists of several individuals and it is a subset of the whole searching space.

3) Fitness function

Fitness function is the evaluation function to guide the search in genetic algorithm [21] [22]. In the issue of genetic algorithm-based data placement, the objective function is denoted as $\Gamma(B)$, and the fitness function is the reciprocal of the objective function, that is $F = 1/\Gamma(B)$.

4) Genetic operators

① Selection: Roulette wheel selection is a genetic operator used in genetic algorithms for selecting potentially useful solutions for recombination [23], chromosomes with higher fitness level are more likely to be selected. The steps of Roulette wheel selection are as follows:

Step 1: Obtain the fitness value $f(i)$ of each individual in a N size population.

Step 2: Suppose there is an individual k and its probability of being selected is $p(k)$:

$$p(k) = f(k) \bigg/ \sum_{i=1}^{N-1} f(i); \quad k = 1, 2, \cdots, N \tag{16}$$

Step 3: Suppose $q(0) = 0$, $q(k) = p(1) + p(2) + \cdots + p(k); k = 1, 2, \cdots N$;

Step 4: Generate a random number $r(0 \leq r < 1)$, if $q(k-1) < r < q(k)$, then individual k is selected.

② Crossover: In Genetic algorithm, crossover operator is used to vary the programming of a chromosome or chromosomes from one generation to the next [24]. Before crossover, individuals in the population should be paired randomly and choose the crossover point and then exchange some genes. Assume that B_1 pairs with B_2, generate two random number r_1, r_2 $(0 < r_1 < r_2 < n)$ as the crossover point, then exchange the genes between the two points, the resulting organisms are the children. **Figure 2** is the schematic of the two-point crossover in a 4*3 placement matrix.

③ Mutation: Mutation alters one or more genes in a chromosome from its initial state. For a binary string, if the genome bit is 1, it is changed to 0 and vice versa. When the mutation operator is used in a placement matrix, a random number r_1 $(0 \leq r_1 < n)$ is generated, and the placement of dataset d_{r_1} is to be changed, then generate two random number r_2, r_3 $(0 \leq r_2 \neq r_3 < l)$, If $\beta_{r_1 r_2}$ is 1, then change it from 1 to 0, and $\beta_{r_1 r_3}$ from 0 to 1; if

$$
\begin{array}{cc}
\begin{array}{ccc}
1 & 0 & 0 \\
0 & 0 & 1 \\
0 & 1 & 0 \\
1 & 0 & 0
\end{array}
&
\begin{array}{ccc}
0 & 0 & 1 \\
0 & 1 & 0 \\
1 & 0 & 0 \\
0 & 1 & 0
\end{array}
\end{array}
\qquad
\begin{array}{cc}
\begin{array}{ccc}
1 & 0 & 0 \\
0 & 1 & 0 \\
1 & 0 & 0 \\
1 & 0 & 0
\end{array}
&
\begin{array}{ccc}
0 & 0 & 1 \\
0 & 0 & 1 \\
0 & 1 & 0 \\
0 & 1 & 0
\end{array}
\end{array}
$$

$$\qquad \mathrm{B}_1 \qquad\qquad \mathrm{B}_2 \qquad\qquad\qquad \mathrm{B'}_1 \qquad\qquad \mathrm{B'}_2$$

Before two-point crossover   After two-point crossover

Figure 2. Perform two-point crossover operator on placement matrixes.

$\beta_{r_1 r_2}$ is 0, then change it from 0 to 1, meanwhile change another 1 in the same row from 1 to 0, to ensure that each row has only one 1, thus change the placement of dataset d_{r_1} in data center. **Figure 3** is the schematic of the mutation in a 4*3 placement matrix.

2.3. Process of Data Placement Based on Genetic Algorithm

Step 1: Determine the size of population (G), crossover rate (P_c) and mutation rate (P_m) according to the actual situation.

Step 2: Generate the initial population: Initial population BG (0) consists of G placement matrices. To generate an individual matrix B_i, all the elements of the matrix is set to 0, then n random numbers $\{r_1, r_2, r_3, \cdots, r_i, \cdots, r_n\}$ $(0 \leq r_i < l)$ are produced, random number r_i indicates dataset d_i is to be placed into data center S_{r_i}, then placement factor β_{ir_i} is changed from 0 to 1. If the generated matrix does not meet the constraint condition in Equation (10), then abandon it and generate a new one.

Step 3: Calculate the fitness of each individual in population $BG(T)$, $T = 0, 1, 2, \cdots, MaxGen$: Get matrix Z by matrix multiplication, that is $Z = A*B$. The number of non-zero elements of row i in matrix Z is the times of accessing all data centers during the execution of the computation c_i, when computation c_i is executed one time, the number of data scheduling is $\left(\sum_{k=1}^{l} u(z_{ik}) - 1\right)$. Then we can work out the total number of data schedule ing in B_t during the execution of all computations in the system in unit interval, that is:

$$\Gamma(B_t) = \sum_{i=1}^{m}\left(\sum_{k=1}^{l} u(z_{ik}) - 1\right) \times \mu_i \tag{17}$$

Step 4: Calculate the number of data scheduling $\Gamma(B_t)$ of each individual in population $BG(T)$, the fitness value of B_t is denoted as $F = 1/\Gamma(B_t)$. After the fitness value of each individual and the probabilities being chosen are calculated, select G individuals from $BG(T)$ by roulette wheel selection.

Step 5: Perform crossover operator on the selected placement matrices: Crossover rate P_c represents the percentage of the chromosomes taking part in the crossover operation [18] [19]. The process of crossover is as follows:

```
Begin
i=0. num= 0.j=0;
ifi<G
                    Generate a random number r_i, (0≤r_i≤1)
ifr_i<P_c
                    Select B_i as a father and put it into the matching pool
num=num +1;
end
i=i+1;
end
ifj<num/2
                    Generate a random number r_k, (num/2≤r_k≤num).r_k≠ j
Change the gene segments ofB_{r_k}.B_j
j =j+1;
                End
            End
```

$$
\begin{array}{ccc}
0 & 0 & 1 \\
0 & 1 & 0 \\
\hline
1 & 0 & 0 \\
0 & 1 & 0
\end{array}
\qquad
\begin{array}{ccc}
0 & 0 & 1 \\
0 & 0 & 1 \\
\hline
1 & 0 & 0 \\
0 & 1 & 0
\end{array}
$$

B   B'

Before mutation   After mutation

Figure 3. Perform mutation operator on placement matrixes.

Step 6: Perform mutation operator on the selected placement matrices: Mutationrate P_m represents the percentage of the chromosomes taking part in the mutation operation [25] [26]. If the size of a population is G and each individual has n genes, the number of genes to be mutated is $G*n*P_m$. We can generate random number (0 $\leq r \leq 1$), if $r < P_m$, the corresponding gene is to be mutated. The process of mutation is as follows:

```
              Begin
i= 0;
ifi<G
                        Generate a random number r_i (0≤r_i≤1)
ifr_i<P_m
                    Mutate B_i
              End
i=i+1;
          End
      End
```

Step 7: Abandon the new individuals that do not meet the requirements of the storage capacity limitation $\sum_{j=1}^{n} z\beta_{jk} \times \varepsilon_j \leq s_k$ and no replicas $\sum_{k=1}^{l} \beta_{jk} = 1 = 1$. If the generation does not exceed *MaxGen*, return Step 3 and continue the evolution, otherwise terminate the iteration and find the individual with highest fitness, the individual is regard as the approximate optimal solution.

Step 8: From the definition of placement factor β_{jk} in Equation (7), we get to know that $\beta_{jk} = 1$ denotes dataset d_j is placed in data center S_k. After we find the approximate optimal solution B^*, the placement of dataset d_j can be determined by the placement factor β_{jk} in B^*.

3. Experiment and Simulation

3.1. Simulation Environment

To test the data placement strategy based on genetic algorithm proposed in this paper, a "digital city" oriented data storage and access platform is constructed. The platform is composed of 20 Dell Power Edge T410 servers. Each of them has 8 Intel Xeon E5606 CPU (2.13 GHz), 16G DDR3 memory and 3TB SATA disk. Every server acts as a data center and we deploy VMware and independent Hadoop distributed file system on each data center. Under the environment of Gigabit Ethernet, users can submit data and perform computations through digital city application demonstration system developed by Flex 4.5.

3.2. Simulation Result and Analysis

In this paper, genetic algorithm is applied to the placement of big data, and comprehensive performance test has been done. To verify the feasibility of genetic algorithm in data placement, we compared the data scheduling between data centers of solutions searched by genetic algorithm with exhaustive search algorithm when the number of datasets was small, the relationship between the minimum number of data scheduling of different number of datasets and the generation are represented by a line chart. We ran 10 test computations randomly for 400 times on 3 data centers and compared the data scheduling between data centers of solutions searched by different algorithms when the number of datasets changed. In genetic algorithm the size of initial population was 200, the maximum generations was set to 1000, and the crossover rate and the mutation rate were 0.5 and 0.05 respectively. The number of iterations of the Monte Carlo algorithm was 10^6.

The data scheduling between data centers of the three algorithms is shown in **Figure 4**. From **Figure 4**, we can find the results of the three algorithms are exactly the same in each case as the number of datasets changes. The results of exhaustive search algorithm are obtained by traversing, thus the corresponding results are the optimal data placement matrices, so using genetic algorithm and Monte Carlo algorithm can also find the optimal data placement matrices.

As **Figure 5** schematically shows, with the increase of generation, the minimum number of data scheduling becomes smaller and smaller, optimization results get more and more close to the optimal solutions. When the number of datasets is 8, the convergence generation is around 400, the convergence generations of different number of datasets are different from each other.

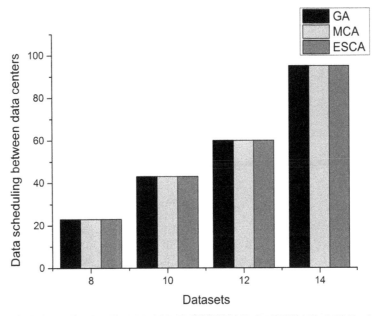

Figure 4. Data scheduling between data centers with different number of datasets.

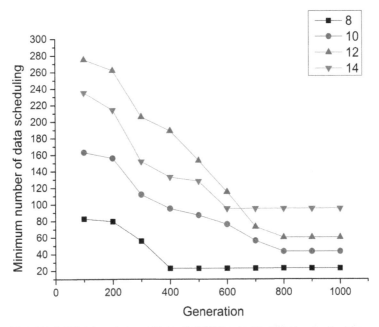

Figure 5. Minimum number of data scheduling in the evolution.

With the increase of the number of datasets, exhaustive search algorithm became infeasible because of the computation complexity. Then we compared the data scheduling between data centers of approximate optimal solutions searched by genetic algorithm with the results searched by Monte Carlo algorithm when the number of datasets was large, the optimization time of each algorithm were also compared. We ran 30 different test computations randomly for 2500 times on 5 data centers with different number of datasets, then we ran the test computations on different numbers of data centers when the number of datasets was 60. In genetic algorithm the size of initial population was 5000, the maximum generations was set to 2000, and the crossover rate and the mutation rate were 0.6 and 0.1 respectively. The number of iterations of the Monte Carlo algorithm was 10^9.

From the **Figure 6** and **Figure 7**, we can see the increase of datasets or data centers leads to the growth of da-

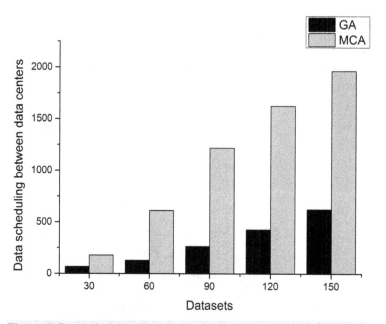

Figure 6. Data scheduling between data centers with different number of datasets.

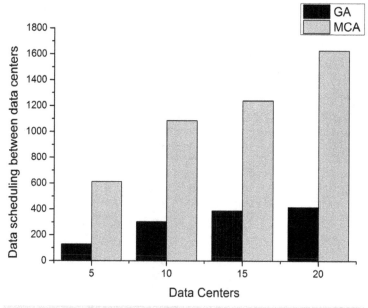

Figure 7. Data scheduling between data centers with diffferent number of data centers.

ta scheduling between data centers. By comparing the data, we find that the data scheduling between data centers of approximate optimal data placement matrices searched by genetic algorithm are always smaller than Monte Carlo algorithm in each case. So for data placement issue, in the case of large datasets, the search results of genetic algorithm are better than Monte Carloalgorithm.

Figure 8 schematically shows the relationship between the minimum number of data scheduling of different number of datasets and the generation. In the experiment, the number of data center was fixed as 5. It appears that the convergence generations of different number of datasets are different from each other. Then the number of datasets was fixed as 60 and we ran 30 test computations randomly for 2500 times on different numbers of data centers, as shown in **Figure 9**. With the increase of generation, the minimum number of data scheduling becomes smaller, and optimization results get more close to the optimal solutions.

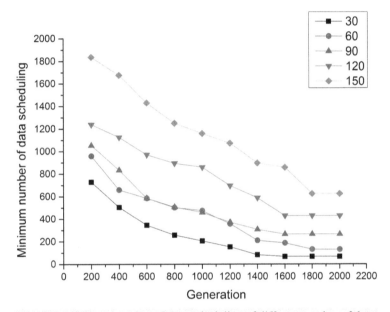

Figure 8. Minimum number of data scheduling of different number of datasets in the evolution.

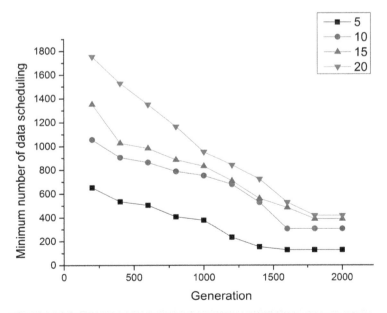

Figure 9. Minimum number of data scheduling of different number of data centers in the evolution.

The optimization time of the two algorithms are showed in **Figure 10** and **Figure 11**. We can find either the increase of datasets or the number of data centers would lead to the increase of the optimization time, and the growth rate of optimization time of Monte Carlo algorithm is much higher than genetic algorithm. It is time costly for Monte Carlo algorithm to find an approximate optimal data placement matrix when the number of datasets or data centers increase to a certain degree. In the case of large number of datasets, the characteristics of inherent parallelism and convergence of genetic algorithm made it possible to find a better solution within an acceptable time.

4. Summary and Future Work

In the environment of distributed cloud computing, placing data to the appropriate data center has become a

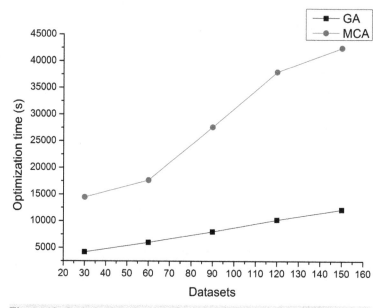

Figure 10. Optimization time of the two algorithms in different number of datasets.

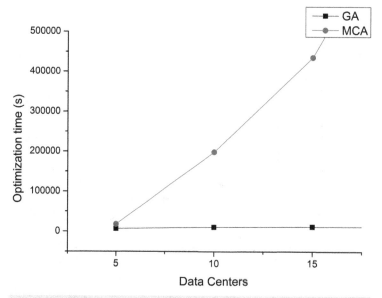

Figure 11. Optimization time of the two algorithms in different number of data centers.

critical issue. Reasonable placement of datasets in data centers can minimize the number of data scheduling between the data centers. In this paper, a mathematical model is built to illustrate the relationship among datasets, data centers and computations. Three different algorithms are used to search the approximate optimal data placement matrices. By comparing genetic algorithm with exhaustive search algorithm and the Monte Carlo algorithm, we can work out the truth that under verifiable conditions, genetic algorithm can find the optimal data placement matrix; when the number of datasets is large enough, genetic algorithm can find an approximate optimal data placement matrix in a reasonable time, and the optimization result is better than Monte Carlo algorithm.

Currently, the focus of our research is to find an optimal data placement matrix, making the number of data scheduling between the data centers as small as possible. During the research, the impact of data access history and access heat on data placement are out of our consideration. The heat of the data and the execution frequency of computations are not constant over time, then data placement needs to update which increases the cost of data management for enterprise; this issue needs further study. In terms of genetic algorithms, the selection is an important operator. There are many selection methods, such as Roulette wheel selection method, league selection method, expectations selection method. In this paper we use Roulette wheel selection method. Different methods of genetic selection affect the performance of the algorithm which requires further study.

Acknowledgements

This paper is part of the research undertaken by Qiang Xu to obtain the Master's Degree in communication and information system at Wuhan University, also as part of the complex application environments oriented theoretical study for data storage funded by the same university.

References

[1] Labrinidis, A. and Jagadish, H. (2012) Challenges and Opportunities with Big Data. *Proceedings of the VLDB Endowment*, **5**, 2032-2033. http://dx.doi.org/10.14778/2367502.2367572

[2] (2008) Big Data. *Nature*, **455**, 1-136.

[3] Manyika, J., Chui, M., Brown, B., *et al.* (2011) Big Data: The Next Frontier for Innovation, Competition, and Productivity. McKinsey Global Institute.

[4] Qiu, L., Padmanabhan, V.N. and Voelker, G.M. (2001) On the Placement of Web Server Replicas. *Proceedings—IEEE INFOCOM*, Anchorage, 22-26 April 2001, 1587-1596.

[5] Wolf, J. and Pattipati, K. (1990) A File Assignment Problem Model for Extended Local Area Network Environments. *Proceedings of 10th International Conference on Distributed Computing Systems*, Paris, 28 May-1 Jun 1990, 554-561.

[6] Scheuermann, P., Weikum, G. and Zabback, P. (1998) Data Partitioning and Load Balancing in Parallel Disk Systems. *The VLDB Journal*, **7**, 48-66. http://dx.doi.org/10.1007/s007780050053

[7] Zhou, X. and Xu, C. (2002) Optimal Video Replication and Placement on a Cluster of Video-on-Demand Servers. *Proceedings of International Conference on Parallel Processing* (*ICPP*), 2002, 547-555. http://dx.doi.org/10.1109/ICPP.2002.1040912

[8] Doraimani, S. and Iamnitchi, A. (2008) File Grouping for Scientific Data Management: Lessons from Experimenting with Real Traces. *Proceedings of the 17th International Symposium on High Performance Distributed Computing*, ACM, Boston, 2008, 153-164.

[9] Fedak, G., He, H. and Cappello, F. (2008) BitDew. A Programmable Environment for Large-Scale Data Management and Distribution. *ACM/IEEE Conference on Supercomputing*, Austin, 15-21 November 2008, 1-12. http://dx.doi.org/10.1109/SC.2008.5213939

[10] Kosar, T. and Livny, M. (2005) A Framework for Reliable and Efficient Data Placement in Distributed Computing Systems. *Journal of Parallel and Distributed Computing*, **65**, 1146-1157. http://dx.doi.org/10.1016/j.jpdc.2005.04.019

[11] Yuan, D., Yang, Y., Liu, X. and Chen, J.J. (2010) A Data Placement Strategy in Scientific Cloud Workflows. *Future Generation Computer Systems*, **26**, 1200-1214. http://dx.doi.org/10.1016/j.future.2010.02.004

[12] Zheng, P., Cui, L.Z., Wang, H.Y. and Xu, M. (2010) A Data Placement Strategy for Data-Intensive Applications in Cloud. *Chinese Journal of Computers*, **33**, 1472-1480. http://dx.doi.org/10.3724/SP.J.1016.2010.01472

[13] Nukarapu, D.T., Tang, B., Wang, L.Q. and Lu, S.Y. (2011) Data Replication in Data Intensive Scientific Applications with Performance Guarantee. *IEEE Transactions on Parallel and Distributed Systems*, **22**, 1299-1306.

[14] Agrawal, D., Das, S. and El Abbadi, A. (2011) Big Data and Cloud Computing: Current State and Future Opportunities.

Proceedings of the 14*th International Conference on Extending Database Technology*, Uppsala, 21-25 March 2011, 530-533.

[15] Goldberg, D.E. (1989) Genetic Algorithms in Search, Optimization and Machine Learning. Addison-Wesley Longman Publishing Co., Boston.

[16] Goldberg, D.E. (1989) Genetic Algorithms in Search, Optimization and Machine Learning. Addison-Wesley, Reading, MA.

[17] Grant, K. (1995) An Introduction to Genetic Algorithms. *C/C++ Users Journal*, **13**, 45-58.

[18] Zhou, M. and Sun, S.D. (1999) Genetic Algorithms and Applications. National Defense Industry Press, Beijing.

[19] Mitchell, M. (1996) Introduction to Genetic Algorithm. MIT Press, Cambridge, MA.

[20] Pan, W., Diao, H.Z. and Jing, Y.W. (2006) A Improved Real Adaptive Genetic Algorithm. *Control and Decision*, **21**, 792-795.

[21] Polgar, O., Fried, M., Lohner, T. and Barsony, I. (2000) Comparison of Algorithms Used for Evaluation of Ellipsometric Measurements Random Search, Genetic Algorithms, Simulated Annealing and Hill Climbing Graph-Searches. *Surface Science*, **457**, 157-177. http://dx.doi.org/10.1016/S0039-6028(00)00352-6

[22] Tan, B.C., *et al.* (2008) A Kind of Improved Genetic Algorithms Based on Robot Path Planning Method. *Journal of Xi'an University of Technology*, **28**, 456-459.

[23] Bäck, T. (1996) Evolutionary Algorithms in Theory and Practice. Oxford University Press, Oxford, 120.

[24] Liu, Z.G., Wang, J.H. and Di, Y.S. (2004) A Modified Genetic Simulated Annealing Algorithm and Its Application. *China Journal of System Simulation*, **16**, 1099-1101.

[25] Deb, K., Pratap, A., Agarwal, S. and Meyarivan, T. (2002) A Fast and Elitist Multiobjective Genetic Algorithm: NSGA-II. *IEEE Transactions on Evolutionary Computation*, **6**, 182-197.

[26] Wong, M. and Wong, T. (2009) Implementation of Parallel Genetic Algorithms on Graphics Processing Units. *Intelligent and Evolutionary Systems*, **187**, 197-216.

6

Brain as an Emergent Finite Automaton: A Theory and Three Theorems

Juyang Weng[1,2]

[1]Department of Computer Science and Engineering, Michigan State University, East Lansing, MI, USA
[2]School of Computer Science and Engineering, Fudan University, Shanghai, China
Email: weng@cse.msu.edu

Abstract

This paper models a biological brain—excluding motivation (e.g., emotions)—as a Finite Automaton in Developmental Network (FA-in-DN), but such an FA emerges incrementally in DN. In artificial intelligence (AI), there are two major schools: symbolic and connectionist. Weng 2011 [1] proposed three major properties of the Developmental Network (DN) which bridged the two schools: 1) From any complex FA that demonstrates human knowledge through its sequence of the symbolic inputs-outputs, a Developmental Program (DP) incrementally develops an emergent FA inside DN through naturally emerging image patterns of the symbolic inputs-outputs of the FA. The DN learning from the FA is incremental, immediate and error-free; 2) After learning the FA, if the DN freezes its learning but runs, it generalizes optimally for infinitely many inputs and actions based on the neuron's inner-product distance, state equivalence, and the principle of maximum likelihood; 3) After learning the FA, if the DN continues to learn and run, it "thinks" optimally in the sense of maximum likelihood conditioned on its limited computational resource and its limited past experience. This paper gives an overview of the FA-in-DN brain theory and presents the three major theorems and their proofs.

Keywords

Brain, Mind, Connectionist, Automata Theory, Finite Automaton, Symbolic Artificial Intelligence

1. Introduction

Our computational theory [2] of brain and mind includes two major parts rooted in the rich literature about biological brains [3] [4]: (A) dynamically emerging, motivation-free circuits and functions; and (B) motivation based on such circuits and functions.

The computation in the former (A) is carried out by target-precise neuron-to-neuron signal transmissions. Weng & Luciw 2012 [5] and Weng *et al.* 2013 [6] presented a computational theory for such brain circuits to process information spatial and temporal, respectively, using their distributed, emergent, and non-symbolic representations. As reviewed in those two articles, such brain circuits are also fundamentally different from many existing neural networks cited therein—the brain circuits are not only locally recurrent as many neural networks, but also globally recurrent in the sense that they all use motor as input concepts. As explained in Weng & Luciw [7], the brain motors (or actions) correspond to all possible concepts that a human can learn and express from conception, through prenatal life, birth, childhood, infancy, and adulthood—such as location, type, scale, temporal context, goal, subgoal, intent, purpose, price, ways to use, and so on. These concepts are used by the brain circuits as states, like states in a Finite Automaton (FA) [8], but such an FA is emergent and non-symbolic to be explained below.

The computation in the latter (B) is based on target-imprecise diffusion of neural transmitters that diffuse across brain tissue. Weng *et al.* 2013 [9] proposed a model for how reinforcement learning is carried out in such emergent brain circuits through two types of transmitter systems—serotonin and dopamine. Wang *et al.* 2011 [10] present a model about how individual neurons use two other types of transmitter systems—acetylcholine and norepinephrine—to automatically estimate uncertainty and novelty, so that each neuron can decide where it gets inputs from. These four types of neural transmitter systems—serotonin, dopamine, acetylcholine and norepinephrine—along with other neural transmitters but seemingly relatively less important than these four types [11], amount to what we know as motivation. Various emotions are special cases of motivation [3] [4].

This paper will not further discuss the motivation part of a biological brain and will instead concentrate on the former—(A) the basic brain circuits and functions. In other words, the theory below models any emotion-free brain. DNs with emotion such as pain avoidance and pleasure seeking will be only briefly discussed in Section 9.

This theory here does not claim that the FA-based brain model is indeed complete for an emotion-free brain, because there is no widely accepted and rigorous definition of a natural phenomenon such as a brain and therefore, there is always some limitation for any theory to explain a natural phenomenon. As such, as any theory can only approximate a natural phenomenon but can never exhaust such an approximation. The Newtonian physics is a good example because it is refined by the relativity theory.

All computational networks fall into two categories: Symbolic Networks (SNs) and Emergent Networks. The former category uses symbolic representations and the latter uses emergent representations. See the review for symbolic models and emergent models in Weng 2012 [12] which tried to clarify some common misconceptions on representations.

The class of SN [13] includes Finite Automata (FA), Markov Chains, Markov Models, Hidden Markov Models (HMM), Partially Observable Markov Decision Processes (POMDP), Belief Networks, Graphical Models, and all other networks that use at least some symbolic representations. The HMM and other probability-based models in the above list are symbolic because they add probability to the symbolic FA basis and therefore the basic nature of their representations is still symbolic—adding probability does not change the nature of symbolic representation. We will use FA as an example for SN because any SN includes FA as its basis.

The class of Emergent Network includes all neural networks that use exclusively emergent representations, such as Feed-forward Networks, Hopfield Networks, Boltzmann Machines, Restricted Boltzmann Machines, Liquid State Machines, and Reservoir Computing, and the newer Developmental Networks (DNs) [14]. However, traditional neural networks are not as powerful and complete as DN, because they do not have the logic of FA as explained first in [14] and we will be proved for DN in this paper.

The major differences between a Symbolic Network (SN) and a Developmental Network (DN) are illustrated in **Figure 1**.

Marvin Minsky 1991 [15] and others correctly argued that symbolic models were logical and clean, while connectionist models were analogical and scruffy. Neural networks are called emergent networks here because some networks were not emergent and partially symbolic. Michael Jodan 2014 [16] correctly raised fundamental questions that many researchers have not paid sufficient attention to. The logic capabilities of emergent networks are still unclear, categorically. This paper addresses some fundamental issues that Michael Jordan raised [16] recently.

Computationally, feed-forward connections serve to feed sensory features [17] to motor area for generating behaviors. It has been reported that feed-backward connections can serve as class supervision [18], attention [19], and storage of time information.

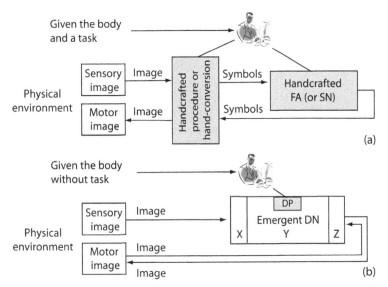

Figure 1. Comparison between a symbolic FA (or SN) and an emergent DN. (a) Given a task, an FA (or SN), symbolic, handcrafted by the human programmer using a static symbol set; (b) A DN, which incrementally learns the FA but takes sensory images directly and produces motor images directly. Without given any task, a human designs the general-purpose Developmental Program (DP) which resides in the DN as a functional equivalent of the "genome" that regulates the development—fully autonomous inside the DN.

The work of Finite Automata (FA) played a major role in our theory about the brain. The work of Weng 2011 [14] and 2013 [20] was not the first to relate a network with an FA. Some researchers used neural networks to batch-com- pile a special kind of FA. Frasconi *et al.* 1995 [21] used a feed-forward network to explicitly compute the state transition function $\delta : Q \times \Sigma \mapsto Q$ of an FA. Their network requires: 1) a special canonical binary coding of the states so that the Hamming distance is 1 between any source state q and any target state q'; 2) an additional intermediate state is added if the source state q and target state q are the same; 3) the entire state transition function δ is known a priori so that their algorithm can directly compute all the weights as a batch (*i.e.,* programmed, instead of learned incrementally). This compiled network uses a layer of logic-AND nodes followed by a layer of logic-OR nodes. Frasconi *et al.* 1996 proposed a radial basis function as an alternative batch-compiled feed-forward network for the above logic network [22] since a finite number of samples are sufficient for completely characterizing the FA due to its symbolic nature. Omlin & Giles 1996 [23] proposed a second-order network for computing the state transition function of a fully given FA. By second order, the neuronal input contains the sum of weighted multiplications (hence the second order), between individual state nodes and individual input nodes. There does not seem to be known evidence that a biological neuron uses such a product. The network Omlin & Giles 1996 is also statically "programmed" by a human programmer based on a fully given FA. They positively contributed to neural network studies.

The above studies aimed successfully compute the state transition function using a programmed network, but they do not generate emergent representations, do not learn from observations of FA operations, do not deal with natural input images (or patterns), and do not deal with natural motor images (or patterns), and not incrementally learn.

As far as we know, the DN in Weng 2011 [14] was the first general-purpose emergent FA that

1) uses fully emergent representations,

2) allows natural sensory firing patterns,

3) allows the motor area to have subareas where each subarea represents either an abstract concept (location, type, scale, etc.) or natural muscle actions (e.g., driving a car or riding a bicycle),

4) uses a general-purpose and unified area function that does not need interactive approximation and does not have local minima in its high dimensional and nonlinear but non-iterative approximation,

5) learns incrementally—taking one-pair of sensory pattern and motor pattern at a time to update the network and discarding the pair immediately after—and,

6) uses an optimization scheme in which every update of the network realizes the maximum likelihood estimate of the network, conditioned on the limited computational resources in the network and the limited learning experience in the network's "life time".

Explained in Weng 2012 [2], the DN model is inspired by biological brains, especially brain anatomy (e.g., [24] [26]) and brain physiological experiments (e.g. [19] [26]). But we will use computational language in the following material, so that the material is understandable by an analytical reader.

In the following, we analyze how the DN theory bridges the symbolic school and the connectionist school in artificial intelligence (AI). First, Section 2 presents the algorithm for the Developmental Program (DP) of the DN. Section 3 gives a temporal formulation of FA to facilitate understanding the brain theory. Then, Section 4 proposes that the framework for FA is complete. All FAs in this paper are Deterministic FA. So, we call them simply FAs. How a DN learns incrementally from an FA is discussed in Section 5. The three theorems are presented and proved in Section 6 through Section 8.

Theorem 1 states that for any FA that operates in real time, there is an emergent DN that learns the FA incrementally. It observes one state-and-input pair from the FA at a time, learns immediately and becomes error-free for all the FA transitions that it has learned, regardless how many times a transition has been observed—one is sufficient but more results in better optimality in the real world. The DN is equivalent to the part of FA that corresponds to all transitions that have demonstrated so far.

Theorem 2 establishes that if the FA-learned DN is frozen—computing responses only but not updating its adaptive parts, the frozen DN is optimal in the sense of maximum likelihood when it takes inputs from infinitely many possible cases in the world.

Theorem 3 asserts that the FA-learned DN, if it is allowed to continue to learn from infinitely many possible cases in the world, is optimal in the sense of maximum likelihood.

Section 9 briefly discusses experiments of DN. Section 10 provides concluding remarks and discussion.

2. Algorithm for Developmental Program

The small DP algorithm self-programs logic of the world into a huge DN based on experiences in its physical activities. A DN has its area Y as a "bridge" for its two banks, X and Z, as illustrated in **Figure 2(b)**.

Biologically, a DP algorithm models the collective effects of some genome properties of the cells of the nervous system—neurons and other types of cells in the nervous system [3] [4] [27]. Thus, in nature, the DP is a result of evolution across many generations of a species. The DP seems to be a more systematic way to understand natural intelligence than studies the response of a child or adult brain.

In artificial intelligence, a DP algorithm is the result of human understanding of the development of natural intelligence followed by a human DP design based such understanding. This approach, known as developmental approach [2] [28], short-cuts the long and expensive process of cross-generation evolution.

Some parameters of DP (e.g., the number of cells in Y) could be experimentally selected by a genetic algorithm, but the DP as a whole seems to be extremely expensive for any artificial genetic algorithm to reach without handcrafting (e.g., see the handcrafted area function below).

Human design of DP algorithm [28] seems to be a more practical way to reach human-like mental capabilities and human-level performance in robots and computers for two main reasons: 1) Fully automatic development of intelligence (*i.e.*, task-nonspecific and fully automatic learning) is the approach that the natural intelligence takes and has demonstrated success; 2) The design of the DP algorithm is a clean task, in contrast to traditional AI—modeling intelligence itself—which is a muddy task [2] [29].

The quality in a human-designed DP, when the DP is widely used in the future, greatly affects all the capabilities in the developmental robots and computers that use the DP.

In the DN, if Y is meant for modeling the entire brain, X consists of all receptors and Z consists of all effectors—muscle neurons and glands. Additionally, the Y area of the DP can also model any Brodmann area in the brain and if so, the X and Z correspond to respectively, the bottom-up areas and top-down areas of the Brodemann area. From the analysis below, we can also see that the Y area of the DN can model any closely related set of neurons—Brodmann area, a subset, or a superset.

The most basic function of an area Y seems to be prediction—predict the signals in its two vast banks X and Z through space and time.

Algorithm 1 (DP) Input areas: X and Z. Output areas: X and Z. The dimension and representation

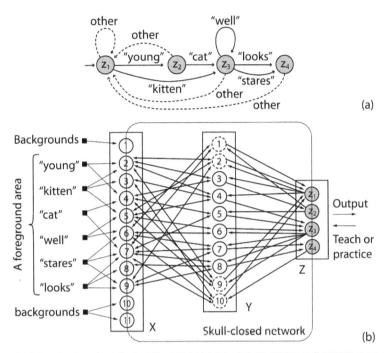

Figure 2. Conceptual correspondence between an Finite Automaton (FA) with the corresponding DN. (a) An FA, handcrafted and static; (b) A corresponding DN that simulates the FA. It was taught to produce the same input-output relations as the FA in (a). A symbol (e.g., z_2) in (a) corresponds to an image (e.g., $(z_1, z_2, \cdots, z_4) = (0,1,0,0)$) in (b).

of X and Y areas are hand designed based on the sensors and effectors of the species (or from evolution in biology). Y is the skull-closed (inside the brain), not directly accessible by the outside.

1) At time $t = 0$, for each area A in $\{X, Y, Z\}$, initialize its adaptive part $N = (V, G)$ and the response vector $\mathbf{r}$, where V contains all the synaptic weight vectors and G stores all the neuronal ages. For example, use the generative DN method discussed below.

2) At time $t = 1, 2, \cdots$, for each A in $\{X, Y, Z\}$ repeat:

a) Every area A performs mitosis-equivalent if it is needed, using its bottom-up and top-down inputs $\mathbf{b}$ and $\mathbf{t}$, respectively.

b) Every area A computes its area function f, described below,

$$(\mathbf{r}', N') = f(\mathbf{b}, \mathbf{t}, N)$$

where $\mathbf{r}'$ is its response vector and N and N' are the adaptive part of the area defined above, before and after the area update, respectively. Note that $\mathbf{r}$ is not part of the domain of f because f is the model for any area A, not just for an individual neuron of A. Thus, f does not use iterations, efficiently approximating lateral inhibitions and internal excitations.

c) For every area A in $\{X, Y, Z\}$, A replaces: $N \leftarrow N'$ and $\mathbf{r} \leftarrow \mathbf{r}'$.

The DN must update at least twice for the effects of each new signal pattern in X and Z, respectively, to go through one update in Y and then one update in Z to appear in X and Z.

In the remaining discussion, we assume that Y models the entire brain. If X is a sensory area, $\mathbf{x} \in X$ is always supervised. The $\mathbf{z} \in Z$ is supervised only when the teacher chooses to. Otherwise, $\mathbf{z}$ gives (predicts) motor output.

The area function f, which is based on the theory of Lobe Component Analysis (LCA) [30], is a model for self-organization by a neural area. Each area A has a weight vector $\mathbf{v} = (\mathbf{v}_b, \mathbf{v}_t)$. Its pre-response vector is:

$$r(\mathbf{v}_b, \mathbf{b}, \mathbf{v}_t, \mathbf{t}) = \frac{\mathbf{v}_b}{\|\mathbf{v}_b\|} \cdot \frac{\mathbf{b}}{\|\mathbf{b}\|} + \frac{\mathbf{v}_t}{\|\mathbf{v}_t\|} \cdot \frac{\mathbf{t}}{\|\mathbf{t}\|} = \dot{\mathbf{v}} \cdot \dot{\mathbf{p}} \tag{1}$$

which measures the degree of match between the directions of $\dot{\mathbf{v}} = \left(\mathbf{v}_b / \|\mathbf{v}_b\|, \mathbf{v}_t / \|\mathbf{v}_t\| \right)$ and $\dot{\mathbf{p}} = \left(\dot{\mathbf{b}}, \dot{\mathbf{t}} \right) = \left(\mathbf{b} / \|\mathbf{b}\|, \mathbf{t} / \|\mathbf{t}\| \right)$.

To simulate lateral inhibitions (winner-take-all) within each area A, only top-k winners are among the c competing neurons fire. Considering $k = 1$, the winner neuron j is identified by:

$$j = \arg \max_{1 \le i \le c} r \left(\mathbf{v}_{bi}, \mathbf{b}, \mathbf{v}_{ti}, \mathbf{t} \right) \qquad (2)$$

The area dynamically scale top-k winners so that the top-k respond with values in $(0,1]$. For $k = 1$, only the single winner fires with response value $y_j = 1$ and all other neurons in A do not fire. The response value y_j approximates the probability for $\dot{\mathbf{p}}$ to fall into the Voronoi region of its $\dot{\mathbf{v}}_j$ where the "nearness" is $r \left(\mathbf{v}_{bj}, \mathbf{b}, \mathbf{v}_{tj}, \mathbf{t} \right)$.

All the connections in a DN are learned incrementally based on Hebbian learning—cofiring of the pre-synaptic activity $\dot{\mathbf{p}}$ and the post-synaptic activity y of the firing neuron. If the pre-synaptic end and the post-synaptic end fire together, the synaptic vector of the neuron has a synapse gain $y\dot{p}$. Other non-firing neurons do not modify their memory. When a neuron j fires, its firing age is incremented $n_j \leftarrow n_j + 1$ and then its synapse vector is updated by a Hebbian-like mechanism:

$$\mathbf{v}_j \leftarrow w_1 \left(n_j \right) \mathbf{v}_j + w_2 \left(n_j \right) y_j \dot{\mathbf{p}} \qquad (3)$$

where $w_2 \left(n_j \right)$ is the learning rate depending on the firing age (counts) n_j of the neuron j and $w_1 \left(n_j \right)$ is the retention rate with $w_1 \left(n_j \right) + w_2 \left(n_j \right) \equiv 1$. Note that a component in the gain vector $y_j \dot{\mathbf{p}}$ is zero if the corresponding component in $\dot{\mathbf{p}}$ is zero.

The simplest version of $w_2 \left(n_j \right)$ is $w_2 \left(n_j \right) = 1/n_j$ which corresponds to:

$$\mathbf{v}_j^{(i)} = \frac{i-1}{i} \mathbf{v}_j^{(i-1)} + \frac{1}{i} 1 \dot{\mathbf{p}} \left(t_i \right), \quad i = 1, 2, \cdots, n_j, \qquad (4)$$

where t_i is the firing time of the post-synaptic neuron j. The above is the recursive way of computing the batch average:

$$\mathbf{v}_j^{(n_j)} = \frac{1}{n_j} \sum_{i=1}^{n_j} \dot{\mathbf{p}} \left(t_i \right) \qquad (5)$$

The initial condition is as follows. The smallest n_j in Equation (3) is 1 since $n_j = 0$ after initialization. When $n_j = 1$, the initial value of $\mathbf{v}_j$ on the right side of Equation (3) is used for pre-response competition to find this winner j, but the initial value of $\mathbf{v}_j$ does not affect the first-time updated $\mathbf{v}_j$ on the left side since $w_1 (1) = 1 - 1 = 0$.

In other words, any initialization of weight vectors will only determine who win (*i.e.*, which newly born neurons take the current role) but the initialization will not affect the distribution of weights at all. In this sense, all random initializations of synaptic weights will work equally well—all resulting in weight distributions that are computationally equivalent. Biologically, we do not care which neurons (in a small 3-D neighborhood) take the specific roles, as long as the distribution of the synaptic weights of these neurons lead to the same computational effect. This neuronal learning model leads to the following conjecture.

Conjecture 1 In a small 3-D neighborhood (e.g., of a hundred nearby neurons), neural circuits are so different across different biological brains that mapping the detailed neuron wiring of brain is not informative at the level of individual neuron.

The NIH Connectome program aims to "map the neural pathways ... about the structural and functional connectivity of the human brain. ... resulting in improved sensitivity, resolution, and utility, thereby accelerating progress in the emerging field of human connectomics". The DN theory and the above conjecture predict that such an NIH program is not as scientifically useful as the NIH program hoped in terms of understanding how the brain works and future studies of abnormal brain circuits. For the brain, "more detailed connectomics data" seems to be not as productive as more complete and clear theories.

3. FA as a Temporal Machine

In this section, we present an FA as a temporal machine, although traditionally an FA is a logic machine, driven by discrete event of input.

As we need a slight deviation from the standard definition of FA, let us look at the standard definition first.

Definition 1 (Language acceptor FA) A finite automaton (FA) M is a 5-tuple $M = (Q, \Sigma, q_0, \delta, A)$, where Q is a finite set of states, consists of symbols. Σ is a finite alphabet of input symbols. $q_0 \in Q$ is the initial state. $A \subset Q$ is the set of accepting states. $\delta : Q \times \Sigma \mapsto Q$ is the state transition function.

This classical definition is for a language acceptor, which accepts all strings x from the alphabet Σ that belongs to a language L. It has been proved [8] that given any *regular language L* from alphabet Σ, there is an FA that accepts L, meaning that it accepts exactly all $\mathbf{x} \in L$ but no other string not in L. Conversely, given any FA taking alphabet Σ, the language L that the FA accepts is a regular language. However, a language FA, just like any other automata, only deals syntax not semantics. The semantics is primary for understanding a language and the syntax is secondary.

We need to extend the definition of FA for agents that run at discrete times as follows.

Definition 2 (Agent FA) A finite automaton (FA) M for a finite symbolic world is a 4-tuple $M = (Q, \Sigma, q_0, \delta)$, where Σ and q_0 are the same as above and Q is a finite set of states, where each state $q \in Q$ is a symbol, corresponding to a set of concepts. The agent runs through discrete times $t = 1, 2, \cdots$, starting from state $q(t) = q_0$ at $t = 0$. At each time $t-1$, it reads input $\sigma(t-1) \in \Sigma$ and transits from state $q(t-1)$ to $q(t) = \delta(q(t-1), \sigma(t-1))$, and outputs $q(t)$ at time t, illustrated as $q(t-1) \xrightarrow{\sigma(t-1)} q(t)$.

The inputs to an FA are symbolic. The input space is denoted as $\Sigma = \{\sigma_1, \sigma_2, \cdots, \sigma_l\}$, which can be a discretized version of a continuous space o input. In sentence recognition, the FA reads one word at a time. The number l is equal to the number of all possible words—the size of the vocabulary. For a computer game agent, l is equal to the total number of different percepts.

The outputs (actions) from a language acceptor FA are also symbolic, $A = \{a_1, a_2, \cdots, a_n\}$ which can also be a discretized version of a continuous space of output. For a sentence detector represented by an FA, when the FA reaches the last state, its action reports that the sentence has been detected.

An agent FA is an extension from the corresponding language FA, in the sense that it outputs the state, not only the acceptance property of the state. The meanings of each state, which are handcrafted by the human programmer but are not part of the formal FA definition, are only in the mind of the human programmer. Such meanings can indicate whether a state is an accepting state or not, along many other meanings associated with each state as our later example will show. However, such concepts are only in the mind of the human system designer, not something that the FA is "aware" of. This is a fundamental limitation of all symbolic models. The Developmental Network (DN) described below do not use any symbols, but instead (image) vectors from the real-world sensors and real-world effectors. As illustrated in **Figure 2**, a DN is grounded in the physical environment but an FA is not.

Figure 3 gives an example of the agent FA. Each state is associated with a number of cognitive states and actions, shown as text in the lower part of **Figure 3**, reporting action for cognition plus a motor action. The example in **Figure 3** shows that an agent FA can be very general, simulating an animal in a micro, symbolic world. The meanings of each state in the lower part of **Figure 3** are handcrafted by, and only in the mind of, the human designer. These meanings are not a part of the FA definition and are not accessible by the machine that simulates the FA.

Without loss of generality, we can consider that an agent FA simply outputs its current state at any time, since the state is uniquely linked to a pair of the cognition set and the action set, at least in the mind of human designer.

4. Completeness of the FA-in-DN Framework

The FA-in-DN framework is useful for understanding how a DN works. However, FA itself is handcrafted by a human teacher, or in other words, the behaviors of an autonomously developed human teacher.

It has been proved [8] that an FA with n states partitions all the strings in Σ into n sets. Each set is called equivalence class, consisting of strings that are indistinguishable by the FA. Since these strings are indistinguishable, any string x in the same set can be used to denote the equivalent class, denoted as $[x]$. Let Λ denote an empty string. Considering **Figure 3**, the FA partitions all possible strings into 6 equivalent classes. $[\Lambda] = ["calculus"]$ as the agent does not know about "calculus" although it is in Σ. All the strings in the equivalent class $[\Lambda]$ end in z_1. All strings in the equivalent class $["kitten'""looks"]$ end in z_4, etc.

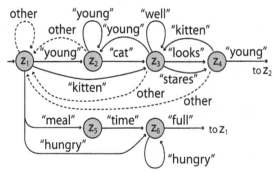

z₁: report "start"   z₂: report "young"
z₃: report "kitten-equiv." z₄: report "kitten-looks equiv."
z₅: report "meal"   z₆: report "hungry-equiv." and eat

Figure 3. An FA simulates an animal. Each circle indicates a context state. The system starts from state z_1. Supposing the system is at state q and receives a symbol σ and the next state should be q', the diagram has an arrow denoted as $q \xrightarrow{\sigma} q'$. A label "other" means any symbol other than those marked from the out-going state. Each state corresponds to a set of actions, indicated below the FA. The "other" transitions from the lower part are omitted for brevity.

From the above discussion, we can see that the key power of an FA is to lump very complex equivalent (q, σ) contexts into equivalent classes.

A Turing Machine (TM) [8] [31] is a 5-tuple $T = (Q, \Sigma, \Gamma, q_0, \delta)$, where Q is the set of states, Σ and Γ are the input and tape alphabets, respectively, with $\Sigma \subseteq \Gamma$, q_0 is the initial state, and δ is the transition function:

$$\delta : Q \times (\Gamma \cup \{\Delta\}) \to (Q \cup \{h\}) \times (\Gamma \cup \{\Delta\}) \times \{R, L, S\}$$

where Δ is the blank symbol not in Γ, h denotes the halt state, and R, L, S denote the head motion, right, left, and stationary, respectively. Consider the following two definitions:

1) Define Q' to include also the tape write action w and the head move action m:

$$Q' = (Q \cup \{h\}) \times (\Gamma \cup \{\Delta\}) \times \{R, L, S\}$$

Each state in Q' is a three tuple (q, w, m) where w and m can be empty.

2) Let $\Sigma' = \Gamma \cup \{\Delta\}$.

The above transition function δ for TM becomes the transition function δ' of an FA: $\delta' = Q' \times \Sigma' \to Q'$.

Therefore, the controller of any TM is an FA. A grounded DN can learn the FA perfectly. It takes input $\sigma \in \Sigma'$ from the real word and its action can include head write and head motion. A TM is not grounded, but the DN is grounded: A TM senses from, and acts on, a tape but a DN senses from, and acts on, its real-world physical environment.

The completeness of agent FA-in-DA can be described as follows. Given a vocabulary Σ' representing the elements of a symbolic world, a natural language L is defined in terms of Σ' where the meanings of all sentences (or events) in L are defined by the set of equivalent classes, determined by Q' of FA-in-DN. When the number of states is sufficiently large, a properly learned FA-in-DN can sufficiently characterize the cognition and behaviors of an agent living in the real physical world with vocabulary Σ'.

This argument is based on the following observation: as long as the context state $q(t-1)$ is properly learned so that it contains all the information that is necessary and sufficient for generating the following states, then $q(t-1)$ with sensory input $\sigma(t-1)$ correctly selected from a cluttered scene should be sufficient to generate the next state: $q(t-1) \xrightarrow{\sigma(t-1)} q(t)$.

As a simple example, an FA-in-DN can accept the context-free language $L = \{a^n b^n \mid n \geq 0\}$, the set of all strings that consist of n a's followed by the same number of b's, by simulating how a TM works on a tape to accept the language L.

The Chomsky hierarchy [31] after the work of Norm Chomsky in particular and the automana and languages theory in classical computer science [8] [31] regard only Turing Machines as general-purpose programming machine because they mainly consider only the syntax of a computer language, not the rich semantics that a symbol can represent. However, a symbolic state q and an input symbol σ can practically represent any set of meanings. Yet, the meanings of general purpose with Turing Machines and FA-in-DN are different: with a TM, it means what kind of sequence of computations the TM program can represent. With the latter FA-in-DN, it means the richness of meaning any symbol (q and σ) can represent so that the FA-in-DN can represent any emergent state-based agent that has a finite memory.

In particular, it is important to note that a state can remember very early event [2] [6]: e.g. an event needed by $q(t)$ can be contained in $q(t-1)$, $q(t-2)$, etc.

But FA-in-DN goes beyond the symbolic AI, because it automatically develop internal representations—emergent.

5. DN Incrementally Learns FA

Next, let us consider how a DN learns from any FA. First we consider the mapping from symbolic sets Σ and Q to vector spaces X and Z.

Definition 3 (Symbol-to-vector mapping) A symbol-to-vector mapping m is a one-to-one mapping $m : \Sigma \mapsto X$. We say that $\sigma \in \Sigma$ and $\mathbf{x} \in X$ are equivalent, denoted as $\sigma \equiv \mathbf{x}$ if $\mathbf{x} = m(\sigma)$.

A binary vector of dimension d is such that all its components are either 0 or 1. It simulates that each neuron, among d neurons, either fires with a spike $(s(t) = 1)$ or without $(s(t) = 0)$ at each sampled discrete time $t = t_i$. From discrete spikes $s(t) \in \{0, 1\}$, the real valued firing rate at time t can be estimated by

$v(t) = \sum_{t-T < t_i \leq t} \frac{s(t_i)}{T}$, where T is the temporal size for averaging. A biological neuron can fire at a maximum

rate around $v = 120$ spikes per second, producible only under a laboratory environment. If the brain is sampled at frequency $f = 1000\,\text{Hz}$, we consider the unit time length to be $1/f = 1/1000$ second. The timing of each spike is precise up to $1/f$ second at the sampling rate f, not just an estimated firing rate v, which depends on the temporal size T (e.g., $T = 0.5\,\text{s}$). Therefore, a firing-rate neuronal model is less temporally precise than a spiking neuronal model. The latter, which DN adopts, is more precise for fast sensorimotor changes.

Let B_p^d denote the d-dimensional vector space which contains all the binary vectors each of which has *at most* p components to be 1. Let $E_p^d \subset B_p^d$ contains all the binary vectors each of which has *exactly* p components to be 1.

Definition 4 (Binary-p mapping) Let $Q = \{q_i | i = 1, 2, \cdots, n\}$. A symbol-to-vector mapping $m : Q \mapsto B_p^d$ is a binary-p mapping if m is one to one, that is, if $\mathbf{z}_i \equiv m(q_i)$ then $q_i \neq q_j$ implies $\mathbf{z}_i \neq \mathbf{z}_j$.

The larger the p, the more symbols the space of Z can represent. However, through a binary-p mapping, each symbol q_i always has a unique vector $\mathbf{z} \in Z$. Note that different q's are mapped to different directions of unit $\mathbf{z}$'s.

Suppose that a DN is taught by supervising binary-p codes at its exposed areas, X and Z. When the motor area Z is free, the DN performs, but the output from Z is not always exact due to (a) the DN outputs in real numbers instead of discrete symbols and (b) there are errors in any computer or biological system. The following binary conditioning can prevent error accumulation by suppressing noise and normalizing the spikes as 1, which the brain seems to use through spikes.

Definition 5 (Binary conditioning) For any vector from $\mathbf{z} = (z_1, z_2, \cdots, z_d)$, the binary conditioning of $\mathbf{z}$ forces every real-valued component z_i to be 1 if the pre-response of z_i is larger than the machine zero—a small positive bound estimating computer round-off noise.

The binary conditioning must be used during autonomous performance as long as the Z representations use spikes, instead of firing rates. Machines zeros are noises from computer finite precision in representing a number. The binary conditioning suppresses the accumulation of such computer generated round-off errors. Because the Z representation is binary by definition, the binary conditioning forces the real numbers to become 0 or 1 only. However, the actual value of machine zero is computer dependent, depending on the length to represent a real number. In particular, the case of a constant Z vector of all ones will not appear incorrectly because all noises components that are meant to be 0 are set back to 0.

The output layer Z that uses binary-p mapping must use the binary conditioning, instead of top-k competition with a fixed k, as the number of firing neurons ranges from 1 to p.

Algorithm 2 (DP for GDN) A GDN is a DN that gives the following specific way of initialization. It starts from pre-specified dimensions for the X and Z areas, respectively. X represents receptors and is totally determined by the current input. But it incrementally generates neurons in Y from an empty Y (computer programming may use dynamic memory allocation). Each neuron in Z is initialized by a synaptic vector $\mathbf{v}$ of dimension 0, age 0. Suppose $V = \left\{ \mathbf{v}_i = (\mathbf{x}_i, \mathbf{z}_i) \middle| \mathbf{x} \in X, \mathbf{z} \in Z, i = 1, 2, \cdots, c \right\}$ is the current synaptic vectors in Y. Whenever the network takes an input $\mathbf{p} = (\mathbf{x}, \mathbf{z})$, compute the pre-resppnses in Y. If the top-1 winner in Y has a pre-response lower than 2 (*i.e.*, $\mathbf{p} \notin V$), simulate mitosis-equivalent by doing the following:

1) Increment the number of neurons $c \leftarrow c + 1$,

2) Add a new Y neuron. Set the weight vector $\mathbf{v} = \dot{\mathbf{p}}$, its age to be 0, and its pre-response to be 2 since it is the perfect match based on Equation (1). There is no need to recompute the pre-responses.

The response value of each Z neuron is determined by the starting state (e.g., background class). As soon as the first Y neuron is generated, every Z neuron will add the first dimension in its synaptic vector in the following DN update. This way, the dimension of its weight vector continuously increases together with the number c of Y neurons.

6. Theorem 1: DN Learns FA Perfectly

In this section, we establish the most basic theorem of the three, **Theorem 1**. First, we give an overview. Next, we establish a lemma to facilitate the proof of **Theorem 1**. Then, we present **Theorem 1**. Finally, we discuss grounded DN.

6.1. Overview

We first give an overview to facilitate the understanding of the proofs. **Figure 4** is our graphic guide of this section. It has two parts, **Figure 4(a)** having a four-state and two-input FA as a small example of SN, and **Figure 4(b)** being a general purpose DN that can implement the FA in **Figure 4(a)** as only a special case but a DN can learn any FA autonomously from physically emerging patterns.

Although an FA is a temporal machine, the classic way to run an FA at discrete events that correspond to the time when the FA receives a symbolic input [8]. In order to explain how a continuously running DN learns an FA we run both FA and DN through discrete time indices.

An FA, such as the one in **Figure 4(a)** is handcrafted by a human programmer for a specific given task. However, a DN in **Figure 4(b)** can learn any FA, including the one in **Figure 4(a)**. The DN observes one pair of symbol (q, σ) at a time from the FA but the DN only uses the physically consistent pattern $(\mathbf{z}, \mathbf{x})$ corresponding to (q, σ), instead of (q, σ) itself. By physically consistent, we mean, e.g., $\mathbf{z}$ is a muscle neuron firing pattern and $\mathbf{x}$ is an image in the eyes. Therefore, we say that $(\mathbf{z}, \mathbf{x})$ is emergent (*i.e.*, directly emerge from the physical world) but (q, σ) is not (*i.e.*, handcrafted by the human programmer in the design document).

Because all three areas X, Y, Z in the DN all compute in parallel in **Algorithm 1**, we have two parallel computation flows in **Figure 4(b)**:

1) The first flow corresponds to $(\mathbf{z}, \mathbf{x})$ in the first column, $\mathbf{y}$ in the second column, and $(\mathbf{z}, \mathbf{x})$ in the third column.

2) The second flow has $\mathbf{y}$ in the first column, $(\mathbf{z}, \mathbf{x})$ in the second, and $\mathbf{y}$ in the third.

Both flows satisfy the real-world events, but for the FA logic here we let the second flow simply repeat (retain) the first flow. Therefore, due to these two flows, the DN must update at least twice for each pair (q, σ) for the effect of a new $(\mathbf{z}, \mathbf{x})$ to reach the next $(\mathbf{z}, \mathbf{x})$, once for the new $\mathbf{y}$ computation and once for the new $(\mathbf{z}, \mathbf{x})$ computation. In the real world, DN should be updated as fast as the computational resources allow so as to respond to the real world as fast as it can.

The X area is always supervised by $\mathbf{x}$ as the binary pattern of σ.

The number of Z firing neurons depends on the number of different physical patterns required for Z, but we assume that the Z area uses binary representations. Each firing Z neuron, supervised by the current q from the FA as vector $\mathbf{z}$, accumulates the firing frequency of the current single firing Y neuron as the corresponding Y-to-Z synaptic weights of the Z neuron. The incremental average in the Hebbian learning of Equation (4) is ex-

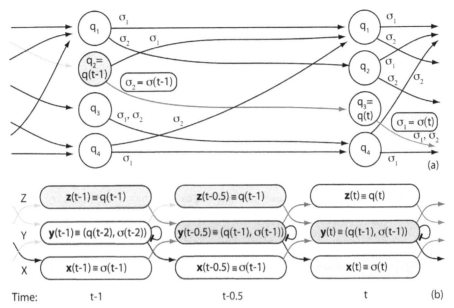

Figure 4. Symbolic Network (SN) and model the brain mapping, DN. In general, the brain performs external mapping $b(t): X(t-1) \times Z(t-1) \mapsto X(t) \times Z(t)$ on the fly. (a) An SN samples the vector space Z using symbolic set Q, and X using Σ, to compute symbolic mapping $Q(t-1) \times \Sigma(t-1) \mapsto Q(t)$. This example has four states $Q = \{q_1, q_2, q_3, q_4\}$, with two input symbols $\Sigma = \{\sigma_1, \sigma_2\}$. Two conditions (q, σ) (e.g., $q = q_2$ and $\sigma = \sigma_2$) identify the active outgoing arrow (e.g., red). $q_3 = \delta(q_2, \sigma_2)$ is the target state pointed to by the (red) arrow. (b) The grounded DN generates the internal brain area Y as a bridge, its bidirectional connections with its two banks X and Z, the inner products distance, and adaptation, to realize the external brain mapping. It performs at least two network updates during each unit time. To show how the DN learns a SN, the colors between (a) and (b) match. The sign $\equiv$ means "image code for". In (b), the two red paths from $q(t-1)$ and $\sigma(t-1)$ show the condition $(\mathbf{z}(t-1), \mathbf{x}(t-1)) \equiv (q(t-1), \sigma(t-1))$. At $t-0.5$, they link to $\mathbf{y}(t-0.5)$ as internal representation, corresponding to the identification of the outgoing arrow (red) in (a) but an SN does not have any internal representation. At time t, $\mathbf{z}(t) \equiv q(t) = \delta(q(t-1), \sigma(t-1))$ predicts the action. But the DN uses internal $\mathbf{y}(t-0.5)$ to predict both state $\mathbf{z}(t)$ and input $\mathbf{x}(t)$. The same color between two neighboring horizontal boxes in (b) shows the retention of (q, σ) image in (a) within each unit time, but the retention should be replaced by temporal sampling in general. The black arrows in (b) are for predicting X. Each arrow link in (b) represents many connections. When it is shown by a non-black color, the color indicates the corresponding transition in (a). Each arrow link represents excitatory connections. Each bar link is inhibitory, representing top-k competition among Y neurons.

actly what is needed to compute this firing frequency. This firing frequency is equal to the discrete probability required for the optimality in the later **Theorems 2** and **3**.

The Y area of the GDN is empty to start with. Whenever there is a new input $(\mathbf{z}, \mathbf{x})$, the DN automatically assigns a new Y neuron that memorizes $(\mathbf{z}, \mathbf{x})$ as its weight vector $(\mathbf{v}_t, \mathbf{v}_b)$. Later, this Y neuron will not win in the top-1 competition unless when the same input $(\mathbf{z}, \mathbf{x})$ appears again. The incremental average in the Hebbian learning of Equation (4) implies that every Y neuron never changes its weight vector after it is initialized using the input—average over the same vectors. Therefore, the number of Y neurons needed by the DN to learn an FA is equal to the number of different FA transitions.

With this overview, we are ready for **Lemma 1**.

6.2. Lemma 1

This subsection is a little long because of the detailed and complete proof, but I use the top-level Case 1 (new Y input) and Case 2 (old Y input) in the proof to organize the material. Each Case first considers Y and then Z. When we consider Z, we have Case (i,a) and Case (i,b) for the case where the Z neuron under consideration should fire and not fire, respectively, where i corresponds to 1 or 2 in the above Cases 1 or 2.

Lemma 1 (Properties of a GDN) Suppose a GDN simulates any given FA using top-1 competition for Y, binary-p mapping, and binary conditioning for Z, and update at least twice in each unit time. Each input $\mathbf{x}(t-1)$ is retained during all DN updates in $(t-1,t]$. Such a GDN has the following properties for $t=1,2,\cdots$:

1) The winner Y neuron matches perfectly with input $\mathbf{p}(t-1) \equiv (q(t-1),\sigma(t-1))$ with $\mathbf{v} = \dot{\mathbf{p}}$ and fires, illustrated in **Figure 4(a)** as a single transition edge (red).

2) All the synaptic vectors in Y are unit and they never change once initialized, for all times up to t. They only advance their firing ages. The number of Y neurons c is exactly the number of learned state transitions up to time t.

3) Suppose that the weight vector $\mathbf{v}$ of each Z neuron is $\mathbf{v} = \left(p_1, p_2, \cdots, p_{c(Y)} \right)$, and Z area uses the learning rate straight recursive average $w_2(n_j) = 1/n_j$. Then the weight p_j from the j-th Y neuron to each Z neuron is

$$p_j = \text{Prob}\left(j\text{-th } Y \text{ neuron fires} \mid \text{the } Z \text{ neuron fires} \right) = f_j/n \tag{6}$$

$j=1,2,\cdots,c(Y)$, where f_j is the number of times the j-th Y neuron has fired conditioned on that the Z neuron fires, and n is the total number of times the Z neuron has fired.

4) Suppose that the FA makes transition $q(t-1) \xrightarrow{\sigma(t-1)} q(t)$, as illustrated in **Figure 4(a)**. After the second DN update, Z outputs $\mathbf{z}(t) \equiv q(t)$, as long as Z of DN is supervised for the second DN update when the transition is received by Z the first time. Z then retains the values automatically till the end of the first DN update after t.

Proof. The proof below is a constructive proof, instead of an existence one. To facilitate understanding, the main ideas are illustrated in **Figure 4**. Let the X of the DN take the equivalent inputs from Σ using a symbol-to-vector mapping. Let Z be supervised as the equivalent states in Q, using a binary-p mapping. The number of firing neurons Z depends on the binary-p mapping. The DN lives in the simulated sensori-motor world $X \times Z$ determined by the sensory symbol-to-vector mapping: $m_x : \Sigma \mapsto X$ and the binary-p symbol-to-vector mapping $m_z : Q \mapsto Z$.

We prove it using induction on integer t.

Basis: When $t=0$, set the output $\mathbf{z}(0) \equiv q(0) = q_0$ for the DN. Y has no neuron. Z neurons have no synaptic weights. All the neuronal ages are zeros. The properties 1, 2, 3 and 4 are trivially true for $t=0$.

Hypothesis: We hypothesize that the above four properties are true up to integer time t. In the following, we prove that the above properties are true for $t + 1$.

Induction step: During t to $t + 1$, suppose that the FA makes transition $q(t) \xrightarrow{\sigma(t)} q(t+1)$. The DN must do the equivalent, as shown below.

At the next DN update, there are two cases for Y: Case 1: the transition is observed by the DN as the first time; Case 2: the DN has observed the transition.

Case 1: new Y input. First consider Y. As the input $\mathbf{p}(t) = (\mathbf{x}(t),\mathbf{z}(t))$ to Y is the first time, $\dot{\mathbf{p}} \notin V$. Y initializes a new neuron whose weight vector is initialized as $\mathbf{v}_j = \dot{\mathbf{p}}(t)$ and age $n_j = 0$. The number of Y neurons c is incremented by 1 as this is a newly observed state transition. From the hypothesis, all previous Y neurons in V are still their originally initialized unit vectors. Thus, the newly initialized $\mathbf{v}_j$ is the only Y neuron that matches $\dot{\mathbf{p}}(t)$ exactly. With $k=1$, this new Y neuron is the unique winner and it fires with $y_j = 1$. Its Hebbian learning gives age advance $n_j \leftarrow n_j + 1 = 0 + 1 = 1$ and Equation (3) leads to

$$\mathbf{v}_j \leftarrow w_1(n_j)\dot{\mathbf{p}} + w_2(n_j) \cdot 1 \cdot \dot{\mathbf{p}} = \left(w_1(n_j) + w_2(n_j) \right)\dot{\mathbf{p}} = 1 \cdot \dot{\mathbf{p}} = \dot{\mathbf{p}} \tag{7}$$

As DN updates at least twice in the unit time, Y area is updated again for the second DN update. But X and Z retain their values within each unit time, per simulation rule. Thus, the Y winner is still the same new neuron and its vector still does not change as the above expression is still true. Thus, properties 1 and 2 are true for the first two DN updates within $(t,t+1]$.

Next consider Z. Z retains its values in the first DN update, per hypothesis. For the second DN update, the response of Z is regarded the DN's Z output for this unit time, which uses the above Y response as illustrated in

Figure 4. In Case 1, Z must be supervised for this second DN update within the unit time. According to the binary-p mapping from the supervised $q(t+1)$, Equation (3) is performed for up to p firing Z neurons:

$$\mathbf{v}_j \leftarrow w_1(n_j)\dot{\mathbf{v}}_j + w_2(n_j)\cdot 1\cdot\dot{\mathbf{p}}. \tag{8}$$

We can see that Equations (7) and (8) are the same Hebbian learning, but the former is for Y and the latter is for Z. Note that Z has only bottom input $\mathbf{p} = \mathbf{y}$ and the normalized vector $\dot{\mathbf{p}}$ is binary. That is, only one component (the new one) in $\dot{\mathbf{p}}$ is 1 and all other components are zeros. All Z neurons do not link with this new Y neuron before the second DN update. Consider two subcases, subcase (1.a) the Z neuron should fire at the end of this unit time, and subcase (1.b) the Z neuron should not fire.

Subcase (1.a): the Z neuron should fire. All Z neurons that should fire, up to p of them, are supervised to fire for the second DN update by the Z area function. Suppose that a supervised-to-fire Z neuron has a synapse vector $\mathbf{v} = (p_1, p_2, \cdots, p_c)$ with the new p_c just initialized to be 0 since the new Y neuron $j = c$ now fires. From the hypothesis, $p_i = f_i/n$, $i = 1, 2, \cdots, c-1$. But, according to the Z initialization in GDN, $p_c = 0$ for the new dimension initialization. Then from $0 = p_c = f_c/n$, we have $f_c = 0$ which is correct for f_c. From Equation (3), the c-th component of $\mathbf{v}$ is

$$v_c \leftarrow \frac{n}{n+1}\cdot\frac{f_c}{n} + \frac{1}{n+1}\cdot 1\cdot 1 = \frac{f_c+1}{n+1} = \frac{1}{n+1} \tag{9}$$

which is the correct count for the new v_c, and the other components of $\mathbf{v}$ are

$$v_i \leftarrow \frac{n}{n+1}\cdot\frac{f_i}{n} + \frac{1}{n+1}\cdot 1\cdot 0 = \frac{f_i+0}{n+1} = \frac{f_i}{n+1} \tag{10}$$

for all $i = 1, 2, \cdots, c-1$, which is also the correct count for other components of the $\mathbf{v}$ synaptic vector. Every firing Z neuron advances its age by 1 and correctly counts the firing of the new c-th Y neuron. As Y response does not change for more DN updates within $(t, t+1]$ and the firing Y neuron meets a positive $1/n_j$ weight to the firing Z neuron with age n_j, the Z area does not need to be supervised after the second DN update within $(t, t+1]$.

Subcase (1.b): the Z neuron should not fire. All Z neurons that should not fire must be supervised to be zero (not firing). All such Z neurons could not be linked with the new Y neuron because the new Y neuron was not present until now. However, in computer programming or hardware circuits, each non-firing Z neuron must add a zero-weight link from this new Y neuron. Otherwise, the Z neuron never "sees" the new Y neuron and can never link from it when the Z neuron fires in the future. All these non-firing neurons keep their counts and ages unchanged. As Y response does not change for more DN updates within $(t, t+1]$, the Z area does not need to be supervised after the second DN update within $(t, t+1]$, since the only firing Y neuron meets a 0 weight to the Z neuron.

The binary conditioning for Z makes sure that all the Z neurons that have a positive pre-response to fire fully. That is, the properties 3 and 4 are true from the first two DN updates within $(t, t+1]$.

Case 2: old Y input. First consider Y. To Y, $\mathbf{p}(t) = (\mathbf{x}(t), \mathbf{z}(t))$ has been an input before. From the hypothesis, the winner Y neuron j exactly matches $\dot{\mathbf{p}}(t)$, with $\mathbf{v}_j = \dot{\mathbf{p}}(t)$. Equation (7) still holds using the inductive hypothesis, as the winner Y neuron fires only for a single $\dot{\mathbf{p}}$ vector. Thus, properties 1 and 2 are true from the firstD N update within $(t, t+1]$.

Next consider Z. Z retains its previous vector values in the first DN update, per hypothesis. In the second DN update, the transition is not new, we show that Z does not need to be supervised during the unit time $(t, t+1]$ to fire perfectly. From Equation (1), the Z pre-response is computed by

$$r(\mathbf{v}_b, \mathbf{b}) = \frac{\mathbf{v}_b}{\|\mathbf{v}_b\|}\cdot\frac{\mathbf{b}}{\|\mathbf{b}\|} = \frac{\mathbf{v}_b}{\|\mathbf{v}_b\|}\cdot\frac{\mathbf{y}}{\|\mathbf{y}\|} \tag{11}$$

where $\dot{\mathbf{y}}$ is binary with only a single positive component and $\mathbf{t}$ is absent as Z does not have a top-down input. Suppose that Y neuron j fired in the first DN update. From the hypothesis, every Z neuron has a synaptic vector $\mathbf{v} = (p_1, p_2, \cdots, p_c)$, where $p_j = f_j/n$ counting up to time t, where f_j is the observed frequency (occurrences) of Y neuron j firing, $j = 1, 2, \cdots, c$, and n is the total number of times the Z neuron has fired.

Consider two sub-cases: (2.a) the Z neuron should fire according to the transition, and (2.b) the Z neuron should not.

For sub-case (2.a) where the Z neuron should fire, we have

$$r(\mathbf{v}_b,\mathbf{b}) = r(\mathbf{v},\mathbf{y}) = \dot{\mathbf{v}}\cdot\dot{\mathbf{y}} = \frac{p_j}{\|\mathbf{v}\|}\cdot 1 = \frac{p_j}{\|\mathbf{v}\|} = \frac{f_j/n}{\|\mathbf{v}\|} = \frac{f_j}{n\|\mathbf{v}\|} > 0$$

because the Z neuron has been supervised at least the first time for this transition and thus $f_j \geq 1$. We conclude that the Z neuron guarantees to fire at 1 after its binary conditioning. From Equation (3), the j-th component of $\mathbf{v}$ is:

$$v_j \leftarrow \frac{n}{n+1}\cdot\frac{f_j}{n} + \frac{1}{n+1}\cdot 1\cdot 1 = \frac{f_j+1}{n+1} \tag{12}$$

which is the correct count for the j-th component, and the other components of $\mathbf{v}$ are:

$$v_i \leftarrow \frac{n}{n+1}\cdot\frac{f_i}{n} + \frac{1}{n+1}\cdot 1\cdot 0 = \frac{f_i+0}{n+1} = \frac{f_i}{n+1} \tag{13}$$

for all $i \neq j$, which is also the correct count for all other components in $\mathbf{v}$. The Z neuron does not need to be supervised after the second DN update within $(t,t+1]$ but still keeps firing. This is what we want to prove for property 3 for every firing Z neuron.

Next consider sub-case (2.b) where the Z neuron should not fire. Similarly we have $r(\mathbf{v}_b,\mathbf{b}) = r(\mathbf{v},\dot{\mathbf{y}}) = f_j/(n\|\mathbf{v}\|) = 0$, from the hypothesis that this Z neuron fires correctly up to time t and thus we must have $f_j = 0$. Thus, they do not fire, change their weights, or advance their ages. The Z neuron does not need to be supervised after the second DN update within $(t,t+1]$ but keeps not firing. This is exactly what we want to prove for property 3 for every non-firing Z neuron.

Combining the sub-cases (2.a) and (2.b), all the Z neurons act perfectly and the properties 3 and 4 are true for the first two DN updates. We have proved for Case 2, old Y input.

Therefore, the properties 1, 2, 3, 4 are true for first two DN updates. If DN has time to continue to update before time $t+1$, we see that we have always Case 2 for Y and Z within the unit time and Y and Z re- tain their responses since the input $\mathbf{x}$ retains its vector value. Thus, the properties 1, 2, 3, 4 are true for all DN updates within $(t,t+1]$.

According to the principle of induction, we have proved that the properties 1, 2, 3 and 4 are all true for all t. □

6.3. Theorem 1

Using the above lemma, we are ready to prove:

Theorem 1 (Simulate any FA as scaffolding) The general-purpose DP incrementally grows a GDN to simulate any given FA $M = (Q,\Sigma,q_0,\delta,A)$, error-free and on the fly, if the Z area of the DN is supervised when the DN observes each new state transition from the FA. The learning for each state transition completes within two network updates. There is no need for a second supervision for the same state transition to reach error-free future performance. The number of Y neurons in the DN is the number of state transitions in the FA.

Proof. Run the given FA and the GDN at discrete time t, $t = 1,2,\cdots$. Using the lemma above, each state transition $q \xrightarrow{\sigma} q'$ is observed by the DN via the mappings m_x and m_z. Update the DN at least twice in each unit time. In DN, if $\mathbf{p} = (\mathbf{z},\mathbf{x})$ is a new vector to Y, Y adds a new neuron. Further, from the proof of the above lemma, we can see that as soon as each transition in FA has been taught, the DN has only Case 2 for the same transition in the future, which means that no need for second supervision for any transition. Also from the proof of the lemma, the number of Y neurons corresponds to the number of state transitions in the FA. □

If the training data set is finite and consistent (the same (q,σ) must go to the unique next state q'), re-substitution test (using the training set) corresponds to simulating an FA using pattern codes. **Theorem 1** states that for the GDN any re-substitution test for consistent training data is always immediate and error-free. Conventionally, this will mean that the system over-fits data as its generalization will be poor. However, the GDN does not over-fit data as the following **Theorem 2** states, since the nature of its parameters is optimal and the size of the parameter set is dynamic. In other words, it is optimal for disjoint tests.

6.4. Grounded DN

Definition 6 (Grounded DN) Suppose that the symbol-to-vector mapping for the DN is consistent with the real sensor of the a real-world agent (robot or animal), namely, each symbol σ for FA is mapped to an sub-image $\mathbf{x}$ from the real sensor, excluding the parts of the irrelevant background in the scene. Then the DN that has been trained for the FA is called grounded.

For a grounded DN, the SN is a human knowledge abstraction of the real world. After training, a grounded DN can run in the real physical world, at least in principle. However, as we discussed above, the complexity of symbolic representation for Σ and Q is exponential in the number of concepts. Therefore, it is intractable for any SN to sufficiently sample the real world since the number of symbols required is too many for a realistic problem. The fact that there are enough symbols to model the real world causes the symbolic system to be brittle. All the probability variants of FA can only adjust the boundaries between any two nearby symbols, but the added probability cannot resolve the fundamental problem of the lack of sufficient number of symbols.

7. Theorem 2: Frozen DN Generalizes Optimally

The next theorem states how the frozen GDN generalizes for infinitely many sensory inputs.

Theorem 2 (DN generalization while frozen) Suppose that after having experienced all the transitions of the FA from time $t = t_0$, the GDN turns into a DN that

1) freezes: It does not generate new Y neurons and does not update its adaptive part.

2) generalizes: It continues to generate responses by taking sensory inputs not restricted to the finite ones for the FA.

Then the DN generates the Maximum Likelihood (ML) action $\mathbf{z}_n(t)$, recursively, for all integer $t > t_0$:

$$n(t) = \arg\max_{\mathbf{z}_i \in Z} h\left(\dot{\mathbf{p}}(t-1) \middle| \mathbf{z}_i(t), \mathbf{z}(t-1)\right) \tag{14}$$

where the probability density $h\left(\dot{\mathbf{p}}(t-1) \middle| \mathbf{z}_i(t), \mathbf{z}(t-1)\right)$ is the probability density of the new last observation $\dot{\mathbf{p}}(t-1)$, with the parameter vector $\mathbf{z}_i$, conditioned on the last executed action $\mathbf{z}(t-1)$, based on its experience gained from learning the FA.

Proof. Reuse the proof of the lemma. Case 1 does not apply since the DN does not generate new neurons. Only Case 2 applies.

First consider Y. Define c Voronoi regions in $X \times Z$ based on now frozen $V = (\mathbf{v}_1, \mathbf{v}_2, \cdots, \mathbf{v}_c)$, where each R_j consisting of $\dot{\mathbf{p}}$ vectors that are closer to $\dot{\mathbf{v}}_j$ than to other $\dot{\mathbf{v}}_i$:

$$R_j = \left\{ \dot{\mathbf{p}} \middle| j = \arg\max_{1 \leq i \leq c} \dot{\mathbf{v}}_i \cdot \dot{\mathbf{p}} \right\}, \quad j = 1, 2, \cdots, c$$

Given observation $\dot{\mathbf{p}}(t-1)$, V has two sets of parameters, the X synaptic vectors and the Z synaptic vectors. They are frozen.

According to the dependence of parameters in DN, first consider c events for area Y: $\dot{\mathbf{p}}(t-1)$ falls into R_i, $i = 1, 2, \cdots, c$ partitioned by the c Y vectors in V. The conditional probability density $g\left(\dot{\mathbf{p}}(t-1) \middle| \dot{\mathbf{v}}_i, \mathbf{z}(t-1)\right)$ is zero if $\dot{\mathbf{p}}(t-1)$ falls out of the Voronoi region of $\dot{\mathbf{v}}_i$:

$$g\left(\dot{\mathbf{p}}(t-1) \middle| \mathbf{v}_i, \mathbf{z}(t-1)\right) = \begin{cases} g_i\left(\dot{\mathbf{p}}(t-1) \middle| \mathbf{v}_i, \mathbf{z}(t-1)\right), & \text{if } p(t-1) \in R_i; \\ 0, & \text{otherwise} \end{cases} \tag{15}$$

where $g_i\left(\dot{\mathbf{p}}(t-1) \middle| \mathbf{v}_i, \mathbf{z}(t-1)\right)$ is the probability density within R_i. Note that the distribution of $g_i\left(\dot{\mathbf{p}}(t-1) \middle| \mathbf{v}_i, \mathbf{z}(t-1)\right)$ within R_i is irrelevant as long as it integrates to 1.

Note that $\mathbf{p}(t-1) = (\mathbf{x}(t-1), \mathbf{z}(t-1))$. Given $\dot{\mathbf{p}}(t-1)$, the ML estimator for the binary vector $\mathbf{y}_j \in E_1^c$ needs to maximize $g\left(\dot{\mathbf{p}}(t-1) \middle| \mathbf{v}_i, \mathbf{z}(t-1)\right)$, which is equivalent to finding

$$j = \arg\max_{1 \leq i \leq c} g\left(\dot{\mathbf{p}}(t-1) \middle| \mathbf{v}_i, \mathbf{z}(t-1)\right) = \arg\max_{1 \leq i \leq c} \dot{\mathbf{v}}_i \cdot \dot{\mathbf{p}}(t-1) \tag{16}$$

since finding the ML estimator j for Equation (15) is equivalent to finding the Voronoi region to which $\dot{\mathbf{p}}(t-1)$ belongs to. This is exactly what the Y area does, supposing $k=1$ for top-k competition.

Next, consider Z. The set of all possible binary-1 Y vectors and the set of producible binary-p Z vectors have a one-to-one correspondence: $\mathbf{y}_j$ corresponds to $\mathbf{z}_n$ if and only if the single firing neuron in $\mathbf{y}_j$ has non-zero connections to all the firing neurons in the binary-p $\mathbf{z}_n$ but not to the non-firing neurons in $\mathbf{z}_n$. Namely, given the winner Y neuron j, the corresponding $\mathbf{z} \in Z$ vector is deterministic. Furthermore, for each Y neuron, there is only unique $\mathbf{z}$ because of the definition of FA. Based on the definition of probability density, we have:

$$g\left(\dot{\mathbf{p}}(t-1)\middle|\mathbf{v}_i, \mathbf{z}(t-1)\right) = h\left(\dot{\mathbf{p}}(t-1)\middle|\mathbf{z}_n(t), \mathbf{z}(t-1)\right)$$

for every $\mathbf{v}_j$ corresponding to $\mathbf{z}_n(t)$. Thus, when the DN generates $\mathbf{y}(t-0.5)$ in Equation (16) for ML estimate, its Z area generates ML estimate $\mathbf{z}_n(t)$ that maximizes Equation (14). □

8. Theorem 3: DN Thinks Optimally

There seems no more proper terms to describe the nature of the DN operation other than "think". The thinking process by the current basic version of DN seems similar to, but not exactly the same as, that of the brain. At least, the richness of the mechanisms in DN that has demonstrated experimentally to be close to that of the brain.

Theorem 3 (DN generalization while updating) Suppose that after having experienced all the transitions of the FA from time $t = t_0$, the GDN turns into a DN that

1) fixes its size: It does not generate new Y neurons.
2) adapts: It updates its adaptive part $N = (V, A)$.
3) generalizes: It continues to generate responses by taking sensory inputs not restricted to the finite ones for the FA.

Then the DN "thinks" (*i.e.*, learns and generalizes) recursively and optimally: for all integer $t > t_0$, the DN recursively generates the Maximum Likelihood (ML) response $\mathbf{y}_j(t-0.5) \in E_1^c$: with

$$j = \arg \max_{1 \le i \le c} g\left(\dot{\mathbf{p}}(t-1)\middle|\dot{\mathbf{v}}_i(t-1), \mathbf{z}(t-1)\right) \tag{17}$$

where $g\left(\dot{\mathbf{p}}(t-1)\middle|\dot{\mathbf{v}}_i(t-1), \mathbf{z}(t-1)\right)$ is the probability density, conditioned on $\dot{\mathbf{v}}_i(t-1)$, $\mathbf{z}(t-1)$. And the Z has the pre-response vector $\mathbf{z}(t) = \left(r_1, r_2, \cdots, r_{c(Z)}\right)$, where r_n, $n = 1, 2, \cdots, c(Z)$, is the conditional probability for the n-th Z neuron to fire:

$$r_n = p_{nj}(t) = \text{Prob}\left(j\text{-th } Y \text{ neuron fires at time } t-0.5 \middle| n\text{-th } Z \text{ neuron fires at time } t\right) \tag{18}$$

The firing of each Z neuron has a freedom to choose a binary conditioning method to map the above the pre-response vector $\mathbf{z} \in R^{c(Z)}$ to the corresponding binary vector $\mathbf{z} \in B^{c(Z)}$.

Proof. Again, reuse the proof of the lemma with the synaptic vectors of Y to be $V(t-1) = (\mathbf{v}_1, \mathbf{v}_2, \cdots, \mathbf{v}_c)$ now adapting.

First consider Y. Equation (16) is still true as this is what DN does but V is now adapting. The probability density in Equation (15) is the currently estimated version based on past experience but V is now adapting. Then, when $k=1$ for top-k Y area competition, the Y response vector $\mathbf{y}_j(t-0.5) \in E_1^c$ with j determined by Equation (16) gives Equation (17). In other words, the response vector from Y area is again the Maximum Likelihood (ML) estimate from the incrementally estimated probability density. The major difference between Equation (16) and Equation (17) is that in the latter, the adaptive part of the DN updates.

Next, consider Z. From the proof of the **Lemma 1**, the synaptic weight between the j-th Y neuron and the n-th Z neuron is

$$p_{nj} = \text{Prob}\left(j\text{-th } Y \text{ neuron fires in the last DN update} \middle| n\text{-th } Z \text{ neuron fires in the next DN update}\right) \tag{19}$$

The total pre-response for the n-th neuron is

$$r_n = r(\mathbf{v}_n, \mathbf{y}) = \dot{\mathbf{v}}_n \cdot \dot{\mathbf{y}} = p_{nj} y_j = p_{nj} 1 = p_{nj}$$

since the j-th neuron is the only firing Y neuron at this time. The above two expressions give Equation (18). □

The last sentence in the theorem gives the freedom for Z to choose a binary conditioning method but a binary conditioning method is required in order to determine which Z neurons fire and all other Z neurons do not. In the brain, neural modulation (e.g., expected punishment, reward, or novelty) discourages or encourages the recalled components of **z** to fire.

The adaptive mode after learning the FA is autonomous inside the DN. A major novelty of this theory of thinking is that the structure inside the DN is fully emergent, regulated by the DP (*i.e.*, nature) and indirectly shaped (*i.e.*, nurture) by the external environment.

The neuronal resource of Y gradually re-distribute according to the new observations in $Z \times X$. It adds new context-sensory experience and gradually weights down prior experience. Over the entire life span, more often observed experience and less often observed experience are proportionally represented as the synaptic weights.

However, an adaptive DN does not simply repeat the function of the FA it has learned. Its new thinking experience includes those that are not applicable to the FA. The following cases are all allowed in principle:

1) Thinking with a "closed eye": A closed eye sets $\mathbf{x} = \mathbf{u}$ where **u** has 0.5 for all its components (all gray image). The DN runs where Y responses mainly to **z** as **x** has little "preference" in matching.

2) Thinking with an "open eye": In the sensory input **x** is different from any prior input.

3) Inconsistent experience: from the same $(\mathbf{z},\mathbf{x}) \equiv (q,\sigma)$, the next $\mathbf{z}' \equiv q'$ may be different at different times. FA does not allow any such inconsistency. However, the inconsistencies allow occasional mistakes, update of knowledge structures, and possible discovery of new knowledge.

The neuronal resources of Y gradually re-distribute according to the new context-motor experience in $Y \times Z$. The learning rate $w_2(n_j) = 1/n_j$ amounts to equally weighted average for past experience by each neuron. Weng & Luciw 2009 [30] investigated amnesic average to give more weight to recent experience.

In the developmental process of a DN, there is no need for a rigid switch between FA and the real-world learning. The mitosis-equivalent of Y neurons is gradually realized by gradual mitosis and cell death, neuronal migration and connection, neuronal spine growth and death, and other neuronal adaptation. DN can also switch between neuronal initialization and adaptation smoothly. The rigid switches between neuronal initialization and neuronal adaptation and between FA learning and the real-world learning above are meant to facilitate our understanding and analysis only.

The binary conditioning is suited only when Z is supervised according to the FA to be simulated. As the "thinking" of the DN is not necessarily correct, it is not desirable to use the binary conditioning for Z neurons. For example, a dynamic threshold can be used for v_n to pass in order for the n-th neuron to fire at value 1. This threshold can be related to the punishment and reward from the environment. In general, the threshold is related to the neural modulatory system.

The thinking process by the current basic version of DN seems similar to, but not exactly the same as, that of the brain. At least, the richness of the mechanisms in an experimental DN is not yet close to that of an adult brain. For example, the DN here does not use neuromodulators so it does not prefer any signals from receptors (e.g., sweet vs bitter).

9. Experimental Results

Due to the focused theoretical subject here and the space limitation, detailed experimental results of DN are not included here. The DN has had several versions of experimental embodiments, called Where-What Networks (WWNs), from WWN-1 [32] to WWN-7 [33]. Each WWN has multiple areas in the Z areas, representing the location concept (Location Motor, LM), type concept (Type Motor, TM), or scale concept (Scale Motor, SM), and so on.

A learned WWN can simultaneously detect and recognize learned 3-D objects from new unobserved cluttered natural scenes [5] [34].

The function of this space-time machine DN differs depending on the context information in its Z area [7]. If there is no Z signal at all, the WWN is in an (emergent) free-viewing mode and it detects any learned object from the cluttered scene and tells its location from LM, type from TM, and scale from SM. If the LM area fires representing a location (intent or context), the WWN recognizes the object near that intended location from the cluttered scene and tells its type from TM and scale from SM. If the TM area fires representing an object type (intent or context) the WWN finds (*i.e.*, detects) an intended object type from the cluttered scene and tells its location from LM and scale from SM.

A WWN can also perform autonomous attention. If the DN suppresses the firing neuron that represents an object type in TM, the WWN switches attention from one object type to another object type that barely lost in the previous Y competition—feature-based autonomous attention. If the DN suppresses the firing neuron in LM, the WWN switches attention from one object location to another object location that barely lost in the previous Y competition—location-based autonomous attention.

The WWN has also performed language acquisition for a subset of natural language and also generalized and predicted [35]. For example, predict from one person Joe to his hierarchical properties such as male and human, and predict from Penguin to its hierarchical properties such as non-flying and bird.

The WWNs have versions that are motivated, such as pain avoidance and pleasure seeking, so that its learning does not need to be supervised [9]. The learned tasks include object recognition under reinforcement learning and autonomous foraging (wandering around) in the presence of a friend and an enemy.

However, the experimental results from such DN experiments are difficult to understand and to train without a clear theoretical framework here that links DNs with the well-known automata theory and the mathematical properties presented as the three theorems that have been proved here.

10. Conclusions and Discussion

Proposed first in Weng 2011 [14], the DN framework seems to be, as far as I know, the first brain-scale computational and developmental theory for the brain and mind. By developing, we mean that the model regards brain areas should automatically emerge from activities, instead of fully specified rigidly by the genome. This view is supported by a great deal of cross-modal plasticity found in mammalian brains, from eye deprivation by Torsten N. Wiesel and David H. Hubel [36], to the auditory cortex that processes visual information by Mriganka Sur *et al.* [37], to the reassignment of modality—visual cortex is reassigned to audition and touch in the born blind as reviewed by Patrice Voss [38].

Therefore, it appears that a valid brain model at least should not assume a static existence of—genome rigidly specified—Brodmann areas. This static existence has been prevailing in almost all existing biologically inspired models for sensorimotor systems. Instead, a brain model should explain the emergence and known plasticity of brain areas. DP enables areas to emerge in DN and adapt. The genome provides the power of cells to move and connect. The genome also plays a major role in early and coarse connections of a brain. However, fine connections in the brain seem to be primarily determined by the statistics of activities from the conception of the life all the way up to the current life time.

In conclusion, this paper provides an overarching theory of the brain and mind, although the complexity of the mind is left to the richness of the environment and the activities of DN—task nonspecific [28]. The paper also provides the proofs of the three basic theorems in an archival form. At this early time of the computational brain theory, we predict that the landscape of AI and understanding of natural intelligence would both fundamentally change in the future.

Acknowledgements

The author would like to thank Hao Ye at Fudan University who carefully proof-read the proofs presented here and raised two gaps that I have filled since then. The author would also like to thank Z. Ji, M. Luciw, K. Miyan and other members of the Embodied Intelligence Laboratory at Michigan State University; Q. Zhang, Yuekai Wang, Xiaofeng Wu and other members of the Embodied Intelligence Laboratory at Fudan University whose work has provided experimental supports for the theory presented here.

References

[1] Weng, J. (2011) Three Theorems: Brain-Like Networks Logically Reason and Optimally Generalize. *International Joint Conference on Neural Networks*, San Jose, 31 July-5 August 2011, 2983-2990.

[2] Weng, J. (2012) Natural and Artificial Intelligence: Introduction to Computational Brain-Mind. BMI Press, Okemos.

[3] Kandel, E.R., Schwartz, J.H., Jessell, T.M., Siegelbaum, S. and Hudspeth, A.J., Eds. (2012) Principles of Neural Science. 5th Edition, McGraw-Hill, New York.

[4] Gluck, M.A., Mercado, E. and Myers, C., Eds. (2013) Learning and Memory: From Brain to Behavior. 2nd Edition, Worth Publishers, New York.

[5] Weng, J. and Luciw, M. (2012) Brain-Like Emergent Spatial Processing. *IEEE Transactions on Autonomous Mental Development*, **4**, 161-185. http://dx.doi.org/10.1109/TAMD.2011.2174636

[6]   Weng, J., Luciw, M. and Zhang, Q. (2013) Brain-Like Temporal Processing: Emergent Open States. *IEEE Transactions on Autonomous Mental Development*, **5**, 89-116. http://dx.doi.org/10.1109/TAMD.2013.2258398

[7]   Weng, J. and Luciw, M.D. (2014) Brain-Inspired Concept Networks: Learning Concepts from Cluttered Scenes. *IEEE Intelligent Systems Magazine*, **29**, 14-22. http://dx.doi.org/10.1109/MIS.2014.75

[8]   Hopcroft, J.E., Motwani, R. and Ullman, J.D. (2006) Introduction to Automata Theory, Languages, and Computation. Addison-Wesley, Boston.

[9]   Weng, J., Paslaski, S., Daly, J., VanDam, C. and Brown, J. (2013) Modulation for Emergent Networks: Serotonin and Dopamine. *Neural Networks*, **41**, 225-239. http://dx.doi.org/10.1016/j.neunet.2012.11.008

[10]   Wang, Y., Wu, X. and Weng, J. (2011) Synapse Maintenance in the Where-What Network. *International Joint Conference on Neural Networks*, San Jose, 31 July-5 August 2011, 2823-2829.

[11]   Krichmar, J.L. (2008) The Neuromodulatory System: A Framework for Survival and Adaptive Behavior in a Challenging World. *Adaptive Behavior*, **16**, 385-399. http://dx.doi.org/10.1177/1059712308095775

[12]   Weng, J. (2012) Symbolic Models and Emergent Models: A Review. *IEEE Transactions on Autonomous Mental Development*, **4**, 29-53. http://dx.doi.org/10.1109/TAMD.2011.2159113

[13]   Russell, S. and Norvig, P. (2010) Artificial Intelligence: A Modern Approach. 3rd Edition, Prentice-Hall, Upper Saddle River.

[14]   Weng, J. (2011) Why Have We Passed "Neural Networks Do Not Abstract Well"? *Natural Intelligence: The INNS Magazine*, **1**, 13-22.

[15]   Minsky, M. (1991) Logical versus Analogical or Symbolic versus Connectionist or Neat versus Scruffy. *AI Magazine*, **12**, 34-51.

[16]   Gomes, L. (2014) Machine-Learning Maestro Michael Jordan on the Delusions of Big Data and Other Huge Engineering Efforts. *IEEE Spectrum*, Online Article Posted 20 October 2014.

[17]   Olshaushen, B.A. and Field, D.J. (1996) Emergence of Simple-Cell Receptive Field Properties by Learning a Sparse Code for Natural Images. *Nature*, **381**, 607-609. http://dx.doi.org/10.1038/381607a0

[18]   Hinton, G.E., Osindero, S. and Teh, Y-W. (2006) A Fast Learning Algorithm for Deep Belief nets. *Neural Computation*, **18**, 1527-1554. http://dx.doi.org/10.1162/neco.2006.18.7.1527

[19]   Desimone, R. and Duncan, J. (1995) Neural Mechanisms of Selective Visual Attention. *Annual Review of Neuroscience*, **18**, 193-222. http://dx.doi.org/10.1146/annurev.ne.18.030195.001205

[20]   Weng, J. (2013) Establish the Three Theorems: DP Optimally Self-Programs Logics Directly from Physics. *Proceedings of International Conference on Brain-Mind*, East Lansing, 27-28 July 2013, 1-9.

[21]   Frasconi, P., Gori, M., Maggini, M. and Soda, G. (1995) Unified Integration of Explicit Knowledge and Learning by Example in Recurrent Networks. *IEEE Transactions on Knowledge and Data Engineering*, **7**, 340-346. http://dx.doi.org/10.1109/69.382304

[22]   Frasconi, P., Gori, M., Maggini, M. and Soda, G. (1996) Representation of Finite State Automata in Recurrent Radial Basis Function Networks. *Machine Learning*, **23**, 5-32. http://dx.doi.org/10.1007/BF00116897

[23]   Omlin, C.W. and Giles, C.L. (1996) Constructing Deterministic Finite-State Automata in Recurrent Neural Networks. *Journal of the ACM*, **43**, 937-972. http://dx.doi.org/10.1145/235809.235811

[24]   Felleman, D.J. and Van Essen, D.C. (1991) Distributed Hierarchical Processing in the Primate Cerebral Cortex. *Cerebral Cortex*, **1**, 1-47. http://dx.doi.org/10.1093/cercor/1.1.1

[25]   Sur, M. and Rubenstein, J.L.R. (2005) Patterning and Plasticity of the Cerebral Cortex. *Science*, **310**, 805-810. http://dx.doi.org/10.1126/science.1112070

[26]   Bichot, N.P., Rossi, A.F. and Desimone, R. (2006) Parallel and Serial Neural Mechanisms for Visual Search in Macaque Area V4. *Science*, **308**, 529-534. http://dx.doi.org/10.1126/science.1109676

[27]   Campbell, N.A., Reece, J.B., Urry, L.A., Cain, M.L., Wasserman, S.A., Minorsky, P.V. and Jackson, R.B. (2011) Biology. 9th Edition, Benjamin Cummings, San Francisco.

[28]   Weng, J., McClelland, J., Pentland, A., Sporns, O., Stockman, I., Sur, M. and Thelen, E. (2001) Autonomous Mental Development by Robots and Animals. *Science*, **291**, 599-600. http://dx.doi.org/10.1126/science.291.5504.599

[29]   Weng, J. (2009) Task Muddiness, Intelligence Metrics, and the Necessity of Autonomous Mental Development. *Minds and Machines*, **19**, 93-115. http://dx.doi.org/10.1007/s11023-008-9127-1

[30]   Weng, J. and Luciw, M. (2009) Dually Optimal Neuronal Layers: Lobe Component Analysis. *IEEE Transactions on Autonomous Mental Development*, **1**, 68-85. http://dx.doi.org/10.1109/TAMD.2009.2021698

[31]   Martin, J.C. (2003) Introduction to Languages and the Theory of Computation. 3rd Edition, McGraw Hill, Boston.

[32]   Ji, Z., Weng, J. and Prokhorov, D. (2008) Where-What Network 1: "Where" and "What" Assist Each Other through

Top-Down Connections. *IEEE International Conference on Development and Learning*, Monterey, 9-12 August 2008, 61-66.

[33] Wu, X., Guo, Q. and Weng, J. (2013) Skull-Closed Autonomous Development: WWN-7 Dealing with Scales. *Proceedings of International Conference on Brain-Mind*, East Lansing, 27-28 July 2013, 1-8.

[34] Luciw, M. and Weng, J. (2010) Where What Network 3: Developmental Top-Down Attention with Multiple Meaningful Foregrounds. *IEEE International Conference on Neural Networks*, Barcelona, 18-23 July 2010, 4233-4240.

[35] Miyan, K. and Weng, J. (2010) WWN-Text: Cortex-Like Language Acquisition, with What and Where. *IEEE 9th International Conference on Development and Learning*, Ann Arbor, 18-21 August 2010, 280-285.

[36] Wiesel, T.N. and Hubel, D.H. (1965) Comparison of the Effects of Unilateral and Bilateral Eye Closure on Cortical Unit Responses in Kittens. *Journal of Neurophysiology*, **28**, 1029-1040.

[37] Von Melchner, L., Pallas, S.L. and Sur, M. (2000) Visual Behaviour Mediated by Retinal Projections Directed to the Auditory Pathway. *Nature*, **404**, 871-876. http://dx.doi.org/10.1038/35009102

[38] Voss, P. (2013) Sensitive and Critical Periods in Visual Sensory Deprivation. *Frontiers in Psychology*, **4**, 664.

7

Biological Neural Network Structure and Spike Activity Prediction Based on Multi-Neuron Spike Train Data

Tielin Zhang[1,2]*, Yi Zeng[1]*, Bo Xu[1]

[1]Institute of Automation, Chinese Academy of Sciences, Beijing, China
[2]University of Chinese Academy of Sciences, Beijing, China
Email: zhangtielin2013@ia.ac.cn, yi.zeng@ia.ac.cn

Abstract

The micro-scale neural network structure for the brain is essential for the investigation on the brain and mind. Most of the previous studies typically acquired the neural network structure through brain slicing and reconstruction via nanoscale imaging. Nevertheless, this method still cannot scale well, and the observation on the neural activities based on the reconstructed neural network is not possible. Neuron activities are based on the neural network of the brain. In this paper, we propose that multi-neuron spike train data can be used as an alternative source to predict the neural network structure. And two concrete strategies for neural network structure prediction based on such kind of data are introduced, namely, the time-ordered strategy and the spike co-occurrence strategy. The proposed methods can even be applied to *in vivo* studies since it only requires neural spike activities. Based on the predicted neural network structure and the spreading activation theory, we propose a spike prediction method. For neural network structure reconstruction, the experimental results reveal a significantly improved accuracy compared to previous network reconstruction strategies, such as Cross-correlation, Pearson, and the Spearman method. Experiments on the spikes prediction results show that the proposed spreading activation based strategy is potentially effective for predicting neural spikes in the biological neural network. The predictions on the neural network structure and the neuron activities serve as foundations for large scale brain simulation and explorations of human intelligence.

Keywords

Neural Network Structure Prediction, Spike Prediction, Time-Order Strategy, Co-Occurrence Strategy, Spreading Activation

---

*These authors contributed to the work equally and should be regarded as co-first authors.

1. Introduction

The micro-scale brain anatomy and activities of the neurons are essential for understanding how the brain works and the nature of human intelligence. The general motivation of this paper comes from the fact that neuronal structure and activities are closely connected with each other even though it is usually very hard to get both neural anatomical structure and spike activity by electrophysiology or imaging method at the same time. The general idea is that even without nanoscale imaging techniques (which cannot scale well), it is still possible to reconstruct the neural network structure and predict spike activities by analyzing the spike train data.

From the structure perspective, we propose that multi-neuron spike train data can be used as an alternative source to predict the neural network structures, and here we discuss two concrete strategies for neural network structure prediction based on this kind of data. Multi-neuron spike train data is composed of spike trains from multiple neurons recorded in the same time interval. The data typically shows whether a specific neuron generates a spike or not at a specific time. Two strategies are proposed for neural network structure prediction: 1) the time-ordered strategy: synapses exist between neurons that generate spikes at the two neighborhood time points (*i.e.* the time point N and N-1); 2) the spike co-occurrence strategy: synapses exist between neurons that fire together at the same time slot. This strategy is consistent with the Hebb's law "cells that fire together, wire together".

From the function perspective, for each neuron in a neural network, its behavior is not only decided by its own property, but also very relevant to its contexts (e.g. other neurons in the same network). Hence, effective prediction of neural spike activities in a network context requires at least the following three major efforts: 1) response prediction of a single neuron towards a stimulus; 2) obtaining the detailed network structure, with synapse information among neurons; 3) modeling signal transmission based on the neural network. We use the neuron simulator to build detailed single pyramidal cells for the first effort. The network structure is built by the methods introduced above, while the spreading activation method based on the two previous efforts is introduced for the third effort. We use part of the spike train data to build the neural network structure and the model for neural activity prediction and the rest is for validation.

In order to validate the proposed methods and strategies, we use the data based on calcium imaging technology. Among different kinds of calcium imaging method, one of them is named functional Multi-neuron Calcium Imaging (fMCI), namely, multi-neurons loading of calcium fluorophores. The advantages of fMCI include: 1) recording en masse from hundreds of neurons in a wide area; 2) single-cell resolution; 3) identifiable location of neurons; and 4) detection of non-active neurons during the observation period. These advantages enables us acquire necessary spike train data discussed above to support the investigation and validation of proposed problems and methods. The paper is structured as follows: Section 2 briefly introduce related work, Section 3 explain the detailed neural network structure and spikes prediction method as well as their relationships, and Section 4 describes the experiments and results to show the prediction accuracy, finally conclusion is made in Section 5. This paper refines and extends the work introduced in [1] and [2].

2. Related Work

From the structure perspective, most common approaches for obtaining the micro-level neural network structure is typically based on brain slicing and reconstruction with nanoscale imaging [3] [4]. This method can accurately locate the position of neurons, synapses and even dendritic spines. But at the same time, complex and weak nanoscale images make image repairing, synapse recognition and 3D structure reconstruction cost too much time. Based on current brain slicing and imaging techniques, it is still difficult to get synaptic scale neural network structures for a small group of neurons, let alone bigger network. In addition, tissues after slicing are with no functional reactions any more. This makes advanced research on neuronal functions based on the reconstructed neural network nearly impossible.

From the activity perspective at the nanoscale, electrophysiology techniques and calcium imaging techniques are frequently used. The electrophysiology techniques detect and save the neurons' time dependent soma voltage [5]. This technique is with accurate temporal resolution but poor space resolution. In addition, it can only record few neurons' voltage at one time. While calcium fluorescence imaging techniques detect the changes on neurons' voltage values by monitor cell calcium changes, it can monitor the activity of a hundred to thousand neurons simultaneously both *in vitro* and *in vivo* [6]. The maximum number of neurons monitored by calcium fluorescence is around 100,000 cells for zebrafish [7]. Stetter uses transfer entropy method to reconstruct the network which requires no prior statistics and connections assumptions, and the work focuses on excitatory synaptic links, and network clustering topology [8]. Takahashi investigates the calcium imaging experiments including imaging, spikes detection and some network analysis tasks. He and coauthors conclude that the network fits for power-law scaling of synchronization properties and network connection probability varies from different network scales [6].

3. Methodology

Although the functional data are collected by functional multi-neuron calcium imaging techniques, the missing of relevant structures from anatomical method still makes analysis about the dynamic causality for the whole network hard. Here we propose architecture to analyze the spike train data to predictively reconstruct the micro-level network structure, and predict neuronal activities based on the reconstructed network.

The methodology introduced here relies on spike train data generated by various kinds of techniques (e.g. fMCI and electrophysiology experiments). In this paper, we use the experimental data from the mouse memory task [6]. Spontaneous spiking activities are still happening in slices of the mouse brain hippocampus CA1 area when it was taken out of the body for not a long time. These spikes show the special task related network function in hippocampus, such as memory retention. The understanding of these kinds of data can greatly speed up the procedure of memory research.

As **Figure 1** shows, calcium images and neuron voltages from mouse slices data are collected by fMCI method. Neural voltage signals based on the fMCI technique are with low Signal to Noise Ratio (SNR). Hence, signal processing to filter noise is necessary. Here we use Fast Fourier Transform (FFT) and Inverse Fast Fourier Transform (IFFT) methods to filter the high frequency noises so that spiking signals can be detected precisely. Then two methods to convert neural spike signals to neural structure are introduced, namely, the co-occurrence strategy and the time-ordered strategy. As a step forward, we propose a spike activity prediction method based on the predicted neural network, the spreading activation theory and single pyramidal neuron models.

3.1. Voltages Signal Processing

Voltages signals from calcium imaging are so closed combined with noise that high frequency filter must be applied for further spikes detection. The processing procedure mainly includes the following four parts: 1) using FFT to transform time sequence signals to frequency signals; 2) using high frequency filters to eliminate signal

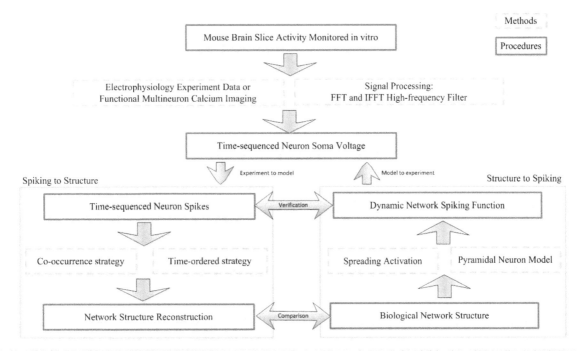

Figure 1. The overall architecture for predicting neural network structure and neuronal activities based on spike train data.

noises; 3) using IFFT to transform frequency signals back to time series signals; 4) deciding the voltage threshold to detect spiking signals. As **Figure 2** shows, after signal transformation from time series to frequency and back again by FFT and IFFT, high frequency noises are filtered and spike signals are detected.

3.2. From Spikes to Neuronal Structures

In this paper, two strategies are discussed and used to realize the procedure of converting spike signals to neural network structure:

1) The time-ordered strategy: synapses exist between neurons that generate spikes at the two neighborhood time points (the time point N and N-1);

2) The spike co-occurrence strategy: synapses exist between neurons that fire together at the same time slot. This strategy is consistent with the Hebb's law "cells that fire together, wire together".

Based on the proposed two different strategies, two neurons that may share a connection might be connected from tens to hundreds of times. Each time of connection is with the same unit strength. However, more times of connection between neurons indicate the higher probability for the existence of synapse. As shown in **Figure 3**, the network is rebuilt by combination of two methods. The upper panel in **Figure 3** shows the spikes states of 62

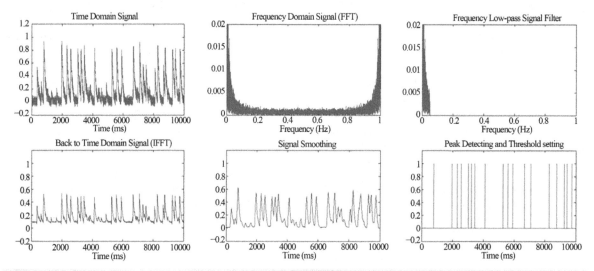

Figure 2. Neural activity signal processing. a) Original time series signals; b) FFT frequency signals; c) High frequency filter; d) IFFTtime series signals; e) Signal smooth process; f) Voltage threshold method of spiking detection.

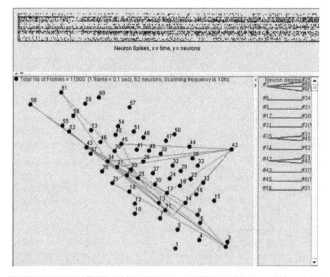

Figure 3. Network structure prediction procedure.

neurons in different time slot. The bottom left panel shows the present spike transfer (in green line). The bottom right panel shows the connection probability of different neurons.

3.3. Spike Prediction Based on Spreading Activation

With the reconstructed micro-level neural network based on the methods proposed in Section 3.2, combined with single neuron models, we can predict spike activities for the neurons in observation. Here we first introduce a single neuron model as a foundation. Then we propose a spreading activation based spike prediction method, which utilize the single neuron model and the predicted neural network.

Since pyramidal neuron is widely distributed in mouse hippocampus (more than 90%) [9], here we introduce the single neuron model of a kind of pyramidal neuron in mouse brain hippocampus CA1 area for the simulation of the neuronal activities. Its neural structure obtained from http://neuromorpho.org/ (ID: NMO_08800) is shown in **Figure 4(a)**. Neuron model contains three basic kinds of ion channels, namely potassium channel, sodium channel and calcium channel. Potassium ion channels mainly include four subtypes, namely K^+-A^+ channel, basic potassium channel, slow Ca^{2+}-dependent potassium channel and calcium-activated potassium channel. The calcium ion channel contains l-calcium channel and basic calcium channel. The sodium ion channel is H-current kind of sodium channel. In addition, detailed ion channel parameters in different model sections such as soma, axon and dendrite are varied from each other. Neuron response with given voltage stimuli is shown in **Figure 4(b)**. Special response from high stimuli voltage can be found in **Figure 4(c)**, which shows the detailed neuron model with more ion channels (not only basic H-H kind of Na^+, K^+, Ca^{2+}), not just leaky integrate-and-fire kind of spiking model. It is able to describe the property of neuronal refractory period well in this model. This detailed pyramidal neuron model built in neuron [10] [11] is essential to understanding and simulation of brain network function.

Spreading activation (SA) was proposed in cognitive psychology for understanding human memory. It is also widely used for searching associative network, neural network or semantic network [12]. The SA network is briefly illustrated in **Figure 5**. In this paper, this method is applied to the micro scale for understanding neural network activities and predicting spikes.

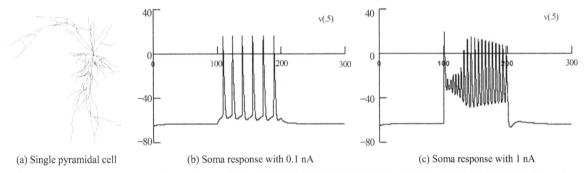

(a) Single pyramidal cell   (b) Soma response with 0.1 nA   (c) Soma response with 1 nA

Figure 4. Single pyramidal cell's reaction with voltage stimulus (0.1 nA to 1 nA). The morphology of the pyramidal cell (a) is from http://neuromorpho.org/ (ID: NMO_08800).

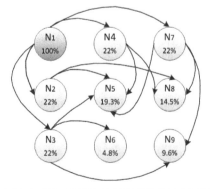

Figure 5. An illustration of the SA network mechanism.

Here we utilize some biology evidence to enhance SA method. The two important variables in SA is the decay factor D and the voltage threshold F. As **Figure 6** shows, electrical stimulation action experiment is simulated by Neuron software on real pyramidal cell in mouse hippocampus CA1 area introduced above. Both voltages in soma and dendrites are monitored. As Equation (1) shows, since the voltage decay between two neurons is mainly caused by dendrites instead of axons, we can calculate the average voltage decay range as the universal decay which is fit for the decay factor in SA method. Based on the calculation, the value of D should be 0.22. As Equation (2) shows, voltage threshold F can be the neuron spiking threshold which is set as −56 mv based on [13].

$$D = \frac{\max\left[\dfrac{\sum_1^{N_{dend}} V_{dend} - V_{th}}{N_{dend}}\right]}{\max\left[V_{soma} - V_{th}\right]} \tag{1}$$

$$F = V_{th} \tag{2}$$

D is the decay factor in SA method which can be biologically described as the voltage decay. N_{dend} is the number of neuronal dendrites. V_{dend} is the voltage of the dendrite section. V_{th} is the resting potential of neuron. F, which represents the spreading threshold factor in SA, is described by pyramidal cell voltage threshold.

The SA method is initiated by activating some neurons as source nodes and then iteratively propagates or spreads that activation to other neurons. During the propagation procedure, the values from original neurons decay according to different weights of neighbor neurons. The activation will terminate when the values go below the threshold for activation [12]. The detailed SA based method for spike prediction is described as follows.

Spreading Activation Based Method for Spike Prediction:
[1] Initialize the main parameters including voltage threshold F (ranging from zero to one) and decay factor D (ranging from zero to one).
[2] Initialize the network and set all neuron activation value $A[i]$ to zero. Set some origin nodes in $A[i]$ a larger number compared to the voltage threshold F.
[3] For each links $[i, j]$, connect the source $[i]$ with target $[j]$, adjust $A[i] = A[j] + A[i] * W[i, j] * D$
[4] If a target neuron activation value is larger than threshold F, adjust activation value to F_{max}.
[5] Once a neuron has fired, it may not fire again for preventing repeated firing and loops in a refractory period (experimentally set as 10 iteration times).
[6] Neurons whose activation values exceed the voltage threshold F should be marked for firing on the next spreading activation cycle.
[7]Procedure terminates when no more neurons fire or the number of iterations exceeds the maximum value (experimentally set as 10 iteration times).

4. Experiments and Results

4.1. The Pathway Prediction Results

Data of the rat hippocampus CA1 pyramidal cell layer based on fMCI is used for neural network structure prediction (including 8 datasets, and each of them records spike activities for 62 to 226 neurons. The datasets were imaged with the frequency of 10 Hz [6] [14]) using the upper two proposed strategies.

We validate the accuracy of the neural network structure prediction strategies based on the following steps. The overall prediction accuracy is an average value based on the 8 dataset. For each of the dataset: 1) Equally divide one dataset as 20 sub datasets according to the time intervals (The sub datasets are denoted as S1,...,S20). Select the first 80% of the sub datasets (S1,...,S16) for neural network structure construction, and validate the pathway using the rest of the 20% sub dataset (Here we assume that if the predicted pathway is correct, it should cover the neuronal connections based on the rest of the 20% sub datasets); 2) Select another 80% of the sub datasets for neural network structure construction, and the rest for validation, and repeat this step until all the sub datasets have been selected for validation. 3) The prediction accuracy is the average value of the 20 predictions.

There are several important observations and indications based on the prediction results. 1) Although the two prediction strategies seem entirely different, the neural network structures based on the two different strategies are very relevant (The correlation is significant with the Pearson correlation value 0.958). It indicates that al-

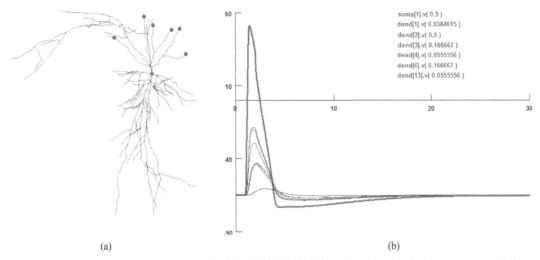

Figure 6. Pyramidal cell morphology and electrical activity simulation. a) Single pyramidal cell voltage, probe method to ensure the section voltages in soma (red point) and dendrites (blue points); b) Different synapse sections and soma voltage changing by multi stimuli from six neurons. Both soma [*i*], v[*j*] and dendrite [*i*], v[*j*] sections are built in this model, *i* stands for the section id, *j* denotes the detection probe position. The average decay factor is calculated by means of these six voltages.

though the proposed strategies are different, the results from the two different strategies do not have major conflicts, instead they are very consistent, and support each other. 2) The neural network structure prediction accuracy for the time-ordered strategy is 83.4%, and the accuracy for the spike co-occurrence strategy is 80.5%. When we group the two neural network structures together (denoted as the merged strategy), the prediction accuracy reaches 89.3%. **Figure 7** shows the prediction accuracy for each of the dataset using the proposed strategies. This result indicates that better prediction can be made when the predicted pathways from the two strategies are combined together. 3) 27% of the possible connections among neurons are selected for the time-ordered strategy, while 25% of the connections are selected by the spike co-occurrence strategy. If the two results are grouped together, 32% of the possible connections are included. The results seem good, since the coverage is not high (and is consistent with the observation by using electro-microscopy techniques [15] [16]), while the predicted accuracy for possible neural network structure reaches 89%. Comparing with other correlation strategies, merged strategy shows better prediction accuracy results as **Figure 8** shows.

The proposed method is validated on the data in which the distance of two neurons is within approximately 400 μm [17]. Whether the proposal is applicable when the distance goes further needs to be validated. In addition, our current result is based on fMCI data from rat brain slices. In our future work, we will investigate the possibility of using the proposed method on fMCI *in-vivo* imaging data.

4.2. Spike Prediction Results

Assume a specific neuron (denoted as n1) is connected with N neurons in the network and its action potential is V, the post synaptic neurons of n1 receive transmitted signals from n1. When one synaptic transmission is done and the signal reaches the post synaptic soma, its contribution to this soma is around 5 mv [18]. The overall contribution to the voltage of the soma (denoted as P) is represented as $P = N \times 5\,\text{mv}$, which is obtained by summing up all the contribution from each of the post synaptic potential, while P is used as the stimulus to generate next action potentials. Each of the potential P for the N neurons that connects to a specific neuron can be obtained through the upper calculation process. Having the structure of the neural network, we predict the neuron which owns the largest value of P will generate a spike in a refractory period (experimentally set as 10 iteration times).

In order to validate the proposed method, the data from the rat hippocampus CA1 pyramidal cell layer using fMCI is used (including 8 datasets, and each of them records spike activities from 62 to 226 neurons. The datasets were pictured with the frequency of 10 Hz [6] [14]). Since the time slot during two neighborhood pictures is 100 ms, signal transmissions may have looped for several rounds. Hence, iterations of the spreading activation process are needed. The spike prediction accuracy for each of the dataset is shown in **Figure 9**.

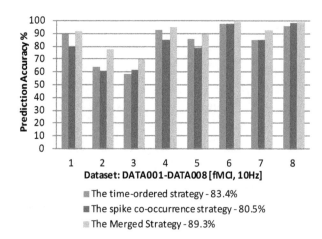

Figure 7. Neural pathway prediction accuracy based on fMCI multi-neuron spike train dataset.

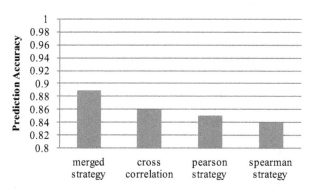

Figure 8. Accuracy made by the merged strategy and other correlation strategies.

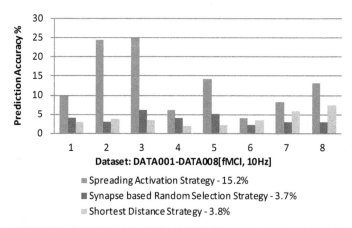

Figure 9. Neural spike prediction accuracy based on different strategies.

As a comparative study, we introduce two alternative strategies, namely the shortest distance strategy (the neuron which owns the shortest distance compared to other post synaptic neurons will be fired), and the synapse based random selection strategy (randomly select a neuron from the set of post synaptic neurons). As shown in **Figure 1**, the spreading activation based strategy outperforms other two strategies and the average prediction accuracy on 8 datasets is around 15.2%, at least three times better than the other two strategies (the average prediction accuracy for shortest distance strategy is 3.8%, while the synapse based random selection strategy is 3.7%). The validation shows that the proposed spreading activation strategy is potentially effective for predicting neural spikes in the neural network.

5. Conclusion

In this paper, two strategies to predict neural network structure ares proposed and high accuracy experiment results are showed in Section 4.1 and proved their efficiency. This effort makes the rebuilt network structure without anatomy slicing possible. Although restricted by the experimental data, the size of the rebuilt network is around hundred neurons, it still shows great potential for handling larger network reconstruction tasks. Further, the spiking prediction method gives us a view point to analyze the special condition in which we can acquire only structure data. As the first try, this paper only compared with some commonly used methods, such as cross correlation, Pearson and Spearman strategies. More methods will be taken into consideration for comparative studies in the future, such as Granger causality method. One further potential efforts for this work is that spiking functional activities from prediction model can further be used to guide biological experiment signal processing, such as which kind of spikes are noises while others are not.

Acknowledgements

This paper is supported by the Brain Engineering project funded by Institute of Automation, Chinese Academy of Sciences. The authors would like to thank anonymous reviewers for constructive comments.

References

[1]   Zeng, Y., Zhang, T.L. and Xu, B. (2014) Neural Pathway Prediction Based on Multi-Neuron Spike Train Data. *Proceedings of the 23rd Annual Computational Neuroscience Meeting* (*CNS* 2014), Québec City, 26-31 July 2014, 6.

[2]   Zhang, T.L., Zeng, Y. and Xu, B. (2014) Neural Spike Prediction Based on Spreading Activation. *Proceedings of the 23rd Annual Computational Neuroscience Meeting* (*CNS* 2014), Québec City, 26-31 July 2014, 7.

[3]   Sporns, O., Tononi, G. and Kötter, R. (2005) The Human Connectome: A Structural Description of the Human Brain. *PLoS Computational Biology*, **1**, e42. http://dx.doi.org/10.1371/journal.pcbi.0010042

[4]   Arenkiel1, B.R. and Ehlers, M.D. (2009) Molecular Genetics and Imaging Technologies for Circuit-Based Neuroanatomy. *Nature*, **461**, 900-907. http://dx.doi.org/10.1038/nature08536

[5]   Mukamel, R. and Fried, I. (2011) Human Intracranial Recordings and Cognitive Neuroscience. *Annual Review of Psychology*, **63**, 511-537. http://dx.doi.org/10.1146/annurev-psych-120709-145401

[6]   Takahashi, N., Sasaki, T., Usami, A., Matsuki, N. and Ikegaya, Y. (2007) Watching Neuronal Circuit Dynamics through Functional Multineuron Calcium Imaging (fMCI). *Neuroscience Research*, **58**, 219-225. http://dx.doi.org/10.1016/j.neures.2007.03.001

[7]   Kettunen, P. (2012) Calcium Imaging in the Zebrafish. In: Islam, S., Ed., *Calcium Signaling*, Springer Netherlands, Heidelberg, 1039-1071.

[8]   Stetter, O., Battaglia, D., Soriano, J. and Geisel, T. (2012) Model-Free Reconstruction of Excitatory Neuronal Connectivity from Calcium Imaging Signals. *PLoS Computational Biology*, **8**, e1002653. http://dx.doi.org/10.1371/journal.pcbi.1002653

[9]   Mira, J. and Sánchez-Andrés, J.V. (1999) Foundations and Tools for Neural Modeling. *Proceedings of International Work-Conference on Artificial and Natural Neural Networks*, Vol. I, Alicante, 2-4 June 1999, 29.

[10]   Carnevale, N.T. and Hines, M.L. (2006) The Neuron Book. Cambridge University Press, Cambridge, UK. http://dx.doi.org/10.1017/CBO9780511541612

[11]   Dayan, P. and Abbott, L.F. (2001) Theoretical Neuroscience: Computational and Mathematical Modeling of Neural Systems. MIT Press, Cambridge.

[12]   Anderson, J.R. (1983) A Spreading Activation Theory of Memory. *Journal of Verbal Learning and Verbal Behavior*, **22**, 261-295. http://dx.doi.org/10.1016/S0022-5371(83)90201-3

[13]   Yue, C.Y., Remy, S., Su, H.L., Beck, H. and Yaari, Y. (2005) Proximal Persistent Na^+ Channels Drive Spike Afterdepolarization and Associated Bursting in Adult CA1 Pyramidal Cells. *The Journal of Neuroscience*, **25**, 9704-9720. http://dx.doi.org/10.1523/JNEUROSCI.1621-05.2005

[14]   Yue, C.Y., Remy, S., Su, H.L., Beck, H. and Yaari, Y. (2011) High-Speed Multi-Neuron Calcium Imaging Using Nipkow-Type Confocal Microscopy. *Current Protocols in Neuroscience*, **2**, Unit 2.14. http://www.hippocampus.jp/data

[15]   Gómez-Di Cesare, C.M., Smith, K.L., Rice, F.L. and Swann, J.W. (1997) Axonal Remodeling during Postnatal Matu-

ration of CA3 Hippocampal Pyramidal Neurons. *Journal of Comparative Neurology*, **384**, 165-180.

[16] Fujisawa, S., Matsuki, N. and Ikegaya, Y. (2006) Single Neurons Can Induce Phase Transitions of Cortical Recurrent Networks with Multiple Internal States. *Cerebral Cortex*, **16**, 639-654. http://dx.doi.org/10.1093/cercor/bhj010

[17] Sasaki, T., Matsuki, N. and Ikegaya, Y. (2007) Metastability of Active CA3 Networks. *The Journal of Neuroscience*, **27**, 517-528. http://dx.doi.org/10.1523/JNEUROSCI.4514-06.2007

[18] Lodish, H., Berk, A., Zipursky, S.L., Matsudaira, P., Baltimore, D. and Darnell, J. (2000) Molecular Cell Biology. 4th Edition, Freeman and Company, New York.

8

Modeling Neuromorphic Persistent Firing Networks

Ning Ning[1*], Guoqi Li[2,3*], Wei He[1], Kejie Huang[4], Li Pan[1], Kiruthika Ramanathan[1], Rong Zhao[4], Luping Shi[2,3]

[1]Data Storage Institute, Agency for Science, Technology and Research, Singapore
[2]Department of Precision Instrument, Tsinghua University, Beijing, China
[3]Center for Brain-Inspired Computing Research (CBICR), Tsinghua University, Beijing, China
[4]Singapore University of Technology and Design, Dover, Singapore
Email: lpshi@tsinghua.edu.cn

Abstract

Neurons are believed to be the brain computational engines of the brain. A recent discovery in neurophysiology reveals that interneurons can slowly integrate spiking, share the output across a coupled network of axons and respond with persistent firing even in the absence of input to the soma or dendrites, which has not been understood and could be very important for exploring the mechanism of human cognition. The conventional models are incapable of simulating the important newly-discovered phenomenon of persistent firing induced by axonal slow integration. In this paper, we propose a computationally efficient model of neurons through modeling the axon as a slow leaky integrator, which captures almost all-known neural behaviors. The model controls the switching of axonal firing dynamics between passive conduction mode and persistent firing mode. The interplay between the axonal integrated potential and its multiple thresholds in axon precisely determines the persistent firing dynamics of neurons. We also present a persistent firing polychronous spiking network which exhibits asynchronous dynamics indicating that this computationally efficient model is not only bio-plausible, but also suitable for large scale spiking network simulations. The implications of this network and the analog circuit design for exploring the relationship between working memory and persistent firing enable developing a spiking network-based memory and bio-inspired computer systems.

Keywords

Neuron Model, Neuromorphic, Persistent Firing, Slow Integration, Spiking Network, Working Memory

*The authors contribute equally to this work.
This work is funded by Brain Inspired Computing Research, Tsinghua University (20141080934).

1. Introduction

Understanding how human brain represents, stores, and processes information is one of the greatest unsolved mysteries and fundamental challenges of science today. Over the past century, since Lapicque introduced the integrate-and-fire model of the neuron in 1907 [1], computational neuroscientists have developed several mathematical and computational neural models. Generally, one approach in computational neuroscience involves creating biologically realistic models, where information about the biological details of neurons including their electrochemistry, biochemistry, and detailed morphology and connectivity are also included [2], such as Hodgkin-Huxley [3] and compartment models [4]. Another approach involves building qualitative models to capture the spiking nature and the essential elements of the behavior with simplified complexity, for example, leaky integrate-and-fire [5], FitzHugh-Nagumo [6], Morris-Lecar [7], Hindmarsh-Rose [8], Wilson [9], Resonate-and-Fire [10] and Izhikevich [11] neuron models.

However, as neuroscience continues to advance rapidly, more and more complex neuronal behaviors and brain dynamics are revealed. This has posed challenges for neural modeling as conventional neuron models fail to reflect the newly-discovered complexity of neural systems, such as the persistent firing phenomenon recently observed in rodent hippocampal inhibitory neurons [12]. In the classic viewpoint about the information flow in the nervous system, synaptic inputs are received and integrated in the dendrites only on a timescale of milliseconds to seconds, and when the depolarized somatic membrane potential exceeds the threshold, action potentials are triggered at the axon hillock and propagate along the axon. However, recent discovery reveals that some action potential began at the distal end of axon instead of at the axon hillock. A much slower form of potential integration is observed which leads to persistent firing in distal axons of rodent hippocampal and neocortical interneurons [12]. The slow integration lasts from tens of seconds to minutes in distal axon, so does the persistent firing. During the persistent firing, the somatic depolarization is not observed, implying that axon may perform its own neural computations without any involvement of the soma or dendrites.

In this paper, we propose a new computationally-efficient artificial neuron model that account for all-known neural behaviors. In this model, axon is an independent computational unit complementary to the classic somatic computational unit which evokes action potentials. Compared to the soma which integrates dendritic inputs in a timescale of milliseconds to seconds, the axon integrates the spikes evoked by soma in a timescale of tens of second to minutes, and consequently determines the persistent firing behavior of the axon. Besides the computational model, a neuromorphic model of persistent firing neurons and its analog circuit are also proposed. In addition, a polychronous spiking network [13] with persistent firing inhibitory interneurons is simulated, which may assist the development of spiking network-based memory and bio-inspired computer system.

2. Persistent Firing Neuron Model

The conventional models such as Izhikevich neuron model [11] are incapable of simulating the important newly-discovered phenomenon of persistent firing induced by axonal slow integration, as a recent discovery in neurophysiology reveals that interneurons can slowly integrate spiking, share the output across a coupled network of axons and respond with persistent firing even in the absence of input to the soma or dendrites. To this end, we extend the Izhikevich neuron model by modeling the axonal slow integration, which can be mathematically described by Equations (1)-(6):

$$v' = 0.04v^2 + 5v + 140 - u + I \tag{1}$$

$$u' = a(bv - u) \tag{2}$$

$$w' = -fw \tag{3}$$

with the auxiliary resettings:

$$\text{if } v \geq 30 \text{ mV, then } v \leftarrow c, \ u \leftarrow u + d, \ w \leftarrow w + e \tag{4}$$

$$\text{if } w \geq w_p, \text{ then } (a,b,c,d,e) \leftarrow (a,b,c,d,e)_p \tag{5}$$

$$\text{if } w \leq w_n, \text{ then } (a,b,c,d,e) \leftarrow (a,b,c,d,e)_n \tag{6}$$

where $' = \mathrm{d}/\mathrm{dt}$, t is the time, w describes the hyper theoretical potential of the axonal leaky integrator, v

and u are the dimensionless variables that describe the membrane potential, the membrane recovery, respectively. Parameters a, b, c, d, e and f are dimensionless, a describes the timescale of u, b represents the sensitivity of u to the subthreshold fluctuations of v, c is the after-spike reset value of the membrane potential, d describes the after-spike reset of u, e represents the after-somatic-spike axonal accumulation in the passive conduction mode, and f is the value describing the rate of the axonal leak. In Equations (5) and (6), w_p is the high threshold (rising edge) value of w to trigger the persistent firing mode of axon, and w_n is the low threshold (falling edge) value of w for the axon to return to passive conduction mode. $(a,b,c,d,e)_p$ and $(a,b,c,d,e)_n$ describe the parameter sets of a, b, c, d, e variables when the axon is in the persistent firing mode and passive conduction mode, respectively.

This model extends the Izhikevich neuron model [11] described by Equations (1)-(2), which well captures the somatic spiking dynamics. By modifying the a, b, c, d variables in Equations (1), (2), and (4), different firing patterns can be generated. One important concept of our model is the axon-dependent switch of the axonal firing patterns through dynamically selecting different variable set of a, b, c and d.

The axon is modeled as a slow leaky integrator, which is capable to alter the axonal functions between passive conduction and persistent firing modes, depending on the potential of axonal integrator. In the passive conduction mode, the axon acts as a transmission cable in which stable propagation occurs once an action potential is evoked by synaptic inputs. In the persistent firing mode, in which the parameters in the model are chosen to set the dynamical system to be self-oscillatory, axon acts as a bistable oscillator which does not require stimulus from dendrites to sustain the persistent firing of action potentials.

In contrast to the somatic leaky integrator which accounts for the integration of dendritic inputs, the axonal leaky integrator has a larger time constant for its integration and leakage, integrating incoming spikes generated in the axon hillock in the timescale from tens of seconds to minutes, due to its slow rate of leakage f, as described in Equation (3). When the potential in the axonal leaky integrator exceeds w_p, which denotes the high threshold (rising edge), the persistent firing will be triggered, and the firing pattern is determined by the parameter set of $(a,b,c,d,e)_p$. If there are no somatic spikes accumulated in the axon, the potential w decreases at the rate of f. When w reaches the low threshold (falling edge), the axon w_n returns to passive conduction mode, and the a, b, c, d, e variables in the model are reset to $(a,b,c,d,e)_n$.

We have simulated the persistent firing neuronal behaviors under two stimulation protocols, with the parameters summarized in **Table 1**. The simulation results under step/pause stimulation protocol [12] are shown in **Figure 1**. We applied 1-second current step of 500 pA during each 10-second sweep to the simulation model. During the sweeps of the step/pause input stimulus, it is observed that the somatically evoked action potentials appear when the synaptic input stimulus is presented and disappear when the stimulus is removed (**Figure 1(a)**). When w accumulates to a level higher than the high threshold w_p, persistent firing occurs (**Figure 1(a)**), 12th sweep), after which w decreases monotonically due to axonal leakage and no stimulus (**Figure 1(d)**). The persistent firing ends when w is lower than the low threshold w_n. It should be noted that in this model, the resting potential of persistent firing spikes is about 20 mV below the one of somatically evoked action potentials, which fits well with the data from current-clamp recordings in the persistent firing neurons [12] [14]. We emulate this phenomenon through switching the parameter c in Equation (4) between c_p and c_n.

The variation of persistent firing frequency was also simulated (**Figure 1(b)** and **Figure 1(c)**). As the firing frequency can be tuned by the parameter b in Equation (2), the decrease of persistent firing frequency observed in the current-clamp experiment can be emulated in the model through defining the following relationship between parameter b and f.

Table 1. Simulation parameters.

Step/Pause protocol	Long Pulse protocol
$(a,b,c,d,e)_p = (0.1, 5, -85, 0, 0)$	$(a,b,c,d,e)_p = (0.1, 0.3, -85, 0, 0)$
$(a,b,c,d,e)_n = (0.1, 0.2, -65, 2, 0.001)$	$(a,b,c,d,e)_n = (0.1, 0.2, -65, 2, 0.012)$
$f = 5 \times 10^{-4}$	$f = 8 \times 10^{-4}$
$w_n = 0.2$, $w_p = 0.84$	$w_n = 0.2$, $w_p = 2.1$
$I = 500 \, \text{pA}$	$I = 15 \, \text{pA}$

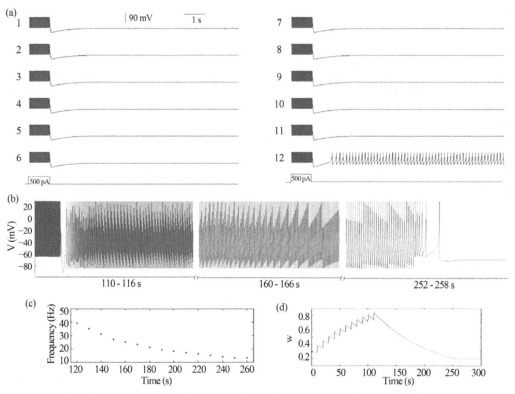

Figure 1. Simulation of persistent firing neuron model. (a) The waveform of membrane potential. The simulation used the same stimulation protocol as the experiment of whole-cell current-clamp recording by Sheffield *et al* [12]. To evoke persistent firing, 1-s current step of 500 pA was delivered to the neuron during each 10-s sweep (left, sweeps 1 - 6; right, sweeps 7 - 12). In this simulation, persistent firing was evoked after the 12th sweep, and the total number of evoked action potentials before persistent firing was 1278. (b) The waveform of persistent firing, which lasted over 2 minutes. The total number of evoked axonal action potentials was 3073. The simulation reflects the decrease of instantaneous firing frequency, which was shown in the current-clamp experiment. (c) The instantaneous firing frequency of persistent firing action potentials, which decreased from 40 Hz at the onset of persistent firing to 12 Hz at the end of persistent firing as the parameter b decreased in this simulation. (d) The time response of w, which represents the hypertheoretical potential of the axonal leaky integrator.

$$\text{if persistent firing action potential is generated, then } b \leftarrow b(1-f) \tag{7}$$

The instantaneous firing frequency of axon-evoked action potentials attains its maximum (40 Hz) at the onset of persistent firing, and decreases over time till the end of persistent firing.

We also applied the stimulation with a 40-second long pulse of 15 pA current to the persistent firing neuron model described by Equations (1)-(7) with a different parameter set (**Table 1**). The simulation results are shown in **Figure 2**. The repeated somatic current stimuli eventually trigger the persistent firing that outlasts the current stimuli by more than 30 seconds.

By tuning the parameters of e, f, w_p and w_n, we can set different time scales for the axonal slow integration, allowing the model to accommodate different types of neurons with different persistent firing behaviors.

3. Model Analysis

In this section, we present the mathematical analysis on the conditions which guarantee the existence of the persistent firing behavior in the neuron. Let $X = [uvw]'$. Equations (1)-(3) can be rewritten as:

$$X' = F(X) + HI = X^{\mathrm{T}}AX + BX + C + HI \tag{8}$$

where I is the input current, A, B, C and H are the corresponding matrices determined by

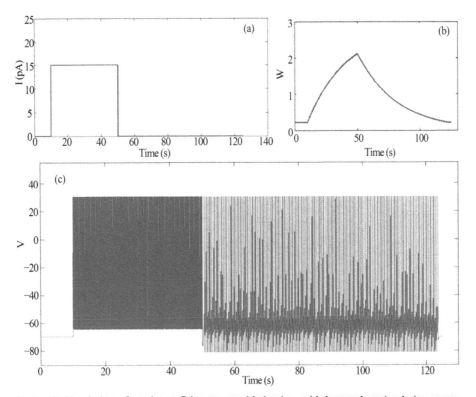

Figure 2. Simulation of persistent firing neuronal behaviors with long pulse stimulation protocol. (a) The input stimulus. A pulse of current with 15 pA amplitude lasts 40 seconds as the synaptic input to the neuron. (b) Time response of w, the variable describing the potential of the axonal leaky integrator. (c) Time response of v, which describes the membrane or axon potential. The first part is the fast spiking waveform of v when the 15pA current step is present, and the second part is the persistent firing waveform of v.

Equations (1)-(3). When the input current I is not present, the equilibrium points of the dynamic system in Equation (8) are the solutions of the Equation $F(X) = 0$, the two equilibrium points are obtained

$$X_1 = \left[-12.5\left(5 - b + \sqrt{\Delta}\right) - 12.5\left(5 - b + \sqrt{\Delta}\right) 0 \right]' \quad \text{and} \quad X_2 = \left[-12.5\left(5 - b - \sqrt{\Delta}\right) - 12.5\left(5 - b - \sqrt{\Delta}\right) 0 \right]'.$$

Here, we assume that $\Delta = 2.6 + b^2 - 10b > 0$ and it is noted that X_1 is a stable equilibrium point while X_2 is unstable. Based on the analysis of stability of the equilibrium points and the nonlinear dynamic characteristic of Equation (8), the following conditions can be summarized to guarantee the existence of the persistent firing behavior.

Condition 1. The input current I satisfies that $\forall v \in R$ such that $0.04v^2 + (5 - b)v + 140 \geq 0$, i.e,

$$I \geq \left| \min\left\{0.04v^2 + (5 - b)v + 140\right\} \right|.$$

Condition 2. The condition $w > w_p$ is satisfied no later than the time when I is removed.

Condition 3. When $w > w_p$, the parameter c is denoted as c_p in Equation (5) (during the persistent firing period) is chosen to be the value such that $c > -12.5\left(5 - b - \sqrt{\Delta}\right)$.

Condition 1 means that there is no equilibrium point for the equation $F(X) + HI = 0$ which gives $X' AX + BX + C + HI = 0$. Otherwise, X may approach the equilibrium point and not change any more when I is present. In this case, it is impossible for persistent firing to exist. **Condition 2** requires that the neuron fires a sufficient number of spikes to ensure that $w > w_p$ before I is removed. **Condition 3** implies that, during the persistent firing period, $0.04v^2 + (5 - b)v + 140 > 0$ should be guaranteed at the interval

$$-12.5\left(5 - b - \sqrt{\Delta}\right) \leq v \leq c_p.$$

In the above analysis, we choose b to be such that $\Delta > 0$. Now we analyze the case that $\Delta \leq 0$. It can be shown that there is no real equilibrium point or at most a unstable equilibrium point for the equation $F(X) = 0$. Then **Condition 1** is achieved even if $I = 0$. The persistence firing can be always observed no matter whether the **Conditions 2** and **3** are satisfied or not. However, in this case, the nonlinear system $X = F(X) + HI$ is unstable. This is the reason that generally b is suggested to be chosen as a value such that $\Delta > 0$.

The geometrical approach provides a clear and insightful perspective of investigating the characteristics of dynamical system of neuron [15], and is therefore adopted to analyze the persistent firing model. We choose conveniently to conduct geometrical analysis on the phenomenon of persistent firing due to a long-lasting pulse stimulation (**Figure 2** and **Figure 3(a)**) rather than on that due to a pulse train (**Figure 1**), since the geometry of the former is less complicated yet retains significant information regarding the time evolution of the dynamical

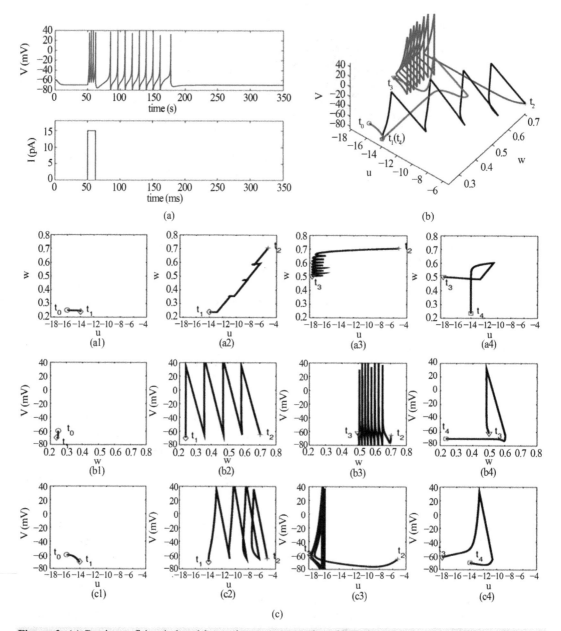

Figure 3. (a) Persistent firing induced by an input current pulse; (b) Trajectory of state variables u, v, w in three-dimensional phase space; (c) The three rows are projections of the 3-D trajectory. Figure 3(b) of persistent firing on the uw (a1-a4), wv (b1-b4), and uv (c1-c4) phase planes, respectively; the four columns represent the four stages of the whole process of persistent firing: stage 1 (a1, b1, c1), stage 2 (a2, b2, c2), stage 3 (a3, b3, c3), and stage 4 (a4, b4, c4), respectively.

system of neuron, such as the stable equilibrium and the threshold values, as shown in **Figure 3(b)** where the geometrical trajectory of the state variables u, v, w is plotted in three-dimensional phase space. It is worth mentioning that a new set of values in **Table 2** is assigned to the model's parameters to further reduce the complexity of the geometry, as shown in **Figure 3(a)** and **Figure 3(b)**. For the convenience of analysis, the projections of the 3-D trajectory on the uw, wv, and uv phase planes are illustrated in **Figure 3(c)**, where five points in time (t_0, t_1, t_2, t_3, t_4) are labeled on the curves, so as to partition the whole course of persistent firing into four temporal stages:

Stage 1: During the time range of $t_0 \rightarrow t_1$, the system begins with its initial state at t_0, converges to a stable equilibrium, stay there until t_1. The stable equilibrium can be calculated to be $[-70, -14, 0]'$.

Stage 2: During the time range of $t_1 \rightarrow t_2$, the system exhibits action potential evoked by a rectangular current signal, which also leads to the persistent firing in the next stage.

Stage 3: During the time range of $t_2 \rightarrow t_3$, the system exhibits persistent firing, which is triggered at t_2 when w reaches the upper threshold $w_p = 0.7$, and terminates at t_3 when w reaches the lower threshold value $w_n = 0.5$.

Stage 4: During the time range of $t_3 \rightarrow t_4$, the system returns to the state of stable equilibrium and rests there.

4. Neuromorphic Model of the Artificial Neuron

Since the last two decades, there has been a continuing interest in developing the neuromorphic circuits and systems that mimic the operation of biological neurons and brains, which enables considerably faster and more energy-efficient emulations of the neurons and neural systems. Due to the computational simplicity of our model, it is rather straightforward to implement the proposed neuron model in hardware, either in digital circuits or analog circuits. There have been several circuit implementations of Izhikevich neuron model and its variants [16] [17]. Thus in our case it is intuitive to add a leaky integrator emulating the axon, as well as the switching devices for selecting one of two sets of a, b, c, d, e parameters, which may be stored in memory devices, e.g. non-volatile memory.

A conceptual design of the proposed artificial neuron are shown in **Figure 4**, where the axonal spikes are originated from the unstable state of the neuron circuit and the artificial neuron is considered as a parameter-dependent dynamic system. The parameters of such dynamic system can be stored in non-volatile memory devices. Through modifying the parameter values in the memory, the spiking neuron unit can alter the axonal dynamics between the passive conduction mode and the persistent firing mode.

We have built the neuromorphic model based on the concept design with SPICE and Verilog-A languages, and simulated the model in Synopsys® HSPICE Simulator. The circuit model is shown in **Figure 5(a)** and **Figure 5(b)**. The soma membrane circuit (**Figure 5(a)**) essentially implements the Izhikevich neuron model [10], which includes a SPICE block describing Equations (1)-(2), an adder, a Schmitt trigger and two NMOS transistors (M1, M2) as switches. The stimulus I is the only external input to the soma unit, which also requires to fetch a parameter set of a, b, V_p and c from its memory during the operation. The Schmitt trigger implemented in Verilog-A, compares the membrane potential v with V_p (peak of the spike, typically 30 mV) and c (rest potential, typically −65 mV), and produces the output C_v, of VDD only when $> V_p$, and GND only when $v < c$. When c_v is high (VDD), which means a spike is generated, the two NMOS switches (M1, M2) are turned on thus the potentials of u and v are reset to u_{new} and c, respectively. When C_v is low (GND), the potentials of u and v remain to be solely determined by Equations (1)-(2) in the SPICE block.

Table 2. Simulation parameters.

$(a, b, c, d, e)_p$	=	$(0.1, 0.3, -85, 0, 0)$
$(a, b, c, d, e)_n$	=	$(0.1, 0.2, -85, 2, 0.12)$
f	=	5×10^{-4}
w_n	=	0.5
w_p	=	0.7
I	=	15 pA

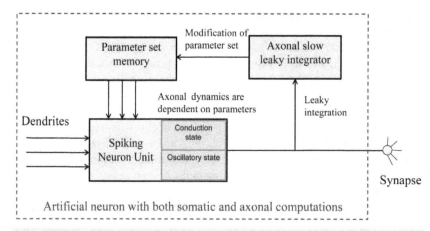

Figure 4. Conceptual design of the proposed artificial neuron.

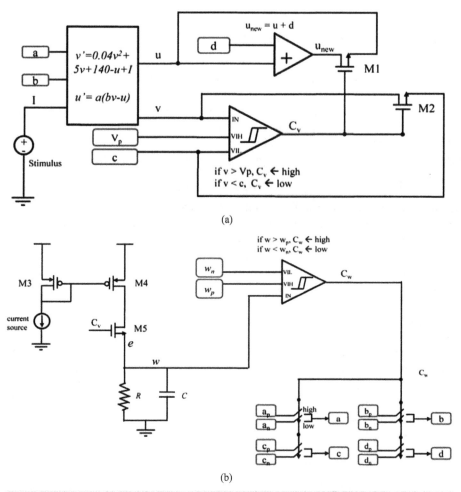

Figure 5. (a) The soma membrane circuit; (b) The axon circuit.

In the axon circuit (**Figure 5(b)**), a parallel RC circuit implements the axonal leaky integrator. When the soma membrane is generating a spike, C_v is high (VDD) and NMOS M5 will be turned on and pull the current from the current mirror (M3, M4), and charge the RC leaky integrator, increasing the axon potential w. The potential w is compared with w_n and w_p by a Schmitt trigger, which produces the output C_w of VDD when $w > w_p$ (the persistent firing should start) and GND when $w < w_n$ (the persistent firing should stop). The C_w signal controls five 2-way switches, which subsequently determine the value of x to be x_n or x_p, where

$x \in \{a,b,c,d,e\}$, and the neuron spiking dynamics.

Based on the long-pulse stimulation protocol and the circuit parameters given in **Table 3**, the simulation results of the circuit are shown in **Figure 6**. It should be noted that the values of the stimulus current I and simulation time here are different from those discussed in the previous section, with the purpose of achieving simpler implementation in the circuits. Nevertheless, it can be clearly seen that after we continuously applied the stimulus current for a period of time and stopped the input, the persistent firing of spikes was triggered, lasted for a similar duration, and finally stopped, depending on the level of axonal integrator potential w.

5. Persistent Firing Spiking Network

We have used this model to simulate a spiking network of 1000 randomly connected neurons. The network takes into account of axonal conduction delays [18] and spike-timing-dependent plasticity (STDP), which is considered to be "polychromous" [13]. The network consists of 800 excitatory neurons with regular spiking pattern [11] and 200 inhibitory neurons. As around 80% of EGFP-positive interneurons were found to have persistent firing behavior by repeated somatic current injection [12], we set in the 80% simulation, or 160 of the inhibitory neurons to be capable of persistent firing while the remaining 20% are fast spiking inhibitory neurons.

Each excitatory neuron is connected to 100 random neurons, and each inhibitory neuron, including persistent firing neuron, is randomly connected to 100 excitatory neurons only. Each synaptic connection has a fixed integer conduction delay between 1 ms and 20 ms. The conduction delay in the range of 1 - 20 ms is randomly as-

Table 3. Circuit simulation parameters.

$(a,b,c,d,e)_p$	=	$(0.1\text{ V}, 0.3\text{ V}, -85\text{ mV}, 0\text{ V}, 0.1\text{ mA})$
$(a,b,c,d,e)_n$	=	$(0.1\text{ V}, 0.2\text{ V}, -65\text{ mV}, 2\text{ mV}, 0.1\text{ mA})$
f	=	0.2
w_n	=	40 mV
w_p	=	90 mA

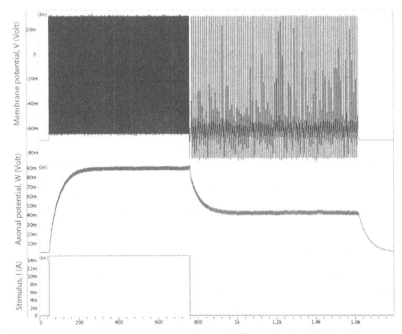

Figure 6. Circuit simulation results of the artificial neuron, showing that after a continuous applied stimulus stops, the slow integration in the axon leads to persistent firing of spikes. Top: the membrane potential v; Middle : the potential of axonal integrator w; Bottom: the stimulus current I.

signed to all excitatory synapses, while the 1 ms delay are assigned to all inhibitory synapses [13]. The synaptic connections are modified according to the STDP rule [19]. The implementation of the STDP function is based on Equation (9):

$$W(\Delta t) = \begin{cases} A^+ e^{-\Delta t/\tau^+}, & \text{for } \Delta t > 0 \\ -A^- e^{\Delta t/\tau^-} & \text{for } \Delta t < 0 \end{cases} \qquad (9)$$

where $\Delta t = t_{post} - t_{pre}$, $W(\Delta t)$ represents the strength of synapse connection, A^+ and A^- depend on the maximum synaptic strength, and τ^+ and τ^- are time constants determining the time window of STDP.

A simplified example of the spiking network structure is illustrated in **Figure 7(a)**. The raster plots of 1-second firing activities in the 1000-neuron spiking network with persistent firing inhibitory interneurons are shown in **Figure 7(b)**. One can see from **Figure 7(b)** that the network exhibits asynchronous dynamics. Different rhythmic activities can be identified, ranging from 3 Hz to 8 Hz. Dense vertical columns indicate there are occasional episodes of synchronized firings. As the firing rate of the inhibitory neurons (fast spiking) is higher than that of excitatory neurons (regular spiking), there are generally more firings for inhibitory neurons. The

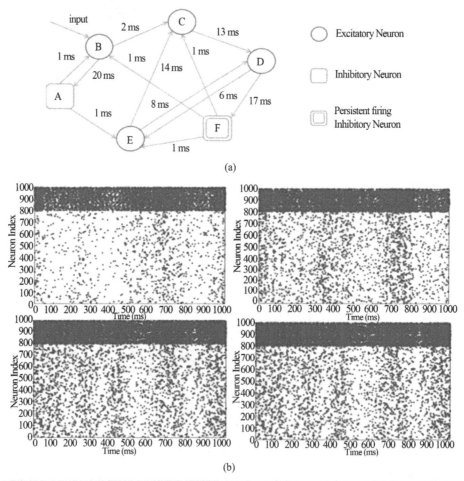

Figure 7. (a) A simplified example of the persistent firing spiking network structure. Among the neurons ranging from A to F in the network, (B, C, D, E) represent the excitatory neurons, and (A, F) represent inhibitory neurons in which F is capable for persistent firing. (b) Raster plots of spike activities in the spiking network of 1000 neurons including persistent firing inhibitory interneurons. Each raster plot shows the 1-second segment of the firing activity. Neurons indexed from 1 to 800 are excitatory neurons, and neurons indexed from 801 to 1000 are inhibitory. Within the 200 inhibitory neurons, there are 160 randomly selected neurons with persistent firing capability. Horizontally continuous dotted lines with neuron index in the range of 801 - 1000 indicate there are persistent firings of action potentials in inhibitory neurons.

persisting firing of inhibitory interneurons in the network, leads to reciprocal inhibition in a longer timescale and thus shut down the activities for a longer period (**Figure 7(b)** middle column). The synchronization of persistent firing interneurons could contribute to the beta and gamma oscillation, whose frequency ranges are close to the persistent firing frequency [20].

6. Discussion

The possible functions of the persistent firing were suggested to be related to working memory [12]. The ability to maintain the persistent firing of action potentials without on-going stimulation provides a mechanism of storing the information for a short period of time. This mechanism is similar to our working memory [21]-[23], which actively holds a limited amount of information [24] in the absence of stimuli. Working memory has been extensively explored from perspectives of highly abstract top levels in the domains of psychology, neuroscience and anatomy, but there are much less work from perspectives of bottom level of biological neurons [25]-[30]. It is still unknown how working memory is represented within a population of cortical neurons.

The presented simple model of persistent firing neurons enables further investigation of possible functions of persistent firing, especially the relationship between working memory and persistent firing, and the neural correlate of working memory. Recently, we have proposed a model of short term persistent habituation [31], consisting of a persistent firing neuron and a habituating synapse, to explore the presynaptic learning and memory. The interaction of persistent firing axonal and presynaptic processes increases the retention time of the synaptic conductance and therefore the recovery time, and continues the learning of short term habituation for the duration of persistent firing. This leads to a working memory for habituation.

Through incorporating the persistent firing dynamics in spiking networks with axonal delays and STDP learning rules, we can further investigate the interaction of polychronization and persistent neural activities. In the polychronous spiking network, the number of co-existing polychronous groups far exceeds the number of neurons in the network, resulting in an unprecedented memory capacity of the system [13]. Thus it would be interesting to investigate how working memory is presented in the polychronous network, and simulate a bioplausible working memory system with increased memory capacity. To this end, we are working towards the development of artificial cognitive memory with the objective of developing a novel function-driven memory technology in comparison to conventional density-driven storage technology [32]. The models of persistent firing neuron and spiking network presented in this paper can be used in the simulation of cognitive memory architectures.

Due to the computational simplicity of our model, it is straightforward to implement the model in hardware. We have developed a neuromorphic model of persistent firing neurons [33], which reproduces the neuronal persistent firing behavior by integrating somatic and axonal computational processes of different timescales. Considering there are many existing VLSI implementations of Izhikevich neuron model and its variants [16] [34]-[36], the proposed neuron model can be conveniently implemented in silicon by incorporating the axonal leaky integrator into the Izhikevich VLSI designs, enabling a considerably faster emulation of the neural systems with persistent neural activity in a highly parallel manner.

7. Conclusion

Based on the recent discovery in neurophysiology which revealed that interneurons can slowly integrate spiking, share the output across a coupled network of axons and respond with persistent firing even in the absence of input to the soma or dendrites, we proposed a new model of persistent firing neuron to bridge the gap between the conventional models and the newly-discovered phenomenon. In this work, we presented and discussed the mathematical and neuromorphic models of the artificial neuron, as well as a persistent firing polychronous spiking network which exhibits asynchronous dynamics. The artificial neuron we proposed, being computationally efficient yet bio-plausible, would be useful to construct and simulate the large scale models of animal or human cortex, which provides a neuromorphic platform for further investigation of the possible functions of persistent firing and their roles in animal and human brain, especially for exploring the relationship between working memory and persistent firing spiking network-based memory and the bio-inspired computer systems.

References

[1]   Lapicque, L. (1907) Recherches quantitatives sur l'excitation electrique des nerfs traitee comme une polarization. *Jour-*

nal of Physiol Pathol Générale, **9**, 620-635.

[2]   Sandberg, A. and Bostrom, N. (2008) Whole Brain Emulation: A Roadmap. Future of Humanity Institute, Oxford University, Technical Report #2008-3.

[3]   Hodgkin, A.L. and Huxley, A.F. (1952) A Quantitative Description of Membrane Current and Its Application to Conduction and Excitation in Nerve. *The Journal of Physiology*, **117**, 500-544. http://dx.doi.org/10.1113/jphysiol.1952.sp004764

[4]   Brette, R., Rudolph, M., Carnevale, T., Hines, M., Beeman, D., Bower, J.M., Diesmann, M., Morrison, A., Goodman, P.H., Harris Jr., F.C, *et al.* (2007) Simulation of Networks of Spiking Neurons: A Review of Tools and Strategies. *Journal of Computational Neuroscience*, **23**, 349-398. http://dx.doi.org/10.1007/s10827-007-0038-6

[5]   Mihalas, S. and Niebur, E. (2009) A Generalized Linear Integrate-and-Fire Neural Model Produces Diverse Spiking Behaviors. *Neural Computation*, **21**, 704-718. http://dx.doi.org/10.1162/neco.2008.12-07-680

[6]   Fitzhugh, R. (1961) Impulses and Physiological States in Theoretical Models of Nerve Membrane. *Biophysical Journal*, **1**, 445-466. http://dx.doi.org/10.1016/S0006-3495(61)86902-6

[7]   Morris, C. and Lecar, H. (1981) Voltage Oscillations in the Barnacle Giant Muscle Fiber. *Biophysical Journal*, **35**, 193-213. http://dx.doi.org/10.1016/S0006-3495(81)84782-0

[8]   Rose, R.M. and Hindmarsh, J.L. (1989) The Assembly of Ionic Currents in a Thalamic Neuron I. The Three-Dimensional Model. *Proceedings of the Royal Society of London. Series B. Biological Sciences*, **237**, 267-288. http://dx.doi.org/10.1098/rspb.1989.0049

[9]   Wilson, H.R. (1999) Simplified Dynamics of Human and Mammalian Neocortical Neurons. *Journal of Theoretical Biology*, **200**, 375-388. http://dx.doi.org/10.1006/jtbi.1999.1002

[10]   Izhikevich, E.M. (2001) Resonate-and-Fire Neurons. *Neural Networks*, **14**, 883-894. http://dx.doi.org/10.1016/S0893-6080(01)00078-8

[11]   Izhikevich, E.M. (2003) Simple Model of Spiking Neurons. *IEEE Transactions on Neural Networks*, **14**, 1569-1572. http://dx.doi.org/10.1109/TNN.2003.820440

[12]   Sheffield, M.E.J., Best, T.K., Mensh, B.D., Kath, W.L. and Spruston, N. (2011) Slow Integration Leads to Persistent Action Potential Firing in Distal Axons of Coupled Interneurons. *Nature Neuroscience*, **14**, 200-207. http://dx.doi.org/10.1038/nn.2728

[13]   Izhikevich, E.M. (2006) Polychronization: Computation with Spikes. *Neural Computation*, **18**, 245-282. http://dx.doi.org/10.1162/089976606775093882

[14]   Ning, N., Yi, K.J., Huang, K.J. and Shi, L.P. (2011) Axonal Slow Integration Induced Persistent Firing Neuron Model. *Lecture Notes in Computer Science*, **7062**, 469-476. http://dx.doi.org/10.1007/978-3-642-24955-6_56

[15]   Izhikevich, E.M. (2007) Dynamical Systems in Neuroscience: The Geometry of Excitability and Bursting. The MIT Press, Cambridge.

[16]   Wijekoon, J.H. and Dudek, P. (2008) Compact Silicon Neuron Circuit with Spiking and Bursting Behaviour. *Neural Networks*, **21**, 524-534. http://dx.doi.org/10.1016/j.neunet.2007.12.037

[17]   Wijekoon, J.H. and Dudek, P. (2008) Integrated Circuit Implementation of a Cortical Neuron. *Proceedings of the IEEE International Symposium on Circuits and Systems*, Seattle, 18-21 May 2008, 1784-1787.

[18]   Swadlow, H.A. (1985) Physiological Properties of Individual Cerebral Axons Studied *in Vivo* for as Long as One Year. *Journal of Neurophysiology*, **54**, 1346-1362.

[19]   Song, S., Miller, K.D. and Abbott, L.F. (2000) Competitive Hebbian Learning through Spike-Timing-Dependent Synaptic Plasticity. *Nature Neuroscience*, **3**, 919-926. http://dx.doi.org/10.1038/78829

[20]   Bartos, M., Vida, I. and Jonas, P. (2007) Synaptic Mechanisms of Synchronized Gamma Oscillations in Inhibitory Interneuron Networks. *Nature Reviews Neuroscience*, **8**, 45-56. http://dx.doi.org/10.1038/nrn2044

[21]   Baddeley, A. (1992) Working Memory. *Science*, **255**, 556-559. http://dx.doi.org/10.1126/science.1736359

[22]   Durstewitz, D., Seamans, J.K. and Sejnowski, T.J. (2000) Neurocomputational Models of Working Memory. *Nature Neuroscience*, **3**, 1184-1191. http://dx.doi.org/10.1038/81460

[23]   Egorov, A.V., Hamam, B.N., Fransen, E., Hasselmo, M.E. and Alonso, A.A. (2002) Graded Persistent Activity in Entorhinal Cortex Neurons. *Nature*, **420**, 173-178. http://dx.doi.org/10.1038/nature01171

[24]   Miller, G.A. (1956) The Magical Number Seven, Plus or Minus Two: Some Limits on Our Capacity for Processing Information. *Psychological Review*, **63**, 81-97. http://dx.doi.org/10.1037/h0043158

[25]   D'Esposito, M., Detre, J.A., Alsop, D.C., Shin, R.K., Atlas, S. and Grossman, M. (1995) The Neural Basis of the Central Executive System of Working Memory. *Nature*, **378**, 279-281. http://dx.doi.org/10.1038/378279a0

[26]   Goldman-Rakic, P.S. (1995) Cellular Basis of Working Memory. *Neuron*, **14**, 477-485.

http://dx.doi.org/10.1016/0896-6273(95)90304-6

[27] Miller, E.K., Erickson, C.A. and Desimone, R. (1996) Neural Mechanisms of Visual Working Memory in Prefrontal Cortex of the Macaque. *The Journal of Neuroscience*, **16**, 5154-5167.

[28] Amit, D. and Mongillo, G. (2003) Spike-Driven Synaptic Dynamics Generating Working Memory States. *Neural Computation*, **15**, 565-596. http://dx.doi.org/10.1162/089976603321192086

[29] O'Reilly, R.C. and Frank, M.J. (2006) Making Working Memory Work: A Computational Model of Learning in the Prefrontal Cortex and Basal Ganglia. *Neural Computation*, **18**, 283-328. http://dx.doi.org/10.1162/089976606775093909

[30] Szatmary, B. and Izhikevich, E.M. (2010) Spike-Timing Theory of Working Memory. *PLoS Computational Biology*, **6**, e1000879. http://dx.doi.org/10.1371/journal.pcbi.1000879

[31] Ramanathan, K., Ning, N., Dhanasekar, D., Li, G., Shi, L.P. and Vadakkepat, P. (2012) Presynaptic Learning and Memory with a Persistent Firing Neuron and a Habituating Synapse: A Model of Short Term Persistent Habituation. *International Journal of Neural System*s, **22**, Article ID: 1250015. http://dx.doi.org/10.1142/S0129065712500153

[32] Shi, L.P., Yi, K.J., Ramanathan, K., Zhao, R., Ning, N., Ding, D. and Chong, T.C. (2011) Artificial Cognitive Memory—Changing from Density Driven to Functionality Driven. *Applied Physics A*, **102**, 865-875. http://dx.doi.org/10.1007/s00339-011-6297-0

[33] Ning, N., Huang, K.J. and Shi, L.P. (2012) Artificial Neuron with Somatic and Axonal Computation Units: Mathematical and Neuromorphic Models of Persistent Firing Neurons. *Proceedings of the* 2012 *International Joint Conference on Neural Networks* (*IJCNN*), Brisbane, 10-15 June 2012, 1-7.

[34] van Schaik, A., Jin, C., McEwan, A. and Hamilton, T.J. (2010) A Log-Domain Implementation of the Izhikevich Neuron Model. *Proceedings of* 2010 *IEEE International Symposium on Circuits and Systems* (*ISCAS*), Paris, 30 May-2 June 2010, 4253-4256.

[35] Li, G.Q., Ning, N., Ramanathan, K., Wei, H., Pan, L. and Shi, L.P. (2013) Behind the Magical Numbers: Hierarchical Chunking and the Human Working Memory Capacity. *International Journal of Neural Systems*, **23**, Article ID: 1350019. http://dx.doi.org/10.1142/S0129065713500196

[36] Li, G.Q., Wen, C.Y., Li, Z.G., Zhang, A.M., Yang, F. and Mao, K.Z. (2013) Model-Based Online Learning with Kernels. *IEEE Transactions on Neural Networks and Learning Systems*, **24**, 356-369. http://dx.doi.org/10.1109/TNNLS.2012.2229293

9

A Decision Support System Based on Multi-Agent Technology for Gene Expression Analysis

Edna Márquez[1], Jesús Savage[1], Jaime Berumen[2], Christian Lemaitre[3],
Ana Lilia Laureano-Cruces[4], Ana Espinosa[2], Ron Leder[1], Alfredo Weitzenfeld[5]

[1]Facultad de Ingeniería, Universidad Nacional Autónoma de México, México D.F., México
[2]Unidad de Medicina Genómica, Hospital General de México, México D.F., México
[3]Departamento de Ciencias de la Comunicación, Universidad Autónoma Metropolitana, México D.F., México
[4]Departamento de Sistemas, Universidad Autónoma Metropolitana, México D.F., México
[5]Department of Computer Science and Engineering, University of South Florida, Tampa, FL, USA
Email: cednam@gmail.com, robotssavage@gmail.com, jaimeberumen@hotmail.com, lemaitre@gmail.com, clc@azc.uam.mx, anaesga@hotmail.com, rleder@ieee.org, aweitzenfeld@usf.edu

Abstract

The genetic microarrays give to researchers a huge amount of data of many diseases represented by intensities of gene expression. In genomic medicine gene expression analysis is guided to find strategies for prevention and treatment of diseases with high rate of mortality like the different cancers. So, genomic medicine requires the use of complex information technology. The purpose of our paper is to present a multi-agent system developed in order to improve gene expression analysis with the automation of tasks about identification of genes involved in a cancer, and classification of tumors according to molecular biology. Agents that integrate the system, carry out reading files of intensity data of genes from microarrays, pre-processing of this information, and with machine learning methods make groups of genes involved in the process of a disease as well as the classification of samples that could propose new subtypes of tumors difficult to identify based on their morphology. Our results we prove that the multi-agent system requires a minimal intervention of user, and the agents generate knowledge that reduce the time and complexity of the work of prevention and diagnosis, and thus allow a more effective treatment of tumors.

Keywords

Multi-Agent Systems, Machine Learning, Bioinformatics, Gene Expression Analysis

1. Introduction

In genomic medicine the knowledge derived from gene expression analysis could help to understand the function of normal and neoplastic cells and to identify molecular markers with diagnostic value and medical prognosis in cancers, in order to develop effective prevention, early diagnostic and therapeutic strategies. Two important goals of genomic medicine, in particular in cancer studies, are to search new molecular subtypes of cancer and predict membership to predefined cancer classes [1]. Classification of samples is important because it contributes to the prognosis of cancer.

Our work was designed in order to achieve these objectives, because current medicine requires non-trivial information processing like pre-processing data, filtering data, data mining, characterizing of genes, and visualization of results. Also our system proposed through intelligent agents and machine learning can contribute to these types of tasks that are in the area of Bioinformatics.

The use of agent technology is viewed as an emerging area in Bioinformatics [2]. In Bioinformatics almost all of the applications of agents are dedicated in the integration of resources using different sources that are distributed in different nodes like data bases or web sites. In our multi-agent system for gene expression analysis (**MAS-GEN**), we are interested in the automation of complete whole process of gene expression analysis through distribution of activities in a group of specialized agents with different abilities.

In the first section we present a background of gene expression in microarrays and the relation between agents and gene expression analysis, and the machine learning methods applied. In the second section we present the architecture implemented in MAS-GEN. In the third section are some example outcomes with study case of cervical cancer and finally the conclusions and the discussion.

1.1. DNA Microarray

Since the deoxyribonucleic acid microarrays appeared in 90's the studies based in molecular biology can have the expression of thousands of genes in a single matrix. In a typical experiment the study includes dozens of microarrays with the measure of the expression levels of large numbers of genes simultaneously and the comparison of the information extracted from them.

This microarray technology demands to computer science methods and techniques at different levels, like data analysis and statistical information processing, information standardization, and automation of the whole information processes involved in each experiment.

Through the analysis of microarrays is possible for researchers to know which genes are active in a cell at particular situation. The comparison of genes expression patterns (which genes are active) of two cells of the same type, one normal cell and the other belonging to a tumor tissue, can be of great help in understanding what are the genes that might be involved in the tumor formation.

In many cases, for researchers in gene expression analysis, it is not trivial to use several software programs to complete the microarray analyses that we can find in most experiments. The problems include matching of data output and input formats understanding the software performance/limitations, and finding one or more special software programs; this is usually not an easy task given their training. We propose an agent system platform for automating the information analysis process of microarray samples.

1.2. Related Work

Many groups of research have been interested in combining Bioinformatics (where gene expression analysis is included) and intelligent agent software. In [3] we found a Group on Agents in Bioinformatics, BioAgents, which promote the agent work in Bioinformatics fields. In [4] the project Geneweaverthe, agents work with external databases. Another system for gene expression analysis using multi-agent technology is in [5]. They propose three stages of gene expression analysis: pre-processing, statistical analysis and biological inference. With agents they want to get automation and parallel processing. In BioMas [6] the agents work with the sequence and function of genes. A multi-agent system for gene expression classification is presented in [7]. The system searches for significant genes to classify samples of some cancers. The genes are grouped by couples; that are tested with clustering methods if they could classify types of cancer.

In our application we are interested in the automation of complete whole process of gene expression analysis, since the reading of profiles expression data to selection of relevant genes and sample classification, through distribution of activities in a group of specialized agents with different abilities.

At difference with the previous multi-agent systems, MAS-GEN joins in its agents the knowledge of experts with the use of statistical and machine learning methods for supporting decisions in gene expression analysis in samples classification and identification of relevant genes for a not expert user. The intervention of the user could be minimal, he only must give the files with gene expression intensity and MAS-GEN makes all tasks to find relevant genes and create groups of samples.

1.3. Agent Technology

An agent is a computer system that is situated in some environment, and that is capable of autonomous action in this environment in order to meet its design objectives [8]-[10].

Some characteristics of intelligent agents are:
- Autonomy, agents can exercise control over their internal state and actions without direct human or other interaction.
- Reactive, they have to react timely and appropriately to unexpected events.
- Proactive are goal-oriented and take the initiative where appropriate
- Planning, the agents can plan their own actions, they have to solve tasks through plans
- Adaptive, can learn and change their behavior on the basis of their previous experience to adapt to changing environmental conditions
- Mobile, have the ability to transport themselves from one machine to another
- Sociability, agents deal with interactions, positive and negative, with other agents.

Agent technology represents a paradigm of software development, which improves the development of systems in solving complex and real world problems [11].

A multi-agent system is composed of a number of interacting agents. Multi-agent technology offers an alternative to building software in bioinformatics, where the complexity of required systems can be divided into well-defined sub components that can be handled by agents. Decomposition of complex problems into autonomous agents is an effective way of partitioning a problem [11]. In the systems where using different data resources and need an ontology, multi-agent technology has been adopted in several research projects for integration of Bioinformatics resources [12].

1.4. Machine Learning

The data obtained from digital image files of multiple microarrays with thousands of genes must be transformed and organized in a gene expression matrix, where each row represents the expression of one gene in many samples represented by columns. After the matrix of gene expression profiles has been generated, we can begin the analysis which in non trivial doubt the dimension of data. Machine learning contributes with the supervised and non-supervised algorithms in order to make groups of similar data, genes or samples according of gene expression levels.

In our system we applied non-supervised machine learning algorithms through the clustering algorithms: fuzzy c-means, self-organizing maps, vector quantization, hierarchical clustering and principal component analysis, for discovering similarities in the samples and/or behavior of genes.

Fuzzy C-means algorithm has been used as an alternative to k-means in the analysis of genes, while in k-means one gene must belong just to one cluster in C-means one element could be in two or more classes with different degree of belonging. For this algorithm must choose the number of clusters not less than 2, also select the distance metric and the degree to which possessions are shared in the clusters (diffusivity). With the centroids of each cluster fuzzy will get the diffuse array, the metric distance is applied to view the difference between the current diffusivity matrix with the previous and verified with a threshold value until the distance were less than or equal to threshold value. For our aim, in classification of samples this algorithm permits to find degrees of membership to few types of cancers for each case or person.

Algorithm of Fuzzy C-means
Input: md = the data set of gene expression profiles, c = number of clusters, u = threshold of fuzzy value
1) *Randomly create c clusters*
2) *Repeat*
3) *For i = 1 to c do*

4) *Calculate the C-centroid*
5) *Get fuzziness matrix, md(n), with all centroids*
6) *calculate the distance d(md(n − 1), md(n))*
7) *End_For*
8) *Until u > d(md(n − 1), md(n))*

Self-organizing maps (SOM) is a type of clustering is based on the Kohonen neural network [13]. Corresponds to the non-hierarchical clustering split because there is no dependency between the different clusters formed and begins with the full set of objects (genes or samples) to be grouped by their similarity. In SOM the objects are assigned to a partition group by their similarity, and the partitions are defined according to a geometric shape established at the beginning. With a lattice are created the number of neurons to classify for the NxM dimensions and initialize the weight vector for each neuron to the input vector, during the iterations the winner neuron is looking for, that represents the input vector, its weights and weights of its neighbours are updated; the iteration continue until a detention criteria is satisfied, when the map has minimal changes.

Algorithm of SOM:
Input: data set of genes expression profiles, u = threshold of difference
1) *Create a lattice with N neurons,*
2) *Initialize randomly the weight vector for each k neuron, $W_{ik,}$ connected to input i*
3) *Repeat*
4) *Presents an input vector V to network*
5) *Compute distance $d(V_i, W_{ik})$,*
6) *Get the winner neuron, with the smallest $d(V_i, W_{ik})$, which represents the input vector,*
7) *Refresh the weight of the winner neuron and the neighbors*
8) *Until $(d(V_i, W_{ik}) < u)$.*

Vector quantization method (VQ) is also applicable like non-hierarchical clustering, in the process the space is divided into several connected regions, also called Voronoi regions. Each region is represented by a centroid, which bind the closest input vectors according to a distance measure. Vector quantization used here is designed so that you can create any number of centroids not only in power of 2. We have N input vectors with G dimensions to be grouped into M centroids. The algorithm begins with an initial centroid, which is the average of all vectors, the current centroids are divided in each iteration, each vector is associated to its nearest centroid, the centroids are recalculated as the arithmetic mean of the vectors associated with it, and repeat the iterations until criteria of error are satisfied.

Algorithm of VQ:
Input: N is data set of genes expression profiles, ε = threshold of distortion
1) *Find an initial codebook D_1, with one centroid C_1, by averaging all the vectors p_j, with $L_m = 1$;*
2) *Repeat*
3) *For i = 1 to M do*
4) *Modify each $C_i, C_i = C_i + \varphi$ of small magnitude to generate new centroids from each of them, generating a new codebook $D_m + 1, L_m + 1$;*
5) *End_For*
6) *Compute the difference $d(p_j, C_k)$, between the input vector p_j and the cluster R_k whose centroid is Ck;*
7) *Assign each input vector into the cluster with minimal distortion measure;*
8) *Recompute the centroids C_k for each of the cluster, by averaging all the vectors p_j that belong to R_k;*
9) *Compute the average distortion, A*
10) *Until L_m > codebook_size and A < ε*

The codebook size is the number of clusters in the environment.

The principal component analysis (PCA) is a technique widely used in fields such as recognition of images and to find patterns in large data. Another use of PCA is the reduction of dimension of data vectors with no loss of information. Variables that represent those dimensions are chosen to collect the percentage of variability that is sufficient, called principal components. The algorithm for PCA gets the covariance matrix of the initial data with its eigenvalues and eigenvectors, the columns of the eigenvectors are sorted according to the values of the eigenvalues. Finally N columns take the eigenvector according to the N dimensions that you want to keep.

Hierarchical Clustering is an agglomerative clustering algorithm, where the genes that are separated in groups, forming a hierarchical tree with clusters of genes. The hierarchical clustering algorithm consists in calculating the distances between all pairs of objects (genes or samples), this is the same as assuming that every object is a cluster: {C1, ..., CN}, two closest clusters (C_i, C_j) are selected to form one, C_{ij}, you have to repeat the selection of clusters until there are no pairs of comparison. For calculating the distance between clusters is calculated by 3 ways: simple linkage, corresponds to the minimum distance between elements in the clusters, emerging clusters are linked by very long branches may be less significant clusters; average linkage is the average distance between all elements of both clusters is complex for processing large amounts of data, like in the case of genes; complete linkage is the maximum distance between elements of the clusters. With the final group of clusters it is creating a dendogram or tree diagram that helps the visualization of clusters, you can find different levels of clusters and therefore relationship between the elements that comprise them.

Cluster validation was made with Cross-validation is very useful in gene expression analysis with microarrays because the number of samples is reduced by the cost and it is not possible have training and testing samples for all studies. Here the agents apply 10-fold cross-validation, for evaluating and comparing the results of clustering methods, where the samples are divided in two sets: training and testing. With 10-fold cross-validation the samples are divided into 10 equally sized segments, the groups are going to be used for 10 iterations of training and validation such that within each iteration 9 folds are used for learning while one fold of the data is held-out for validation. In sample classification the agent uses 10-fold cross-validation to measure the accuracy classification of samples, calculated according the number of right classified in testing sets.

2. MAS-GEN Architecture

The gene expression analysis through the microarray data could be improved by automation of many tasks. In the proposed system MAS-GEN, to reach the goals of gene identification and tumor classification is distributed in operational agents and many tasks could be solver in parallel with the knowledge of other experts. We intended to create a simple and transparent system for the user to do gene expression analysis without a lot experience. The biomedical experts for MAS-GEN integrate the team of Genomic Medicine in the General Hospital of México [14].

MAS-GEN has four operational agents and one manager. In this multi-agent system the agents have some properties of individual intelligent agents and collaborate to reach a main goal. This is why communication and coordination between the agents is necessary. Some agents have autonomy to make own decisions according their internal state and the information received from the environment to solve his tasks. The autonomy of agents could be adjustable [15] in order to give part of the process control to the user the agent autonomy could be limited to respond to user needs.

Our operational agents are Pre-processing agent, Gene Identification agent, Sample Classification agent and Databases agent they are coordinated by a Manager agent.

Agents' decision making is based on a system of production rules, where each agent has a base of facts and a set of rules implemented in the programming language Clips [16].

The agent platform uses a set of functions or procedures to analyze the expression of thousands of genes in many experimental conditions. This set of statistical and machine learning methods is independent of the agents. The use of microarrays for gene expression analysis is a field that it is improving continuously with new or better methods and techniques, so, it is possible to increase the capacity of the system with the incorporation or modification of new functions for preprocessing or processing data, and presentation of data, without introducing conflicts in agents' operation. In **Figure 1**, we present the MAS-GEN architecture.

With this independence processes and functions have been implemented in different programming languages such as Java, C++ and R.

MAS-GEN is integrated by four operational agents (Pre-processing agent, Gene Identification agent, Sample Classification agent and Database agent), which are coordinated by a master agent who interacts with the user. The set of statistical and machine learning methods are implemented out of platform agent and all agents can use them.

2.1. Pre-Processing Agent

The Pre-processing agent's activity begins with the reading of data intensity files of expressed genes in experiments from microarrays. This agent uses functions for reading, normalizing and standardizing data, already implemented in the R language by Bioconductor [17].

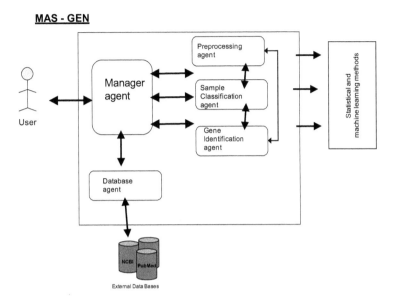

Figure 1. Architecture of MAS-GEN.

According the problem to be solves: sample classification or selection of genes the agent must give the format of data matrix, the matrix must be complete does not have missing values for all samples in all genes, and the data matrix has data normalized. To keep up with the dynamic field of Bioinformatics, the preprocessing agent can incorporate new methods for reading other gene Chips or data normalization, so the system facilitates the incorporation of new pre-processing processes. This is an autonomous agent because have motivations to act.

2.2. Gene Identification Agent

This agent makes one of the main tasks of MAS-GEN, has the goal of creating lists of genes from which genes potentially involved in the diseases investigated can be identified. It also requires the collaboration of the databases agent to characterize the genes, and the collaboration of the sample classification agent to review the capacity of classification samples with the selected lists. The use case diagram for gene identification is in **Figure 2**.

In the aim of identification of genes all the agents of MAS-GEN collaborate. Identification of genes begins with a user request to manager agent, which presents the requests to pre-processing agent and gene identification agent to create lists of genes and manager agent to the user system presents the results.

This agent applies filters based in the experience of the experts in this task. The agent works with statistical and machine-learning methods, like vector quantization and self-organizing maps, for creation of lists of genes. The agent has to make different clusters of genes to decide what clusters are promising in order to include the most important genes to the research. Gene Identification agent evaluates the lists of genes generated according the knowledge given by sample classification agent and databases agent. In the selection of a list of genes the gene identification agent looks upon if the genes in the list can make a correct classification with the samples and the previous knowledge about relation between the genes and the disease from external databases.

2.3. Sample Classification Agent

The agent of sample classification makes groups with the microarray samples based in the quantitative data of gene expression profiles. The results of this agent help to do the difference between healthy and diseased samples, as well as the identification of cancer type and tumor variants. The creation of groups of samples is using machine learning through clustering methods: 1) self-organizing maps (SOM); 2) vector quantization (VQ) [18], and 3) c-means and principal component analysis (PCA). In **Figure 3** is the use case for sample classification task.

Sample Classification agent responds to request and applies clustering methods to make the groups of samples

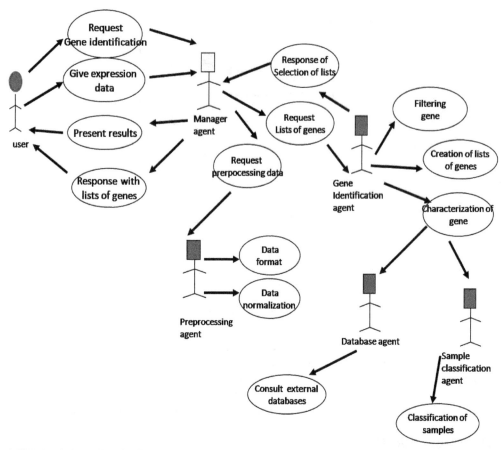

Figure 2. Use case diagram for identification of genes.

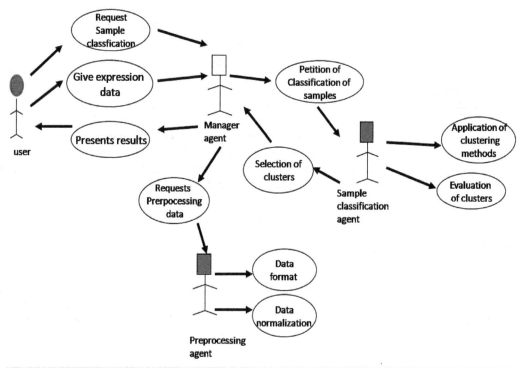

Figure 3. Use case diagram for classification of samples.

using the numerical data of gene expression. With the knowledge about the groups of samples, another task for this agent is to classify new samples, if the sample is a tumor or not, or what kind of tumor represents, this knowledge is relevant in medicine to determine the state and accurate treatment for a diseases.

Also, Sample Classification agent collaborates in the goal of identification of relevant genes, this agent tests if the lists of genes given by the gene identification agent can classify properly the samples.

2.4. Database Agent

The gene expression analysis to obtain a list of important genes requires the characterization of selected genes. Database agent is specialized in selecting and gathering information of genes using several resources of databases with genomic information through the Internet, through NCBI [19] and other tools like DAVID [20]. Database agent interacts with external databases. Databases agent must select only the relevant information about genes that could be important in the user decision. Finally that agent standardizes and prepares the information about genes to present it to the user. This agent is not autonomous because it works by requisition of other agent, gene identification agent or sample classification agent.

2.5. Manager Agent

MAS-GEN has a manager agent, which coordinates all activities. This agent interacts with the user, gets his requests and gives him the results, coordinates the interaction among agents, has the register of the agents into the system, where the agents presents their abilities to others to respond of their desires.

According with Luck [21] we can classify the entities in an environment in objects, agents and autonomous agent. Autonomous agents are the agents motivated by self to act in the environment, like the agents sample classification, preprocessing and gene identification are autonomous. The database agent is not autonomous because other agents to make its tasks call it. Then in our system we have agents and autonomous agents, since we think all the entities have a goal to reach. This technique has been utilized with success for the organization of agents in different subjects like: 1) a pedagogical context; 2) geothermal wells; 3) video games; and 4) planning and schedule [9] [10] [22]-[25].

Pre-processing agent:
Autonomous Agent
Goal-type: active.
Goal: provide the data genes.
Perception:
Perceiving actions: gene expression data read from files.
Can Perceive: state of expression data, aims for data.
Will Perceive: new necessities of other agents with data.
Actions:
Reading files of gene expression data.
Creation a matrix of data.
Data normalization, and standardization in the matrix.
Format the data genes.

Sample Classification Agent:
Autonomous Agent
Goal-type: Active.
Goal: Create sets of samples.
Perception:
Perceiving actions: need to create sets of samples, creation of lists of genes to identification of genes.
Can Perceive: Sets of genes, sets of samples.
Will Perceive: Sample differentiation.
Actions:
Create sets of samples using gene expression profiles through machine learning methods.

Gene Identification Agent:

Autonomous Agent

Goal-type: Active.

Goal: Create sets of relevant genes.

Perception:

Perceiving actions: Need to create sets of genes to get relevant genes.

Can Perceive: profiles expression of genes.

Will Perceive: grade of correlated of genes in the lists, sample differentiation, and characterization of joined genes in the lists.

Actions:

Create sets of genes using gene expression profiles through machine learning methods, evaluated the relation of genes into a list, evaluation of information gotten by Database Agent about genomic medicine.

Data Bases Agent:

Non autonomous Agent

Goal-type: Pasive.

Goal: Characterization of genes.

Perception:

Perceiving actions: Request of characterization of lists of genes to identification of genes.

Can Perceive: Messages from manager agent.

Actions: Consult of public databases to integrate the knowledge about genes related with the disease of study.

Manager agent:

Autonomous Agent

Goal-type: Active.

Goal: Facilitate the communication between agents, interaction with the user

Perception:

Perceiving actions: Request of autonomous agents to non-autonomous, requests of the user, conflicts between agents.

Can Perceive: Communication of the user, results from other agents.

Will Perceive:

Actions:

    Interaction with the user system, communication with agents, registration of agents,
    and resolution of conflicts.

3. Case Study-Cervical Cancer

3.1. Data

For this paper we use MAS-GEN for identifying relevant genes for cervical cancer. The data of gene expression was generated using the Affymetrix HGFocus Gen Chip of mRNA that contains ~8600 genes. The data are from 42 Mexican women with a diagnosis of cervical cancer with Human Papillomavirus 16 (HPV16). Biological samples were collected during the course of routine clinical practice at the oncology service at the General Hospital of Mexico (Mexico City) and also from 12 controls (non-malignant conditions or for non-cervical cancer were included). The tumor samples are of two cervical cancer subtypes: 14 adenocarcinoma (ACC) and 28 squamous cell carcinoma (SCC), given the histopathological point of view. The assay microarrays were performance in the unit of Genomic Medicine in the General Hospital of Mexico [14].

3.2. Process for Selecting Relevant Genes

The selection of relevant genes is with minimal intervention of the user. At the beginning the user selects the files with the intensity of expression of ~8600 genes for 52 samples and requests the goal of selecting relevant genes. This instruction generates the user query for initializing the work of manager agent, which creates a plan to reach the goal and the operational agents execute the plan. Pre-processing agent reads files with expression of thousands of genes, review the state of data, if the data matrix is complete, apply tests of normalization data and gives the format to data in order to other agent can analysis the gene expression profiles.

The gene identification agent with the data like a matrix with a dimension of N rows of genes and M columns of samples applies filters to reduce the number of genes. With this task the number of genes is reduced only, which have differential expression for the study. The filtering methods, like SAM and t-test, use a threshold to select a list, this threshold is a parameter recommended by an expert but that the user can modify and the agent could propound one according the data. The user could view and use this first a priori list, that also other agents could use it to solve a problem.

For this study case were selected the best fifty genes upregulated from the genes with differential expression. After, for generating sub lists, the gene identification agent creates clusters of genes using machine learning like VQ and SOM algorithms. To evaluate the adequacy of a selected list of genes, the agents test if a list of genes has the capacity to divide the samples in the basic groups: control and cases. After, the list of genes is selected to continue with the characterization of genes using external databases. Data base agent consults information about the disease or a related problem, biological functions and biological processes in which the genes are involved. In **Table 1** are the 3 best lists of genes generated by MAS-GEN with the clusters of genes according the results from the tasks of gene identification, sample classification and database agents. Some of the genes had been reported already about cervical cancer according PubMed [14]. In **Figure 4** the patterns of genes expression of the three best lists selected compare with the expression pattern of the reported genes.

The expression patterns of four lists of genes: a) genes already reported with cervical cancer; b) genes of selected list-1; c) genes of selected list-2; and d) genes of selected list-3. In b), c) and d) are the three best-selected lists of genes by MAS-GEN. The three lists selected by MAS-GEN were grouped by clustering methods so their genes have very similar expression in each one.

The user can review the results through some tables and graphics presented by manager agent with the knowledge obtained by the operational agents. The knowledge given by MAS-GEN could support decision making by the user about a set of genes. In **Table 2** show the principal biological process obtained by data base

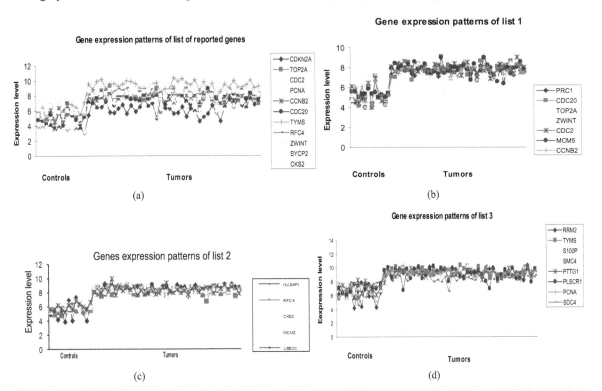

Figure 4. Expression patterns with the lists of genes.

Table 1. Genes of the best selected lists.

List	Genes	# Reported genes
List 1 (7 genes)	• PRC1, CDC20, TOP2A, ZWINT, CDC2, MCM5, CCNB2.	5
List 2 (5 genes)	• NUSAP1, RFC4, CKS2, MCM2, UBE2C.	4
List 3 (8 genes)	• RRM2, TYMS, S100P, SMC4, PTTG1, PLSCR1, PCNA, SDC4.	6

Table 2. Participation of genes in biological processes.

Biological Process	% genes List 1	% genes List 2	% genes List 3
Cell cycle	28.6	-	40.0
Death	28.6	-	28.6
Cell división	14.3	-	-
Gene expression	14.3	20.0	14.3
Transcription	14.3	-	-
Primary metabolic process	28.6	20.0	28.6
Regulation of gene expression	14.3	-	14.3
Transcription	-	-	14.3
Viral reproduction	-	-	14.3

agent for some gene lists. The knowledge from Internet databases about important biological processes of genes selected by MAS-GEN is reported with the percentage of genes involved of the three selected lists. **Table 3** has information about important biological functions of genes selected by MAS-GEN, these results were gotten also by Database agent by consulting databases in internet.

3.3. Process for Sample Classification

For this aim the principal actor is sample classification agent, which applies, clustering methods and cross validation with 10-fold. In this paper, the sample classification agent makes two kind of classification of samples: a) classification in 2 basic classes: tumors and controls, and b) in subtypes of cervical cancer: SCC and ACC. We use a list of genes already reported with relation of cervical cancer and one list obtained by gene identification agent. After pre-processing data, the sample classification agent gets a matrix with N rows of samples and M columns of genes; to create groups of samples.

The classification of subtypes given by the agent is comparing to histopathological classification, which is according the subjective direct observation of the cellular tissue made by the pathology expert. However, the use of molecular biology through the intensity of gene expression is not equals in many cases of cancers but it could give new forms of classification [26]. The aptitude of dividing the samples with the list of already reported genes in PubMed (*CDKN2A, TOP2A, CDC2, PCNA, CCNB2, CDC20, TYMS, RFC4, ZWINT, SYCP2, CKS2*) and the 3 lists of selected genes obtained by Gene Identification agent are in **Table 4**, the results of the clustering methods validated with 10-fold cross-validation for the basic classification: tumors and controls, and for two types of cervical cancer: ASC and SCC. **Figure 5** presents the graphics of PCA and **Figure 6** has the dendograms for sample classification between tumors and controls given by MAS-GEN with the 3 selected lists of genes and with the list of reported genes. Using reported genes and the best lists of genes selected by MAS-GEN, a) visualization with PCA graphics of 2 principal components; and b) visualization with dendograms, both for classification of control and tumor samples.

4. Discussion and Future Work

The results achieved in the classification of samples between cases and controls have a minimal misclassifica-

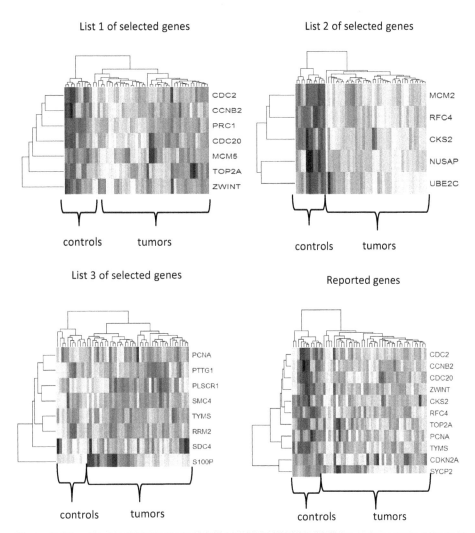

Figure 5. Visualization with dendograms of sample classification between tumors and controls.

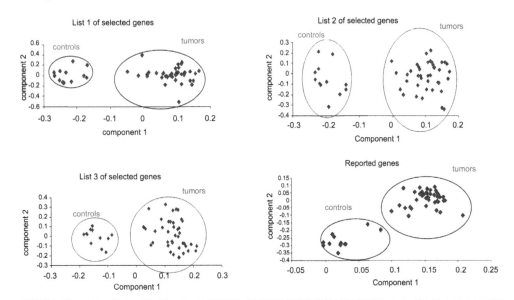

Figure 6. Visualization with PCA of sample classification between tumors and controls.

Table 3. Biological functions of genes selected in gene identification.

List of genes	Biological Functions	% genes
1	Cyclin-dependent protein kinase activity	14.3
	Protein kinase binding	14.3
	Ubiquitin binding	14.3
	DNA binding	28.6
	Atpase activity	57.1
	Protein binding	57.1
2	DNA replication origin binding	20.0
	Protein kinase regulator activity	20.0
	DNA binding	40.0
	Nucleotide binding	40.0
	Atpase activity	80.0
3	DNA binding	12.5
	Mismatch repair complex binding	12.5
	Nucleic acid binding	12.5
	DNA polymerase processivity factor activity	25.0
	Ion binding	37.5

Table 4. Accurate classification samples with selected lists and reported genes.

Genes	Method	Tumors Vs. Controls	Adenos vs. Squamous
Reported	SOM	96%	58%
(CDKN2A,TOP2A,CDC2,PCNA,CCNB2,CDC20, TYMS,RFC4,ZWINT,SYCP2,CKS2)	VQ	97%	63%
	C-means	99%	67%
List 1 of genes	SOM	95%	70%
(PRC1, CDC20, TOP2A, ZWINT, CDC2, MCM5, CCNB2)	VQ	100%	73%
	C-means	100%	74%
List 2 of genes	SOM	92%	52%
(RRM2, TYMS, S100P, SMC4, PTTG1,	VQ	100%	53%
PLSCR1, PCNA, SDC4)	C-means	100%	54%
List 3 of genes	SOM	97%	59%
(NUSAP1, RFC4, CKS2, MCM2, UBE2C)	VQ	100%	55%
	C-means	100%	61%

tion, so the clusters could be used to the determinate if a sample is healthy or not. In the classification of samples into subtypes of cervical cancer like adenocarcinoma and squamous cell carcinoma the rate of misclassification is high due to know disagreement between the histological classifications cytologic morphology of the tumor and the quantitative data of the microarrays. For deterministic sub classification it is necessary to do more processing and research to correctly interpret the results of classification of tumors by molecular biology.

MAS-GEN is an intelligent system to help biologists and medical teams in the analysis of gene expression to understand the genetic details of disease, represents a significant improvement in the state of gene expression analysis. Like a multi-agent system MAS-GEN, provides a flexible tool, using coordinated and specific goal-directed agents that naturally allow decomposition of the complex problem in a single software system. Key advantages over using several different software applications are the time saved and error reduction in managing the process through different data format and reduced amount of user intervention.

For future work we propose implementing more learning and statistical methods to improve gene identification and tumor classification. We propose to create a method to combine the current presumptive results with validating qRT-PCR for selecting genes.

5. Conclusions

In MAS-GEN through the interaction of the agents we can contribute to giving solution of two present questions of genomic medicine: selecting a list of relevant genes and identification and classification of samples, applying many methods in different steps like an expert with the minimal intervention of the user. The advantage for the user of MAS-GEN is that he does not need to do himself all the steps for the analysis of the matrix going through different applications nor to know all the parameters and methods for pre-processing the data expression of genes. All this knowledge is part of the agents' expertise. The results generated by MAS-GEN about the identification of genes is a proposal of relevant genes based on the quantitative evaluation of gene expression levels; after that the user might apply biological methods to validate them like quantitative reverse-transcription polymerase chain reaction (qRT-PCR) and immunochemistry, in order to define marker genes. MAS-GEN is a tool for supporting the decisions.

The distribution in several specialized agents doing the tasks of gene expression analysis (pre-processing methods, data filtering, machine learning, and presentation and display of results) provides a versatile system that can be conveniently adapted to the rapidly changing area of bioinformatics.

The analysis of gene expression is feasible through multi-agent collaboration of operational agents (of data pre-processing, gene identification, classification of samples, and database management), and a single management agent assigns tasks and controls data flow. Operational agent can execute in parallel some tasks because the agents have sufficient independence.

Also, we achieved great flexibility with the implementation of the agents using Java for the platform and Clips in the use of decision rules. By keeping separated the machine learning technics and other methods of the agents' platform, we can modify, add or delete these components without affecting the operation, functionality or design of agents involved in the gene expression analysis. This is important in Bioinformatics field where, to avoid obsolescence, a system must be easy to adapt to frequently emerging new or improved procedures.

Multi-agent technology allows gathering several tasks into one software tool that can simplify, with the minimal user intervention, to automate the selection of relevant genes from large amount of microarray data, and classify tumor samples based on principles of molecular biology, supported by statistical and machine learning techniques and genetic information available on the Internet.

Acknowledgements

This paper is part of the research being carried out by Edna Márquez—to obtain her PhD in Posgrado en Ciencia e Ingeniería de la Computación at the Universidad Nacional Autónoma de México. It is supported by CONACYT, by PAPIIT-DGAPA UNAM under Grant IN-117612. Also the authors thank to Hospital General de México.

References

[1]   Tinker, A.V., Boussioutas, A. and Bowtell, D.D.L. (2006) The Challenges of Gene Expression Microarrays for the Study of Human Cancer. *Cancer Cell*, **9**, 333-339.

[2]   Merelli, E. and Luck, M. (2005) Agents in Bioinformatic. *Knowledge Engineering Review*, **20**, 117-125.

[3]   Merelli, E., Armano, G., Cannata, N., Corradini, F., d'Inverno, M., Doms, A., Lord, P., Martin, A., Milanesi, L., M öller, S., Schroeder, M. and Luck, M. (2006) Agents in Bioinformatics, Computational and Systems Biology. *Briefings in Bioinformatics*, **8**, 45-59.

[4]   Bryson, K., Luck, M., Joy, M. and Jones, D. (2000) Applying Agents to Bioinformatics in GeneWeaver. *Lecture Notes in Computer Science*, **1860**, 60-71. http://dx.doi.org/10.1007/978-3-540-45012-2_7

[5]   Lam, H.C., Garcia, M.V., Juneja, B., Fahrenkrug, S. and Boley, D. (2006) Gene Expression Analysis in Multi-Agent Environment. *International Transactions on Systems Science and Applications*, **1**.

[6]   Jin, L., Steiner, K., Schmidt, C. and Situ, G. (2005) A Multiagent Framework to Integrate and Visualize Gene Expression Information. *IEEE ICDM Workshop on MADW & MADM*, 1-7. http://www.eecis.udel.edu/~kamboj/pubs/kamboj.madw.05.pdf

[7]   Štiglic, G. and Kokol, P. (2004) Using Multi-Agent System for Gene Expression Classification. *Proceedings of the 26th Annual International Conference of the IEEE EMBS*, San Francisco, 1-5 September 2004, 2952-2955.

[8]   Wooldridge, M. (2002) An Introduction to Multiagent Systems. John Wiley, USA.

[9]   Laureano-Cruces, A.L., Ramírez-González, T., Sánchez-Guerrero, L. and Ramírez-Rodríguez, J. (2014) Multi-Agent System for Real Time Planning Using Collaborative Agents. *International Journal of Intelligence Science*, **4**, 91-103.

[10]   Laureano-Cruces, A.L. and Espinoza-Paredes, G. (2005) Behavioral Design to Model a Reactive Decision of an Expert in Geothermal Wells. *International Journal of Approximate Reasoning*, **39**, 1-28. http://dx.doi.org/10.1016/j.ijar.2004.08.002

[11]   Jennings, N. (2001) An Agent-Based Approach for Building Complex Software Systems. *Communications of the ACM*, **44**, 35-41. http://dx.doi.org/10.1145/367211.367250

[12]   Koutkias, V., Malousi, A. and Maglaveras, N. (2007) Engineering Agent-Mediated Integration of Bioinformatics Analysis Tools. *Multiagent and Grid Systems*, **3**, 245-258.

[13]   Kohonen, T. (1995) Self Organizing Maps. Springer, Berlin.

[14]   Espinosa, A., Alfaro, A., Roman-Basaure, E., Guardado-Estrada, M., Palma, Í., Serralde, C., *et al.* (2013) Mitosis Is a Source of Potential Markers for Screening and Survival and Therapeutic Targets in Cervical Cancer. *PLoS ONE*, **8**, e55975. http://dx.doi.org/10.1371/journal.pone.0055975

[15]   Karasavvas, K., Burger, A. and Baldock, R. (2004) Bioinformatics Integration and Agent Technology. *Journal of Biomedical Informatics*, **37**, 205-219. http://dx.doi.org/10.1016/j.jbi.2004.04.003

[16]   Clips (2014) http://clipsrules.sourceforge.net/

[17]   Gentleman, R., Carey, V., Huber, W., Irizarry, R. and Dudoit, S. (2005) Bioinformatics and Computational Biology Solutions Using R and Bioconductor. Springer. http://www.bioconductor.org/

[18]   Márquez, E., Savage, J., Espinosa, A., Berumen, J. and Lemaitre, C. (2008) Gene Expression Analysis for Tumor Classification Using Vector Quantization. *3rd IAPR International Conference on Pattern Recognition in Bioinformatics (PRIB 2008)*, Melbourne, 15-17 October 2008, 95-103.

[19]   National Center for Biotechnology Information (2014) http://www.ncbi.nlm.nih.gov/

[20]   DAVID Bioinformatics Resources (2014) http://david.abcc.ncifcrf.gov/

[21]   Luck, M. and d'Inverno, M. (2001) A Conceptual Framework for Agent Definition and Development. *The Computer Journal*, **44**, 1-20.

[22]   Sánchez-Guerrero, L., Laureano-Cruces, A.L., Mora-Torres, M., Ramírez-Rodríguez, J. and Silva-López, R. (2013) A Multi-Agent Intelligent Learning System: An Application with a Pedagogical Agent and Learning Objects. *Creative Education*, **4**, 181-190. http://www.scirp.org/journal/ce

[23]   Laureano-Cruces, A.L., Acevedo-Moreno, D.A., Mora-Torres, M. and Ramirez-Rodriguez, J. (2012) A Reactive Behavior Agent: Including Emotions for a Video Game. *Journal of Applied Research and Technology* (CCADET-UNAM), **10**, 651-672.

[24]   Sánchez-Guerrero, L., Laureano-Cruces, A.L., Mora-Torres, M. and Ramírez-Rodríguez, J. (2011) Multiagent Architecture for Errors Management in Content Organized in Learning Objects. *Proceedings of World Conference on E-Learning in Corporate, Government, Healthcare, and Higher Education* 2011, Hawai, 17-21 October 2011, 2462-2467. www.EdiTLib.org

[25]   Laureano-Cruces, A.L. and Verduga-Palencia, D.O. (2010) Simulación de un juego de futbol utilizando una arquitectura Multiagente-Reactiva. In Libro: Desarrollo Tecnológico. (Alfa-Omega), *XXIII Congreso Nacional y XI Congreso Internacional de Informática y Computación de la ANIEI*, Puerto Vallarta, 11-15 de octubre, 485-493.

[26]   Berman, J. (2004) Tumor Classification: Molecular Analysis Meets Aristotle. *BMC Cancer*, **4**, 10.

10

Extending Qualitative Probabilistic Network with Mutual Information Weights

Kun Yue[1], Feng Wang[2], Mujin Wei[1], Weiyi Liu[1]

[1]Department of Computer Science and Engineering, School of Information Science and Engineering, Yunnan University, Kunming, China
[2]Yunnan Computer Technology Application Key Lab, Kunming University of Science and Technology, Kunming, China
Email: kyue@ynu.edu.cn

Academic Editor: Prof. Zhongzhi Shi, Institute of Computing Technology, Chinese Academy of Sciences, China

Abstract

Bayesian network (BN) is a well-accepted framework for representing and inferring uncertain knowledge. As the qualitative abstraction of BN, qualitative probabilistic network (QPN) is introduced for probabilistic inferences in a qualitative way. With much higher efficiency of inferences, QPNs are more suitable for real-time applications than BNs. However, the high abstraction level brings some inference conflicts and tends to pose a major obstacle to their applications. In order to eliminate the inference conflicts of QPN, in this paper, we begin by extending the QPN by adding a mutual-information-based weight (MI weight) to each qualitative influence in the QPN. The extended QPN is called MI-QPN. After obtaining the MI weights from the corresponding BN, we discuss the symmetry, transitivity and composition properties of the qualitative influences. Then we extend the general inference algorithm to implement the conflict-free inferences of MI-QPN. The feasibility of our method is verified by the results of the experiment.

Keywords

Qualitative Probabilistic Network (QPN), Inference Conflict, Mutual Information, Influence Weight, Superposition

1. Introduction

Bayesian network (BN) is a well-accepted model to represent a set of random variables and their probabilistic relationships via a directed acyclic graph (DAG) [1] [2]. There is a conditional probability table (CPT) associated with each node to represent the quantitative relationships among the nodes. BN has been widely used in different aspects of intelligent applications including representation, prediction, reasoning, and so on [1] [3]. However, exact inference in an arbitrary BN is NP hard [4], and even the approximate inference is also very difficult [5]. As a result, BN's inferences are not very efficient, which is doomed to pose limits to BN-related applications, especially for real-time situations. Fortunately, as the qualitative abstraction of BN, QPN was proposed by Wellman [6] and can be appropriately used to remedy the above drawbacks of a BN. A QPN adopts a DAG to encode random variables and their relationships, which are not quantified by conditional probabilities, but are summarized by qualitative signs [7]. The most important thing is that there has been an efficient QPN inference (reasoning) algorithm, which is based on sign propagation and run in polynomial time [8].

However, the high abstraction level of QPN results in the problem that there is no information left to compare two different qualitative influences in a QPN. Thus, when a node receives two inconsistent signs from its two different neighbor nodes during inferences, it is hard to know which sign is more suitable for the node, so that the "? (*i.e.*, unknown)" sign is obtained as the result sign on the node. This means that there are inference conflicts generated on the node, which lead to less powerful expressiveness and inference capabilities than expected for real-world prediction and decision-making of uncertain knowledge in economics, health care, traffics, etc [9]-[16]. Worst of all, when the ambiguous results caused by inference conflicts are produced, they will be spread to most parts of the network with the reasoning algorithm going on.

To provide a conflict-free inference mechanism of QPN is paid much attention. Various approaches have been proposed from various perspectives. However, in some representative methods [9] [11] [13], the original sample data or threshold values are required or predefined when the influences are weighted quantitatively. This is not consistent with the BN-based applications that focus on probabilistic inferences taking as input BN without the original sample data. Furthermore, a BN is frequently defined by experts instead of learned from data. Even though the original data are available, the efficiency of the process of deriving influence weights is sensitive to the data size. Meanwhile, the uncertainty of the influence weight has not been well incorporated, and the propagation of influence weights lacks solid theoretical foundations during QPN inferences.

Therefore, in this paper we are to consider eliminating the inference conflicts of general QPNs and developing a conflict-free inference method. We derive the quantitative QPN by adding a weight to each qualitative influence from the corresponding BN, while sample data and threshold values are not required. The weight is adopted as the information to compare two different qualitative signs. Therefore, when a node in a general QPN faces an inference conflict, a trade-off will be incorporated to avoid the conflict based on the weights.

Mutual information (MI) is a quantity that measures the mutual dependence of the two random variables [17] [18]. As well, MI is widely applied to test the association degree among the BN nodes [19]-[21]. When node A receives two inconsistent signs from its two different neighbor nodes, say B and C, we can naturally think that the result sign on A is more dependent on the sign propagated from B than that from C, if the mutual information between A and B is larger than that between A and C. Based on the above idea, we adopt MI as the weight to quantify the degree of the mutual dependence between two nodes linked by a directed edge.

Generally speaking, the main contributions of this paper can be summarized as follows:

- We define the MI-based weight of a qualitative influence, called MI weight, and extend the traditional QPN by adding a MI weight to each qualitative influence. We call the extended QPN as MI-QPN.
- We propose an efficient algorithm to derive MI weights from the conditional probability tables and prior probability distributions in the corresponding BN instead of the sample data.
- We discuss the symmetry, transitivity and composition properties of qualitative influences in the MI-QPN. Then, we extend the general QPN's inference algorithm to achieve conflict-free inferences with the MI-QPN.
- We give preliminary experiments to verify the feasibility and correctness of our method.

2. Related Work

BN has been successfully established as a framework to describe, manage uncertainty using the probabilistic graphical approach [2] [3]. As the qualitative abstraction of BN, QPN [6] was proposed by Wellman and widely used in decision making, industrial control, forecasting, and so on [22]-[24]. The methods to construct QPNs mainly include deriving QPNs from the corresponding existing BNs [15] or giving QPNs by the domain experts. As for the QPN's inference, an efficient algorithm was proposed by Druzdzel *et al.* [8]. The inference conflict has become a common problem for QPNs and how to resolve the inference conflicts is the subject that was paid much attention in recent years. Various methods were proposed from various perspectives.

Lv *et al.* [9] proposed the ambiguity reduction method by associating a qualitative mutual information weight to each qualitative influence in the QPN, but the weight can only be obtained from the given or generated sample data. This is not always feasible, since the BN may be not learned from data, or the sample data cannot be available. Parsons [10] introduced the concept of categorical influence, which is either an influence that serves to increase a probability to 1 or an influence that decreases a probability to 0, regardless of any other influences. By this approach, only some of the inference conflicts can be resolved.

Renooij *et al.* [11] [15] proposed two methods to solve the inference conflicts by using both kappas values and pivots to zoom upon inferences. The kappas value based method distinguishes the strong and weak influences by the interval values that do not have solid theoretical basis for interval value propagation during QPN inferences. Renooij *et al.* [12] presented an enhanced QPN that differs from a regular QPN to distinguish between strong and weak influences. This method is only suitable for the binary-variable situation. A threshold value is required in these methods except that exploits context-specific information. Renooij *et al.* [13] proposed SQPN (semi-QPN) by associating a probability interval value with each qualitative influence to quantify the qualitative influences. De Campos *et al.* [25] discussed the complexity of inferences in polytree-shaped SQPNs. Renooij *et al.* [14] extended QPNs by providing the inclusion of context-specific information about influences and showed that exploiting this information upon inference had the ability to forestall unnecessarily weak results. By this method, a threshold value should be given to distinguish the strong and weak influences.

We extended QPN to solve inference conflicts by adding the weights to qualitative influences based on the rough set theory and interval probability theory respectively in [16] and [26]. By the method in [16], the dependency degree was computed based on the threshold value, but the corresponding sample data was required to obtain the weights. By the method in [26], the interval-probability weights were derived from the corresponding BN's CPT, but the calculation of interval probability during inferences led to approximate results.

3. Preliminaries and Problem Statement

3.1. The Concept of QPN

A QPN has the same graphical structure as the corresponding BN, also represented by a DAG. In a QPN, each node accords with a random variable, and the influence between each pair of the nodes can only be one of the signs including "+", "−", "?" and "0", where "+" ("−") means the probability of a higher (lower) value for the corresponding variable increases, sign "?" denotes the unknown influence by giving an evidence and "0" represents initial state of the variable without observations. Each edge with a qualitative sign means the qualitative influence between two corresponding variables. The definition of the qualitative influence [6] is given as follows.

Definition 3.1 We say that A positively influences C, written $S^+(A,C)$, if for all values $a_1 > a_2$, c_0 and x, which is the set of all of $C's$ parents other than A, $P(C > c_0|a_1 x) \geq P(C > c_0|a_2 x)$.

This definition means the probability of a higher value of C is increased when given a higher value of A, regardless of any other direct influences on C. A negative qualitative influence S^- and a zero qualitative influence S^0 are defined analogously, by replacing $\geq$ in the above formula by $\leq$ and $=$ respectively. If the qualitative influence between A and C does not belong to the above three kinds, written $S^?(A,C)$.

Example 3.1 Based on **Definition 3.1** and from the BN shown in **Figure 1**, we derive a QPN shown in **Figure 2**.

3.2. QPN Inference and Inference Conflicts

It is known that the qualitative influence of a QPN exhibits various useful properties [6]. The *symmetry* prop-

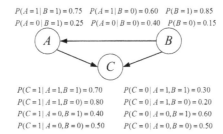

$$P(A=1|B=1)=0.75 \quad P(A=1|B=0)=0.60 \quad P(B=1)=0.85$$
$$P(A=0|B=1)=0.25 \quad P(A=0|B=0)=0.40 \quad P(B=0)=0.15$$

$$P(C=1|A=1,B=1)=0.70 \quad P(C=0|A=1,B=1)=0.30$$
$$P(C=1|A=1,B=0)=0.80 \quad P(C=0|A=1,B=0)=0.20$$
$$P(C=1|A=0,B=1)=0.40 \quad P(C=0|A=0,B=1)=0.60$$
$$P(C=1|A=0,B=0)=0.50 \quad P(C=0|A=0,B=0)=0.50$$

Figure 1. An simple BN.

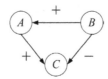

Figure 2. QPN derived from the BN in **Figure 1**.

erty expresses if there is $S^\delta(A,B)$ in a QPN, then we have $S^\delta(B,A)$. The *transitivity* property can be used to combine qualitative influences along a trail without a head-to-head node into a single influence with the $\otimes$-operator. The *composition* property asserts that multiple qualitative influences between two nodes along parallel chains combine into a single influence with the $\oplus$-operator. The ambiguous results ("?") maybe appear by $\oplus$-operator during inference, and then will be propagated to other nodes by $\otimes$-operator.

Building on these three properties and operators, Druzdzel *et al.* proposed an efficient inference algorithm based on sign propagation [8]. The algorithm traces the effect of observing a value for one node on the other nodes by message-passing between neighbors. When the evidences are given to the network, each node receiving a message updates its sign and subsequently sends a message to each (induced) neighbor node that is independent of the observed node. The sign propagation reach all the nodes that are not d-separated with the evidence nodes. During the process of sign propagation, each node has changed its sign at most twice.

The inference conflicts take place when a node receives two different kinds of qualitative signs ("+" and "−"). In fact, the weights of qualitative influences in a QPN are not always equivalent. Thus, in this paper, we will add a weight to each qualitative influence so that a node facing a conflict will take a sign ("+" or "−") instead of "?" by comparing the corresponding weights.

4. Constructing MI-QPN

4.1. Concepts of Mutual Information

It is well known that information entropy quantifies the information contained in a message and is a measure of the uncertainty associated with a random variable. Now we introduce relevant definition [17] and properties [1].

Definition 4.1 The information entropy H of a discrete random variable X with possible values $\{x_1, x_2, \cdots, x_n\}$ is

$$H(X) = -\sum_{i=1}^{n} P(X = x_i)\log_2 P(X = x_i) \tag{1}$$

Definition 4.2 The conditional information entropy of Y given X is

$$H(Y|X) = -\sum_{i=1}^{I}\sum_{j=1}^{J} P(X = x_i)P(Y = y_i|X = x_i)\log_2 P(Y = y_i|X = x_i) \tag{2}$$

where X and Y are two discrete random variables, $x_i \in \{x_1, \cdots, x_I\}$, $y_i \in \{y_1, \cdots, y_J\}$ and I (or J) denotes the total number of possible values of X (or Y).

We know $H(X)$ is regarded as a measure of uncertainty about a random variable X, and $H(X|Y)$ denotes the amount of uncertainty remaining about X when Y is known. The mutual information is just defined as the difference between $H(X)$ and $H(X|Y)$, which is to denote the amount of uncertainty in X that is removed by knowing Y.

Definition 4.3 The mutual information of two discrete random variables X and Y is defined as

$$I(X,Y) = H(Y) - H(Y|X) \tag{3}$$

4.2. Defining MI-QPN

It is known that the dependency quantity X on Y is the same with that of Y on X. However, the same dependency degree may have different influences on X and Y respectively. This means that the weight of $S^\delta(X,Y)$ does not always equal that of $S^\delta(Y,X)$, although we always have $I(X,Y) = I(Y,X)$. Intuitively, for any node Y with two different neighbor nodes X and Z, if the degree of the mutual dependence between Y and X is greater than that between Y and Z, then the weight of $S^\delta(X,Y)$ should be greater than that of $S^{\delta}(Z,Y)$. Consequently, we know the weights of qualitative influences should satisfy the following properties: 1) $MI(X \rightarrow Y)$ does not always equal $MI(Y \rightarrow X)$; 2) For any X, Y and Z,

$$I(X,Y) > (=) I(Z,Y) \Leftrightarrow MI(X \rightarrow Y) > (=) MI(Z \rightarrow Y).$$

Now, we define the weight of a quantitative influence based on a normalized variant of the mutual information. The weight is called MI weight that satisfies the above properties.

Definition 4.4 The MI weight of a qualitative influence $S^{\delta}(X,Y)$ is defined as

$$MI(X \rightarrow Y) = \begin{cases} 0, & I(X,Y) = 0; \\ \dfrac{I(X,Y)}{H(Y)}, & I(X,Y) > 0. \end{cases} \tag{4}$$

From the above definition, we know that the MI weight further satisfies the third property: 3) $MI(X \rightarrow Y) \in [0,1]$. Especially, $MI(X \rightarrow Y) = 1$ when X depends on Y completely, and $MI(X \rightarrow Y) = 0$ when X and Y are independent.

Then, we consider the concerned computation in each of the three properties of the MI weight as follows:

- For the first property, if $I(X,Y) = I(Y,X) = 0$, we have $MI(X \rightarrow Y) = MI(Y \rightarrow X)$. If $I(X,Y) = I(Y,X) \neq 0$ and $H(X) \neq H(Y)$, we know $H(X) \neq 0$ and $H(Y) \neq 0$. Thus, we have $MI(X \rightarrow Y) \neq MI(Y \rightarrow X)$.

- For the second property, if $I(X,Y) > I(Z,Y)$, we have $I(X,Y) > 0$, since $I(Z,Y) \geq 0$. Then, we have

$$MI(X \rightarrow Y) = I(X,Y)/H(Y), \quad MI(Z \rightarrow Y) = I(Z,Y)/H(Y) \tag{5}$$

since if $I(Z,Y) = 0$, otherwise $MI(Z \rightarrow Y) = 0$. Then, we have

$$MI(X \rightarrow Y) - MI(Z \rightarrow Y) = (I(X,Y) - I(Z,Y))/H(Y) > 0, \quad MI(X \rightarrow Y) > MI(Z \rightarrow Y) \tag{6}$$

If $I(X,Y) = I(Z,Y) = 0$, then we have

$$MI(X \rightarrow Y) - MI(X \rightarrow Y) = 0 \tag{7}$$

If $I(X,Y) = I(Z,Y) \neq 0$, we have $MI(X \rightarrow Y) = MI(Z \rightarrow Y)$ since

$$MI(X \rightarrow Y) - MI(Z \rightarrow Y) = (I(X,Y) - I(Z,Y))/H(Y) = 0 \tag{8}$$

Therefore, the second property can be derived from **Definition 4.4**.

- For the third property, if $I(X,Y) = 0$, we have

$$MI(X \rightarrow Y) = 0 \tag{9}$$

If $I(X,Y) > 0$, we have

$$MI(X \rightarrow Y) = I(X,Y)/H(Y) = (H(Y) - H(Y|X))/(H(Y)) = 1 - H(Y|X)/H(Y) \tag{10}$$

Thus, we have $I(X,Y) = H(Y) - H(Y|X) \geq 0$, $H(Y) \geq 0$ and $H(Y|X) \geq 0$, and if $H(Y) \neq 0$, we have

$$0 \leq H(Y|X)/H(Y) \leq 1 \tag{11}$$

By Formulae (9), (10) and (11), we can obtain $0 \leq MI(X \rightarrow Y) \leq 1$.

Definition 4.5 If we have $S^{\delta}(A,B)$, we denote the qualitative influence with an MI weight as $S_{MI(B \rightarrow A)}^{\sigma}(A,B)$, where $\delta \in \{+,-,?,0\}$.

By the symmetry property of the qualitative influence, we know $S^{\delta}(A,B)$ implies $S^{\delta}(B,A)$. Based on **Definition 4.5**, we know $S_{MI(B \rightarrow A)}^{\sigma}(B,A)$. Therefore, two MI weights are added to each QPN edge to represent bidirectional qualitative influences with the MI weights between the corresponding two nodes.

Definition 4.6 MI-QPN is a DAG $G = (V, Q^w)$, where V is a set of variables (nodes) in the graph, and Q^w is a set of qualitative relations and each qualitative influence in Q^w is associated with a MI weight.

4.3. Deriving MI Weights from BN

We can obtain a prior probability distribution from each orphans node and a CPT from each non-orphans one taking as input the BN directly. If B_0 is a orphans node, we denote the prior probability distribution as set $PT(B_0) = \{P(B_0 = s_0) | 1 \le s_0 \le S_0\}$. Otherwise, we denote the CPT of node B_0 with parents $B_1, \cdots, B_n$ as the probability set $CT(B_0 | B_1, \cdots, B_n) = \{P(B_0 = s_0 | B_1 = s_1, \cdots, B_n = s_n) | 1 \le i \le n, 1 \le s_i \le S_i, 1 \le s_0 \le S_0\}$, where S_i denotes the total number of possible states of B_i, and s_i means the s_i-th state of B_i. It is worth noting that $B_1, \cdots, B_n$ are independent given the value s_0 of their child node B_0.

In order to derive the MI weights between B_0 and its parent B_i $(1 \le i \le n)$, it is necessary to obtain the conditional probability sets associated with B_0 and B_i, denoted as

$$CT(B_0 | B_i) = \{P(B_0 = s_0 | B_i = s_i) | 1 \le s_i \le S_i, 1 \le s_0 \le S_0\}.$$

It is also necessary to compute the prior probability distribution of B_0 and B_i, denoted as

$PT(B_0) = \{P(B_0 = s_0) | 1 \le s_0 \le S_0\}$, $PT(B_i) = \{P(B_i = s_i) | 1 \le s_i \le S_i\}$. Then, we can use $CT(B_0 | B_i)$, $PT(B_0)$ and $PT(B_i)$ to compute the MI weights of the qualitative influences associated with B_0 and B_i according to **Definition 4.4**. Let s_i and S_i be the s_i-th state and the total number of possible states of random variable B_i $(0 \le i \le n)$, respectively, $s_i \in \{1, \cdots, S_i\}$. Let $D_i = \{1, \cdots, S_i\}$, if $P(B_1 = s_1, \cdots, B_n = s_n) > 0$, for all s_i and for any $m \in \{1, \cdots, n\}$, we have

$$P(B_0 = s_0 | B_1 = s_1, \cdots, B_m = s_m) = \sum_{s_{m+1}=1}^{S_{m+1}} \sum_{s_{m+2}=1}^{S_{m+2}} \cdots \sum_{s_n=1}^{S_n} P(B_0 = s_0 | B_1 = s_1, \cdots, B_m = s_m) \prod_{j=m+1}^{n} P(B_j = s_j)$$

where $P(B_0 = s_0 | B_1 = s_1, \cdots, B_m = s_m)$ denotes the probability of B_0 taking the s_0-th state, given B_i taking the s_i-th state for each i $(i \in \{1, \cdots, m\})$, i.e., $P(B_0 = s_0 | B_1 = s_1 \cap \cdots \cap B_m = s_m)$.

It can be seen that we need traverse the CPT once to derive the conditional probability set associated with one node and one of its parents. With the CPTs and the prior probability distributions of a BN, we propose **Algorithm 1** to compute the MI weights for each qualitative influence in the MI-QPN.

As the basic operation in **Algorithm 1**, the multiplication operation for computing relevant probabilities in *get conditional probability* is the most time-consuming operation. Let m and n be the number of non-orphans nodes and the maximal in-degree of these nodes respectively. For convenience, we suppose the number of each node's possible values, denoted as s, is the same as that in the corresponding BN. Thus, the total number of rows of each orphans node's CPT is s^{m+1}. For each orphans node, the multiplication operation can be expressed for $f(m,s) = 2 * f(m/s) + s^{m+1}$ times, which leads to the time complexity of **Algorithm 1** in the worst case is $n * f(m,s) < \log 2^{(m)} * s^{m+1} * n$. This means that to compute the MI weights for a QPN, we need scan each conditional probability table in the relevant BN for $\log_2 m$ times at most.

Example 4.3 We consider the MI weights for the QPN in **Figure 2**. By **Algorithm 1**, we can obtain the corresponding MI-QPN shown in **Figure 3**.

5. Conflict-Free Inference with the MI-QPN

It is known that $S^\delta(A, B)$ implies $S^\delta(B, A)$ according to the *symmetry* property. Then, we know there exist $S^\delta_{MI(B,A)}(B, A)$ in the MI-QPN by **Definition 4.4**, since $S^\delta(B, A)$ exists in the corresponding QPN. We can obtain

$$S^\delta_{MI(A \to B)}(A, B) \Rightarrow S^\delta_{MI(B \to A)}(B, A) \tag{12}$$

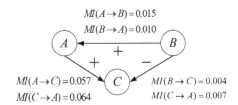

Figure 3. MI-QPN.

Algorithm 1. Deriving MI weights from a BN.

Input: A BN
Output: All the MI weights of the MI-QPN
Symbol Description:

- B_0: an orphans node in a BN or a non-orphans one with parents $B_1, \cdots, B_n$

- $TP(B_k, \cdots, B_m) = \{ PT(B_k), \cdots, PT(B_m) \}$: the prior probability distribution set of nodes $B_k, \cdots, B_m$

- $CT(B_0 | B_k, \cdots, B_m) = \{ P(B_0 = s_0 | B_k = s_k, \cdots, B_m = s_m) | 1 \le s_0 \le S_0, k \le i \le m, 1 \le s_i \le S_i \}$: the CPT of B_0 with some of its parents $B_k, \cdots, B_m$

- $TC(B_0 | B_k, \cdots, B_m) = \{ CT(B_0 | B_k), \cdots, CT(B_0 | B_m) \}$: the set of conditional probability sets

Steps:
1. Obtain a topological sequence of all the nodes in the BN
2. **for** each node B_0 in the topological sequence **do**
3. if B_0 is a non-orphans node **then**
4. $CT(B_0|B_1,...,B_n) \leftarrow$ *get conditional probability* $(B_0, TP(B_1, ..., B_n), CT(B_0|B_1, ..., B_n))$
5. Compute $PT(B_0)$ with $TC(B_0|B_1)$ and $PT(B_1)$
6. **for** $i \leftarrow 1$ to n **do**
7. Compute $MI(B_0 \rightarrow B_i)$ and $MI(B_i \rightarrow B_0)$ with $TP(B_0|B_1,...,B_n)$ and $CT(B_0|B_1,..., B_n)$.
8. **end for**
9. **end if**
10. **end for**
Get conditional probability $(B_0, TP(B_k,...,B_m), CT(B_0|B_1, ..., B_n))$
1. if $m < n$ **then**
2. $mid \leftarrow \lceil m-k/2 \rceil$
3. $CT(B_0|B_k, ..., B_{mid}) \leftarrow \{ P(B_0|B_k = s_k, ..., B_{mid} = s_{mid}) | 1 \le s_0 \le S_0, k \le i \le mid, 1 \le s_i \le S_i \}$
4. $CT(B_0|B_{mid+1}, ..., B_m) \leftarrow \{ P(B_0|B_{mid+1} = s_{mid+1}, ..., B_n = s_m) | 1 \le s_0 \le S_0, mid+1 \le i \le n, 1 \le s_i \le S_i \}$
5. $TC(B_0|B_k, ..., B_{mid}) \leftarrow$ *get conditional probability*$(B_0, TP(B_k, ..., B_{mid}), CT(B_0|B_1, ..., B_{mid}))$
6. $TC(B_0|B_{mid+1}, ..., B_m) \leftarrow$ *get conditional probability*$(B_0, TP(B_{mid+1}, ..., B_{mid}), CT(B_0|B_{mid+1}, ..., B_m))$
7. **return** $TC(B_0|B_k, ..., B_{mid}) \cup TC(B_0|B_{mid+1}, ..., B_m)$
8. **end if**
9. **return** $CT(B_0|B_k)$

In order to address the *transitivity* property, we consider the MI-QPN fragment in **Figure 4**, where X denotes the predecessors of B other than A, and Y represents the predecessors of C other than B. From this network, we have $S_{MI(A \rightarrow B)}^{\delta_1}(A,B)$ and $S_{MI(B \rightarrow C)}^{\delta_2}(B,C)$. Based on $S_{MI(A \rightarrow B)}^{\delta_1}(A,B)$ and $S_{MI(B \rightarrow C)}^{\delta_2}(B,C)$, we are to derive the qualitative influence of A on C with an MI weight, denoted as $S_{MI(A \rightarrow C)}^{\delta}(A,C)$.

First, based on QPN's *transitivity* property, we can obtain $\delta = \delta_1 \otimes \delta_2$. Then, we derive the MI weight of qualitative influence A on C, $MI(A \rightarrow C)$. The transitivity property is denoted as

$$S_{MI(A \rightarrow B)}^{\delta_1}(A,B) \& S_{MI(B \rightarrow C)}^{\delta_2}(B,C) \Rightarrow S_{MI(A \rightarrow C) = MI(A \rightarrow B) * MI(B \rightarrow C)}^{\delta = \delta_1 \otimes \delta_2}(A,C) \tag{13}$$

In order to discuss the *composition* property, we consider the MI-QPN fragment in **Figure 5**, where X denotes the predecessors of C other than A and B. From the MI-QPN, we have $S_{MI(A \rightarrow C)}^{\delta_1}(A,C)$ and $S_{MI(B \rightarrow C)}^{\delta_2}(B,C)$. Then, we are to derive the combination influence of $S_{MI(A \rightarrow C)}^{\delta_1}(A,C)$ and $S_{MI(B \rightarrow C)}^{\delta_2}(B,C)$, denoted as

$$S_{MI(X \rightarrow C)}^{\delta}(X,C) = S_{MI(A \rightarrow C)}^{\delta_1}(A,C) \vee S_{MI(B \rightarrow C)}^{\delta_2}(B,C) \tag{14}$$

where $X = AB$, $MI(A \rightarrow C)$ denotes the composition weight and "$\vee$" is the composition operator.

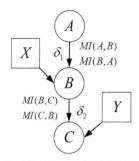

Figure 4. MI-QPN fragment.

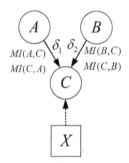

Figure 5. MI-QPN MI-QPN fragment.

Intuitively, the composition operator "∨" ought to satisfy the following properties: 1) The composition weight belongs to [0, 1]; 2) The composition operation is commutative; 3) The composition operation is associative; 4) Combining two influences with the same qualitative signs (e.g., two "+" signs or two "−" signs) will result in an influence with a greater MI weight; 5) Combining two influences with different qualitative signs will result in an influence dependent on but less than the larger one. Inspired by the evidence theory and the basic idea of evidence combination [27], we define the composition operator "∨" based on evidence superposition.

Definition 5.1 $S^{\delta}_{MI(X \to C)}(X,C) = S^{\delta_1}_{MI(A \to C)}(A,C) \vee S^{\delta_2}_{MI(B \to C)}(B,C)$, defined as follows:

- if $\delta_1 = \delta_2$, then

$$\delta = \delta_1 \quad \text{and} \quad MI(X \to C) = MI(A \to C) + MI(B \to C) - MI(A \to C) * MI(B \to C) \quad (15)$$

- if $\delta_1 \neq \delta_2$ and $MI(A \to C) \geq MI(B \to C)$, then

$$\delta = \delta_2 \quad \text{and} \quad MI(X \to C) = MI(A \to C) - MI(B \to C) + MI(A \to C) * MI(B \to C) \quad (16)$$

- if $\delta_1 \neq \delta_2$ and $MI(A \to C) < MI(B \to C)$, then

$$\delta = \delta_2 \quad \text{and} \quad MI(X \to C) = MI(B \to C) - MI(A \to C) + MI(A \to C) * MI(B \to C) \quad (17)$$

- if $\delta_1 \neq \delta_2$ and $MI(A \to C) = MI(B \to C)$, then

$$\delta = \delta_1 \oplus \delta_2 \quad \text{and} \quad MI(X \to C) = MI(A \to C) \quad (18)$$

Based the above properties, we give **Algorithm 2** for conflict-free inferences with the MI-QPN.

Now, we discuss the time complexity of **Algorithm 2** for MI-QPN inferences. First, whether a node will be visited is determined by its node sign whose changes are specified in QPN's general inference algorithm [8], while the influence weights are just used to decide the node sign during inferences. Second, **Algorithm 2** is the same as the general QPN's inference algorithm if there does not exist "?" during inferences [8]. However, **Algorithm 2** can be used to avoid the "?" results as possible by means of weighting influences quantitatively, where each time of weight computation w.r.t. the composition property can be fuelled by Step 5 in Merge-Sign in $O(1)$ time. Therefore, the time complexity of **Algorithm 2** will be the same as that for the general QPN's inferences.

Algorithm 2. Conflict-free inference with an MI-QPN.

Input: an MI-QPN MQ
Output: Sign of the influence of evidence node e on each node in MQ
Steps:
1. **for** each node $n \in MQ$ **do**
2. $sign[n] \leftarrow 0$, $MIweight[n] \leftarrow 0$, Propagate-Sign($\phi, e, e, sign, 1$)
3. **end for**
Propagate-Sign(*trail, from, to, msgsign, msgMIweight*)
1. Merge-Sign (*tosign, toMIweight, msgsign, msgMIweight*)
2. $sign[to] \leftarrow tosign$, $MIweight[to] \leftarrow toMIweight$, $trail \leftarrow trail \cup \{to\}$
3. **for** each (induced) neighbor of *to* **do**
4. $linksign \leftarrow$ sign of influence between *to* and *n*
5. $msgsign \leftarrow linksign \otimes sign[to]$
6. $msgMIweight \leftarrow MIweight[to] * MI(to \rightarrow n)$
7. Merge-Sign($nsign \leftarrow sign[n]$, $nMIweight \leftarrow MIweight[n]$, *msgsign, msgMIweight*)
8. **if** $n \notin trail$ and $sign[n] \neq nsign$ **then**
9. Propagate-Sign(*trail, to, n, msgsign, msgMIweight*)
10. **end if**
11. **end for**
Merge-Sign(*tosign, toMIweight, msgsign, msgMIweight*)
/**tosign* and *toMIweight* denotes both input parameters and return values*/
1. **if** $tosign \neq msgsign$ **then**
2. **if** $toMIweight \geq msgMIweight$ **then**
3. $toMIweight \leftarrow toMIweight - msgMIweight + toMIweight * msgMIweight$
4. **else if** $toMIweight < msgMIweight$ **then**
5. $tosign \leftarrow msgsign$, $toMIweight \leftarrow msgMIweight - toMIweight + toMIweight * msgMIweight$
6. **else**
7. $tosign \leftarrow tosign \oplus msgsign$
8. **end if**
9. **else**
10. $toMIweight \leftarrow msgMIweight + toMIweight - toMIweight * msgMIweight$
11. **end if**

---

6. Experimental Results

To test the performance of our method in this paper, we implemented our algorithms for constructing and inferring MI-QPN. We take BN's inference results obtained from Netica [28] as the criteria to decide whether the increase (or decrease) trends of the nodes indicated by the inference results of the corresponding MI-QPN are correct.

It is well known that Wet-Grass network is a classic BN for whether the *Our Grass* is wet, related to *Our Wall*, *Rain*, *Our Sprinkler* and *Neighbor's Grass* status, containing 5 binary variables and 6 edges [2] [28]. From the Wet-Grass BN, we know the qualitative influences between *node Rain* and *Neighbor's Grass* and the ones between *Rain* and *Our Grass* are the same. To illustrate our methods and show the results straightforwardly, we modify the knowledge in the network by removing node *Neighbor's Grass* and the corresponding edge, which will not affect the rest part of the original network and we denote the possible values of the nodes *wet*, *was on*, *rained* as 1, and *dry*, *was off*, *didn't rain* as 0. Moreover, we rename *Our Wall* as *Wall* or *W*, *Our Grass* as *Grass* or *G* and *Our Sprinkler* as *Sprinkler* or *S* for short. Then, the modified network is shown in **Figure 6**.

First, we derive the corresponding QPN and MI-QPN shown in **Figure 7** and **Figure 8** respectively. Then, we compare the inference results of the QPN and those of the MI-QPN to verify the feasibility of our algorithms. By using the general QPN's inference algorithm [8] and our inference algorithm for an MI-QPN, we take each node in the QPN and the MI-QPN as evidence and record the inference results of other nodes. The comparisons are shown in **Table 1**, from which we can see all possible inference conflicts have been eliminated in the MI-QPN.

Then, we compare the inference results on the modified Wet-Grass BN and those on the derived MI-QPN. We take each node of the BN as evidence, and then record the inference results of other nodes shown in **Table 2**, where E-Node and E-Sign denotes the evidence and corresponding sign respectively. The E-sign $0 \rightarrow 1$ represents that the state of the evidence node changes from 0 to 1, indicating that the probability of state 1 is changed from 0 to 1. If a node in the MI-QPN takes sign "+" ("−") as the final inference result and the increase (decrease) of the probability of state 1 of the corresponding node in the BN, we can conclude that the inference result is correct.

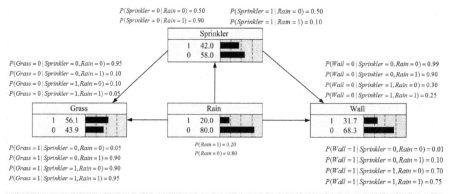

Figure 6. The modified Wet-Grass BN.

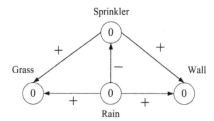

Figure 7. Wet-Grass QPN.

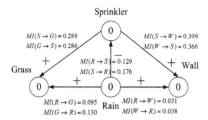

Figure 8. Wet-Grass MI-QPN.

Table 1. Comparisons of inference results between QPN and MI-QPN.

Evidence		QPN				MI-QPN			
Node	Sign	Rain	Sprinkler	Grass	Wall	Rain	Sprinkler	Grass	Wall
Rain	+	+	−	?	?	+	−	+	−
Sprinkler	+	−	+	?	?	−	+	+	+
Grass	+	?	?	+	?	+	+	+	+
Wall	+	?	?	?	+	+	−	+	+

Table 2. Comparisons of inference results between the modified BN and the derived MI-QPN.

	E-Node	E-Sign	Rain	Sprinkler	Grass	Wall
BN	Rain	0 → 1	0 → 1	0.5 → 0.10	0.475 → 0.905	0.355 → 0.165
	Sprinkler	0 → 1	0.31 → 0.0476	0 → 1	0.314 → 0.902	0.0379 → 0.702
	Grass	0 → 1	0.0433 → 0.323	0.0934 → 0.676	0 → 1	0.0782 → 0.504
	Wall	0 → 1	0.245 → 0.104	0.183 → 0.931	0.408 → 0.892	0 → 1
MI-QPN	Rain	+	+	−	+	−
	Sprinkler	+	−	+	+	+
	Grass	+	+	+	+	+
	Wall	+	−	+	+	+

7. Conclusions and Future Work

In this paper, we introduced mutual-information based weights (MI weights) to qualitative influences in QPNs to resolve conflicts during the inferences. We first defined the MI weights based on mutual information and MI-QPN by extending the traditional QPN. Then, we proposed the method to derive the MI weights for the MI-QPN from the corresponding BN without sample data or threshold values. By theoretic analysis, we know the method for deriving MI weights is effective. Furthermore, we discussed the symmetry, transitivity and composition properties in the MI-QPN, and extended the general influence algorithm to implement the conflict-free inferences of MI-QPN. The feasibility of our method was verified by the results of the preliminary experiment.

Our work in this paper also leaves open some other interesting research issues. We are to further consider adding the MI weights to the qualitative synergies and discussing the method to resolve the inference conflicts caused by two inconsistent signs with the same MI weight. As well, we will further resolve the conflicts that take place during the fusion or integration of multiple QPNs by adding the MI weights to the qualitative influences in the QPNs. These are exactly our future work.

Acknowledgements

This work was supported by the National Natural Science Foundation of China (61472345), the Natural Science Foundation of Yunnan Province (2014FA023, 2013FA013), the Yunnan Provincial Foundation for Leaders of Disciplines in Science and Technology (2012HB004), and the Program for Innovative Research Team in Yunnan University (XT412011).

References

[1]   Liu, W.Y., Li, W.H. and Yue, K. (2007) Intelligent Data Analysis. Science Press, Beijing.

[2]   Pearl, J. (1988) Probabilistic Reasoning in Intelligent Systems: Network of Plausible Inference. Morgan Kaufmann, San Mateo.

[3]   Li, W.H., Liu, W.Y. and Yue, K. (2008) Recovering the Global Structure from Multiple Local Bayesian Networks. *International Journal on Artificial Intelligence Tools*, **17**, 1067-1088. http://dx.doi.org/10.1142/S0218213008004308

[4]   Cooper, G.F. (1990) The Computational Complexity of Probabilistic Inference Using Bayesian Belief Networks. *Artificial Intelligence*, **42**, 393-405. http://dx.doi.org/10.1016/0004-3702(90)90060-D

[5]   Dagum, P. and Luby, M. (1993) Approximating Probabilistic Inference in Bayesian Belief Networks Is NP-Hard. *Artificial Intelligence*, **60**, 141-153. http://dx.doi.org/10.1016/0004-3702(93)90036-B

[6]   Wellman, M.P. (1990) Fundamental Concepts of Qualitative Probabilistic Networks. *Artificial Intelligence*, **44**, 257-303. http://dx.doi.org/10.1016/0004-3702(90)90026-V

[7]   Bolt, J.H., Renooij, S. and Van der Gaag, L.C. (2003) Upgrading Ambiguous Signs in QPNs. *Proceedings of the 19th Conference in Uncertainty in Artificial Intelligence*, Acapulco, 7-10 August 2003, 73-80.

[8]   Druzdzel, M.J. and Henrion, M. (1993) Efficient Reasoning in Qualitative Probabilistic Networks. *Proceedings of the 11th National Conference on Artificial Intelligence*, Washington DC, 11-15 July 1993, 548-553.

[9]   Lv, Y.L. and Liao, S.Z. (2011) Ambiguity Reduction Based on Qualitative Mutual Information in Qualitative Probabilistic Networks. *Pattern Recognition and Artificial Intelligence*, **24**, 123-129.

[10] Parsons, S. (1995) Refining Reasoning in Qualitative Probabilistic Networks. *Proceedings of the 11th Conference on Uncertainty in Artificial Intelligence*, Montreal, 18-20 August 1995, 427-434.

[11] Renooij, S., Parsons, S. and Pardieck, P. (2003) Using Kappas as Indicators of Strength in Qualitative Probabilistic Networks. *Proceedings of European Conferences on Symbolic and Quantitative Approaches to Reasoning with Uncertainty*, Aalborg, 2-5 July 2003, 87-99.

[12] Renooij, S. and Van der Gaag, L.C. (1999) Enhancing QPNs for Trade-Off Resolution. *Proceedings of the 15th Conference on Uncertainty in Artificial Intelligence*, Stockholm, 30 July-1 August 1999, 559-566.

[13] Renooij, S., Van der Gaag, L.C. and Parsons, S. (2002) Context-Specific Sign-Propagation in Qualitative Probabilistic Networks. *Artificial Intelligence*, **140**, 207-230. http://dx.doi.org/10.1016/S0004-3702(02)00247-3

[14] Renooij, S., Van der Gaag, L.C., Parsons, S. and Green, S. (2000) Pivotal Pruning of Trade-Off in QPNs. *Proceedings of the 16th Conference in Uncertainty in Artificial Intelligence*, Stanford, 30 June-3 July 2000, 515-522.

[15] Renooij, S. and Van der Gaag, L.C. (2002) From Qualitative to Quantitative Probabilistic Network. *Proceedings of the 18th Conference on Uncertainty in Artificial Intelligence*, Edmonton, 1-4 August 2002, 422-429.

[16] Yue, K., Yao, Y., Li, J. and Liu, W.Y. (2010) Qualitative Probabilistic Networks with Reduced Ambiguities. *Applied Intelligence*, **33**, 159-178. http://dx.doi.org/10.1007/s10489-008-0156-5

[17] Cover, T.M. and Thomas, J.A. (1993) Elements of Information Theory. John Wiley & Sons, Inc., Hoboken.

[18] Shannon, C.E. and Weaver, W. (1949) The Mathematical Theory of Communication. University of Illinois Press, Champaign.

[19] Chen, X.W., Anantha, G. and Lin, X.T. (2008) Improving Bayesian Network Structure Learning with Mutual Information-Based Node Ordering in the K2 Algorithm. *IEEE Transactions on Knowledge and Data Engineering*, **20**, 628-640. http://dx.doi.org/10.1109/TKDE.2007.190732

[20] De Campos, L.M. (2006) A Scoring Function for Learning Bayesian Networks Based on Mutual Information and Conditional Independence Tests. *Journal of Machine Learning Research*, **7**, 2149-2187.

[21] Nicholson, A.E. and Jitnah, N. (1998) Using Mutual Information to Determine Relevance in Bayesian Networks. *Proceedings of the 5th Pacific Rim International Conference on Artificial Intelligence*, Singapore, 22-27 November 1998, 399-410.

[22] Ibrahim, Z.M., Ngom, A. and Tawk, A.Y. (2011) Using Qualitative Probability in Reverse-Engineering Gene Regulatory Networks. *IEEE/ACM Transactions on Computational Biology and Bioinformatics*, **8**, 326-334. http://dx.doi.org/10.1109/TCBB.2010.98

[23] Liu, W.Y., Yue, K., Liu, S.X. and Sun, Y.B. (2008) Qualitative-Probabilistic-Network-Based Modeling of Temporal Causalities and Its Application to Feedback Loop Identification. *Information Sciences*, **178**, 1803-1824. http://dx.doi.org/10.1016/j.ins.2007.11.021

[24] Yue, K., Qian, W.H., Fu, X.D., Li, J. and Liu, W.Y. (2014) Qualitative-Probabilistic-Network-Based Fusion of Time-Series Uncertain Knowledge. *Soft Computing*, Published Online. http://dx.doi.org/10.1007/s00500-014-1381-y.

[25] De Campos, C.P. and Cozman, F.G. (2013) Complexity of Inferences in Polytree-Shaped Semi-Qualitative Probabilistic Networks. *Proceedings of the 27th AAAI Conference on Artificial Intelligence*, Bellevue, 14-18 July 2013, 217-223.

[26] Yue, K., Liu, W. and Yue, M. (2011) Quantifying Influences in the Qualitative Probabilistic Network with Interval Probability Parameters. *Applied Soft Computing*, **11**, 1135-1143. http://dx.doi.org/10.1016/j.asoc.2010.02.013

[27] Shafer, G. (1986) The Combination of Evidence. *International Journal of Intelligent Systems*, **1**, 155-179. http://dx.doi.org/10.1002/int.4550010302

[28] Norsys Software Corp. (2007) Netica 3.17 Bayesian Network Software from Norsys. http://www.norsys.com

11

A Physiologically-Based Adaptive Three-Gaussian Function Model for Image Enhancement

Zilong Xu, Kaifu Yang, Yongjie Li*

Key Laboratory for Neuroinformation of Ministry of Education, School of Life Science and Technology, University of Electronic Science and Technology of China, Chengdu, China
Email: *liyj@uestc.edu.cn

Academic Editor: Prof. Zhongzhi Shi, Institute of Computing Technology, Chinese Academy of Sciences, China

Abstract

Image enhancement is an important pre-processing step for various image processing applications. In this paper, we proposed a physiologically-based adaptive three-Gaussian model for image enhancement. Comparing to the standard three-Gaussian model inspired by the spatial structure of the receptive field (RF) of the retinal ganglion cells, the proposed model can dynamically adjust its parameters according to the local image luminance and contrast based on the physiological findings. Experimental results on several images show that the proposed adaptive three-Gaussian model achieves better performance than the classical method of histogram equalization and the standard three-Gaussian model.

Keywords

Image Enhancement, Receptive Field, Visual System, Three-Gaussian Model

1. Introduction

Images play an important role in transferring information. In order to obtain more information from collected images, image enhancement techniques are commonly required to improve image quality. Traditional image enhancement methods can be roughly divided into two categories: 1) spatial domain methods, such as gray-level transformation, piecewise-linear transformation, and histogram equalization, etc. 2) frequency domain methods,

---

*Corresponding author.

which include high-pass filtering, high-frequency emphasizing filtering, and homomorphic filtering etc. However, these methods mentioned above are in general difficult to balance well among various requirements of image quality, such as contour enhancement, dynamic range, denoising and so on. In addition, the ability of traditional image enhancement methods is far behind the human visual system in almost all aspects.

Early physiological studies have revealed that the retinal ganglion cells have a receptive field (RF) consisting of concentric regions, *i.e.*, an approximately circular center and an annular surround [1] [2]. DOG model was proposed by Rodieck to describe the classical receptive field (CRF) of the ganglion cells [1]. Li *et al.* found that the cells at some distance from the contrast borders were less affected, while the border enhancement might become quite stronger when the centre was close to the corner of a bright contour [2]. Ramachandran found that the luminance gradients of an area are essential for producing perception of three-dimensional visual scenes [3]. By analyzing the length-response functions of lateral geniculate neurons in the cat, Li *et al.* have demonstrated an extensive disinhibitory region (DIR, *i.e.*, non-CRF) outside the classical inhibitory surround of the receptive field [4]. According to this finding, a three-Gaussian function model was proposed in [5]. By setting appreciate parameters of the three-Gaussian model, good fit could be obtained almost for all data that show disinhibitory phenomenon [5]. Functionally, the three-Gaussian model can not only enhance the edge information but also transmit brightness information with low spatial frequency [5] [6].

However, the three-Gaussian model cannot dynamically adjust its parameters according to the local stimulus. In fact, the adaptation to the stimulus features (e.g., the luminance contrast) of the receptive field in the visual system has been deeply studied [7]-[12]. Some experiments [7] showed that the responses of retinal ganglion cells first increased abruptly, and then decayed exponentially to a lower value following the abrupt increase in stimulus contrast. Based on extracellular recordings from 69 LGN cells in the anesthetized cat, Nolt *et al.* found that the spatial summation within their receptive fields was dependent on the contrast of the stimuli presented. They reported that the contrast-dependency in the retinal ganglion cells directly resulted from a reduction in the size of the center mechanism due to an increase in contrast [8]. By characterizing the adaptation of neurons in the cat lateral geniculate nucleus (LGN) to changes in stimulus contrast and correlations, Lesica *et al.* found that the space constant of the excitatory center increased with a decreasing in stimulus contrast [9]. In addition, it has been shown that spatial summation in the primary visual cortex of the cat and monkey is strongly dependent on stimulus contrast; the area (length and width) over which responses summate generally increases as the stimulus contrast decreases; fitting summation curves with a DOG model shows that this contrast-dependent spatial summation seems to derive from a change in the actual size of the receptive field [10]-[12].

To simulate the dynamic properties of the RF, in this work we present an adaptive three-Gaussian function model to automatically adjust its parameters according to the properties of local stimulus, *i.e.*, local contrast and luminance, for image enhancement.

2. Computational Model

2.1. Three-Gaussian Function Model

Figure 1 shows the model of three-Gaussian model, in which the center and surround denote respectively the excitatory region (Center) and inhibitory region (Surround) of CRF. The disinhibitory region usually covers a larger range of visual field. The response amplitude of cells with stimulus radius is shown in the top-right corner of **Figure 1**. The three-Gaussian function model is described as [5]

$$f(x,y) = A_1 e^{\frac{-(x^2+y^2)}{\sigma_1^2}} - A_2 e^{\frac{-(x^2+y^2)}{\sigma_2^2}} + A_3 e^{\frac{-(x^2+y^2)}{\sigma_3^2}} \tag{1}$$

where A_1 and σ_1 are the strength and space constant of the excitatory center, A_2 and σ_2 are the strength and space constant of the inhibitory surround, and A_3 and σ_3 are the strength and space constant of the disinhibitory outer-surround region.

This three-Gaussian model assumes that the sensitivity profiles of the three regions (*i.e.*, center, surround and outer-surround) are distributed as Gaussians, which are circularly concentric with their peaks overlapped at the center point of the RF center region. This model also assumes that the three parts summate linearly from all parts of the receptive field. Functionally, the combination of the first two Gaussians (*i.e.*, the DOG model) serves to detect and enhance the edges, and the third Gaussian serves for the brightness information transmission by compensating the loss of the low frequency components resulted from the almost balanced center and surround mechanisms in the DOG model of most cells [5].

2.2. Adaptive Mechanism

Based on the experimental findings about the stimulus-dependant RF properties, we specifically introduce two dynamic RF features: 1) the excitatory strength of the center (A_1) increases nonlinearly with the increasing of the local contrast; 2) the inhibitory space constant (σ_2) of the RF surround is decreased with the increasing of the local luminance.

In this paper, we define the feature of local luminance contrast as the standard deviation within a small image patch around each pixel in the image. We denote local luminance contrast as Con. In addition, we use a modified sigmoid function to simulate the nonlinear transformation of neural information. The relationship between A_1 and Con is experimentally defined as

$$A_1 = 6 + \frac{1}{1 + e^{-10 \times (Con - 0.5)}} \tag{2}$$

Figure 2 shows the relationship of center excitation (A_1) along with the local contrast (Con).

On the other hand, in order to improve the contrast of shading regions of the image, another parameter (σ_2) is adjusted with local luminance. In our adaptive three-Gaussian function model, we can reduce inhibitory space constant (σ_2) to weaken the surround inhibition when the luminance value of the pixel to be processed is high.

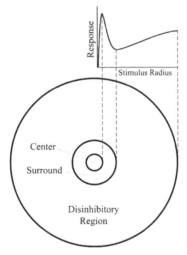

Figure 1. The spatial strucutre of the receptive field of the ganglion cells and LGN cells.

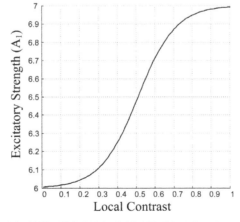

Figure 2. The relatinship of center excitatory (A_1) along with local contrast (*Con*).

We use L to denote local luminance value of each pixel in the image. Similar to Equation (2), we also employ a modified sigmoid function to represent the relationship between the inhibitory space constant (σ_2) and the local luminance feature. The relationship between σ_2 and L is experimentally defined as

$$\sigma_2 = 1.25 + \frac{0.1}{1 + e^{10 \times (L - 0.45)}} \tag{3}$$

Figure 3 shows the relationship between σ_2 and L. Note that a simple smoothing filtering is applied on the map of *Con* and L to removing noises.

As described in Equations (2) and (3), the kernel idea of our adaptive three-Gaussian model is that two important parameters (*i.e.*, A_1 and σ_2 in Equation (1)) are adaptively adjusted based on the features of local contrast and local luminance, respectively.

It should be pointed out that the curves in **Figure 2** and **Figure 3** are sigmoid shaped, because sufficient experimental evidence indicates that the change of receptive field properties (e.g., the sensitivity and spatial size) with the stimulus features (e.g., the luminance contrast) seems nonlinear [7]-[12]. Note that the constants in Equations (2) and (3) determining the shapes of the sigmoid curves (e.g., the slope) were experimentally obtained and we have found that these settings are suitable for most of the real-world images, as indicated by several examples shown in the next section.

3. Results

In this experiment, we compared our adaptive three-Gaussian method with the popular method of histogram equalization and the standard (non-adaptive) three-Gaussian model. Experimental results on several images are shown in **Figure 4**, **Figure 5**, **Figure 6**, and **Figure 7**. Note that the zoomed in view of each test image is also listed in **Figures 4-7**, respectively. From the figures, the results of the standard three-Gaussian model usually include more details than original images, but some regions are over-enhanced (especially in the high contrast place); in addition, the contrast of high-light and shading regions are not enhanced enough. Histogram equalization is efficient in adjusting global dynamic range of images, but it is difficult to obtain good local contrast. In addition, three-Gaussian model usually obtains better performance than histogram equalization.

Our adaptive three-Gaussian function model performs better in both enhancing the local contrast and adjusting global dynamic range. Meanwhile, the proposed method is capable of overcoming the phenomenon of over-enhancement. In addition, the performance of our new approach in edge enhancement is much better than the other two methods mentioned above, which can be clearly seen from **Figures 4-7**, especially from the zoomed in view of each test image.

For quantitative comparison, we employed EME (a measure of enhancement) [13] and SNR (Signal to Noise Ratio) [14] for performance evaluation of image enhancement. SNR is usually defined as the mean target signal to the standard deviation of the noise [13]. In this paper, we define E as the mean value of the all pixels in the

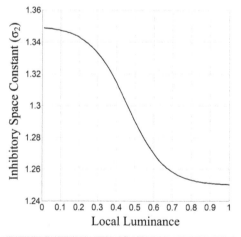

Figure 3. The relatinship of surround space constant (σ_2) along with local lumiance (L).

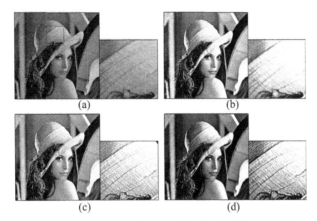

Figure 4. Results on the Lenna image. (a) Original image; (b) Results of histogram equalization; (c) Results of three-Gaussian function model; (d) Results of the proposed method (adaptive three-Gaussian function model). The zoomed in view of the patch in the red rectangle is also shown for each image.

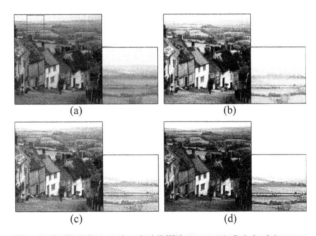

Figure 5. Results on the Goldhill image. (a) Original image; (b) Results of histogram equalization; (c) Results of three-Gaussian function model; (d) Results of the proposed method (adaptive three-Gaussian function model).

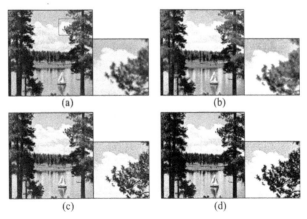

Figure 6. Results on the Sailboat image. (a) Original image; (b) Results of histogram equalization; (c) Results of three-Gaussian function model; (d) Results of the proposed method (adaptive three-Gaussian function model).

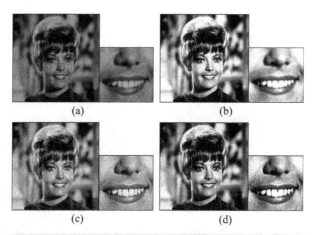

Figure 7. Results on the Zelda image. (a) Original image; (b) Results of histogram equalization; (c) Results of three-Gaussian function model; (d) Results of the proposed method (adaptive three-Gaussian function model).

image and σ as the standard deviation of the all pixels in the image. Therefore, SNR is computed as

$$SNR = 10\log_{10}\frac{E}{\sigma^2} \tag{4}$$

EME is computed as [14]

$$EME = \frac{1}{k_1 k_2}\sum_{l=1}^{k_2}\sum_{k=1}^{k_1} 20\ln\frac{V_{\max,k,l} - V_{\min,k,l}}{V_{\max,k,l} + V_{\min,k,l} + c} \tag{5}$$

where $V_{\min,k,l}$ and $V_{\max,k,l}$ are respectively the minimum and maximum inside a certain block $w(k,l)$ when the whole image is split into $k_1 k_2$ blocks $w(k,l)$ of equal sizes. c is a small constant that equals to 0.0001 to avoid dividing by zero. In general, a higher EME indicates a better enhancement in image details.

EME and SNR of four considered images shown in **Figures 4-7** are listed in **Table 1** and **Table 2**. Note that the EME and SNR were calculated from the whole images. From **Table 1**, the evaluation of EME shows that our adaptive three-Gaussian function model obtains the best performance on edge enhancement. From **Table 2**, we can see that our new approach achieves competitive performance compared with the standard three-Gaussian function model and histogram equalization in suppressing image noise. This indicates that our adaptive model can well balance the requirements of enhancing edges and inhibiting image noises.

4. Discussion

It is generally accepted that the computational image processing methods are far behind the human visual system. They met difficulties to balance well among various requirements of image quality, e.g., contour enhancement and denoising which often cannot be well achieved at the same time. By seeking inspiration from the physiological findings, this paper proposes a physiologically based adaptive three-Gaussian model, which dynamically adjusts the parameters of the three-Gaussian model. The results on several real-world images show that the performance of our new model is better than the standard three-Gaussian function model, especially in overcoming over-enhancement and raising the contrast of highlight and shading regions. Our approach can keep the SNR of an image in an acceptable level; meanwhile, it can effectively enhance the edge profiles and local details of the image. Specifically, in the regions of low luminance, we increase the excitatory strength (A_1) in the regions with high local contrast, which helps enhance the edges with high contrast. Differently, we increase the inhibitory space constant (σ_2) in the regions of low brightness, which helps improve the contrast of shading regions.

Our physiologically-based adaptive three-Gaussian function model only simulates the change of inhibitory space constant (σ_2) and excitatory strength (A_1) based on the local contrast and local brightness, and don't involve inhibitory strength (A_2) and excitatory space constant, (σ_1) which should be improved in the future work. In addition, how to effectively suppress image noise is also an important future direction for us.

Table 1. EME for the testing images.

Index	EME			
Test image	Original image	Histogram equalization	Three-Gaussian	Adaptive three-Gaussian
Lenna	22.9578	55.8410	74.2137	91.6041
Goldhill	16.2290	40.3469	67.6001	130.0269
Sailboat	23.2728	40.4264	81.2151	135.1900
Zelda	17.1172	55.7354	67.2700	94.1577

Table 2. SNR for the testing images.

Index	SNR			
Test image	Original image	Histogram equalization	Three-Gaussian	Adaptive three-Gaussian
Lenna	64.6106	62.6490	61.8363	61.9148
Goldhill	64.9061	62.4141	61.8287	61.5272
Sailboat	62.8929	60.6578	61.8346	60.4178
Zelda	65.6947	61.8349	63.3216	62.8684

Acknowledgements

The authors would like to thank Professor Chaoyi Li for his valuable suggestions. The authors also thank the anonymous reviewers for their helpful comments. This work was supported by the 973 project (#2013CB329401) and the NSFC of China (#61375115 and #91120013).

References

[1] Rodieck, R.W. (1965) Quantitative Analysis of Cat Retinal Ganglion Cell Response to Visual Stimuli. *Vision Research*, **5**, 538-601. http://dx.doi.org/10.1016/0042-6989(65)90033-7

[2] Li, C.I., Chang, Y.J., Chen, P.S., Hsu, H.C. and Wang, H. (1979) Role of Sustained Neurones of Cat Lateral Geniculate Nucleus in Processing Luminance Information. *Scientia Sinica*, **22**, 359-371.

[3] Ramachandran, V.S. (1988) Perceiving Shape from Shading. *Scientific American*, **259**, 76-83. http://dx.doi.org/10.1038/scientificamerican0888-76

[4] Li, C.-Y., Zhou, Y.-X., Pei, X., Qiu, F.-T., Tang, C.-Q. and Xu, X.-Z. (1992) Extensive Disinhibitory Region beyond the Classical Receptive Field of Cat Retinal Ganglion Cells. *Vision Research*, **32**, 219-228. http://dx.doi.org/10.1016/0042-6989(92)90131-2

[5] Li, C.-Y., Pei, X., Zhow, Y.-X. and Von Mitzlaff, H.-C. (1991) Role of the Extensive Area outside the X-Cell Receptive Field in Brightness Information Transmission. *Vision Research*, **31**, 1529-1540. http://dx.doi.org/10.1016/0042-6989(91)90130-W

[6] Keil, M.S., Cristobal, G. and Neumann, H. (2001) A Neurodynamical Retinal Network Based on Reaction-Diffusion Systems. *Proceedings of 11th International Conference on Image Analysis and Processing*, Palermo, 26-28 September 2011, 209-214.

[7] Smirnakis, S.M., Berry, M.J., Warland, D.K., Bialek, W. and Meister, M. (1997) Adaptation of Retinal Processing to Image Contrast and Spatial Scale. *Nature*, **386**, 69-73. http://dx.doi.org/10.1038/386069a0

[8] Nolt, M.J., Kumbhani, R.D. and Palmer, L.A. (2004) Contrast-Dependent Spatial Summation in the Lateral Geniculate Nucleus and Retina of the Cat. *Journal of Neurophysiology*, **92**, 1708-1717. http://dx.doi.org/10.1152/jn.00176.2004

[9] Lesica, N.A., Jin, J.H., Weng, C., Yeh, C.-I, Butts, D.A., Stanley, G.B., *et al.* (2007) Adaptation to Stimulus Contrast and Correlations during Natural Visual Stimulation. *Neuron*, **55**, 479-491. http://dx.doi.org/10.1016/j.neuron.2007.07.013

[10] Kapadia, M.K., Westheimer, G. and Gilbert, C.D. (1999) Dynamics of Spatial Summation in Primary Visual Cortex of Alert Monkeys. *Proceedings of the National Academy of Sciences of the United States of America*, **96**, 12073-12078. http://dx.doi.org/10.1073/pnas.96.21.12073

[11] Song, X.-M. and Li, C.-Y. (2008) Contrast-Dependent and Contrast-Independent Spatial Summation of Primary Visual Cortical Neurons of the Cat. *Cerebral Cortex*, **18**, 331-336. http://dx.doi.org/10.1093/cercor/bhm057

[12] Chen, K., Song, X.-M. and Li, C.-Y. (2013) Contrast-Dependent Variations in the Excitatory Classical Receptive Field and Suppressive Nonclassical Receptive Field of Cat Primary Visual Cortex. *Cerebral Cortex*, **23**, 283-292. http://dx.doi.org/10.1093/cercor/bhs012

[13] Agaian, S.S., Panetta, K. and Grigoryan, A.M. (2000) A New Measure of Image Enhancement. *IASTED International Conference on Signal Processing & Communication*, Marbella, September 2000, 19-22.

[14] Fiete, R.D. and Tantalo, T. (2001) Comparison of SNR Image Quality Metrics for Remote Sensing Systems. *Optical Engineering*, **40**, 574-585.

12

Simulate Human Saccadic Scan-Paths in Target Searching

Lijuan Duan[1,2], Jun Miao[3*], David M. W. Powers[4], Jili Gu[5], Laiyun Qing[6]

[1]Beijing Key Laboratory of Trusted Computing, Beijing Key Laboratory on Integration and Analysis of Large-Scale Stream Data, College of Computer Science and Technology, Beijing University of Technology, Beijing, China

[2]National Engineering Laboratory for Critical Technologies of Information Security Classified Protection, Beijing, China

[3]Key Laboratory of Intelligent Information Processing of Chinese Academy of Sciences(CAS), Institute of Computing Technology, CAS, Beijing, China

[4]School of Computer Science, Engineering & Maths, Flinders University of South Australia, Adelaide, South Australia

[5]Beijing Samsung Telecom R&D Center, Beijing, China

[6]University of Chinese Academy of Sciences, Beijing, China

Email: [*]jmiao@ict.ac.cn

Abstract

Human saccade is a dynamic process of information pursuit. There are many methods using either global context or local context cues to model human saccadic scan-paths. In contrast to them, this paper introduces a model for gaze movement control using both global and local cues. To test the performance of this model, an experiment is done to collect human eye movement data by using an SMI iVIEW X Hi-Speed eye tracker with a sampling rate of 1250 Hz. The experiment used a two-by-four mixed design with the location of the targets and the four initial positions. We compare the saccadic scan-paths generated by the proposed model against human eye movement data on a face benchmark dataset. Experimental results demonstrate that the simulated scan-paths by the proposed model are similar to human saccades in term of the fixation order, Hausdorff distance, and prediction accuracy for both static fixation locations and dynamic scan-paths.

Keywords

Saccadic Scan-Paths, Eye Movement, Fixation Locations, Dynamic Scan-Paths

[*]Corresponding author.

1. Introduction

Searching the localization of targets is still a challenge problem in the fields of computer vision. However, humans perform this task in a more intuitive and efficient manner by selecting only a few regions to focus on, while observers never form a complete and detailed representation of their surroundings [1]. Due to the high efficiency of this biological approach, more and more researchers are devoting increasingly great effort to probing the nature of attention [2].

Usually two kinds of top-down cues are used to predict human gaze location in dynamic scenes [3] and gaze movement control when searching target: cues about bottom-up features such as shape, color, shape, scale [4]-[7] and cues about the top-down visual context that contains the target as well as other relevant objects' spatial relationships and their environmental features [8]-[10].

In classical search tasks, target features are important source of guidance [11]-[15]. Although a natural object, such as an animal (cat or dog), does not have single defining feature, its statistically reliable properties (round head, straight body, legs and others) can be selected by visual attention. There has been little research using visual context in object search. Global context was used by Torralba to predict the region where the target is more detected by [16]. Object detectors are used by Ehinger and Paletta [17] [18] to search the targets in that predicted region detected by [16] for accurate localization. An extended object template containing local context is used by Kruppa and Santana to detect extended targets and infer the location of the targets via the ratio between the size of the target and the size of the extend template in [19]. Most of above methods are just only based on either global context or local context cues. However, Miao *et al.* proposed a serial of neural coding networks in [20]-[23] using both of them.

In this study, the main purpose of our work is to simulate human saccadic scan-paths by the proposed model in [23]. To test the performance of the proposed model, we collect human eye movement data by using an SMI iVIEW X Hi-Speed eye tracker on a face dataset with a sampling rate of 1250 Hz. We compare the saccadic scan-paths generated by the proposed model against actual human eye movement data from the face dataset [28].

The paper is organized as follows: the model of the gaze movement control in target searching proposed in [23] is introduced briefly in Section 2. In Section 3, we compare our saccadic scan-paths with previous methods and scan-paths from eye tracking data. Our conclusions are presented in Section 5.

2. Review of the Gaze Movement Control Model in Target Searching

This paper applies the target searching model in [23] to simulate the eye-motion traces. The feature used in the model is a kind of binary codes called Local Binary Pattern (LBP) [32], which has been proved through our work superior to orientation features used in the same system [33] [34] with respect to search performance. LBP is a simple and fast encoding scheme to map a 3×3 image patch to a local feature pattern in terms of an 8-bit code. This encoding scheme has no parameters to do such mapping, just outputting 0/1 for each bit through comparing the central pixel's value and that of each one of eight surrounding pixels. There are encoding and decoding parameters in the model [23], such as P, which determines how many context coding neurons are activated through competition. Through our experiments, we find the best value of 70% for this parameter. So in this paper, we use the best model with LBP feature and P = 70% to simulate eye-motion traces.

The learning and testing algorithm for target search is illustrated in **Figure 1** and described in Section 2.1 and 2.2. Here the visual context means the visual field image and the spatial relationship from the center of the visual field to the center of the target. In order to encode such context, we need to calculate and store the representation coefficients of the spatial relationship and the visual field images. The model's learning algorithm and test method are introduced in this part. In this experiment, we use head-shoulder image database from the University of Bern [24].

2.1. Model Training

The learning algorithm is described by [23] as follows:

1) Choose a value s from the scale set $\{s_j\}$ for the visual field that will be processed;

2) Choose an initial view point (x_j, y_j) as the center of the visual field from an initial point set $\{(x_j, y_j)\}$ covering the surrounding area of the target;

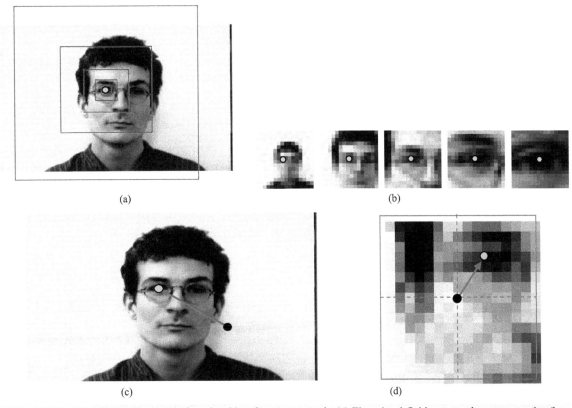

Figure 1. Illustration of learning and testing algorithm for target search. (a) Five visual fields centered at a gaze point (here is the left eye center); (b) Five visual field images (16 × 16 pixels, scales = 5, 4, 3, 2 and 1) sub-sampled from the original image (320 × 214 pixels) with intervals = 16, 8, 4, 2, 1 pixel(s); (c) The spatial relationship between one given starting gaze point and the target center; (d) Memorizing the visual context or predicting between the target center from current gaze points at different scales.

3) Receive signals from the current visual field, and output a relative position evaluation for the target with view point moving distances $(\Delta x, \Delta y)$;

4) If the prediction error err is larger than the limit ERR(s) for the scale s of the current visual field, move the visual field center to a new position randomly; go to 3 until err $\leq$ ERR(s) or the iteration number is larger than a limit;

5) If err > ERR(s), generate a new VF-image encoding neuron (let its response $R_k = 1$); encode the visual context by calculating and memorizing the connecting weights $\{w_{ij, k}\}$ between the new VF-image encoding neuron and the feature neurons and the connection weights $w_{k,uv}$ between the new VF-image encoding neuron and the motion encoding neurons (let their response $R_{uv} = 1$) respectively using the Hebbian learning rule $\Delta w_{a,b} = \alpha R_a R_b$;

6) Go to 2 until all initial view points are chosen;

7) Go to 1 until all scales are chosen.

2.2. Model Prediction

In the test stage, the entire algorithm for view point control for object locating is given as follows:

1) Get a pre-given view point (x, y);

2) Choose a scale s from the set $\{s_i\}$ for the current visual field from the maximum to the minimum;

3) Receive signals from the current visual field, and calculating the response of the feature neurons and the context encoding neurons;

4) Predict a relative position $(\Delta x, \Delta y)$ for the real position of the object;

5) If $(\Delta x, \Delta y) = (0,0)$, object located;

6) If $(\Delta x, \Delta y) \neq (0,0)$, view point moving with $(\Delta x, \Delta y)$, go 2 until all scales are chosen.

3. Experiments

3.1. Participants

Fifteen female and twelve male college students of Beijing University of Technology participated in this study. The age range was 23 - 26 and the average was 24 years old. All of the twenty-seven students had normal or corrected-to-normal vision.

3.2. Stimuli

A set of 30 face pictures are prepared as stimuli. Of this set of 30, 15 are Female-face, 15 are Male-face, and the size of each picture is 1024 × 768 pixels. Pictures are presented on a color computer monitor at a resolution of 1024 by 768 pixels. The monitor size was 41 cm by 33.8 cm, and the participants were sited in a chair about 76 cm in front of the screen.

Stimuli consist of a set of 30 face pictures. There are 15 Female-face and 15 Male-face in this set of 30, and each picture's size is 1024 × 768 pixels. One of the 30 face pictures are presented on a color computer monitor at a resolution of 1024 by 768 pixels.

3.3. Design

A new searching task was used in this study, participants were demanded to search the left and right eyes in a face from a pre-given starting point. Thirty pictures of face were used as stimuli, including 15 female and 15 male faces. The size of each picture was 1024 × 768 pixels. There were four pre-given starting points, named the first, second, third and fourth quadrant respectively in a counterclockwise direction, similar with those in a coordinated system. Searching from a starting point to a target eye decided the searching distance and direction. **Figure 1** illustrated the searching targets and the definition of the quadrants.

3.4. Procedure

For each trial, as shown in **Figure 2**, a black trail indicator was presented initially in the middle of the white screen for 1000 ms to indicate the target of the left or right eye. Then a "+" indicating pre-defined positions was presented in a random order. After that the picture of a face appeared in the middle of the screen for 2000 ms and participants were asked to search the right target eye or the left target eye as accurately and quickly as possible. Participants were told not to look at other part of the picture in the pictures after finding the target.

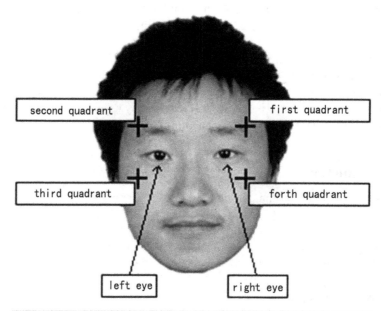

Figure 2. Sketch map of pre-given starting points in the face picture.

4. Experimental Results

4.1. Preprocess

The real fixation points are collected on the images with the size of 1024×768 pixels. However, the model can only deal with the gray images with the size of no more than 320×320 pixels. So when evaluating the performance of the model, we compress the original 1024×768 color images into 320×240 gray images. 10 face images are used in the learning stage and the other 20 face images are used for evaluation. The algorithms for the learning and the prediction stages are described in Section 2. When predicting fixation order and scan-paths, the same initial positions were used in the above experiment. Our model will search left eye and right eye separately from four different initial points that are similar to the above experiment. Each participant is asked to search left and right eyes from four different starting points on a face, and then it would certainly produce 8 eye scan-paths. For 27 subjects and 20 face images, $27 \times 20 \times 8$ scan-paths are totally recoded.

4.2. Evaluation of Fixation Order

We are aware of only a limited literature on computational models of active visual attention, and in particular active visual attention needs further investigation. Lee and Yu's work in [25] provided a conceptual framework but failed to provide a fully implemented solution with experimental results. Renninger *et al.* in [26] simulated scan-paths on novel shapes, but it is not clear how to adapt their method to natural images. However, Itti *et al.* in [27] proposed a scan path generation method from static saliency maps based on winner-takes-all (WTA) and inhibition-of-return (IoR) regulations. Tom Foul sham tried to find the evidence from normal and Gaze-Contingent search tasks in natural scenes in [28] for Itti. Marco Wischnewski proposed a model combining static and dynamic proto-objects in a TVA-based model of visual attention to predict where to look next in [29]. Gert Kootstra proposed a model to predict Eye Fixations on Complex Visual Stimuli Using Local Symmetry [30]. De Croon [31] proposed a novel gaze-control model, named act-detect, which use the information from local image samples in order to shift its gaze towards object locations for detecting objects in images. Our system can automatically generate the fixations, and the fixation can move to the target under the control of learned memory and experience in four or five steps. We here compare the simulated scan-paths generated by the model of [23] with human saccades. We select the initial positions on the four quadrants of the image shown in **Figure 3**. And the experimental results are illustrated in **Figure 4**. We can find that the simulated scan-paths by our model are similar to human saccades.

4.3. Distance of Scan-paths

In order to quantitatively compare the stochastic and dynamic scan-paths, we divide scan-paths into pieces of length 2. We use the Hausdorff distance to evaluate the scan-paths by the model proposed by Miao *et al.* with scan-paths of all subjects recorded by the eye tracker and evaluate the scan-paths between different subjects. The results are shown in **Table 1**.

In **Table 1**, Model-Human means the average of the Hausdorff distances between the scan path generated by model and that from each one of 27 subjects on corresponding images. Human-Human means the average of the Hausdorff distances between the scan-paths generated by any two of 27 subjects. We can know from **Table 1** that the simulated scan-paths by the model of Miao's are similar to human saccades by comparing the Hausdorff distance of scan-paths between the model and the humans: the average of the Hausdorff distances between

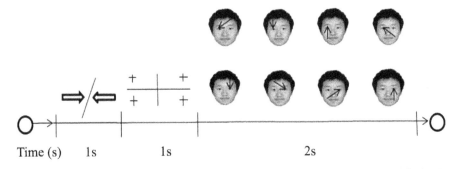

Figure 3. Procedure of the task.

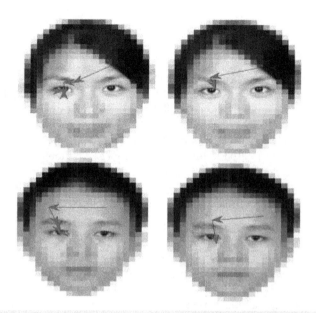

Figure 4. The left column describes fixations predicted by the model proposed in [23]; the right column describes the real Fixations recorded by the SMI iVIEW X Hi-Speed eye tracker (Note: Here example face images are processed with mosaics).

Table 1. The average of the Hausdorff distances between the model to each one of 27 subjects and that between each pair of subjects.

Image	Hausdorff	
	Model-Human	Human-Human
1.bmp	25.83	23.38
2.bmp	26.88	26.06
3.bmp	20.23	23.49
4.bmp	29.02	27.77
5.bmp	28.37	26.84
6.bmp	27.70	25.90
7.bmp	27.94	31.44
8.bmp	28.06	23.50
9.bmp	33.95	30.39
10.bmp	32.11	30.76
11.bmp	25.40	21.67
12.bmp	28.68	27.41
13.bmp	32.90	28.01
14.bmp	30.42	30.18
15.bmp	29.73	22.97
16.bmp	30.60	28.50
17.bmp	30.44	15.46
18.bmp	31.44	26.21
19.bmp	34.39	36.96
20.bmp	29.46	20.29
Average	29.18	26.36

scan-paths generated by the model and each subject on all the corresponding images is 29.18 which is similar to the average (26.36) of the Hausdorff distances between the scan-paths generated by every two subjects of the total 27 subjects. We also compute the average of the Hausdorff distances in the cases of that the initial position is from the second, third and fourth quadrants respectively shown in **Table 2**.

In **Table 2**, Model-Human means the average of the Hausdorff distances between the scan-paths generated by the model and each of 27 subjects on all the corresponding images. Human-Human means the average of the Hausdorff distances between the scan-paths generated by every two of 27 subjects from the first, the second, the third and the fourth quadrants. The average of the Hausdorff distances from all four initial quadrants is 24.09. We conclude that the model of Miao's [23] achieves a good predictive accuracy on both static fixation locations and dynamic scan-paths.

4.4. Evaluation of Search Precision

We also compute the search precision from four different quadrants to left eye and right eye. The results are shown in **Table 3**. We noted that there is a discrepancy of the average value of the search precision between the left eye and right eye. Due to different contextual information which is coded and used by the search model, this case may take place.

5. Discussion and Conclusions

Miao *et al.* presented a new architecture for gaze movement control in target searching in [23]. This paper utilizes the model to simulate human saccadic scan-paths in target searching. To test the performance of the proposed model, we collect human eye movement data by using an SMI iVIEW X Hi-Speed eye tracker at a sample rate of 1250 Hz. We compare the saccadic scan-paths generated by the proposed model against human eye movement data. Experimental results demonstrate that the simulated scan-paths by the proposed model are similar to human saccades in terms of the fixation order and the Hausdorff distance of scan-paths. It can be learned that the model achieves good prediction accuracy on both static fixation locations and dynamic scan-paths.

The model is suitable for target searching in strong-context cases. However, it performs less effectively in weak-context cases. Thus as future work we hope to propose to use a bottom-up saliency map together with a top-down target template to assist context based object searching in weak context cases, in order to achieve good prediction accuracy on both static fixation locations and dynamic scan-paths in weak-context cases.

Table 2. The average of the Hausdorff distances.

Image	Hausdorff	
	Model-Human	Human-Human
First quadrant	29.18	26.36
Second quadrant	21.08	22.59
Third quadrant	18.96	22.10
Fourth quadrant	33.75	25.30
All average	25.74	24.09

Table 3. Search precision from four different quadrants to left eye and right eye.

Quadrant	Target	
	Left eye	Right eye
First quadrant	100%	95%
Second quadrant	100%	100%
Third quadrant	100%	100%
Fourth quadrant	85%	100%
Average	96.25%	98.75%

The current simulation is based on the model with the optimal features and parameters tuned from the real face data. How much do the variation of features and parameters affect the simulation is a valuable question to be investigated? Evaluating the model's performance on the pictures of people's face rather than real face is also an interesting question. These are what we will study in the future work.

Acknowledgements

This research is partially sponsored by Beijing Municipal Natural Science Foundation (4152005 and 4152006), Natural Science Foundation of China (Nos. 61175115, 61370113, 61272320, 61472387 and 61572004), the Importation and Development of High-Caliber Talents Project of Beijing Municipal Institutions (CIT & TCD201304035), Jing-Hua Talents Project of Beijing University of Technology (2014-JH-L06), and Ri-Xin Talents Project of Beijing University of Technology (2014-RX-L06), the Research Fund of Beijing Municipal Commission of Education (PXM2015_014204_500221) and the International Communication Ability Development Plan for Young Teachers of Beijing University of Technology (No. 2014-16).

References

[1]   Rensink, R., O'Regan, K. and Clark, J. (1997) To See or Not to See: The Need for Attention to Perceive Changes in Scenes. *Psychological Sciences*, **8**, 368-373.

[2]   Tsotsos, J.K., Itti, L. and Rees, G. (2005) A Brief and Selective History of Attention. In: Itti, Rees and Tsotsos, Eds., *Neurobiology of Attention*, Academic Press, Salt Lake City, xxiii-xxxii.

[3]   Mital, P., Smith, T., Hill, R. and Henderson, J. (2011) Clustering of Gaze during Dynamic Scene Viewing Is Predicted by Motion. *Cognitive Computation*, **3**, 5-24. http://dx.doi.org/10.1007/s12559-010-9074-z

[4]   Zelinsky, G., Zhang, W., Yu, B., Chen, X. and Samaras, D. (2006) The Role of Top-Down and Bottom-Up Processes in Guiding Eye Movements during Visual Search. *Advances in Neural Information Processing Systems*, Vancouver, 5-8 December 2005, 1407-1414.

[5]   Milanese, R., Wechsler, H., Gil, S., Bost, J. and Pun, T. (1997) Integration of Bottom-Up and Top-Down Cues for Visual Attention Using Non-Linear Relaxation. *Proceedings of IEEE Computer Society Conference on Computer Vision and Pattern Recognition*, Hilton Head, 21-23 June 1994, 781-785.

[6]   Tsotsos, J., Culhane, S., Wai, W., Lai, Y., Davis, N. and Nuflo, F. (1995) Modeling Visual Attention via Selective Tuning. *Artificial Intelligence*, **78**, 507-545. http://dx.doi.org/10.1016/0004-3702(95)00025-9

[7]   Navalpakkam, V., Rebesco, J. and Itti, L. (2005) Modeling the Influence of Task on Attention. *Vision Research*, **45**, 205-221. http://dx.doi.org/10.1016/j.visres.2004.07.042

[8]   Chun, M. and Jiang, Y. (1998) Contextual Cueing: Implicit Learning and Memory of Visual Context Guides Spatial Attention. *Cognitive Psychology*, **36**, 28-71. http://dx.doi.org/10.1006/cogp.1998.0681

[9]   Chun, M. (2000) Contextual Cueing of Visual Attention. *Trends in Cognitive Sciences*, **4**, 170-178. http://dx.doi.org/10.1016/S1364-6613(00)01476-5

[10] Henderson, J., Weeks Jr., P. and Hollingworth, A. (1999) The Effects of Semantic Consistency on Eye Movements during Complex Scene Viewing. *Journal of Experimental Psychology: Human Perception and Performance*, **25**, 210-222. http://dx.doi.org/10.1037/0096-1523.25.1.210

[11] Treisman, A. and Gelade, G. (1980) A Feature Integration Theory of Attention. *Cognitive Psychology*, **12**, 97-136. http://dx.doi.org/10.1016/0010-0285(80)90005-5

[12] Wolfe, J.M. (1994) Guided Search 2.0: A Revised Model of Visual Search. *Psychonomic Bulletin & Review*, **1**, 202-238. http://dx.doi.org/10.3758/BF03200774

[13] Wolfe, J.M. (2007) Guided Search 4.0: Current Progress with a Model of Visual Search. In: Gray, W., Ed., *Integrated Models of Cognitive Systems*, Oxford Press, New York. http://dx.doi.org/10.1093/acprof:oso/9780195189193.003.0008

[14] Wolfe, J.M., Cave, K.R. and Franzel, S.L. (1989) Guided Search: An Alternative to the Feature Integration Model for Visual Search. *Journal of Experimental Psychology: Human Perception and Performance*, **15**, 419-433. http://dx.doi.org/10.1037/0096-1523.15.3.419

[15] Zelinsky, G.J. (2008) A Theory of Eye Movements during Target Acquisition. *Psychological Review*, **115**, 787-835. http://dx.doi.org/10.1037/a0013118

[16] Torralba, A. (2003) Contextual Priming for Object Detection. *International Journal of Computer Vision*, **53**, 169-191. http://dx.doi.org/10.1023/A:1023052124951

[17] Ehinger, K., Hidalgo-Sotelo, B., Torralba, A. and Oliva, A. (2009) Modelling Search for People in 900 Scenes: A Combined Source Model of Eye Guidance. *Visual Cognition*, **17**, 945-978. http://dx.doi.org/10.1080/13506280902834720

[18] Paletta, L. and Greindl, C. (2003) Context Based Object Detection from Video. In: *Proceedings of International Conference on Computer Vision Systems*, Graz, 502-512. http://dx.doi.org/10.1007/3-540-36592-3_48

[19] Kruppa, H., Santana, M. and Schiele, B. (2003) Fast and Robust Face Finding via Local Context. In: *Proceedings of Joint IEEE International Workshop on Visual Surveillance and Performance Evaluation of Tracking and Surveillance*, Nice, France, 11-12 October, 2003, 1-8.

[20] Miao, J., Chen, X., Gao, W. and Chen, Y. (2006) A Visual Perceiving and Eyeball-Motion Controlling Neural Network for Object Searching and Locating. *Proceedings of International Joint Conference on Neural Networks*, Vancouver, 4395-4400.

[21] Miao, J., Zou, B., Qing, L., Duan, L. and Fu, Y. (2010) Learning Internal Representation of Visual Context in a Neural Coding Network. *Proceedings of the International Conference on Artificial Neural Networks*, Thessaloniki, 15-18 September 2010, 174-183. http://dx.doi.org/10.1007/978-3-642-15819-3_22

[22] Miao, J., Qing, L., Zou, B., Duan, L. and Gao, W. (2010) Top-Down Gaze Movement Control in Target Search Using Population Cell Coding of Visual Context. *IEEE Transactions on Autonomous Mental Development*, **2**, 196-215.

[23] Miao, J., Duan, L., Qing, L. and Qiao, Y. (2011) An Improved Neural Architecture for Gaze Movement Control in Target Searching. *Proceedings of the IEEE International Joint Conference on Neural Networks*, San Jose, 31 July-5 August 2011, 2341-2348.

[24] The Face Database of the University of Bern (2008). http://www.iam.unibe.ch/fki/databases/iam-faces-database

[25] Lee, T. and Yu, S. (2002) An Information-Theoretic Framework for Understanding Saccadic Eye Movements. *Advanced in Neural Information Processing System*, **12**, 834-840.

[26] Renninger, L., Verghese, P. and Coughlan, J. (2007) Where to Look Next? Eye Movements Reduce Local Uncertainty. *Journal of Vision*, **7**, 6.

[27] Itti, L., Koch, C. and Niebur, E. (1998) A Model of Saliency Based Visual Attention for Rapid Scene Analysis. *IEEE Transactions on Pattern Analysis and Machine Intelligence*, **20**, 1254-1259.

[28] Foulsham, T. and Underwood, G. (2011) If Visual Saliency Predicts Search, Then Why? Evidence from Normal and Gaze-Contingent Search Tasks in Natural Scenes. *Cognitive Computation*, **3**, 48-63. http://dx.doi.org/10.1007/s12559-010-9069-9

[29] Wischnewski, M., Belardinelli, A., Schneider, W. and Steil, J. (2010) Where to Look Next? Combining Static and Dynamic Proto-Objects in a TVA-Based Model of Visual Attention. *Cognitive Computation*, **2**, 326-343. http://dx.doi.org/10.1007/s12559-010-9080-1

[30] Kootstra, G., de Boer, B. and Schomaker, L. (2011) Predicting Eye Fixations on Complex Visual Stimuli Using Local Symmetry. *Cognitive Computation*, **3**, 223-240. http://dx.doi.org/10.1007/s12559-010-9089-5

[31] de Croon, G., Postma, E. and van den Herik, H. (2011) Adaptive Gaze Control for Object Detection. *Cognitive Computation*, **3**, 264-278. http://dx.doi.org/10.1007/s12559-010-9093-9

[32] Ojala, T., Pietikainen, M. and Harwood, D. (1996) A Comparative Study of Texture Measures with Classification Based on Featured Distribution. *Pattern Recognition*, **29**, 51-59. http://dx.doi.org/10.1016/0031-3203(95)00067-4

[33] Miao, J., Chen, X., Gao, W. and Chen, Y. (2006) A Visual Perceiving and Eyeball-Motion Controlling Neural Network for Object Searching and Locating. *Proceedings of the International Joint Conference on Neural Networks*, Vancouver, 16-21 July 2006, 4395-4400.

[34] Miao, J., Duan, L.J., Qing, L.Y., Gao, W. and Chen, Y.Q. (2007) Learning and Memory on Spatial Relationship by a Neural Network with Sparse Features. *Proceedings of the International Joint Conference on Neural Networks*, Orlando, 12-17 August 2007, 1-6. http://dx.doi.org/10.1109/ijcnn.2007.4371293

13

Compound Hidden Markov Model for Activity Labelling

Jose Israel Figueroa-Angulo[1], Jesus Savage[1], Ernesto Bribiesca[2], Boris Escalante[3], Luis Enrique Sucar[4], Ron Leder[3]

[1]Biorobotics Laboratory, Universidad Nacional Autonoma de Mexico, Mexico City, Mexico
[2]Computer Science Department, Universidad Nacional Autonoma de Mexico, Mexico City, Mexico
[3]Electrical Engineer Department, Universidad Nacional Autonoma de Mexico, Mexico City, Mexico
[4]Computer Science Department, Instituto Nacional de Astrofisica, Optica y Electronica, Puebla, Mexico
Email: jifigueroa@uxmcc2.iimas.unam.mx, savage@servidor.unam.mx, bribiesca@iimas.unam.mx, borises@gmail.com, rleder@ieee.org, esucar@ccc.inaoep.mx

Abstract

This research presents a novel way of labelling human activities from the skeleton output computed from RGB-D data from vision-based motion capture systems. The activities are labelled by means of a Compound Hidden Markov Model. The linkage of several Linear Hidden Markov Models to common states, makes a Compound Hidden Markov Model. Each separate Linear Hidden Markov Model has motion information of a human activity. The sequence of most likely states, from a sequence of observations, indicates which activities are performed by a person in an interval of time. The purpose of this research is to provide a service robot with the capability of human activity awareness, which can be used for action planning with implicit and indirect Human-Robot Interaction. The proposed Compound Hidden Markov Model, made of Linear Hidden Markov Models per activity, labels activities from unknown subjects with an average accuracy of 59.37%, which is higher than the average labelling accuracy for activities of unknown subjects of an Ergodic Hidden Markov Model (6.25%), and a Compound Hidden Markov Model with activities modelled by a single state (18.75%).

Keywords

Hidden Markov Model, Compound Hidden Markov Model, Activity Recognition, Human Activity, Human Motion, Motion Capture, Skeleton, Computer Vision, Machine Learning, Motion Analysis

1. Introduction

In daily life, human beings perform activities to accomplish diverse tasks at different times throughout the day.

These activities are made of one or several simpler actions which are performed at different times, and these simple activities have a chronological relationship to each other.

The motivation for this work is to analyse human behaviour by labelling the activities which are performed by a person. Human activity has the properties of being both complex and dynamic, since a person can be performing any action, which can be a pose or a motion, and change to another action.

The scope of this work is about presenting a method for labelling human activity. The pattern classification algorithm for the skeleton data uses an euclidean measure. The learning model uses a single large Hidden Markov Model, or Compound Hidden Markov Model, to tell the activities of a person from the output of the motion analysis.

The contribution of this work consists of two parts. Firstly, we present a novel way of computing features of a skeleton using distances between certain joints of both upper body and lower body. Secondly, we propose a Compound Hidden Markov Model for labelling cyclic and non-cyclic human activities; the Compound Hidden Markov Model is made of smaller Hidden Markov Models which connect to common states.

1.1. Activity Recognition

The taxonomy of human activities depend on the complexity of the activity [1]. A *gesture* is an elementary movement of a body part. Some examples of gestures are "waving an arm" or "flexing a leg". Gestures are the building blocks for meaningful description of the motion of a person. An *action* is an activity performed by a single person, which is made of several gestures with chronological structure. The actions may involve interaction with objects. Some examples of actions are "walk" or "drink coffee". An *interaction* is a human activity involving two or more persons and/or objects. For example, "two persons dance waltz" is an interaction between two persons, or "one person delivers a briefcase to other person" is an interaction between two persons and an object. A *group activity* is an activity performed by conceptual groups, composed of multiple persons and/or objects.

Some applications of the activity recognition are [1]: Domestic Robotics, where is used for interacting with a robot; in areas of Surveillance is used for detecting suspicious activity, analysing the activities performed in an room; the Gaming applications aim to achieve interaction with a video game without physical input devices; the Health Care area, where the activity recognition can be coupled to systems for emergency response or can be used for physical rehabilitation.

A particular use case for activity labelling on Domestic Robotics could be: for example, a robot helps in cooking. A person is preparing food in the kitchen. The vision system of the robot captures motion data of the person. The Activity Recognition System analyses the motion to get the activities performed. The output of the Activity Recognition System provides information to the Action Planning System, which has information of the world and the robot. The Action Planning System picks a plan of action, such as getting closer to the person and ask to help out.

There is a number of challenges on each stage of the activity recognition. When motion data is acquired, there is noise on the sensor, both from internal and external sources,which alters the captured values of the motion; the occlusion of the sensor by other objects or persons produces inaccurate or incomplete data. There are some issues which are exclusive of the Computer Vision-based systems: the orientation of the body towards the sensor can obscure some body parts, generating inaccurate or incomplete data; bad lighting conditions, if they are not compensated, reduce the accuracy of the capture. The challenges on classifying motion data are: the raw motion data can be high-dimensional, so picking the features which provide the best description is necessary; the position of the person in the motion data is not absolute, that is solved by making the motion data relative to a reference frame. The challenges when recognizing activities is that they can involve interaction with other persons or objects, this is solved by segmenting the data into separate entities and tracking them; several activities can have the same motion, which is solved by segmenting the motion data before training a classification model which provides the input for the recognition model.

1.2. Approaches to Activity Recognition

There are two approaches for activity recognition, according to how the motion data is represented and recognized [1]. The *single-layered approach* represents and recognizes human activities directly from sequences of images. This approach is suitable for gesture recognition and actions with sequential characteristics. In contrast, the *hierarchical approach* represents high-level human activities with a description in terms of simpler activities. This approach is suitable for analysing complex activities, such as interactions and group activities.

The taxonomy of the single-layered approach depends on the way of modelling human activities: space-time approach and sequential approach [1].

The *space-time approach* views an input video as a three-dimensional (*XYT*) volume. This approach can be categorized further depending on the features used for the *XYT* volume: volumes of images [2]-[4], volumes of trajectories [5]-[7], or volumes of local interest point descriptors [8]-[10].

The *sequential approach* uses sequences of features from a human motion source. An activity has occurred if a particular sequence of features which is observed after analysing the features. There are two main types of sequential approaches: exemplary-based and state model-based [1]. This work uses the state model-based approach to human activity recognition.

In the *exemplary-based approach*, human activities are defined as sequences of features which have been trained directly. A human activity is recognized by computing the similarity of a new sequence of features against a set of reference sequences of features, if a similarity is high enough, the system deduces that the new sequence belong to a certain activity. Humans do not perform the same activity at the same rate or style, so the similarity measuring algorithm must account for those details.

An approach to account for those changes is *Dynamic Time Warping* [1] [11], a dynamic programming algorithm which stretches a pattern of motion over the time, to align and match it against a reference pattern of motion. The algorithm returns the cumulative distance between two patterns of motion. When comparing a pattern of motion against a set of reference patterns of motion, the reference pattern which has the highest similarity indicates the most likely activity [12]-[14].

In the *state model-based approach*, human activities are defined as statistical models with a set of states which generate corresponding sequences of feature vectors. The models generate those sequences with a certain probability. This approach accounts for rate and style changes. One of the most used mathematical models for recognizing activities is the Hidden Markov Model [15].

2. Hidden Markov Models

Hidden Markov Models, are statistical Markov Models in which the signal or process to model is assumed to be a Markov Process with unobserved states [15]. A stochastic process is a collection of random variables which represent the evolution of a random values over time, such as the spectra of a sound signal, or the probability of drawing a ball of a certain colour from a set of urns, which have coloured balls in varying amounts [15].

The states in a stochastic process have the distribution probabilities for the collection of random variables, and the transitions from a state to other depend on probabilities (non-determinism).

The Markov property indicates that the probability distribution of future states depends upon the present state; in other words, it does not keep record of past time or future states (memoryless).

The unobserved states in a Hidden Markov Model indicate that the states are not visible directly, but output depends probabilistically on the state (**Figure 1**).

The most common applications of a Hidden Markov Model are temporal pattern recognition, such as speech recognition, handwriting recognition, gesture recognition, speech tagging, following of musical scores, and DNA sequencing.

The output values for the random variables in a Hidden Markov Model can be discrete, originated from a categorical distribution, or continuous, originated from a Gaussian Distribution.

The elements of a Hidden Markov Model (λ) are: $\lambda = \{N, M, A, B, \pi\}$, where N, is the amount of states of the Markov process; M, is the amount of discrete output symbols for the Markov process; A, is the transition probability matrix between states of the Markov process; B, is the emission probability for output symbols per state of the Markov process; and π, is the probability of starting at a certain state of the Markov process.

For a Hidden Markov Model to be useful in real world applications, three basic problems must be solved [15]:

- Evaluation Problem: Given a sequence of observations $O = O_1 O_2 \cdots O_T$ and a model $\lambda = (A, B, \pi)$, how to efficiently compute the probability of the sequence of observations, given the model $P(O|\lambda)$?
- Optimal State Sequence Problem: Given a sequence of observations $O = O_1 O_2 \cdots O_T$ and a model $\lambda = (A, B, \pi)$, how to choose the most likely sequence of states $Q = Q_1 Q_2 \cdots Q_T$ which describes best the sequence of observations?

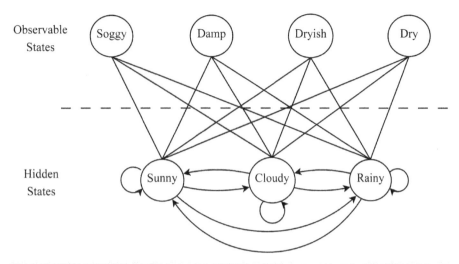

Figure 1. Hidden markov model.

- Training Problem: How to adjust the parameters of the model $\lambda = (A, B, \pi)$ to maximize $P(O|\lambda)$, the probability of a sequence of observations, $O = O_1 O_2 \cdots O_T$, given the model?

2.1. Solution to the Evaluation Problem

The Forward Procedure solves the Evaluation Problem. The forward variable $\alpha_t(i)$ defined as

$$\alpha_t(i) = P(O_1 O_2 \cdots O_t, q_t = S_i | \lambda) \tag{1}$$

indicates the probability of the partial observation sequence, $O_1 O_2 \cdots O_t$, (until time t), and state S_i at time t, given the model λ.

The inductive solution of $\alpha_t(i)$ is the following:

1) Initialization:

$$\alpha_1(i) = \pi_i b_i(O_i), \quad 1 \le i \le N \tag{2}$$

2) Induction:

$$\alpha_{t+1}(j) = \left[\Sigma_i \alpha_t(i) a_{ij} \right] b_j(O_{t+1}), \quad 1 \le t \le T-1, 1 \le j \le N \tag{3}$$

3) Termination:

$$P(O|\lambda) = \sum_{i=1}^{N} \alpha_T(i) \tag{4}$$

The initialization step sets the forward probabilities as the joint probability of state S_i and initial observation O_1. The induction step computes the partial probability at the state S_j, at time $t+1$ with the accompanying partial observations. And, the termination step computes the final forward probability by summing all the terminal forward variables $\alpha_T(i)$.

2.2. Solution to the Most Likely Sequence of States Problem

The evaluation problem is solved by the Viterbi Algorithm, which computes the most likely sequence of connected states $Q = Q_1 Q_2 \cdots Q_T$ which generates a sequence of observations $O_1 O_2 \cdots O_T$, given a model λ.

The Viterbi Algorithm uses the variable δ, which contains the highest probability of a single path, at the time t.

$$\delta_t(i) = \max_{q_1, q_2 \cdots q_{t-1}} P\left[q_1, q_2 \cdots q_{t-1} = i, O_1, O_2 \cdots O_t | \lambda \right] \tag{5}$$

The highest probability along a single path, at time $t+1$, is computed as:

$$\delta_{t+1}(j) = \left[\max_i \delta_t(i)a_{ij}\right]b_j(O_{t+1}) \tag{6}$$

The most likely path is the sequence of these maximized variables, for each time t and each state j. The array $\psi_t(j)$ tracks all the maximized variables $\delta_t(j)$. The most likely state sequence is retrieved by backtracking the variable $\psi_t(j)$.

1) Initialization:

$$\delta_1(i) = \pi_i b_i(O_1), \quad 1 \le i \le N \tag{7a}$$

$$\psi_1(i) = 0. \tag{7b}$$

2) Recursion:

$$\delta_t(j) = \max_i\left[\delta_{t-1}(i)a_{ij}\right]b_j(O_t), \quad 2 \le t \le T, \ 1 \le j \le N \tag{8a}$$

$$\psi_t(j) = \arg\max_i\left[\delta_{t-1}(i)a_{ij}\right], \quad 2 \le t \le T, \ 1 \le j \le N. \tag{8b}$$

3) Termination:

$$P^* = \max_{1 \le i \le N}\left[\delta_T(i)\right] \tag{9a}$$

$$q_t^* = \arg\max_{1 \le i \le N}\left[\delta_T(i)\right]. \tag{9b}$$

4) Backtracking:

$$q_t^* = \psi_{t+1}(q_{t+1}^*), \quad t = T-1, T-2, \cdots, 1 \tag{10}$$

2.3. Solution to the Training Problem

An approach for solving the Training Problem is the Viterbi Learning algorithm [16], which uses the Viterbi Algorithm to estimate the parameters of a Hidden Markov Model. The algorithm can estimate the parameters from a set of multiple sequences of observations. That property makes it different of the Baum-Welch algorithm [15], which requires all the training observation samples to be merged in a single sequence.

The initialization of the transition matrix is done with random values. The random values on each row are normalized, so its sum is equal to one. A bit mask matrix describing the transitions of a specific graph topology can be used to set the probabilities. The transition probabilities under a bit mask value equal to zero get a very small value, while the transition probabilities under a bit mask value equal to one get a random value.

The initialization step for the emission matrix uses one of these approaches: random values or segmented observation sequences. When initializing with random values, all the values must be larger than zero and each row must be normalized, so the sum of each row is equal to one. In the segmented observations sequences approach, the sequence is split by the number of states of the Hidden Markov Model. If the length of the sequence is not a multiple of the number of states, the last state gets less observations. For each state, the emission probability of each symbol is equal to the count of that symbol divided by the total amount of symbols assigned to that state.

The initial probability vector can be initialized either to uniform probabilities or by assigning the larger probability to an state or a number of states. The probabilities are normalized so its sum is equal to one.

In the induction step, for each sequence of observations for training, the Most Likely State Path is computed with the Viterbi Algorithm on the initial Hidden Markov Model, and the Likelihood Probability is computed either with the Viterbi Algorithm or the Forward Algorithm on the initial Hidden Markov Model. The Most Likely State Path of each sequence is stored for computing the parameters of an updated Hidden Markov Model. The Forward Probability of each sequence is accumulated in the variable $prob_{old}$ for computing the condition of termination.

The values of the updated transition matrix A are computed by counting the transitions from the state Q_t, to the next state Q_{t+1}, on the Most Likely State Paths associated to each sequence of observations for training. At the end, the values of each row on the transition matrix are normalized, so its sum is equal to one.

The values of the updated emission matrix B are the frequencies of each observation symbol in the observation sequence, O_t, per state in the Most Likely State Path, Q_t, at the time t, *i.e.*, $B(Q_t)(O_t) = B(Q_t)(O_t) + 1$. The values of each row on the emission matrix are normalized, so its sum is equal to one.

The initial probability vector π is updated by counting the states assigned to the first elements of each Most Likely State Path Q_1.

A new Hidden Markov Model is built from the updated model parameters $\lambda = A, B, \pi$. To check if the model maximizes $P(O|\lambda)$, the Forward Probability of each sequence of observations for training is computed with the model, and accumulated in the variable $prob_{new}$.

The conditions for terminating the algorithm are: either the absolute of the difference of $prob_{new}$ and $prob_{old}$ is smaller than a threshold, or a certain number of iterations has been reached. If any of those conditions is false, the updated Hidden Markov Model is passed to the next iteration of the induction step, otherwise, the algorithm returns the updated Hidden Markov Model.

2.4. Logarithmic Scaling

Both Forward Probability Algorithm and Viterbi Algorithm store the result of floating-point operations in a single variable. The accumulated product of fractional values is a value so small that might fall below the minimum precision of the floating-point variable which stores the result. That variable can be represented in logarithmic scale, where multiplication and division operations are represented as addition and subtraction respectively. The range of values in logarithmic scale goes from $-\infty \cdots +\infty$, where negative logarithmic values represent fractional values and positive logarithmic values represent integral values larger or equal than one. In the case of the elements of a Hidden Markov Model, the values of A, B, and π are converted to negative logarithmic values.

The logarithmic scale in the Forward Algorithm applies at each iteration in the Induction step, a scale variable accumulates the value of the forward variable α, for each state. The forward probability is the sum of the logarithms of the scale for each state.

For the Viterbi Algorithm, the elements of the model $\lambda = A, B, \pi$ are converted to logarithmic scale. In the case of the emission matrix B, the emissions probabilities per states of each observation $O = O_1 O_2 \cdots O_T$ are converted to logarithmic scale. The value of the variable δ is updated by cumulative addition.

Hidden Markov Model Topologies

Depending on the process that generates a signal, the contents of the signal can have a stationary structure, or a chronological structure. The structure of the contents of the signal indicates which is the most suitable Hidden Markov Model [17].

The classical case of the set of bowls containing different proportions of coloured balls is an example of a stationary process: any ball is drawn from any bowl at any time. For this case, the most suitable topology for the Hidden Markov Model is the ergodic model (**Figure 2(a)**), where all the states are fully connected [17].

In automated motion recognition and activity recognition applications, the input data to be processed has a chronological or linear structure [17].

The simplest topology for linear processes is the linear model (**Figure 2(b)**), where each states connects to itself (self-transitions) and to the next state. The self-transitions account for variations in the duration of the patterns in a state [17].

The flexibility in the modelling of the duration can increase if it is possible to skip individual states in the sequence. One of the most used topology variations for automated speech and handwriting recognition is the Bakis model (**Figure 2(c)**). The Bakis model has a transition that skips two states ahead the current state, while the state is not the last state or the next-to-last state [17].

The largest variations in the chronological structure are achieved by allowing a state to have transitions to any posterior states in the chronological sequence. The only forbidden transition is going from a state S_i to a state S_j where $j < i$. This model is called Left-to-Right model (**Figure 2(d)**) [17].

Any of the Hidden Markov Models for signals with chronological structure—Linear, Bakis, Left-to-Right—can model cyclic signals by adding a transition from the last state to the first state (**Figures 2(e)-(f)**) [18].

2.5. Related Work

The *Hidden Markov Model* is one of the most commonly used statistical models in the state model-based

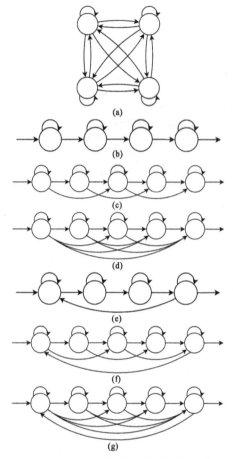

Figure 2. Hidden markov model topologies. (a) Ergodic HMM; (b) Linear HMM; (c) Bakis HMM; (d) Left-to-right HMM; (e) Cyclic linear HMM; (f) Cyclic bakis HMM; (g) Cyclic left-to-right HMM.

approach to Activity Recognition. There are two approaches for recognizing activities with Hidden Markov Models: Maximum Likelihood Probability (MLP) [19]-[23] and Most Likely State Path (MLSP) [24]-[28]. Next we list the main features, advantages and disadvantages of the two approaches.

2.5.1. Maximum Likelihood Probability Activity Recognition
• Features:
-Each Activity has a Hidden Markov Model.
-Each Hidden Markov Model computes the Forward Probability of a sequence of observation symbols.
-The Hidden Markov Model with the largest Forward Probability identifies the activity.
• Advantages:
-New activities can be added easily by training another Hidden Markov Model.
-The evaluation of a sequence of observation symbols can be performed by parallel tasks.
• Disadvantages:
-Motion segmentation is required when recognizing connected activities.

2.5.2. Most Likely State Path Activity Recognition
• Features:
-All the activities are embedded in a single large Hidden Markov Model.
-Each activity is represented by a subset of states.
-A sequence of observation symbols is processed to obtain the sequence of most likely states which generates it.

• Advantages:
-The evaluation of connected activities is possible without motion segmentation.
-Reconstruction of activities from the sequence of most likely states.
• Disadvantages:
-Adding a new activity is complicated: the Hidden Markov Model for the new activity is trained separately, the Hidden Markov Model is merged with the single large Hidden Markov Model and the single large Hidden Markov Model must be retrained to update the probabilities of emission and transition.
-The computation of likelihood probability with Viterbi Algorithm is slower than with Forward Algorithm,
-Reconstruction of activities requires an index which associates each activity with a subset of states.

2.6. Variants of Hidden Markov Models

A limitation of the Hidden Markov Models is that they do not allow for complex activities, interactions between persons and objects, and group interactions. To enhance the probability of recognizing activities with Hidden Markov Models, variations to the model have been studied in previous works.

In the Conditioned Hidden Markov Model [29] [30], the selection of the states is influenced by an external cause. Such cause can be the symbols generated by an external classifier. The probability of those symbols increases the probability of a sequence. This model allows using two streams of different features from the same data.

The Coupled Hidden Markov Model [20] [31] [32] is formed by a collection of Hidden Markov Models. Each Hidden Markov Model handles a data stream. The observations cannot be merged using the Cartesian product of the amount of the symbols of each data stream. The nodes at the time t are conditioned by the nodes at the time $t-1$ of all the related Hidden Markov Models. This model is suitable for recognizing activities using data from multiple sources.

The states of a Hidden Semi-Markov Model [33]-[35] emits a sequence of observations. The next state is predicted based on how long it has remained in the past state. This model relaxes the memoryless property of a Markov Chain.

The Maximum Entropy Markov Model represents [21] [36] the dependence between each state and the full observation system explicitly. The model completely ignores modelling the probability of the state $P(X)$. The learning objective function is consistent with the predictive function $P(Y|X)$. The observation Y sees all the states X, instead of the observation being dependent on the state.

The Compound Hidden Markov Model [17] [37]-[40] is formed by the concatenation of sub-word units Hidden Markov Models. The sub-word units form a lexicon of words. Parallel connections link all the individual sub-word units. The recognized words are subsets of connected states in the most likely state path. The representation of the model can be simplified by the addition of non-emitting states.

The Dynamic Multiple Link Hidden Markov Model [41] is built by connecting multiple Hidden Markov Models. Each Hidden Markov Model models the activities of a single entity. The relevant states between multiple Hidden Markov Models are linked. This model is suitable for group activities.

The Two-Stage Linear Hidden Markov Model [42] is formed by two stages of Linear Hidden Markov Models. The first stage recognizes low-level motions or gestures to generate a sequence of gestures. The sequence of gestures becomes the input for the Hidden Markov Model at the second stage. The second stage recognizes complex activities from the sequences of gestures.

The Layered Hidden Markov Model [28] [43] is a model in which several Hidden Markov Models in layers of increasing activity levels. The layers at the lowest level recognizes simple activities. The simple activities form high-level activities at upper levels. The upper levels use the simple activities to recognize complex activities.

The Hidden Markov Model topology chosen for this work is the Compound Hidden Markov Model, because the purpose of this work is labelling activities performed by a person, during a period of time.

3. Proposed Approach

The method for activity recognition proposed in this work uses a representation of skeleton data based in Euclidean distance between body parts, and a Compound Hidden Markov Model for activity labelling.

3.1. Skeleton Features

The features of the skeleton are a variation of those presented in Glodek *et al.* [30]. The features are made of set of Euclidean distances between joints. The work of Glodek *et al.*, 2012 [30] represents poses from the upper body, as a set of Euclidean distances between these pairs of joints (**Figure 3(a)**): left hand-head, left hand-left shoulder, left hand-left hip, left elbow-torso, right hand-head, right hand-right shoulder, right hand-right hip, and right elbow-torso. This work uses a variation of the features described Glodek *et al.*, 2012 to represent poses of the whole body, as a set of Euclidean distances between these pairs of joints (**Figure 3(b)**): left hand-head, left hand-neck, left hand-left shoulder, left elbow-torso, left foot-hip, left foot-neck, left foot-head, left knee-torso, right hand-head, right hand-neck, right hand-right shoulder, right elbow-torso, right foot-hip, right foot-neck, right foot-head, and right knee-torso.

3.2. Observations for the Hidden Markov Model

The observations for the Hidden Markov Model are computed from the Euclidean Distance between the features of two skeletons. To get the observations of a new sequence of motion data, the skeletons of each frame have their features computed. A set of similarities is computed for each frame of the new sequence of motion data. Those similarities come from the Euclidean Distance of the features of a frame of motion data and the features of each element of the codebook of key frames. The index of the key frame with the smallest Euclidean Distance becomes the observation of each frame.

3.3. Compound Hidden Markov Model

The model proposed for activity labelling is a Compound Hidden Markov Model [37]-[40], which is a Hidden Markov Model where a subset of states represent a pattern, each subset of states is connected to a common initial state and a common final state, and the common final state always connects to the common initial state. The recognized patterns are extracted from the sequence of most likely states, obtained from applying the Viterbi Algorithm to a sequence of observations.

The Compound Hidden Markov Model is formed by several simpler Hidden Markov Models, whose topologies are configured according to the type of activity to model: the stationary activities, like *sit still* and *stand still*, have a single state; the non-periodic activities, like *stand up* and *sit down*, are modelled with Linear Hidden Markov Models; and, the periodic activities, such as *walk*, are modelled by a Cyclical Linear Hidden Markov Model.

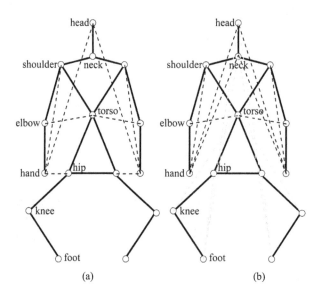

Figure 3. Skeleton Features for pose description. (a) The work of Glodek *et al.*, 2012 [30] represents poses from the upper body, as a set of Euclidean distances between the pairs of joints, which indicated by the black dashed lines; (b) This work uses a variation of the features described Glodek *et al.*, 2012 to represent poses of the whole body, as a set of Euclidean distances between pairs of joints. The black dashed lines indicate the pairs of joints for the upper body, and the grey dashed lines indicate the pairs of joints for the lower body.

The activities are connected using context information. For example, the *sit still* activity connects to the first state of the *stand up* activity, and receives a connection from the last state of the *sit down* activity. The *stand still* activity connects to the first state of the *sit down* activity, and receives a connection from the last state of the *stand up* activity. Also, the *stand still* activity connects to the first state of the *walk* activity and receives a connection from the last state of the *walk* activity (**Figure 4**).

The stationary activities (*sit still*, *stand still*) are modelled with a Hidden Markov Model formed by a single state. The emission probabilities of each Hidden Markov Model are initialized to the averaged frequency of the observations for the corresponding idle activity.

The non-periodic activities (*stand up*, *sit down*) and the periodic activities, (*walk*), are trained using the following procedure: the observations from motion data of each activity are segmented into three sections: the *anticipation* (**Figure 5(a)**), which contains the poses which indicate that a motion is about to start; the *action* (**Figure 5(b)**), which contains the poses which describe a motion; and the *reaction* (**Figure 5(c)**), which contains the poses which indicate the recovery from an action to a neutral position. These three sections, anticipation-action-reaction (AAR), come from the theory of animation [44] [45].

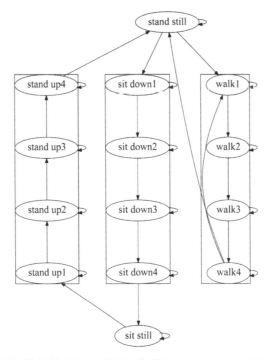

Figure 4. Compound hidden markov model for activity labelling.

Figure 5. An activity has three sections: the motion preceding the activity (anticipation), the motion of the activity (action) and the motion after the activity is performed (reaction). Source: Animal Locomotion, Vol. 1, Plate 154, by Eadweard Muybridge, 1887.

The Hidden Markov Models for stationary activities, non-periodic activities, and periodic activities are merged in a Compound Hidden Markov Model, as specified in the Section 3.3, and its parameters are re-estimated using Viterbi Learning with all the elements of the training set.

4. Experiments

In order to assess the labelling accuracy of both the Compound Hidden Markov Model and some reference Hidden Markov Models, they was tested with a data set of human activities.

4.1. Data Source

The tests were performed using the Microsoft Research Daily Activity 3D Data set (MSRDaily) [46], which was captured by using a Microsoft Kinect device.

The data set is composed by 16 activities, a) drink; b) eat; c) read book; d) call cellphone; e) write on a paper; f) use laptop; g) use vacuum cleaner; h) cheer up; i) remain still; j) toss paper; k) play game; l) lay down on sofa; m) walk; n) play guitar; o) stand up; and p) sit down which are performed by 10 persons, who execute each activity twice, once in standing position, and once in sitting position. There is a sofa in the scene. Three channels are recorded: depth maps (.bin), skeleton joint positions (.txt), and RGB video (.avi). There are $16 \times 10 \times 2 = 320$ files for each channel. The whole set is formed by $320 \times 3 = 960$ files. The position of the joints of the skeleton are computed from the depth map [47].

For the purpose of this work, only the skeleton joint positions were used as input for labelling the actions, as well as a subset of activities: a) remain still (sitting pose) (**Figure 6(a)**); b) remain still (standing pose) (**Figure 6(b)**); c) walk (**Figure 6(c)** and **Figure 6(d)**); d) stand up (**Figure 6(e)** and **Figure 6(f)**); and e) sit down (**Figure 6(g)** and **Figure 6(h)**). Those activities are selected because there is a clear start in the sitting pose or the standing pose , or there are transitions between the sitting pose and the standing pose.

At the training step, the Hidden Markov Model is generated using a training set of motion data. The training set is made of the motion data from the first 6 subjects of the MSRDaily data set, while the motion data of the last 4 subjects constitute the testing set.

4.1.1. Computing the Codebook

The Microsoft Kinect sensor captures the depth map $\vec{D}$ of a motion sequence of an activity performed by a person. The depth map is processed to extract a skeleton $\vec{S} = \{j_1, j_2, \cdots, j_{15}\}, j = \{x, y, z\}$ [47]. During the capture, a skeleton represents a single frame of the motion, therefore, a whole motion sequence contains several skeletons. The training set of an activity is formed by captures of motion sequences of the same activity performed by several people.

First of all, the skeletons have their features extracted, using the algorithm described in the Section 3.1. All the features from the skeletons of the training set are clustered with the k-means algorithm. The centroids of the clusters become the codebook of key frames.

The amount of symbols used in this work is 255, because that is the amount of symbols which provided the best labelling accuracy on the testing set, after performing tests on different amounts of symbols for the codebook, which were $31, 63, 127, 255, 511, 1023, 2047,$ and 4095 centroids[1].

4.1.2. Building the Compound Hidden Markov Model

The Hidden Markov Model for a non-stationary activity has the following structure for its states: the amount of states is N, where $N \geq 3$, so the states can contain all the states of a motion; the state S_1 is for the random variables of the anticipation of the motion (Anticipation State), the state S_N is for the random variables of the reaction of the motion (Reaction State), and the states $S_2 \cdots S_{N-1}$ are for the random variables of the action of the motion (Action States).

The transition probabilities from the Anticipation State to the Action States are initialized to uniform values. There are no transitions from the Action States to the Anticipation State. The transition probabilities from the

---

[1]The reason for those sizes for the codebooks was that for the experiments, the initial amount of symbols were powers of two—32, 64, 128, 256, 512, 1024, 2048, and 4096—but one of the centroids computed by the k-means algorithm had undefined values (NaN values) and had to be removed from the codebook, to avoid arithmetical errors when computing the Euclidean distance between any data object and a centroid with undefined values.

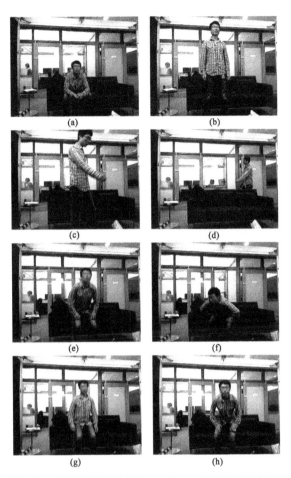

Figure 6. Subset of activities from Microsoft Research Daily Activity 3D used in this work. (a) Idle, sitting position; (b) Idle, standing position; (c) Walk in front of a sofa; (d) Walk behind a sofa; (e) Stand up, frontal orientation; (f) Stand up, three-quarters orientation; (g) Sit down, frontal orientation; (h) Sit Down, three-quarters orientation.

Action States to the Reaction State are initialized to uniform values. And, the transition probabilities from the Reaction State to the Anticipation State are set to uniform values.

The observations from the anticipation section are used for initialize the emission probabilities of the Anticipation State. The observations from the reaction section are used to initialize the emission probabilities of the Reaction State. The emission probabilities of the Action States are initialized to random values.

Both the transition probabilities and the emission probabilities for all the States will be refined after applying Viterbi Learning [16] to the Model.

4.2. Testing Activity Labelling.

The assessment of the quality of a labelled activity is done on the results of computing the Most Likely State Sequence from the observations of an activity.

The joints of the skeleton $\vec{S}$ are converted to vector of features $\vec{c}$ (Section 3.1). The features $\vec{c}$ are classified against a codebook of key frames $F = \{f_1, f_2, \cdots, f_k\}$, using Euclidean Distance.

The key frame with the minimum distance becomes an observation o, which is appended to a sequence of observations $\vec{O} = \{o_1, o_2, \cdots, o_t\}$.

Assessing Labelling Accuracy

The first Hidden Markov Model to test is an Ergodic Hidden Markov Model where each state represent a single activity, giving a total of 5 states (**Figure 7(a)**).

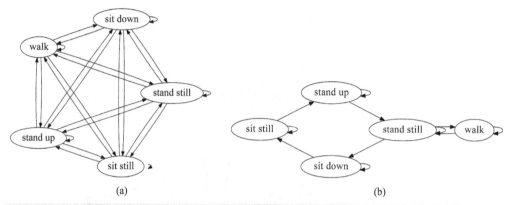

Figure 7. Hidden markov models for activity labelling (reference). (a) Ergodic hidden markov model; (b) Graph-like hidden markov model.

For the second Hidden Markov Model, the proposal is a Hidden Markov Model organized like a Finite State Machine. Each activity is represented by a single state, giving a total of 5 states. The connections between the states of each activity use a language model.

The third Hidden Markov Model is a variation of the second Hidden Markov Model, where its parameters are retrained with Viterbi Learning. The connections between the states of each activity use a language model.

Both the second and the third Hidden Markov Model have a Graph-like structure (**Figure 7(b)**).

The fourth Hidden Markov Model is the Compound Hidden Markov Model proposed in the Section 2.3 (**Figure 8**). The connections between the states at the ends of each activity use a language model.

The language model for connecting coherent activities is the following:
•Sit Still → Sit Still.
•Sit Still → Stand Up → Stand Still.
•Stand Still → Stand Still.
•Stand Still → Sit Down → Sit Still.
•Stand Still → Walk → Stand Still.

The sequence of observations $\bar{O}$ is the input for the Compound Hidden Markov Model. The Viterbi algorithm decodes the sequence of observations to a sequence of most likely states $\bar{Q}$. The states show an activity executed at an instant of time.

The criteria for determining the accuracy of the sequence of most likely states $\bar{Q}$ is *sequence accuracy*. A sequence of states is accurate if the rate between the count of the states which follow the expected sequence of motions and the length of the sequence of states is greater or equal than a threshold of 90%. The language model for connecting coherent activities specifies the expected sequence of motions for an activity. Repeated states are allowed as long as they stay on a expected motion. The sequence accuracy criterion depends on the assessed activity (**Table 1**).

5. Results

The tests were performed on the four different Hidden Markov Models specified in the section 23. Each Hidden Markov Model was tested with the following amount of symbols 31, 63, 127, 255, 511, 1023, 2047, and 4095 , while keeping the amount of states of each Hidden Markov Model topology. The tables show the Hidden Markov Model with the amount of symbols that provided the highest labelling accuracy.

The assessed data was the sequence of most likely states $\bar{Q}$ computed with the Viterbi Algorithm on the observations of the motion data. If all the states match the expected sequence of motions, the activity labelling is correct.

Table 2(a) and **Table 2(b)** show the average labelling accuracy of three codebook sizes for each topology of Hidden Markov Models which gave the highest labelling accuracy for all the activities. **Tables 3(a)-(d)** show the results of the tests on the 6 subjects of the training set from the MSRDaily data set. The first column shows the topology of the Hidden Markov Model, the columns 2-4 show the three sizes of codebooks which gave high accuracy for a first activity, and the columns 5-7 show three sizes of codebooks which gave high accuracy for a second activity.

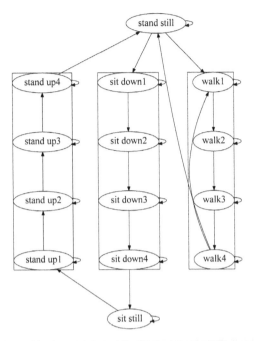

Figure 8. Hidden markov models for activity labelling (proposed). compound hidden markov model.

Table 1. Criteria for sequence accuracy per activity.

Activity	Expected sequence of motions
Sit still	{Sit still}
Stand still	{Stand still}
Stand up	{Sit still, stand up, stand still}
Sit down	{Stand still, sit down, sit still}
Walk	{Stand still, walk, stand still (optional)}

Table 2. Average labelling accuracy for the hidden markov models with highest accuracy. (a) Training set, inter-joint distance features; (b) Testing set, inter-joint distance features.

(a)

	Codebook size		
Model (#states)	255 symbols	511 symbols	2047 symbols
Ergodic (5)	25.00%	37.50%	58.33%
Graph-like (5)	41.66%	43.75%	54.16%
Graph-like retrained (5)	41.66%	43.75%	68.75%
Compound (14)	54.16%	54.16%	77.08%

(b)

	Codebook size		
Model (#states)	255 symbols	511 symbols	2047 symbols
Ergodic (5)	6.25%	15.62%	18.75%
Graph-like (5)	18.75%	12.50%	6.25%
Graph-like retrained (5)	18.75%	18.75%	53.12%
Compound (14)	59.37%	56.25%	53.12%

Table 3. Results on activity labelling accuracy for inter-joint distance features (training set). (a) Number of subjects, out of 6, with correct labelling on "sit" and "stand"; (b) Number of subjects, out of 6, with correct labelling on "walk" and "walk occluded"; (c) Number of subjects, out of 6, with correct labelling on "stand up 1" and "stand up 2"; (d) Number of subjects, out of 6, with correct labelling on "sit down 1" and "sit down 2".

(a)

Subjects tested			6			
Activity		Sit			Stand	
Model (#states, #symbols)	255	511	2047	255	511	2047
Ergodic (5)	4	**6**	**6**	**2**	**3**	**6**
Graph-like (5)	**6**	**6**	**6**	0	0	0
Graph-like retrained (5)	**6**	**6**	**6**	0	0	0
Compound (14)	**6**	**6**	**6**	0	0	0

(b)

Subjects tested			6			
Activity		Walk			Walk occluded	
Model (#states, #symbols)	255	511	2047	255	511	2047
Ergodic (5)	1	4	**6**	0	0	0
Graph-like (5)	**6**	**6**	5	0	0	0
Graph-like retrained (5)	**6**	**6**	**6**	0	0	2
Compound (14)	**6**	**6**	**6**	4	4	3

(c)

Subjects tested			6			
Activity		Stand up 1			Stand up 2	
Model (#states, #symbols)	255	511	2047	255	511	2047
Ergodic (5)	3	4	**6**	0	0	0
Graph-like (5)	**5**	5	5	0	0	0
Graph-like retrained (5)	**5**	5	**6**	0	0	**4**
Compound (14)	**5**	**6**	**6**	**1**	0	**4**

(d)

Subjects tested			6			
Activity		Sit down 1			Sit down 2	
Model (#states, #symbols)	255	511	2047	255	511	2047
Ergodic (5)	2	1	4	0	0	0
Graph-like (5)	**3**	**3**	**6**	0	**1**	4
Graph-like retrained (5)	**3**	**3**	5	0	**1**	4
Compound (14)	**3**	**3**	**6**	**1**	**1**	**6**

Tables 4(a)-(d) show the results of the tests on the 4 subjects of the testing set from the MSRDaily data set. The first column shows the topology of the Hidden Markov Model, the columns 2-4 show the three sizes of codebooks which gave high accuracy for a first activity, and the columns 5-7 show three sizes of codebooks which gave high accuracy for a second activity.

Table 4. Results on activity labelling accuracy for inter-joint distance features (testing set). (a) Number of subjects, out of 4, with correct labelling on "sit" and "stand"; (b) Number of subjects, out of 4, with correct labelling on "walk" and "walk occluded"; (c) Number of subjects, out of 4, with correct labelling on "stand up 1" and "stand up 2"; (d) Number of subjects, out of 4, with correct labelling on "sit down 1" and "sit down 2".

(a)

Subjects tested	4					
Activity	Sit			Stand		
Model (#states, #symbols)	255	511	2047	255	511	2047
Ergodic (5)	0	0	0	1	2	2
Graph-like (5)	0	0	0	1	1	0
Graph-like retrained (5)	0	1	2	1	1	1
Compound (14)	2	2	2	3	2	2

(b)

Subjects tested	4					
Activity	Walk			Walk occluded		
Model (#states, #symbols)	255	511	2047	255	511	2047
Ergodic (5)	1	2	4	0	0	0
Graph-like (5)	4	1	1	0	1	0
Graph-like retrained (5)	4	2	4	1	1	3
Compound (14)	4	4	4	2	2	2

(c)

Subjects tested	4					
Activity	Stand up 1			Stand up 2		
Model (#states, #symbols)	255	511	2047	255	511	2047
Ergodic (5)	0	1	0	0	0	0
Graph-like (5)	0	1	1	0	0	0
Graph-like retrained (5)	0	1	2	0	0	2
Compound (14)	3	2	2	2	2	3

(d)

Subjects tested	4					
Activity	Sit down 1			Sit down 2		
Model (#states, #symbols)	255	511	2047	255	511	2047
Ergodic (5)	0	0	0	0	0	0
Graph-like (5)	0	0	0	1	0	0
Graph-like retrained (5)	0	0	2	0	0	1
Compound (14)	1	1	2	2	3	0

The results for both the training set and the testing set show that the Compound Hidden Markov Model labels correctly a sequence of motion more often than an Ergodic Hidden Markov Model or the Graph-like Hidden Markov Models, when the amount of symbols is lesser than 2047 (**Table 2(a)** and **Table 2(b)**). The Compound Hidden Markov Model which had the highest labelling accuracy on the testing set has a codebook of 255 symbols.

In the Hidden Markov Models whose codebooks are of $\{2047, 4095\}$ symbols, the Retrained Graph-like Hidden Markov Model had a labelling accuracy similar to the Compound Hidden Markov Model (**Table 2(a)** and **Table 2(b)**).

It must be noted that the "Walk Occluded" activity is labelled incorrectly by all the Hidden Markov Models. The reason for such failure is that the skeleton data is incorrect or noisy because a sofa occludes the person who is walking. The algorithm which computes the skeleton [47] only works when the body is completely visible.

6. Conclusion

We present results for labelling human activity from skeleton data of a single Microsoft Kinect sensor. We present a novel way of computing features of a skeleton using distances between certain joints of both upper body and lower body. And, we propose a Compound Hidden Markov Model for labelling cyclic and non-cyclic human activities, which perform better than the reference Hidden Markov Models, an Ergodic Hidden Markov Model and a Graph-like Hidden Markov Model. The results for labelling 5 activities from 4 non-trained subjects show that the Compound Hidden Markov Model, with a codebook of 255 symbols, labels correctly a sequence of motion with an average accuracy of 59.37%, which is higher than the average labelling accuracy for activities of unknown subjects of an Ergodic Hidden Markov Model (6.25%), and a Compound Hidden Markov Model with activities modelled by a single state (18.75%), both with a codebook of 255 symbols. The contributions of this work are the representation of a full body pose with Euclidean distances between certain pairs of body joints, and the method for training a Compound Hidden Markov Model for activity labelling by segmenting the training data with the Anticipation-Action-Reaction sections from theory of animation. The future work involves using a new representation for the skeleton, based on Orthogonal Direction Change Chain Codes [48] [49], for both the codebook and the input samples.

Acknowledgements

This work was supported by PAPIIT-DGAPA UNAM under Grant IN-107609.

References

[1]   Aggarwal, J. and Ryoo, M. (2011) Human Activity Analysis: A Review. *ACM Computing Surveys*, **43**, 16:1-16:43. http://dx.doi.org/10.1145/1922649.1922653

[2]   Bobick, A. and Davis, J. (2001) The Recognition of Human Movement Using Temporal Templates. *IEEE Transactions on Pattern Analysis and Machine Intelligence*, **23**, 257-267. http://dx.doi.org/10.1109/34.910878

[3]   Ke, Y., Sukthankar, R. and Hebert, M. (2007) Spatio-Temporal Shape and Flow Correlation for Action Recognition. *Proceedings of the IEEE Conference on Computer Vision and Pattern Recognition*, Minneapolis, 17-22 June 2007, 1-8. http://dx.doi.org/10.1109/cvpr.2007.383512

[4]   Shechtman, E. and Irani, M. (2005) Space-Time Behavior Based Correlation. *Proceedings of the IEEE Computer Society Conference on Computer Vision and Pattern Recognition*, San Diego, 20-25 June 2005, 405-412. http://dx.doi.org/10.1109/cvpr.2005.328

[5]   Campbell, L. and Bobick, A. (1995) Recognition of Human Body Motion Using Phase Space Constraints. *5th International Conference on Computer Vision*, Cambridge, 20-23 June 1995, 624-630. http://dx.doi.org/10.1109/ICCV.1995.466880

[6]   Rao, C. and Shah, M. (2001) View-Invariance in Action Recognition. In *Proceedings of the 2001 IEEE Computer Society Conference on Computer Vision and Pattern Recognition*, Kauai, 8-14 December 2001, II-316-II-322. http://dx.doi.org/10.1109/cvpr.2001.990977

[7]   Sheikh, Y., Sheikh, M. and Shah, M. (2005) Exploring the Space of a Human Action. *Proceedings of the Tenth IEEE International Conference on Computer Vision*, Beijing, 15-21 October 2005, 144-149. http://dx.doi.org/10.1109/iccv.2005.90

[8]   Ryoo, M.S. and Aggarwal, J. (2009) Spatio-Temporal Relationship Match: Video Structure Comparison for Recogni-

tion of Complex Human Activities. *Proceedings of the 12th IEEE International Conference on Computer Vision*, Kyoto, 27 September-4 October 2009, 1593-1600.

[9] Wong, K.Y.K., Kim, T.-K. and Cipolla, R. (2007) Learning Motion Categories Using Both Semantic and Structural Information. *Proceedings of the IEEE Conference on Computer Vision and Pattern Recognition*, Minneapolis, 18-23 June 2007, 1-6. http://dx.doi.org/10.1109/cvpr.2007.383332

[10] Yilma, A. and Shah, M. (2005) Recognizing Human Actions in Videos Acquired by Uncalibrated Moving Cameras. *Proceedings of the Tenth IEEE International Conference on Computer Vision*, Beijing, 15-21 October 2005, 150-157. http://dx.doi.org/10.1109/iccv.2005.201

[11] Vintsyuk, T. (1968) Speech Discrimination by Dynamic Programming. *Cybernetics*, **4**, 52-57. http://dx.doi.org/10.1007/BF01074755

[12] Darrell, T. and Pentland, A. (1993) Space-Time Gestures. *IEEE Computer Society Conference on Computer Vision and Pattern Recognition*, 335-340. http://dx.doi.org/10.1109/cvpr.1993.341109

[13] Gavrila, D. and Davis, L. (1996) 3-D Model-Based Tracking of Humans in Action: A Multi-View Approach. *Proceedings of the IEEE Computer Society Conference on Computer Vision and Pattern Recognition*, San Francisco, 18-20 June 1996, 73-80.

[14] Yacoob, Y. and Black, M. (1998) Parameterized Modeling and Recognition of Activities. *Proceedings of the Sixth International Conference on Computer Vision*, Bombay, 7 January 1998, 120-127. http://dx.doi.org/10.1109/iccv.1998.710709

[15] Rabiner, L.R. (1989) A Tutorial on Hidden Markov Models and Selected Applications in Speech Recognition. *Proceedings of the IEEE*, **77**, 257-286. http://dx.doi.org/10.1109/5.18626

[16] Rabiner, L. and Juang, B.H. (1993) Fundamentals of Speech Recognition. Prentice Hall, Englewood Cliffs.

[17] Fink, G.A. (2007) Markov Models for Pattern Recognition: From Theory to Applications. Springer E-Books.

[18] Magee, D.R. and Boyle, R.D. (2002) Detecting Lameness Using "Re-Sampling Condensation" and "Multi-Stream Cyclic Hidden Markov Models". *Image and Vision Computing*, **20**, 581-594. http://dx.doi.org/10.1016/S0262-8856(02)00047-1

[19] Chen, H.-S., Chen, H.-T., Chen, Y.-W. and Lee, S.-Y. (2006) Human Action Recognition Using Star Skeleton. *Proceedings of the 4th ACM International Workshop on Video Surveillance and Sensor Networks*, New York, 171-178. http://dx.doi.org/10.1145/1178782.1178808

[20] Starner, T.E. and Pentland, A. (1995) Visual Recognition of American Sign Language Using Hidden Markov Models. *Proceedings of the International Workshop on Automatic Face- and Gesture-Recognition*, Zurich, 26-28 June 1995.

[21] Sung, J., Ponce, C., Selman, B. and Saxena, A. (2012) Unstructured Human Activity Detection from RGBD Images. *Proceedings of the 2012 IEEE International Conference on Robotics and Automation (ICRA)*, Saint Paul, 14-18 May 2012, 842-849.

[22] Xia, L., Chen, C.-C. and Aggarwal, J. (2012) View Invariant Human Action Recognition Using Histograms of 3D Joints. *Proceedings of the 2nd International Workshop on Human Activity Understanding from 3D Data (HAU3D)*, Providence, 16-21 June 2012.

[23] Yamato, J., Ohya, J. and Ishii, K. (1992) Recognizing Human Action in Time-Sequential Images Using Hidden Markov Model. *Proceedings of the IEEE Computer Society Conference on Computer Vision and Pattern Recognition*, Champaign, 15-18 June 1992, 379-385. http://dx.doi.org/10.1109/cvpr.1992.223161

[24] Bobick, A., Ivanov, Y., Bobick, A.F. and Ivanov, Y.A. (1998) Action Recognition Using Probabilistic Parsing. *Proceedings of the IEEE Computer Society Conference on Computer Vision and Pattern Recognition*, Santa Barbara, 23-25 June 1998, 196-202. http://dx.doi.org/10.1109/cvpr.1998.698609

[25] Nergui, M., Yoshida, Y., Imamoglu, N., Gonzalez, J. and Yu, W. (2012) Human Behavior Recognition by a Bio-Monitoring Mobile Robot. In: *Proceedings of the 5th International Conference on Intelligent Robotics and Applications—Volume Part II*, Springer-Verlag, Berlin, Heidelberg, 21-30. http://dx.doi.org/10.1007/978-3-642-33515-0_3

[26] Oh, C.-M., Islam, M.Z., Park, J.-W. and Lee, C.-W. (2010) A Gesture Recognition Interface with Upper Body Model-Based Pose Tracking. *Proceedings of the 2nd International Conference on Computer Engineering and Technology*, Chengdu, 16-18 April 2010, V7-531-V7-534. http://dx.doi.org/10.1109/iccet.2010.5485583

[27] Yu, E. and Aggarwal, J.K. (2006) Detection of Fence Climbing from Monocular Video. In: *Proceedings of the 18th International Conference on Pattern Recognition*, IEEE Computer Society, Washington DC, 375-378. http://dx.doi.org/10.1109/icpr.2006.440

[28] Zhang, D., Gatica-Perez, D., Bengio, S. and McCowan, I. (2006) Modeling Individual and Group Actions in Meetings with Layered HMMS. *IEEE Transactions on Multimedia*, **8**, 509-520.

[29] Glodek, M., Layher, G., Schwenker, F. and Palm, G. (2012) Recognizing Human Activities Using a Layered Markov

Architecture. In: Villa, A., Duch, W., Érdi, P., Masulli, F. and Palm, G., Eds., *Artificial Neural Networks and Machine Learning—ICANN* 2012, Springer, Berlin, 677-684. http://dx.doi.org/10.1007/978-3-642-33269-2_85

[30] Glodek, M., Schwenker, F. and Palm, G. (2012) Detecting Actions by Integrating Sequential Symbolic and Sub-Symbolic Information in Human Activity Recognition. In: *Proceedings of the 8th International Conference on Machine Learning and Data Mining in Pattern Recognition*, Springer-Verlag, Berlin, Heidelberg, 394-404. http://dx.doi.org/10.1007/978-3-642-31537-4_31

[31] Brand, M., Oliver, N. and Pentland, A. (1997) Coupled Hidden Markov Models for Complex Action Recognition. *IEEE Computer Society Conference on Computer Vision and Pattern Recognition*, San Juan, 17-19 June 1997, 994-999. http://dx.doi.org/10.1109/CVPR.1997.609450

[32] Oliver, N., Rosario, B. and Pentland, A. (2000) A Bayesian Computer Vision System for Modeling Human Interactions. *IEEE Transactions on Pattern Analysis and Machine Intelligence*, **22**, 831-843. http://dx.doi.org/10.1109/34.868684

[33] Duong, T.V., Bui, H.H., Phung, D.Q. and Venkatesh, S. (2005) Activity Recognition and Abnormality Detection with the Switching Hidden Semi-Markov Model. *IEEE Computer Society Conference on Computer Vision and Pattern Recognition CVPR* 2005, **1**, 838-845. http://dx.doi.org/10.1109/CVPR.2005.61

[34] Natarajan, P. and Nevatia, R. (2007) Coupled Hidden Semi Markov Models for Activity Recognition. *Proceedings of the IEEE Workshop on Motion and Video Computing*, Austin, 23-24 February 2007, 10. http://dx.doi.org/10.1109/wmvc.2007.12

[35] Shi, Q., Wang, L., Cheng, L. and Smola, A. (2008) Discriminative Human Action Segmentation and Recognition Using Semi-Markov Model. *Proceedings of the IEEE Conference on Computer Vision and Pattern Recognition*, Anchorage, 24-26 June 2008, 1-8.

[36] Sung, J., Ponce, C., Selman, B. and Saxena, A. (2011) Human Activity Detection from RGBD Images. Technical Report, Carnegie Mellon University, Department of Computer Science, Cornell University, Ithaca, NY.

[37] Guenterberg, E., Ghasemzadeh, H., Loseu, V. and Jafari, R. (2009) Distributed Continuous Action Recognition Using a Hidden Markov Model in Body Sensor Networks. In: *Proceedings of the 5th IEEE International Conference on Distributed Computing in Sensor Systems*, Springer-Verlag, Berlin, Heidelberg, 145-158. http://dx.doi.org/10.1007/978-3-642-02085-8_11

[38] Lowerre, B.T. (1976) The Harpy Speech Recognition System. PhD Thesis, Carnegie Mellon University, Pittsburgh.

[39] Ryoo, M.S. and Aggarwal, J.K. (2006) Recognition of Composite Human Activities through Context-Free Grammar Based Representation. *Proceedings of the 2006 IEEE Computer Society Conference on Computer Vision and Pattern Recognition*, New York, 17-22 June 2006, 1709-1718.

[40] Savage, J. (1995) A Hybrid System with Symbolic AI and Statistical Methods for Speech Recognition. PhD Thesis, University of Washington, Seattle.

[41] Gong, S. and Xiang, T. (2003) Recognition of Group Activities Using Dynamic Probabilistic Networks. *Proceedings of the Ninth IEEE International Conference on Computer Vision*, Nice, 13-16 October 2003, 742-749.

[42] Nguyen-Duc-Thanh, N., Lee, S. and Kim, D. (2012) Two-Stage Hidden Markov Model in Gesture Recognition for Human Robot Interaction. *International Journal of Advanced Robotic Systems*, **9**.

[43] Oliver, N., Horvitz, E. and Garg, A. (2002) Layered Representations for Human Activity Recognition. In: *Proceedings of the 4th IEEE International Conference on Multimodal Interfaces*, IEEE Computer Society, Washington DC, 3-8. http://dx.doi.org/10.1109/ICMI.2002.1166960

[44] Lasseter, J. (1987) Principles of Traditional Animation Applied to 3D Computer Animation. *ACM SIGGRAPH Computer Graphics*, **21**, 35-44. http://dx.doi.org/10.1145/37402.37407

[45] Williams, R. (2009) The Animator's Survival Kit. Second Edition, Faber & Faber, London.

[46] Wang, J., Liu, Z., Wu, Y. and Yuan, J. (2012) Mining Actionlet Ensemble for Action Recognition with Depth Cameras. *Proceedings of the 2012 IEEE Conference on Computer Vision and Pattern Recognition (CVPR)*, Providence, 16-21 June 2012, 1290-1297. http://dx.doi.org/10.1109/cvpr.2012.6247813

[47] Shotton, J., Fitzgibbon, A., Cook, M., Sharp, T., Finocchio, M., Moore, R., Kipman, A. and Blake, A. (2011) Real-Time Human Pose Recognition in Parts from Single Depth Images. In: *Proceedings of the 2011 IEEE Conference on Computer Vision and Pattern Recognition*, IEEE Computer Society, Washington DC, 1297-1304. http://dx.doi.org/10.1109/cvpr.2011.5995316

[48] Bribiesca, E. (2000) A Chain Code for Representing 3D Curves. *Pattern Recognition*, **33**, 755-765. http://dx.doi.org/10.1016/S0031-3203(99)00093-X

[49] Bribiesca, E. (2008) A Method for Representing 3D Tree Objects Using Chain Coding. *Journal of Visual Communication and Image Representation*, **19**, 184-198. http://dx.doi.org/10.1016/j.jvcir.2008.01.001

14

Intelligent Agent Technologies: The Work Horse of ERP E-Commerce

Anne T. Galante

Department of Computing Systems, SUNY Farmingdale State College, Farmingdale, USA
Email: galanta@farmingdale.edu

Abstract

Agents are the new defacto standard for inclusion in modules of today's software systems such as ERP systems, mobile applications and operating systems. Agents are an integral part of today's software design. The question is how do intelligent agents work in the specific area of ERP credit card processing e-commerce models? To answer this question, a specific area of ERP systems will be analyzed: credit card processing for merchants. One specific merchant credit card processor will be specifically investigated: EVO Merchants. This paper will research how exactly does ERP systems interact using Application Programing Interface or "API" specified by a credit card clearing house. Secure Socket Layers or SSL, and XML are discussed and elaborated on specifically how intelligent agents play such a pivotal role in ERP e-commerce systems for credit card processing.

Keywords

Intelligent Agents Agent Technologies, ERP, E-Commerce, API, Artificial Intelligence, Decision Making, Enterprise Resource Planning, Application Programing Interface, EVO, Credit Cards, XML, SSL, AIM, W3C, SGML

1. Introduction

Agent technologies are the foundation of software applications that are used in everyday life. Agents are quite flexible and because of this specific attribute, it gives them a particular strength. While agents have a particular quiet and unobtrusive characteristic, they play a crucial hand running in the background or performing automotive activities for specific users. Agents are essential to the current Enterprise Resource Planning or ERP systems specifically in today's environment where the use of credit cards payments is so prevalent.

According to the 2013 Federal Reserve Payment Study, the number of noncash payments (credit, and debit cards excluding electronic funds transfers or "EFT") in 2012 reached a whopping 122.8 billion of transactions, with a value of $79.0 trillion dollars [1]. For ERP systems, agent technologies play a pivotal role in the processing of credit and debit cards.

MIT research first introduced the concept of agent technology in 1961. Agent technologies are found in a vast scope of applications ranging in the field of information sciences, computer science, specifically artificial intelligence, and other diverse traditional areas of science. According to Jennings and Wooldridge [2], an agent is located in a particularly complex environment that is an encapsulated system. An agent's primary focus is its main design objective and because of this, is goal driven and often at times collaborative.

Agents are the new defacto standard for inclusion in modules of today's software systems such as ERP systems, mobile applications and operating systems. Agents are an integral part of today's software design. The question is what advantages to agents give to a software engineer? To answer this question a specific area of ERP systems will be analyzed: credit card processing for merchants.

Agents are helpful because they can perform a variety of tasks, and thus are very flexible. According to Rusbridge [3], agents are responsible for the functions of observation, recognition, planning and or inference and action or execution. Agents are customized for application in complex systems, such as ERP systems. Some of the tasks agents accomplish are the ability to translate, communicate and publish information. Agents also can guide the user's search query from the interface to the appropriate target. Agents also negotiate, and gain access to exchange information with other agents. This negotiation is similar to a conversation that allows agents to determine which tasks are performed within the context of pre-determined tasks. These specialized features allow for the effective management of the user's environment. Agents are systems that facilitate different areas in ERP systems, such as Supply Chain or "SC" and Customer Relationship Management or "CRM" are can be viewed as a network of autonomous and collaborative units that regulate, control and organize all activities contained in the ERP system [4].

Prior research on intelligent agent system architectures has shown that problems exist within highly distributed systems that require synergy of many elements; a solution is multi-agent systems or "MAS" [5] [6]. Additional research investigated intelligent agents and ERP scheduling systems for taxi companies. The conclusion was that agents are a palpable solution for a large taxi company's complex scheduling system in London. This solution gave the ability to schedule a taxi and provide the form of payment by credit card, but it did not go into detail how the agents were involved in the credit card processing in the ERP systems [7]. Exactly how the agent works with credit card processing merchants, the ERP software is the focus of this research.

The intelligent agent plays a pivotal role in the function of using a credit card in an ERP system to pay for goods. The example of a customer ordering goods from an e-commerce site from a specific merchant, where the ERP order application would then call an Application Programing Interface or "API" specified by a credit card clearing house. The API will process the customer's credit or debit card information. An example of a company who provides these types of specifications for API for credit cards is EVO Payments International. EVO founded in 1989, and EVO's corporate office is located in New York. EVO Payments International is among the largest fully integrated merchant acquirer and payment processors in the world. EVO operates as a payment service provider for both face-to-face and e-commerce transactions for all major credit cards, debit cards, commercial cards and electronic bank transfers. EVO can process in nearly 50 markets and 120 currencies around the world. Through its European subsidiary, EVO operates as a principal member of MasterCard Worldwide and Visa Europe [8].

2. Problem Definition

Some of the specific tasks of the EVO credit card system, related to intelligent agents, will be subsequently addressed and discussed. How does agent technology interface with ERP systems and credit card processing merchants? These questions are discussed in the research.

3. Advanced Integration Method—AIM

The API tool EVO provides is a merchant web services API, Advanced Integration Method or "AIM". AIM provides the necessary protocols to connect an e-commerce site or a retail point of sale to the Authorize Net Payment Gateway to submit credit card information by activating the AIM API. AIM will validate credit card information, provide a receipt of the transaction, and will secure all credit card information using a 128 bit Secure Socket Layer or "SSL". According to Bhiogade [9] SSL is a protocol developed by Netscape that establishes a secure communication for a web browser and a web server. The SSL protocol requires the web server to have a digital certificate installed in order for the SSL connection to be created. SSL works by using a public key to encrypt the data transferred over the SSL. **Figure 1** shows the process on how to implement AIM.

Figure 1 begins with Step 1 with a developer creating an application or modifying an existing application to obtain the necessary credit card information. In Step 2, a secure SSL connection is established to EVO's payment gateway. The developer must parse the credit card information into a format specified by AIM. The results are passed back to the merchant software application to initially initiated the transaction.

The parsed credit card information is embedded in an Extensible Markup Language or "XML" document. According to Shanmugasundaram, Tufte, Zhang, He, DeWitt, & Naughton [10], XML is a class of data objects called XML documents and partially and subsequently describes the behavior of the computer programs that are responsible for processing the documents. XML is profile of Standard Generalized Markup Language or "SGML" defined by the World Wide Web Consortium or W3C. The World Wide Web Consortium or "W3C" is an international community run by member organizations, a full-time staff, and the public. The members work together to develop Web standards. Led by Web inventor Tim Berners-Lee and CEO Jeffrey Jaffe, W3C's mission is to lead the Web to its full potential [11]. XML documents contained parsed data and are made up of character data called entities. Markup is the encoded description of the documents storage layout and logical structure. **Figure 2** is an example of test data parsed and encoded in XML.

Figure 2 shows the parsed data collected from the program developed by the software engineer for the purpose of credit card processing. Each piece of data is put into a markup, or encoded, with beginning and ending tags. This is similar to the Hyper Text Markup Language or "HTML" works. For example, the beginning structure is <MerchantAuthentication>. The merchant name is parsed with <name> and an ending </name> tag. The actual merchant name is placed in the markup.

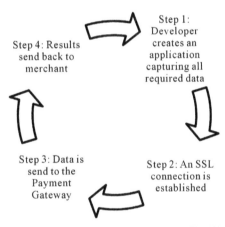

Figure 1. Example of the payment gateway process.

```
<merchantAuthentication>
<name>Shoe World</name>
<transactionKey>123abc</transactionKey>
</merchantAuthentication>
<refId>123456</refId>
<transactionRequest>
<transactionType>authOnlyTransaction</transactionType>
<amount>5</amount>
<payment>
<creditCard>
<cardNumber>5424000000000015</cardNumber>
<expirationDate>1102</expirationDate>
<cardCode>999</cardCode>
</creditCard>
</payment>
```

Figure 2. Example sample test XML data.

4. Conclusions

AIM is an API provided by EVO for merchants to install in ERP systems. There are four steps to credit card approval (parse data, secure SSL, send data, receive a response). Intelligent agents are the workers of the corporate ERP systems, transferring data and performing services established in the software framework. In order to implement AIM, a software developer must write a program or modify and already established system to obtain the necessary credit card information. A SSL certificate is installed on the server. The data is parsed with XML according the vendor's specifications. The data is transmitted to the payment gateway and the AIM API goes to work. AIM validates the data, processes it, and sends results back to the receiver.

The paper researched how the implementation of the AIM API for merchant credit card processing is seamless, transparent, and unobtrusive to users. The use of agent technology gives maximum control over the merchants credit card processing. The implementation of agents in complex environments is a palpable solution for merchants with e-commerce sites. This solution is innovative, scalable, and compatible with today's modern trends for optimization and effectiveness.

References

[1]   (2013) Federal Reserve Bank Service.
      https://www.frbservices.org/files/communications/pdf/research/2013_payments_study_summary.pdf

[2]   Wooldridge, M. and Jennings, N.R. (1995) Intelligent Agents: Theory and Practice. *The Knowledge Engineering Review*, **10**, 115-152. http://dx.doi.org/10.1017/S0269888900008122

[3]   Rusbridge, C. (1998) Towards the Hybrid Library.
      https://www.era.lib.ed.ac.uk/bitstream/handle/1842/1736/DLib98.pdf;jsessionid=54AF601B4AC4262188CE469427A
      A8FC3?sequence=2

[4]   Symeonidis, A.L., Kehagias, D.D. and Mitkas, P.A. (2003) Intelligent Policy Recommendations on Enterprise Resource Planning by the Use of Agent Technology and Data Mining Techniques. *Expert Systems with Applications*, **25**, 589-560. http://dx.doi.org/10.1016/S0957-4174(03)00099-X

[5]   Jennings, N.R., Sycara, K. and Wooldridge, M.J. (1998) A Roadmap of Agent Research and Development. Autonomous Agents and Multi-Agent Systems. Kluwer Academic, Boston.

[6]   Ferber, J. (1999) Multi-Agent Systems: An Introduction to Distributed Artificial Intelligence. Addison Wesley Longman, Harlow.

[7]   Glaschenko, A., Ivaschenko, A., Rzevski, G. and Skobelev, P. (2009) Multi-Agent Real Time Scheduling System for Taxi Companies. *Proceedings of the 8th International Conference on Autonomous Agents and Multiagent Systems*, Budapest, 10-15 May 2009, 29-36.

[8]   (2015) EVO Payments International. http://evopayments.com/about-evo/evo-payments-international

[9]   Bhiogade, M.S. (2001) Secure Socket Layer. *Proceedings of the Computer Science and Information Technology Education Conference*, Cork, June 2002, 85-90. http://dx.doi.org/10.2139/ssrn.291499

[10] Shanmugasundaram, J., Tufte, K., Zhang, C., He, G., DeWitt, D.J. and Naughton, J.F. (1999) Relational Databases for for Querying XML Documents: Limitations and Opportunities. *Proceedings of the 25th International Conference on Very Large Data*, 1999, 302-314.

[11] (2015) About W3C. http://www.w3.org/Consortium/

15

DBpedia-Based Fuzzy Query Recommendation Algorithm and Its Applications in the Resource-Sharing Platform of Polar Samples

Wenfang Cheng[1,2*], Qing'e Wu[3,4], Xiao Cheng[5], Jie Zhang[1,2], Zhuanling Song[6]

[1]Polar Research Institute of China, Shanghai, China
[2]Key Laboratory for Polar Science, State Oceanic Administration, Shanghai, China
[3]School of Computer Science, Fudan University, Shanghai, China
[4]College of Electric and Information Engineering, Zhengzhou University of Light Industry, Zhengzhou, China
[5]College of Global Change and Earth System Science, Beijing Normal University, Beijing, China
[6]The First Institute of Oceanography, SOA, Qingdao, China
Email: *chengwenfang@pric.org.cn

Abstract

In order to continuously promote the polar sample resource services in China and effectively guide the users to access such information as needed, a fuzzy algorithm based on DBpedia has been proposed through the analysis of the characteristics of the query recommendations in search engines, namely, to search similar entry queues by constructing a DBpedia category tree, then use the fuzzy matching algorithm to work out the entry similarity, and then present the example query applications of this algorithm on the resource-sharing platform of polar samples. Comparing the traditional literal character matching method and DBpedia semantic similarity algorithm, the experimental results show that the fuzzy query algorithm based on DBpedia features has a higher search accuracy rate, stronger anti-interference capability, and more flexible algorithm use by virtue of its fuzzy weight adjustment.

Keywords

Search Engine, Fuzzy Query, Semantic Similarity, Wiki

---

*Corresponding author.

1. Introduction

As one of the most important modules of information platforms, each search engine has its query recommendation almost as a standard function for its search module. In particular, when the users are not clear about their search objects, the relevant search results given by the search engine can effectively guide the users to gradually get access to the information they need [1]. During the past decade, the query recommendation technology has obtained fairly satisfactory results in e-commerce platforms; therefore, in order to improve the value of scientific data, this paper examines the application of the query recommendation technology on resource-sharing platform of polar samples (BIRDS). It provides information on major samples collected in the polar regions during previous Chinese polar expeditions with large numbers of valuable samples available, including snow, ice cores, flora and fauna, meteorites, sediments, and rocks. Since the establishment of BIRDS in 2006, it has released 7058 resources, 12,279 pictures and 6.4 GB data. On average, every day it is visited by 895 users from 187 countries with 112 million clicks and 16.6 TB content downloads. However, most users came from the cooperated institutes of BIRDS, and the average PV (pages view) per day per user normally was less than 20. In order to further promote the polar sample resource services in China, to provide more samples and relevant information to scientists who have made an attempt to carry out related polar research but without access to filed study, and to improve the utilization efficiency of polar sample resources, this paper has designed a fuzzy query recommendation algorithm based on Wikipedia knowledge database and applied it to BIRDS [2].

Scientific data platforms have a relatively smaller number of users than e-commerce platforms and thus have a simpler user log; thereby this paper presents the query recommendation [3] based on contents. In addition, this paper has fully considered the fact that search engine is one of the most important factors of information platforms, as well as the character or word association characteristics [4] to have proposed the DBpedia-based fuzzy query algorithm, namely, to search similar entry queues by constructing a DBPedia category tree, then use the fuzzy matching algorithm to work out the entry similarity, and then present the example query applications of this algorithm on BIRDS.

In the past 10 years, many scientific data platforms have offered query recommendation services which received good effect, but this fuzzy query recommendation algorithm based on DBpedia is first presented and applied on scientific data platforms especially on polar data sharing systems. After the application on BIRDS, the platform's daily users increased to thousands, and the daily PV per user was stabled at about 15. More platform visit data show the algorithm proposed better effect than normal query recommendation algorithm.

2. Algorithm of Category Tree on a Knowledge Database

2.1. Construction of Semantically Similar Category Tree

The construction of a knowledge database is a complicated task involving many disciplines. The associated database [5]-[7] constructed in this paper based on DBpedia has the following characteristics:
- Its entries are based on Wikipedia, and are able to develop along with changes of Wikipedia.
- It has extracted structured data from Wikipedia and converted such data into the form of Linked Data.
- Its knowledge database uses the form of ontological construction to organize the entries.
- It has an open API interface, enabling the machine to understand such structural data.
  The DBpedia body mainly consists of four types of system structures [8]:
  (1) "part-of" relationship, indicating the relationship between the part and the whole of a concept.
  (2) "kind-of" relationship, indicating an integrated relationship between concepts.
  (3) "instance-of" relationship, indicating the relationship between the concept and its instances.
  (4) "attribute-of" relationship, indicating that one concept is the attribute of another concept.
  The method in this paper only uses the relationship between "concepts" and "categories" to construct a category tree. For instance, in Chinese Wikipedia, the free encyclopedia:
  Skua category: Gull passerine|Stercorariidae.
  Stercorariidae category: Gull passerine.
  Gull passerine category: Birds|Charadriiformes.
  Emperor penguin category: IUCN threatened species|Antarctica|Spheniscidae.
  Spheniscidae category: birds|Sphenisciformes|Spheniscidae.
  Sphenisciformes category: birds|Sphenisciformes|Spheniscidae.

Finally a knowledge database as below can be obtained:

Skua -> Stercorariidae -> Gull passerine -> Birds.

Emperor penguin -> Spheniscidae -> Sphenisciformes -> Birds.

In the process of the category tree extraction, it is particularly important to set the height of the category tree; if it is too high, the traversal speed will be influenced; if too low, the matching effect will be reduced.

2.2. Construct a Proper Height for the Category Tree

A category tree's error rate will be quite high if it is constructed too small. On the other hand, if the tree is too big, the apparent error rate obtained by means of learning set test is very small, but its true error rate may still be relatively large. Therefore, we need to construct a tree of a proper/appropriate size to minimize the real error rate.

The purpose/aim of decision tree learning is to obtain a simple tree with a strong predictive capacity. When the tree is in its full growth, its predictive capacity will be reduced. In order to solve this problem, we need to obtain a tree of the proper/appropriate size. In generally, there are two methods available.

Method-1: Define the conditions that the tree will stop growing.

1) Partition the number of instances to the minimum. When the size of the data subset corresponding to the current node is smaller than the number of specified minimum partition instances, no further partition is needed even though they do not belong to the same category.

2) Partition threshold value. When the difference between the value obtained by means of the applied partition method and the value of its parent node is smaller than the specified threshold value, no further partition is needed.

3) Maximize tree depth. When the length of further partition will exceed the maximal tree depth, stop partitioning.

Method-2: Carry out pruning after a complete decision tree is generated by evaluating subtrees. The entire decision trees will perform better if a subtree is removed, then the subset is pruned. Specifically, the implementing process in the Breiman CART [9] are as follows:

1) Tree construction

The decision tree is made up of the data sets partitioned by attribute values, and thereby needs to define the measurement partitioned by attribute, namely, according to this measurement, the optimal partitioning attributes for current data subset can be worked out.

When the fuzzy function of calculation cost for node has been selected, during the process of the tree growth, we are always trying to find an optimal bifurcation value to partition the samples in the node, so that the cost could be minimized. The fuzzy function $\phi(P)$ is used to represent the fuzzy degree of the tree node t or error partition index, namely:

$$E(t) = \phi(D) = -\sum_{i \neq l} p_i p_l = 1 - \sum_{i=1}^{c} p_i^2. \tag{1}$$

Here, $D = \{p_1, p_2, \cdots, p_c\}$ is a decision set, c denotes the number of the decision-making categories in the decision set, $p_i \geq 0$ indicates the proportion of the ith decision-making category in the decision set D and $\sum_{i=1}^{c} p_i = 1$.

In the bifurcation tree of the CART algorithm architecture, the amount of changes of fuzzy degree due to bifurcation is as follows:

$$\Delta E(t) = E(t) - p_l E(t_l) - p_r E(t_r) \tag{2}$$

where, t is the bifurcation node; $E(t)$ is the fuzzy degree of the node t; $E(t_l)$ and $E(t_r)$ are the fuzzy degree of the left and right bifurcation node, respectively; p_l and p_r denote the percentage of the node t in the left and right bifurcation samples, respectively. For bifurcation of each internal node t, take the largest change of fuzzy degree in all possible bifurcation ways of t. For other nodes, repeat the same search process.

2) Pruning

The large scale trees are generated by the above algorithm and its apparent error rate is very small, but its true error rate may still be relatively large. We must construct a tree with a small true error rate by means of the pruning technique. We use a certain algorithm to prune the branches of this tree continuously. During the pruning process, we will obtain a list of decresing trees to form a sequence of pruned trees, and each tree in this sequence will have a smaller apparent error rate [9] compared with other subtrees of the same size, and then we can conclude that this sequence is an optimal one. The bifurcation tree can be pruned on the basis of the minimal cost complexity principle as below:

In general, a tree can be expressed by T, the subtree with the root node of t is expressed by T_t, then the pruned subtree T_{t3} will shrink into a terminal node $t3$, the pruned tree can be expressed as $T - T_{t3}$, and there is the $T - T_{t3} \subset T$, which is the subset of T. Use $\bar{T}$ to express the terminal node set in the trees T, and the number of the corresponding terminal nodes is $|\bar{T}|$. The impurity index of the tree T is defined as follows:

$$E(T) = \sum_{t \in \bar{T}} E(t). \tag{3}$$

$E(t)$ denotes the fuzzy index of the tree node t or the square error of the fitting node data set of the node t in the Equation (3), and the error index is the fuzzy function $E(t)$.

The pruning principle of the decision tree, namely, the cost complexity measurement is displayed as:

$$E_a(T) = E(T) + a|\bar{T}| \tag{4}$$

where $E_a(T)$ denotes a linear combination of the tree impurity index cost $E_a(T)$ and its complexity. Therein, a is the complexity parameter resulted from the complexity of a tree and $|\bar{T}|$ indicates the number of the terminal nodes for the tree T.

To find the next smallest tree of the tree T: For each internal node t of the tree T, we need to work out the value a of the penalty factor for the next tree $T - T_t$ wrongly partitioned, and label the value as a_t, which is the ratio between the change amount of the error index before and after the current tree is pruned and the change of the terminal node number:

$$a_t = \frac{E(t) - E(T_t)}{|\bar{T}_t| - 1}. \tag{5}$$

The node we need to select is an internal node with minimal a_t. The whole tree pruning process is to calculate a_t, then seek the smallest a_t, and then select $T - T_t$ as the next pruning object.

For each given value a, a smallest tree $T(a)$ can always be found based on the corresponding to the measurement of its cost complexity:

$$E_a(T(a)) = \min_{T \subset T_{max}} E_a(T). \tag{6}$$

When the value a increases, $T(a)$ always remains smallest until it reaches a jump point a', and then the tree $T(a')$ becomes a new smallest tree.

After the smallest tree $T(a)$ is determined, its height can be defined as $h = n(t_f) - n(t_0) + 1$, where $n(t_f)$ is the number of layers of the final leaf nodes while $n(t_0)$ is the number of layers of the root nodes.

For such cases in this paper, we can work out the appropriate height of a tree as $h = 5$ according to the above algorithm.

3. Similarity Algorithm

The similar degree of traditional category tree is mainly calculated through the following two methods: character direct search method and vector included angle cosine calculation method. However, these two methods are oversimplified and thus the similarity is seriously affected. Therefore, based on the character search method, this paper has proposed a fuzzy query algorithm based on DBpedia.

3.1. Literal Character Matching Method (CCQ)

Literal character matching method is the easiest method, it judges the similarity by the proportionality of common words on two words. For example, there is one common word between *adelie penguins* and *emperor penguin*, then the matching value is 0.5.

Algorithm:

First, get all samples' name from database, named Word$_1$, Word$_2$, ... Word$_i$, ..., Word$_n$;

Second, calculate each correlation for word$_i$, and the value is correlation [word$_j$, word$_i$] = Max (length (common words (word$_j$, word$_i$))/lengh (word$_i$), length (common words (Pinyin (word$_j$), Pinyin (word$_i$)))/lengh (Pinyin (word$_i$))).

3.2. Fuzzy Query Algorithm (WIKIFQ)

If the search contents are classified according to such attributes of a word or a phrase as pronunciation, meaning and relevance, refer to the concrete fuzzy query algorithm [10].

1) Classification of the query contents

Firstly, the samples to be queried are classified appropriately. The query criteria are: the smaller distance between the example that belongs to a certain category and the center within the category is the better; the larger distance that is from the center among categories is the better. According to the attributes of each category, the average value of each category is calculated as the category center $v_i, i = 1, 2, \cdots, n$. Assume u_{ik} is the membership function of the kth sample to the ith category, $0 \leq u_{ik} \leq 1$ and $0 < \sum_{k=1}^{N} u_{ik} < N$, $U = \{u_{ik}\}$. Assume $d_{ik} = \|x_k - v_i\|$ is the distance between the sample x_k and the center v_i of the ith category, and $m > 1$ is a fuzzy weighted exponent. Define the distances within a category and among categories, to make the distances satisfy that the distance is from the center within the category is smaller, and the distance is from the center among categories is larger.

Define the distance within a category

$$J_m(U_i, v_i) = \sum_{j=1}^{N_i} u_{ij}^m d_{ij}^2. \tag{7}$$

Define the distance among categories

$$J_m(U_{\setminus\{U_i\}}, v_i) = \sum_{i=1}^{n} \sum_{j=1}^{N-N_i} u_{ij}^m d_{ij}^2. \tag{8}$$

Synthesize the Equations (7) and (8) to define the objective function $J_m(U, n)$ as

$$J_m(U, n) = \sum_{i=1}^{n} \sum_{j=1}^{N} u_{ij}^m d_{ij}^2 \tag{9}$$

where, $U_i = \{u_{ij}\}$ is applicable to a certain i, while $U = \{u_{ij}\}$ is applicable to all i.

An objective finally needs to be classified into a certain kind of problems according to a certain membership degree, so the objective function satisfies a certain constraints as follows:

$$\sum_{i=1}^{n} u_{ij} = 1, \forall 1 \leq j \leq N. \tag{10}$$

According to the objective function, the following conditions should be met: 1) the defined u_{ij} should be inversely proportional to d_{ij}, namely, u_{ij} is a monotone decreasing function about d_{ij}. 2) u_{ij} is a monotone increasing function about the fuzzy weighted exponent m. 3) u_{ij} is the membership degree, so $0 \leq u_{ij} \leq 1$. Moreover, it requires that each category must contain one sample at least, but the sample may not belong to the same category, so $0 < \sum_{j=1}^{N} u_{ij} < N$ is true. 4) Simultaneously, u_{ij} satisfies the Equation (10).

According to 1)-4), u_{ij} can be defined as follows:

$$u_{ij} = \left\{ \sum_{k=1}^{n} \left(\frac{d_{ij}}{d_{kj}} \right)^{\frac{2}{m-1}} \right\}^{-1}. \tag{11}$$

It can be proved that the Equation (11) satisfies the conditions 1)-4).

Under the constraint (10), the minimal value of the Equation (9) can be obtained by iterating repeatedly the Equation (11) to determine the final u_{ij}.

Based on u_{ij}, assume the center of each category is v_i, and it can be calculated as follows:

$$v_i = \frac{\sum_{j=1}^{N} (u_{ij})^m x_j}{\sum_{j=1}^{N} (u_{ij})^m}. \tag{12}$$

2) Character matching query

For a sample x to be queried, calculate the distance between x and the center v_i, select k characters or words that is closest to x, which are represented by $x_1, x_2, \cdots, x_k$ respectively. Define an ordered pair $\langle x, f(x) \rangle$, and $f(x)$ is the category which the sample x belongs to: $f(x): R \to W$, in which R is a set of samples to be queried, W is a finite set $\{w_1, w_2, \cdots, w_n\}$ of category, w_i is the ith type content of the partition query content, and n is the number of categories. Then $f(x)$ can be calculated as follows:

$$f(x) = \arg\max_{w_j \in W} \sum_{i=1}^{k} \sigma(w_j, f(x_i)), \text{ where } \sigma(w_j, f(x_i)) = \begin{cases} 1, f(x_i) = w_j \\ 0, f(x_i) \neq w_j \end{cases}. \text{ If } f(x) = w_{j*}, \text{ then the sample } x$$

belongs to the category w_{j*}.

The above expressions can also be written as: $S_j = \sum_{i=1}^{k} \sigma(w_j, f(x_i))$, here $f(x) = \arg\max_j S_j$, then x belongs to the category w_{j*}, $j = 1, 2, \cdots, n$.

3.3. Selection of the Fuzzy Weighted Exponent m

For the Equation (11), when $m \to 1$, each u_{ij} in the Equation (11) satisfies $u_{ij} \to 0$ or 1, and when $m = 1$, there is no weighted value u_{ij}; when $m \to +\infty$, each u_{ij} satisfies $u_{ij} \to 1/n$, and the partition is most fuzzy at this time. It is clear that the exponent m directly determines the fuzziness of the classification results.

To classify the search contents, we can use the fuzzy method and algorithm [11]-[13] of target recognition researched by BEZDEK, Lin Qing, Wei Meia and others. The fuzzy degree of classification is defined as follows:

$$F_m(U, n) = \frac{1}{N} \sum_{i=1}^{n} \sum_{j=1}^{N} \left| u_{ij} - (u_{ij})_{0.5} \right| \tag{13}$$

where, BEZDEK [11]

$$(u_{ij})_{0.5} = \begin{cases} 1, u_{ij} \geq 0.5 \\ 0, u_{ij} < 0.5 \end{cases} \tag{14}$$

A fuzzy decision-making problem is formed by the intersection of a given fuzzy target G_f and a fuzzy constraint C_f, i.e.,

$$D = G_f \cap C_f.$$

In this paper, the fuzzy object of a decision-making problem that a keyword or a word is queried is defined as follows:

$$G_f = \min\{J_m(U^*, n) | m \in (1, +\infty)\} \tag{15}$$

where, U^* is the set of the final u_{ij} determined when the Equation (9) reaches a minimal value. In addition, while completing the content fuzzy classification, this algorithm also requires that the content should be partitioned as clearly as possible in order to correctly distinguish the category membership of each sample. Therefore, the selection of the parameter m is subject to another constraint, namely, the selected value can not make the classification results of the fuzzy classification algorithm overly fuzzy. The partition fuzzy degree is a good measurement to evaluate fuzzy classification to partition fuzziness. As a result, the fuzzy constraint of the decision that the parameter m is preferred is as follows:

$$C_f = \min\left\{F_m\left(U^*, n\right) \middle| m \in \left(1, +\infty\right)\right\}. \tag{16}$$

When G_f and C_f are treated as fuzzy sets, they can be characterized by their membership functions respectively. In order to ensure that the membership functions of the fuzzy object G_f and the fuzzy constraint C_f have the same increasing or decreasing extent, the membership functions of G_f and C_f can be defined respectively as follows:

$$\mu_G\left(m\right) = \left(\frac{J_m\left(U^*, n\right)}{\max_{\forall m} J_m\left(U^*, n\right)}\right)^3 \tag{17}$$

$$\mu_C\left(m\right) = F_m\left(U^*, n\right) \tag{18}$$

The membership function of fuzzy decision can be expressed as $\mu_D\left(x\right) = \min\left\{\mu_G\left(x\right), \mu_C\left(x\right)\right\}$, and the final decision-making result is the solution to satisfy $\mu_D\left(x^*\right) = \max_{\forall x}\left\{\mu_D\left(x\right)\right\}$.

Consequently, the optimal weighted index m^* is the m value corresponding to the maximum membership degree of the intersection of fuzzy subsets corresponding to the fuzzy object and fuzzy constraint, respectively. The optimal weighted index m^* can be obtained by the following formula:

$$m^* = \arg_{\forall m}\left\{\max\left\{\min\left\{\mu_G\left(m\right), \mu_C\left(m\right)\right\}\right\}\right\}. \tag{19}$$

The m^* obtained based on the Formula (19) will be able to ensure that the classified objective function and the classified partition fuzziness could be minimized by a larger membership degree, so that the fuzzy classification achieved by the fuzzy classification algorithm could not only express the similar information among samples, but also ensure the clarity of the sample classification. Therefore, a corresponding better fuzzy classification result will be obtained.

4. Experiment

4.1. Data Processing

1) Construct a DBpedia Database

A data rather large in amount cannot be indexed or retrieved if placed directly in a document, so a MYSQL database should be built. Download the XML dump file of 2013 November from Chinese Wikipedia, extract the three files to get zhwiki-latest-categorylinks.sql, zhwiki-latest-pages.sql and zhwiki-latest-redirect.sql (with the total of 1.34 GB), and import such files into the DBpedia Chinese entry database already obtained with approximately 3,102,000 page records, 315,000 category records and 7,736,000 categorylinks records.

2) Get N entries from the database of BIRDS [14]. N = Random (50 - 100)

3) Extract the category tree from DBpedia and then form a weight matrix [15] [16]. The code for a category tree of an individual entry is shown in **Figure 1** and **Figure 2**.

4) Superimpose the fuzzy matching algorithm to get similarity

In the experiment, take the fuzzy weighted exponent $m = 1.75$.

5) Test environment

CPU: 2.5 GHZ × 2 core

Memory: 4.0 GB

OS: Windows 7 - 64 bit

```
#Get category by name
def getCategorysByName(name, printable=False):

    if printable:
        print 'getCategorysByName'
        print u'%s' %name
    cursor = conn.cursor()

    cursor.execute('SELECT page_id, page_is_redirect FROM page where page_namespace=14 and page_title=%s ' , (name))
    page = cursor.fetchone()

    if not page:
        cursor.execute('SELECT page_id, page_is_redirect FROM page where page_namespace=0 and page_title=%s ' , (name))
        page = cursor.fetchone()
        if not page:
            return None
    if page['page_is_redirect']:
        cursor.execute('SELECT rd_title FROM redirect where rd_from=%s ', (page['page_id']))
        redirect = cursor.fetchone()
        if not redirect:
            return None
        return getCategorysByName(redirect['rd_title'], printable)

    categorys = []
    cursor.execute('SELECT cl_to FROM categorylinks where cl_from=%s ', (page['page_id']))
    rows = cursor.fetchall()
    for row in rows:
        if printable:
            print '  ', row['cl_to'].decode('utf8')
        categorys.append(row['cl_to'].decode('utf8'))
    cursor.close()
    return categorys
```

Figure 1. Get category by entry name.

```
#Get categroy tree, the depth <= 5, result is stored in out which is a dictionary.
def getCategoryTree(name,  out={}, depth=0, printable=False):
    if depth == 0:
        if printable:
            print 'getCategoryTree'
            print u'0 %s' %name
        out[name] = 1
    if depth>3:
        return
    depth += 1
    categorys = getCategorysByName(name)
    if not categorys:
        return
    for category in categorys:
        if repr(name) == repr(category):
            continue
        if printable:
            print '  '*depth, depth,category
        if not out.get(category):
            out[category] = 5-depth
        getCategoryTree(category, out, depth, printable)
```

Figure 2. Get category list.

4.2. Experimental Results

In order to verify the efficiency of this algorithm, we compare it with the traditional literal string matching algorithm and DBpedia semanteme-based algorithm (**Table 1**). The results indicate that the fuzzy matching algorithm is more accurate than other algorithms in terms of semantic analysis, and is even capable of detecting certain relationships between two seemingly different words.

4.3. Discussion

From the test result shown in **Table 1**, we can conclude that **WIKIFQA** method can detect similar data more efficiently and more accurately. After the application of the WIKIFQA on 2013 years, users have received more convenient service, and the value of PV, IP increased also (**Figure 3**).

But the algorithm is dependent on wiki database too much, and its accuracy is mostly affected by the quantity and quality of Wikipedia pages. To improve the accuracy, we have to update the database quarterly automatically.

5. Conclusion

This paper provides a DBpedia-based fuzzy query algorithm and gives the feature extraction method for fuzzy algorithm eigenvalue and implementation of semantic matching algorithm based on the analysis of the characteristics of the polar sample data and Wikipedia Chinese data. The experimental results show that this WIKIFQA

Table 1. Comparison of WIKIFQA with CCQ and WIKIQA algorithms.

Word pairs	Literal character matching method (CCQ)	DBpedia semantic algorithm (WIKIQA)	Fuzzy matching algorithm based on DBpedia (WIKIFQA)
Skua-Skue	0.5000	0.0000	1.0000
Skua-Penguin	0.0000	0.2371	0.2371
Stratosphere-Troposphere	0.6667	0.8899	0.8899
Stratosphere-Mesosphere	0.3333	0.8899	0.8899
Stratosphere-Planetary Boundary Layer	0.3333	0.0000	0.0000
Cinerite-Sulfate	0.0000	0.0624	0.0624
Cyclone-Drought	0.0000	0.1346	0.1346
Lightning-Windstorm	0.0000	0.3008	0.3008
Frost-Fog	0.0000	0.2961	0.2961
Rainfall-Natural Phenomena	0.0000	0.3968	0.3968
Rainfall-Rainbow	0.0000	0.2353	0.2353
Rainfall-Storm	0.0000	0.3205	0.3205
Storm-Tornado	0.5000	0.2121	0.2121
Aurora-Rainbow	0.0000	0.3574	0.3574
Desert-Steppe	0.0000	0.8819	0.8819
Desert-Swamp	0.0000	0.5269	0.5269
Desert-Hill	0.0000	0.3971	0.3971
Desert-Island	0.0000	0.3627	0.3627
Desert-Ocean	0.0000	0.3299	0.3299
Ascomycota-Basidiomycota	0.7500	0.5055	0.5055
Auriculariales-Dacrymycetales	0.6667	0.3557	0.6667
Calanoida-Harpacticoida	0.7500	0.9687	0.9687
Calanoida-Cyclopoida	0.7500	0.9687	0.9687
Amphibian-Echinoderm	0.5000	0.3328	0.5000
Amphibian-Reptiles	0.5000	0.6789	0.6789
Molluscs-Reptiles	0.5000	0.3295	0.5000
Molluscs-Vertebrate	0.5000	0.4775	0.5000
Lobopodia-Arthropods	0.5000	0.6184	0.6184
Onychophora-Tardigrade	0.5000	0.9848	0.9848
Nemathelminthes-Arthropods	0.5000	0.7044	0.7044
Geology-Geophysics	0.6667	0.5654	0.5654
Geology-Orography	0.3333	0.5320	0.5320
Geology-Biology	0.3333	0.4715	0.4715
Geology-Literature	0.3333	0.3571	0.3571
Hydrosphere-Lithosphere	0.5000	0.3436	0.3436
Hydrosphere-Atmosphere	0.5000	0.2353	0.2353
Hydrosphere-Biosphere	0.5000	0.4883	0.4883

Continued

Magmatite-Sedimentary	0.6667	0.6360	0.6360
Magmatite-Metamorphic Rock	0.6667	0.4027	0.4027
Magmatite-Gneiss	0.6667	0.4720	0.4720
Metamorphic Rock-Gneiss	0.3333	0.8430	0.8430
Magmatite-Extrusive Rock	0.6667	0.7815	0.7815
Magmatite-Granite	0.6667	0.5101	0.5101
Chlorophyll-Photosynthetic Pigments	0.3333	0.5670	0.5670
Chlorophyll-Photosynthesis	0.0000	0.3865	0.3865
Carbon Dioxide-Photosynthesis	0.0000	0.0300	0.0300
Water-Photosynthesis	0.0000	0.1077	0.1077
Oxygen-Photosynthesis	0.0000	0.0604	0.0604
Carbohydrate-Photosynthesis	0.2000	0.2797	0.2797
Cirque-Moraine	0.5000	0.6373	0.6373
Moraine-Glacier	0.5000	0.7061	0.7061
Glacier-Glacier	0.5000	0.9919	0.9919
Ice Sheet-Glacier	0.5000	0.8654	0.8654
Valley Glacier-Glacier	0.5000	0.6143	0.6143
Oil-Natural Gas	0.0000	0.4948	0.4948
Oil-Coal	0.0000	0.3162	0.3162
Oil-Wind Power	0.0000	0.1924	0.1924
Oil-Solar Power	0.0000	0.1272	0.1272
Oil-Power	0.0000	0.4291	0.4291
Oil -Non-Renewable Energy Resource	0.0000	0.2837	0.2837
Oil-Clean Energy	0.0000	0.1494	0.1494
Earthquake-Tsunami	0.0000	0.8564	0.8564
Earthquake-Landslip	0.0000	0.5799	0.5799
Earthquake-Debris Flow	0.0000	0.3734	0.3734
Earthquake-Volcano	0.0000	0.3636	0.3636
Earthquake-Natural Disaster	0.0000	0.7747	0.7747
Chinese Antarctic Greatwall Station-Greatwall Station	0.4286	0.9940	0.9940
Chinese Antarctic Greatwall Station-China Zhongshan Station	0.7143	0.5826	0.7143
Chinese Antarctic Greatwall Station-China Domea Station	0.7143	0.5199	0.7143
Chinese Antarctic Greatwall Station-China Yellow Station	0.5714	0.6437	0.6437
Yellow River Station-The Arctic Ocean	0.0000	0.3268	0.3268
Yellow River Station-Southern Ocean	0.0000	0.1663	0.1663
Greatwall Station-Antarctica	0.0000	0.1062	0.1062
Greatwall Station-The Arctic Ocean	0.0000	0.0890	0.0890

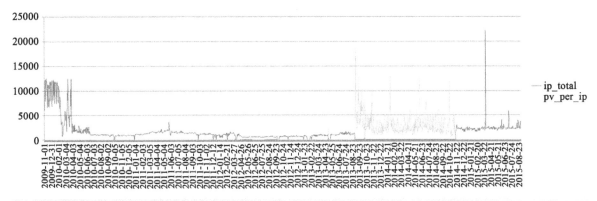

Figure 3. Value of PV, IP on BIRDS.

method can detect similar data more efficiently and more accurately to improve data accuracy, compared with the traditional literal string matching method and DBpedia semantic similarity algorithm. Also, the algorithm application on BIRDS proves its applicability and convenience.

Foundation

This work is supported by National Ocean Public Benefit Research Foundation(201305035); Key Laboratory of Digital Ocean, SOA (KLD0201408) respectively, Platform for Basic Conditions of the Ministry of Science and Technology (2005DKA21406); National postdoctoral science foundation (2013M531120); Project of Henan Province Science and Technology (No. 142300410247); Project of Henan Province Education Department (14A413002); Project of Zhengzhou Scientific and Technology Department (131PPTGG411-4).

References

[1]   Anagnostopoulos, A., Becchetti, L., Castillo, C., *et al.* (2010) An Optimization Framework for Query Recommendation. *Proceedings of the 3rd ACM International Conference on Web Search and Data Mining*, 161-170. http://dx.doi.org/10.1145/1718487.1718508

[2]   Cheng, W.F., Zhang, J., Xia, M.Y., *et al.* (2013) System Design and Implementation of a Resource-Sharing Platform for Polar Samples. *Polar Research*, **25**, 185-196.

[3]   Linden, G., Smith, B. and York, J. (2003) Amazon.com Recommendations: Item-to-Item Collaborative Filtering. *IEEE Internet Computing*, 7, 76-80. http://dx.doi.org/10.1109/MIC.2003.1167344

[4]   Bai, R.J., Yu, X.F. and Wang, X.Y. (2011) The Comparative Analysis of Major Domestic and Foreign Ontology Library. *New Technology of Library and Information Service*, 1, 3-13.

[5]   Gabrilovich, E. and Markovitch, S. (2007) Computing Semantic Relatedness Using Wikipedia-Based Explicit Semantic Analysis. *IJCAI*, 7, 1606-1611.

[6]   Sheng, Z.-C. and Tao, X.-P. (2011) Semantic Similarity Computing Method Based on Wikipedia. *Computer Engineering*, **37**.

[7]   Liu, J. and Yao, T.-F. (2010) Semantic Relevancy Computing Based on Wikipedia. *Computer Engineering*, **36**.

[8]   Chao, L.M., Zhang, Y. and Xing, C.X. (2011) DBpedia and Its Typical Applications. *New Technology of Library and Information Service*, 3, 80-87.

[9]   Breiman, L., Friedman, J.H., Oishen, R.A., *et al.* (1984) Classification and Regression Trees. Wadsworth, Inc.

[10] Chen, Z.W., Wu, Q.E and Yang, W.D. (2015) Target Image Classification through Encryption Algorithm Based on the Biological Features. *International Journal of Intelligence Science (IJIS)*, **5**, 6-12. http://dx.doi.org/10.4236/ijis.2015.51002

[11] Bezdek, J.C. (1981) Pattern Recognition with Fuzzy Objective Function Algorithms. Plenum Press, New York. http://dx.doi.org/10.1007/978-1-4757-0450-1

[12] Qing, L., Xu, X.-D. and Wang, S.-T. (2012) Fuzzy Particle Filter for Object Tracking. *AASRI Procedia*, **3**, 191-196. http://dx.doi.org/10.1016/j.aasri.2012.11.032

[13] Meia, W., Xiao, Y. and Wang, G. (2012) Object Classification Based on a Combination of Possibility and Probability Likelihood in the Bayesian Framework. *Procedia Engineering*, **29**, 9-14.

http://dx.doi.org/10.1016/j.proeng.2011.12.659

[14] Mai, F.-J., Li, D.-P. and Yue, X.-G. (2011) Research on Chinese Word Segmentation Based on Bi-Direction Marching Method and Feature Selection Algorithm. *Journal of Kunming University of Science and Technology* (*Natural Science Edition*), **36**, 47-51.

[15] Martelli, A., Ravenscroft, A. and Ascher, D. (2008) Python Cookbook. O'Reilly.

[16] Wiki API. http://zh.wikipedia.org/w/api.php

Target Image Classification through Encryption Algorithm Based on the Biological Features

Zhiwu Chen[1], Qing E. Wu[1,2*], Weidong Yang[2]

[1]College of Electric and Information Engineering, Zhengzhou University of Light Industry, Zhengzhou, China
[2]School of Computer Science, Fudan University, Shanghai, China
Email: *wqe969699@163.com

Abstract

In order to effectively make biological image classification and identification, this paper studies the biological owned characteristics, gives an encryption algorithm, and presents a biological classification algorithm based on the encryption process. Through studying the composition characteristics of palm, this paper uses the biological classification algorithm to carry out the classification or recognition of palm, improves the accuracy and efficiency of the existing biological classification and recognition approaches, and compares it with existing main approaches of palm classification by experiments. Experimental results show that this classification approach has the better classification effect, the faster computing speed and the higher classification rate which is improved averagely by 1.46% than those of the main classification approaches.

Keywords

Encryption, Palm Recognition, Classification, Feature Extraction

1. Introduction

The occurrence of computer has prompted the development of network and society informationization. On the other hand, the networked and informationized society demands a higher security for the information and systems [1]. The body biometric recognition technology is to use the biological characteristics owned by the human body to carry out an automatic identification, biology recognition technique for short, which is one of fundamental methods which are used for enhancing the security of information and systems. The palmprint recognition technology is an important part of the biology recognition ones [2]. Currently, the palmprint recognition

---

*Corresponding author.

technique has been widely used in police department, military branch and so on.

In 1998, the idea of automatic identification by using palm recognition was described systematically and comprehensively by Hong Kong Polytechnic University and Tsinghua University [3], which summarized comprehensively the characteristic of palm and the palmprint and opened up the research areas of palmprint recognition technology. Based on high resolution palmprint images, You *et al.* used the point of interest in the palmprint to carry out identification [4]. Among algorithms of image segmentation [5]-[7], the Fuzzy C-Means clustering [6] is one of algorithms that has some better features which can meet the human cognition pattern, be described concisely and clearly, and be easy to implement and so on. However, this algorithm has some disadvantages such as its performance depending on the initial clustering center, poor antinoise capability, and slow convergence and so on. From the research of traditional Markov Random Field (MRF) [7], the segmentation effect of MRF to micro texture is better, but the segmentation result of macro texture has many isolated islands or small areas.

Through studying the biological characteristics of palm, this paper analyses the features of texture principal lines, papilla ridges and bifurcation points of palm. At the same time, this paper gives an encryption algorithm and presents a biological classification algorithm based on the encryption process. Moreover, this paper calculates the distance between the characteristic vector of identified palm and that of known palm, and estimates the similarity degree between the two vectors by the distance. According to the minimum distance, the classification result can be obtained. Finally, the comparison of the proposed and existing classification approaches of palm is given.

2. Biological Feature Analysis

An appropriate encryption algorithm is more suitable for the features extraction of biological information, because the encryption to features of biological target is only include the characteristics of biological target, but not involve in some noises and background. Therefore, the analysis to biological feature needs to be discussed firstly in this section. Here, the features of palmprint as a biological feature example are analyzed.

The main research object to palm is the palmprint and fingerprint. The palmprint is the whole human palm excluding fingers, *i.e.*, the part between the finger roots and the wrist. There is a plenty of texture information in this area including several obvious principal lines, irregular wrinkles, trivial papillary ridges and a number of bifurcation points [3], which can be used as the features of palm and extracted by different methods to carry out an identification. In recent years, some researches on palmprint recognition had been attracted special attention, and some progress had been obtained, but further researches are to be made.

The fingerprint refers to the grain generated by the jagged lines on the skin of the finger ends [8] [9]. These lines of the skin in the pattern, break point and intersection are varied, and the morphology of the grain varies with everyone. *i.e.*, the grain line of everyone is different each other, which is called a "feature" in information processing. By comparing a man's fingerprint with previously saved fingerprints, his real identity can be verified. There is a plenty of texture information in fingerprint segment [8] [10] including several obvious grain lines, rotation direction, area coverage, trivial papillary ridges, a number of bifurcation points, break point and intersection, which can be used as the features of fingerprint and extracted by different methods to carry out an identification.

In palm image, the gray level of pixels in the features region and ones in the non-features region are different, as shown in the energy diagrams of **Figure 1**. From the Figure found clearly, the texture feature in the features region is very prominent, which shows a fine feature of energy mutation, but the energy feature diagram of non-features region almost levels off and the mutation is not obvious.

There are a plenty of papillary ridges in a palm, which are analogous to the fingerprints. However, compared with fingerprints, the geometric regularity of papillary ridges is not so evident. Through a large number of observations, these papillary ridges show some certain regularity in specific region of palm exclude fingers. As shown in **Figure 2**, in the lower part of index finger root, middle finger root, ring finger root and little finger root, there are four convergent points called as triangular points, which are formed by the corresponding papillary ridges. Since these triangular points are innate and not susceptible to being damaged, and their positions are very fixed, a palmprint image can be divided up by the positions of these triangular points.

In comparison with most recognition approaches, the fingerprint and palmprint recognition suffers fewer disturbances because of the shape of palm and the acquirement of fingerprint or palmprint image is stable. Thus, a relatively fixed fingerprint or palmprint image can be obtained no matter in when and where, and what state. In a

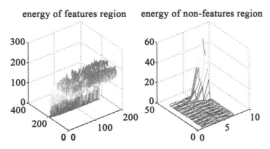

Figure 1. Energy feature of palm image.

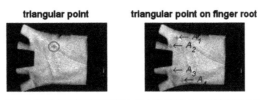

Figure 2. Triangular point in a palm.

concrete extraction, either the one of those features of fingerprint or palmprint may be extracted such as the one of principal lines and bifurcation points, or all features are extracted by high resolution acquisition equipment and fuse them together to construct a high precision palm recognition system.

3. Image Encryption Algorithm Proposed to Target Feature

For carrying out encryption, an encryption algorithm is given as follows:

Assume the current inputted feature is $u(l)$, and also inputted m features are $u(l-1),\cdots,u(l-m)$ before. By the encryption algorithm, the current output information $v(l)$ can be obtained. Their relationship can be denoted by the following formula.

$$v(l) = f\big(u(l),u(l-1),\cdots,u(l-m)\big),\ l=0,1,2,\cdots$$

where f is a binary linear convolution code algorithm, *i.e.*, is a Boolean function composed by modular binary addition operation. Assume the length of u is a constant k bits, and the length of v is a constant n bits, which they are all called one section.

For each k bits input, produce a n bits output. The relation of any input section $u(l-h)$ and any output section $v(l)$ is a special relation of linear block encoding (n,k). There is a $k \times n$ binary matrix denoted by G_h which makes the following formula established.

$$v(l) = u(l-h)*G_h,\ h=0,1,2,\cdots,m$$

Therefore, for each message queue, $u = \big(u(0),u(1),\cdots,u(m),u(m+1),\cdots\big)$, the corresponding output queue is $v = \big(v(0),v(1),\cdots,v(m),v(m+1),\cdots\big)$, and satisfies the requirement of following formula:

$$\begin{cases} v(l) = u(l-m)G_m + u(l-m+1)G_{m-1} + \cdots + u(l-1)G_1 + u(l)G_0 = \sum_{h=0}^{m} u(l-h)*G_h, & l=0,1,2,\cdots \\ u(l) = 0, & l<0 \end{cases} \quad (1)$$

Formula (1) is a convolution code model. The binary linear convolution code (n,k,m), which is denoted by C, is a set of code word v. The set can be denoted by the following formula:

$$C = \left\{ v \,\middle|\, v = \tilde{u}G_\infty, \tilde{u} = \Big(u,\underbrace{0,0,\cdots,0}_{m*k}\Big), u = (u_0,u_1,u_2,\cdots), u_i \in \{0,1\} \right\}$$

where G_∞ is the matrix generated by the convolution code:

$$
G_\infty = \begin{bmatrix}
G_0 & G_1 & G_2 & \cdots & G_{m-1} & G_m & & & \\
 & G_0 & G_1 & G_2 & \cdots & G_{m-1} & G_m & & \\
 & & G_0 & G_1 & G_2 & \cdots & G_{m-1} & G_m & \\
 & & & \cdots & \cdots & \cdots & \cdots & \cdots
\end{bmatrix}
$$

The G_B is a basic generated matrix of convolution code, which is a submatrix of G_∞, composed by front of k rows and $(m+1)n$ columns of G_∞. It can be denoted by:

$$
G_B = \left[G_0 G_1 G_2 \cdots G_{m-1} G_m \right] = \left[g_1, \cdots, g_i, \cdots, g_k \right]^{\mathrm{T}} = \left[g_{it} \right]_{k \times kn}
$$

The i-th row in G_B, denoted by g_i, describes the influence that the i-th input bit in all in-put section versus all out-put bits. Where g_i is the i-th generator of convolution code. It is obvious that the convolution code (n,k,m) has the count of k generators.

Through doing some experiments, the feature extraction based on the proposed encryption algorithm can provide translation, rotation, or scale invariant properties, because the algorithm is only involve in the characteristics of biological target, but not include the position of target.

4. Give Image Classification or Recognition Algorithm

4.1. Propose Algorithm of Classification or Recognition

According to the principal lines, triangular points, irregular wrinkles, trivial papillary ridges and a number of bifurcation points of palmprint feature, some palmprints can be classified. Or if the search fingerprints are classified according to such attributes of fingerprint as grain lines, rotation direction, area coverage, trivial papillary ridges, a number of bifurcation points, break point and intersection, with the N samples classified into n categories $(1 < n < N)$, then such n categories should be the sample sets of $w_1, w_2, \cdots, w_n$, and each category identified should have N_i samples, $i = 1, 2, \cdots, n$. Assume the sample has p attributes, such as the bifurcation points, break point, intersection and so on, then the indexes of sample points can form a p-dimensional characteristic space, and each sample point will have only one corresponding point in the p-dimensional characteristic space. Moreover, for any sample to be identified $x = \langle a_1(x), a_2(x), \cdots, a_p(x) \rangle$, $a_r(x)$ represents the r-th attribute of the sample x. For a sample x to be identified, the k samples that are closest to x are chosen firstly according to the defined distance in the training sample data set, and the k samples are represented by $x_1, x_2, \cdots, x_k$ respectively. Assume $k_1, k_2, \cdots, k_n$ are the number of samples belonging to categories $w_1, w_2, \cdots, w_n$ in the k neighbors. If k_i is the largest one, then the sample x will belong to the w_i category.

Distance definition: Assume the sample $x = \langle a_1(x), a_2(x), \cdots, a_p(x) \rangle$ and the sample $y = \langle a_1(y), a_2(y), \cdots, a_p(y) \rangle$, then the distance can be defined as follows:

$$
d_{xy} = \sum_{j=1}^{p} \left| a_j(x) - a_j(y) \right|
$$

Assume $d_{ik} = \| x_k - v_i \|$ is the distance between the sample x_k and the center v_i of the i-th category, and $m > 1$ is a fuzzy weighted exponent.

The center v_i of each category can be calculated as follows:

$$
v_i = \frac{\sum_{j=1}^{N} (u_{ij})^m x_j}{\sum_{j=1}^{N} (u_{ij})^m} \tag{2}
$$

where u_{ij} can be given by membership function and must satisfy the following conditions:

(1) The defined u_{ij} should be inversely proportional to d_{ij}, namely, u_{ij} is a monotone decreasing function about d_{ij}; (2) u_{ij} is a monotone increasing function about the fuzzy weighted exponent m; (3) u_{ij} is the degree of membership, so $0 \le u_{ij} \le 1$. Moreover, it requires that each category must contain one sample at least,

but the sample may not belong to the same category, so $0 < \sum_{j=1}^{N} u_{ij} < N$ is true; (4) Simultaneously, u_{ij} satis-

fies the equation $\sum_{i=1}^{n} u_{ij} = 1$, $\forall 1 \leq j \leq N$.

For a sample x to be identified, calculate the distance between x and the center v_i, select k features that is closest to x, which are represented by $x_1, x_2, \cdots, x_k$ respectively. Define an ordered pair $\langle x, f(x) \rangle$, and $f(x)$ is the category which the sample x belongs to: $f(x): R \to W$, in which R is a set of samples to be identified, W is a finite set $\{w_1, w_2, \cdots, w_n\}$ of category, w_i is the i-th type feature of the partition identified feature, and n is the number of categories. Then $f(x)$ can be calculated as follows:

$$f(x) = \arg\max_{w_j \in W} \sum_{i=1}^{k} \sigma\big(w_j, f(x_i)\big),$$

here $f(x) = w_{j^*}$, then the sample x belongs to the category w_{j^*}. where, $\begin{cases} \sigma(a,b) = 1 & a = b \\ \sigma(a,b) = 0 & a \neq b \end{cases}$.

4.2. Experiment and Analysis

Here, the Hong Kong Polytechnic University (HKPU) palmprint database is used for evaluating the classification or recognition algorithm. For each palm image, 10 times repeating experiments are carried out by the above feature classification and recognition method in simulation. Moreover, some features of palm here are used for the classification and recognition algorithm, *i.e.*, principal line, irregular wrinkle, trivial papillary ridge, bifurcation point, triangular point features. The number of samples is different in each experiment. The literature [11] provided an updated survey of palmprint recognition methods, and presented a comparative study to evaluate the performance of the state-of-the-art palmprint recognition methods. According to [11], the proposed classification approach compares with those currently usually used approaches such as FCM [6], Median filter [9], Gabor [12] and Fourier transform [13]. The experimental results show that the average correct classification rates of these approaches are 95.57%, 94.11%, 93.24%, 92.45% and 88.17% in simulation of 500 times, respectively. The simulation results are shown in **Figure 3**.

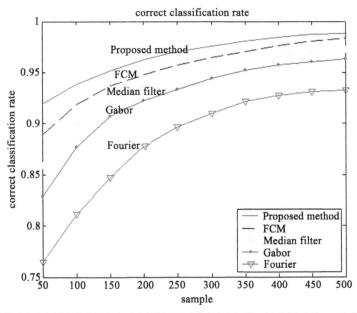

Figure 3. Comparison of correct classification rate for the proposed and other classification approaches

From **Figure 3** concluded, the average correct classification rate of the classification approach based on feature extraction of encryption is the highest among all referred approaches. In experiment, the average correct classification rate increases constantly with the increasing classification samples, and the curve of average correct classification rate gradually levels off as the samples increase when the number of samples reaches a certain value. Through 500 times simulation, the simulation results show that every average correct classification rate is a stable value respectively when the number of samples are enough much. Moreover, the average correct classification rate of the proposed approach based on feature encryption is the highest, and its classification effect is also the best, which is shown in **Table 1**.

To evaluate the comprehensive performance of these approaches, we adopt the combination of quantitative analysis and qualitative analysis method, and synthesize comparison based on some factors such as the computing speed, memory capacity, communications traffic and correct classification rate. We evaluate the merits and demerits of different classification approaches for palm. **Table 1** gives the results of a comprehensive comparison.

In **Table 1**, the computing speed is the mean time obtained by the mean computing time of 10 times repeating test of these approaches at each step in simulation environment, which the computing time is only the computing time of algorithm itself. In simulation, the computer used is the Pentium 4 and 2G memory, and the programming language is Matlab. The memory capacity and the communications traffic are estimated approximately based on the computing course and complexity of every approach. From the results of **Table 1** seen, the memory capacity and communications traffic are close related. The average correct classification rates are the average of two stages which are an average of 500 times simulations and then taking an average of 10 time-steps for every approach under the given simulation environment. In fact, they are the average of the correct classification rates in space and time, so they are an overall average of the correct classification rates.

On the basis of the simulation results, the classification approach based on feature extraction of encryption not only has the faster processing speed, the lower memory capacity and communications traffic, but also has better classification effect.

5. Conclusions

This paper firstly analyzes the features of a palm image such as wrinkles, principal ridges, papillary ridges, triangular points and so on. Then, this paper discusses the biological features of palm, presenting an encryption algorithm based on the features of palm. Moreover, this paper gives the feature extraction based on encryption algorithm, as well as the classification and recognition approach of palm image, at the same time, carrying out the simulation test. Finally, the simulation results prove the feasibility and effectiveness of all proposed algorithms or approaches in each stage.

The advantage of the presented encryption algorithm is that its calculation is small and it programming is simple. However, the combination between this algorithm and other feature extraction algorithms for image will need to be discussed in the future. Moreover, to compare with existing classification or recognition approaches, the classification approach based on feature extraction of encryption in this paper has some advantages, such as the faster processing speed, the lower memory capacity and communications traffic, as well as better recognition effect, etc., and its potential application could include fingerprint recognition, iris recognition, medical image classification, etc., lots of biological classification and recognition. However, more wide applications will be urgently studied in the further work.

Table 1. Comprehensive comparison of different classification approaches for palm.

Approaches	Average correct classification rate $\overline{R}_c$	Computing speed	Memory capacity	Communications traffic
Proposed classification	0.9557	0.426 s	Low	Low
FCM	0.9411	0. 546 s	Middle	Middle
Median filter	0.9324	0.458 s	Middle	Middle
Gabor	0.9245	0.49 s	Lower	Lower
Fourier	0.8817	0.82 s	Middle	Middle

Acknowledgements

This work is supported by Project of Henan Province Science and Technology (No. 142300410247); Key Project of Henan Province Education Department (No: 14A413002, 12A520049, 14A413010); Project funded by China postdoctoral science foundation (No. 2013M531120); Aerospace support fund (No. Chinare 2014-04-07); Project of Zhengzhou Science and Technology (No. 131PPTGG411-4), and fund of ZZULI (No. 2013XJJ013), respectively.

References

[1] Janarthanam, S., Ramalingam, M. and Narendran, P. (2010) Texture Analysis on Low Resolution Images Using Unsupervised Segmentation Algorithm with Multichannel Local Frequency Analysis. *International Conference on Communication and Computational Intelligence* (*INCOCCI*), 4-6 January 2010, 260-265.

[2] Yue, F., Zuo, W.M. and Zhang, D.P. (2010) Survey of Palmprint Recognition Algorithms. *Acta Automatica Sinica*, **36**, 353-365.

[3] Shu, W. and Zhang, D. (1998) Automated Personal Identification by Palmprint. *Optical Engineering*, **37**, 2359-2362. http://dx.doi.org/10.1117/1.601756

[4] You, J., Li, W.X., *et al.* (2002) Hierarchical Palmprint Identification via Multiple Feature Extraction. *Pattern Recognition*, **1**, 847-859. http://dx.doi.org/10.1016/S0031-3203(01)00100-5

[5] Xie, X.Z., Wu, J.T. and Jing, M.G. (2013) Fast Two-Stage Segmentation via Non-Local Active Contours in Multiscale Texture Feature Space. *Pattern Recognition Letters*, **34**, 1230-1239. http://dx.doi.org/10.1016/j.patrec.2013.04.016

[6] Yu, J. (2011) Texture Segmentation Based on FCM Algorithm Combined with GLCM and Space Information. *International Conference on Electric Information and Control Engineering*, Wuhan, 15-17 April 2011, 4569-4572. http://dx.doi.org/10.1109/ICEICE.2011.5778005

[7] Long, Z.L. and Younan, N.H. (2013) Multiscale Texture Segmentation via a Contourlet Contextual Hidden Markov Model. *Digital Signal Processing*, **23**, 859-869. http://dx.doi.org/10.1016/j.dsp.2012.11.009

[8] Jiang, X.B., You, X.E., Yuan, Y. and Gong, M.M. (2012) A Method Using Long Digital Straight Segments for Fingerprint Recognition. *Neurocomputing*, **77**, 28-35. http://dx.doi.org/10.1016/j.neucom.2011.07.018

[9] Kızrak, A.M. and Özen, F. (2011) A New Median Filter Based Fingerprint Recognition Algorithm. *Procedia Computer Science*, **3**, 859-865. http://dx.doi.org/10.1016/j.procs.2010.12.141

[10] Caldwell, T. (2013) Tabletop Combines Image Display and Fingerprint Recognition. *Biometric Technology Today*, **2013**, 1, 12-13. http://dx.doi.org/10.1016/S0969-4765(13)70180-2

[11] Zhang, D., Zuo, W.M. and Yue, F. (2012) A Comparative Study of Palmprint Recognition Algorithms. *ACM Computing Surveys*, **44**, 1-37. http://dx.doi.org/10.1145/2071389.2071391

[12] Pan, X. and Ruan, Q.Q. (2009) Palmprint Recognition Using Gabor-Based Local Invariant Features. *Neurocomputing*, **72**, 2040-2045. http://dx.doi.org/10.1016/j.neucom.2008.11.019

[13] Li, W., Zhang, D. and Xu, Z. (2002) Palmprint Identification Based on Fourier Transform. *Journal of Software*, **13**, 95-97.

17

Converting Instance Checking to Subsumption: A Rethink for Object Queries over Practical Ontologies

Jia Xu[1], Patrick Shironoshita[1], Ubbo Visser[2], Nigel John[1], Mansur Kabuka[1]

[1]Department of Electrical and Computer Engineering, University of Miami, Coral Gables, USA
[2]Department of Computer Science, University of Miami, Coral Gables, USA
Email: j.xu11@umiami.edu, patrick@infotechsoft.com, nigel.john@miami.edu, m.kabuka@miami.edu, visser@cs.miami.edu

Academic Editor: Zhongzhi Shi, Institute of Computing Technology, CAS, China

Abstract

Efficiently querying Description Logic (DL) ontologies is becoming a vital task in various data-intensive DL applications. Considered as a basic service for answering object queries over DL ontologies, instance checking can be realized by using the most specific concept (MSC) method, which converts instance checking into subsumption problems. This method, however, loses its simplicity and efficiency when applied to large and complex ontologies, as it tends to generate very large MSCs that could lead to intractable reasoning. In this paper, we propose a revision to this MSC method for DL $\mathcal{SHI}$, allowing it to generate much simpler and smaller concepts that are specific enough to answer a given query. With independence between computed MSCs, scalability for query answering can also be achieved by distributing and parallelizing the computations. An empirical evaluation shows the efficacy of our revised MSC method and the significant efficiency achieved when using it for answering object queries.

Keywords

Description Logic, Ontology, Object Query, $\mathcal{SHI}$, Most Specific Concept

1. Introduction

Description logics (DLs) play an ever growing role in providing a formal and semantic-rich way to model and represent structured data in various applications, including semantic web, healthcare and biomedical research, etc. [1]. A knowledge base in description logic, usually referred to as a DL ontology, consists of an *assertional* component (ABox $\mathcal{A}$) for data description, where *individuals* (single objects) are introduced and their mutual relationships are described using assertional axioms. Semantic meaning of the ABox data can then be unambiguously specified by a *terminological* component (TBox $\mathcal{T}$) of the DL ontology, where abstract *concepts* and *roles* (binary relations) of the application domain are properly defined.

In various applications of description logics, one of the core tasks for DL systems is to provide an efficient way to manage and query the assertional knowledge (*i.e.* ABox data) in a DL ontology, especially for those data-intensive applications; and DL systems are expected to scale well with respect to (w.r.t.) the fast growing ABox data, in settings such as semantic webs or biomedical systems. The most basic reasoning service provided by existing DL systems for retrieving objects from ontology ABoxes is *instance checking*, which tests whether an individual is a member of a given concept. Instance retrieval (*i.e.* retrieve all instances of a given concept) then can be realized by performing a set of instance checking calls.

In recent years, considerable efforts have been dedicated to the optimization of algorithms for ontology reasoning and query answering [2]-[4]. However, due to the enormous amount of ABox data in realistic applications, existing DL systems, such as HermiT [4] [5], Pellet [6], Racer [7] and FaCT++ [8], still have difficulties in handling the large ABoxes, as they are all based on the (*hyper*) *tableau* algorithm that is computationally expensive for expressive DLs (e.g. up to EXPTIME for instance checking in DL $\mathcal{SHIQ}$), where the complexity is usually measured in the size of the TBox, the ABox and the query [9]-[13]. In practice, since the TBox and the query are usually much smaller compared with the ABox, the reasoning efficiency could be mostly affected by the size of the ABox.

One of the solutions to this reasoning scalability problem is to develop a much more efficient algorithm that can easily handle large amount of ABox data. While another one is to reduce size of the data by either partitioning the ABox into small and independent fragments that can be easily handled in parallel by existing systems [14]-[16], or converting the ABox reasoning into a TBox reasoning task (*i.e.* ontology reasoning without an ABox), which could be "*somewhat*" independent of the data size, the TBox is static and relatively simple, as demonstrated in this paper.

A common intuition about converting instance checking into a TBox reasoning task is the so-called most specific concept (MSC) method [10] [17] [18] that computes the MSC of a given individual and reduces any instance checking of this individual into a *subsumption test* (*i.e.* test if one concept is more general than the other). More precisely, for a given individual, its most specific concept should summarize all information of the individual in a given ontology ABox, and should be specific enough to be subsumed by any concept that the individual belongs to. Therefore, once the most specific concept C of an individual a is known, in order to check if a is an instance of any given concept D, it is sufficient to test if C is subsumed by D. With the MSC of every individual in the ABox, the efficiency of online object queries can then be boosted by performing an offline classification of all MSCs that can pre-compute many instance checks [10]. Moreover, if a large ontology ABox consists of data with great diversity and isolation, using the MSC method for instance checking could be more efficient than the original ABox reasoning, since the MSC would have the tableau algorithm to explore only the related information of the given individual, potentially restricted to a small subset of the ABox. Also, this method allows the reasoning to be parallelized and distributed, since MSCs are independent of each other and each preserves complete information of the corresponding individual.

Despite these appealing properties possessed by the MSC method, the computation of a MSC could be difficult even for a very simple description logic such as $\mathcal{ALE}$. The difficulty arises mainly from the support of qualified existential restrictions (e.g. $\exists R.C$) in DLs, such that when converting a role assertion (e.g. $R(a,b)$) of some individuals into an existential restriction, so that information of that given individual may not be preserved completely. For a simple example, consider converting assertions

$$R(a,b) \text{ and } A(a)$$

into a concept for individual a. In this case, we can always find a more specific concept for a in the form of

$$A \sqcap \underbrace{\exists R.\exists R. \cdots \exists R}_{n}.A$$

by increasing n, and none of them would capture the complete information of individual a. Such information loss is due to the occurrence of cycles in the role assertions, and none of the existential restrictions in DL could impose a circular interpretation (model) unless *nominals* (e.g. $\{a\}$) are involved or (local) reflexivity is presented [5].

Most importantly, due to the support of existential restrictions, computation of the MSC for a given individual may involve assertions of other entities that are connected to it through role assertions. This implies not only the complexity of the computation for MSCs but also the potential that the resulting MSCs may have larger than desired sizes. In fact, in many of the practical ontology ABoxes (e.g. a social network or semantic webs), most of the individuals could be connected to each other through role assertions, forming a huge connected component in the ABox graph. Under this situation, the resulting MSC could be extremely large and reasoning with it may completely degenerate into an expensive reasoning procedure.

In this paper, we propose a revised MSC method for DL $\mathcal{SHI}$ that attempts to tackle the above mentioned problems, by applying a *call-by-need* strategy together with optimizations. That is, instead of computing the most specific concepts that could be used to answer any queries in the future, the revised method takes into consideration only the related ABox information with *current* query and computes a concept for each individual that is only *specific enough* to answer it w.r.t. the TBox. Based on this strategy, the revision allows the method to generate much simpler and smaller concepts than the original MSCs by ignoring irrelevant ABox assertions. On the other hand, the complexity reduction comes with the price of re-computation (*i.e.* online computation of MSCs) for every new coming query, if no optimization is applied. Nevertheless, as shown in our experimental evaluation, the simplicity achieved could be significant in many practical ontologies, and the overhead is thus negligible compared with the reasoning efficiency gained for each instance checking and query answering. Moreover, due to the re-computations, *we do not assume a static ontology or query*, and the ABox data is amenable to frequent modifications, such as insertion or deletion, which is in contrast to the original MSC method where a relatively static ABox is assumed. A procedure for instance retrieval based on our revised MSC method is shown in **Figure 1**.

The revised MSC method could be very useful for efficient instance checking in many practical ontologies, where the TBox is usually small and manageable while the ABox is in large scale as a database and tends to change frequently. Particularly, this method would be appealing to large ontologies in *non-Horn* DLs, where current optimization techniques such as rule-based reasoning or pre-computation may fall short. Moreover, the capability to parallelize the computation is another compelling reason to use this technique, in cases where answering object queries may demand thousands or even millions of instance checking tasks.

Our contributions in this paper are summarized as follows:

1) We propose a call-by-need strategy for the original MSC method, instead of computing the most specific concepts offline to handle any given query, which allows us to focus on the current queries and to generate online much smaller concepts that are sufficient to compute the answers. This strategy makes our MSC method suitable for query answering in ontologies, where frequent modifications to the ontology data are not uncommon;

2) We propose optimizations that can be used to further reduce sizes of computed concepts in practical ontologies for more efficient instance checking;

3) Finally, we evaluate our approach on a range of test ontologies with large ABoxes, including ones generated by existing benchmark tools and realistic ones used in biomedical research. The evaluation shows the efficacy of our proposed approach that can generate significantly smaller concepts than the original MSC. It also

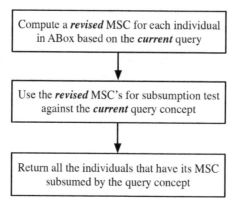

Figure 1. A procedure for instance retrieval for a given query based on our revised MSC method.

shows the great reasoning efficiency that can be achieved when using the revised MSC method for instance checking and query answering.

The rest of the paper is organized as follows: in Section 2, we introduce the background knowledge of a description logic and DL ontology; in Section 3, we give more detailed discussion about the MSC method and our call-by-need strategy; Section 4 presents the technical details of the revised MSC method; Section 5 discusses the related work; Section 6 presents an empirical evaluation on our proposed method; and finally, Section 7 concludes our work.

2. Preliminaries

The technique proposed in this paper is for description logic $\mathcal{SHI}$. For technical reasons, we need a *constrained* use of nominals on certain conditions (*i.e.* assertion cycles), which requires logic $\mathcal{SHIO}$. Thus, in this section, we give a brief introduction to formal syntax and semantics of logic $\mathcal{SHIO}$, DL ontologies, and basic reasoning tasks for derivation of logical entailments from DL ontologies.

2.1. Description Logic $\mathcal{SHIO}$

The vocabulary of description logic $\mathcal{SHIO}$ includes a set $\mathbf{R}$ of named roles with a subset $\mathbf{R}_+ \subseteq \mathbf{R}$ of transitive roles, a set $\mathbf{C}$ of named (atomic) concepts, and a set $\mathbf{I}$ of named individuals.

Definition 2.1 ($\mathcal{SHIO}$ Role) *A role in $\mathcal{SHIO}$ is either a named (atomic) one $R \in \mathbf{R}$ or an inverse one R^- with $R \in \mathbf{R}$, and the complete role set of $\mathcal{SHIO}$ can be denoted $\mathbf{R}^* = \mathbf{R} \cup \{R^- \mid R \in \mathbf{R}\}$. To avoid role representation such as R^{--}, a function $Inv(\cdot)$ is defined, such that $Inv(R) = R^-$ R^- if R is a role name, and $Inv(R) = P$ if $R = P^-$ for some role name P. A role R is transitive, denoted $Trans(R)$, if either R or $Inv(R)$ belongs to $\mathbf{R}_+$.*

Definition 2.2 ($\mathcal{SHIO}$ Concept) *A $\mathcal{SHIO}$-concept is either an atomic (named) concept or a complex one that can be defined using the following constructs recursively*

$$C, D ::= A \mid \{o\} \mid \top \mid \bot \mid \neg C \mid C \sqcap D \mid C \sqcup D \mid \forall R.C \mid \exists R.C$$

where A is an atomic concept in $\mathbf{C}$, o is a named individual, and $R \in \mathbf{R}^*$.

Description logic $\mathcal{SHI}$ is then defined as a fragment of $\mathcal{SHIO}$, which disallows the use of nominal (*i.e.* $\{o\}$) as a construct for building complex concepts.

Definition 2.3 ($\mathcal{SHIO}$ Semantics) *The meaning of an entity in $\mathcal{SHIO}$ is defined by a model-theoretical semantics using an interpretation denoted $\mathcal{I} = (\Delta^{\mathcal{I}}, \cdot^{\mathcal{I}})$, where $\Delta^{\mathcal{I}}$ is referred to as a non-empty domain and $\cdot^{\mathcal{I}}$ is an interpretation function. The function $\cdot^{\mathcal{I}}$ maps every atomic concept in $\mathbf{C}$ to a subset of $\Delta^{\mathcal{I}}$, every ABox individual to an element of $\Delta^{\mathcal{I}}$, and every role to a subset of $\Delta^{\mathcal{I}} \times \Delta^{\mathcal{I}}$. Interpretation for other concepts and role are given below:*

$$\top^{\mathcal{I}} = \Delta^{\mathcal{I}}$$

$$\bot^{\mathcal{I}} = \varnothing$$

$$\{o\}^{\mathcal{I}} = \{o^{\mathcal{I}}\}$$

$$\neg C^{\mathcal{I}} = \Delta^{\mathcal{I}} \setminus C^{\mathcal{I}}$$

$$(R^-)^{\mathcal{I}} = \{(y, x) \mid (x, y) \in R^{\mathcal{I}}\}$$

$$(C \sqcap D)^{\mathcal{I}} = C^{\mathcal{I}} \cap D^{\mathcal{I}}$$

$$(C \sqcup D)^{\mathcal{I}} = C^{\mathcal{I}} \cup D^{\mathcal{I}}$$

$$(\exists R.C)^{\mathcal{I}} = \{x \mid \exists y.(x, y) \in R^{\mathcal{I}} \wedge y \in C^{\mathcal{I}}\}$$

$$(\forall R.C)^{\mathcal{I}} = \{x \mid \forall y.(x, y) \in R^{\mathcal{I}} \wedge y \in C^{\mathcal{I}}\}$$

Definition 2.4 (Simple-Form Concept) *A concept is said to be in simple form, if the maximum level of nested quantifiers in this concept is less than 2.*

For example, given an atomic concept A, both A and $\exists R.A$ are simple-form concepts, while $\exists R_1.(A \sqcap \exists R_2.A)$ is not, since its maximum level of nested quantifiers is two. Notice however, an arbitrary concept can be *linearly* reduced to the simple form by assigning new concept names for fillers of the quantifiers. For example, $\exists R_1.\exists R_2.C$ can be converted to $\exists R_1.D$ by letting $D \equiv \exists R_2.C$ where D is a new concept name.

Assumption: For accuracy of the technique presented in this paper, without loss of generality, we assume all ontology concepts are in simple form as defined previously, and the concept in any concept assertion is atomic.

2.2. DL Ontologies and Reasoning

Definition 2.5 ($\mathcal{SHIO}$ Ontology) *A $\mathcal{SHIO}$ ontology is a tuple, denoted $\mathcal{K} = (\mathcal{T}, \mathcal{A})$, where $\mathcal{T}$ is called a TBox and $\mathcal{A}$ is called an ABox.*

The TBox $\mathcal{T}$ is constituted by a finite set of role inclusion axioms (*i.e.* $R_1 \sqsubseteq R_2$ with R_1, $R_2 \in R^*$) and a finite set of concept inclusion axioms in the form of $C \sqsubseteq D$ and $C \equiv D$, where C, D are $\mathcal{SHI}$ concepts. The former is called a *general concept inclusion axiom (GCI)*, and the latter can be simply converted into two GCIs as $C \sqsubseteq D$ and $D \sqsubseteq C$.

The ABox $\mathcal{A}$ consists of a finite set of assertions, in the form of $A(a)$ (concept assertion) and $R(a,b)$ (role assertion), where A is a concept, R is a role, and a, b are named individuals in I. In a role assertion $R(a,b)$, individual a is referred to as a R-*predecessor* of b, and b is a R-*successor* (or R^--*predecessor*) of a. If b is a R-successor of a, b is also called a R-*neighbor* of a.

An interpretation $\mathcal{I}$ satisfies an axiom $C \sqsubseteq D$ (written $\mathcal{I} \vDash C \sqsubseteq D$), iff $C^{\mathcal{I}} \subseteq D^{\mathcal{I}}$, and $\mathcal{I}$ satisfies an axiom or assertion:

$$R_1 \sqsubseteq R_2 \text{ iff } R_1^{\mathcal{I}} \subseteq R_2^{\mathcal{I}}$$

$$C(a) \text{ iff } a^{\mathcal{I}} \in C^{\mathcal{I}}$$

$$R(a,b) \text{ iff } (a^{\mathcal{I}}, b^{\mathcal{I}}) \in R^{\mathcal{I}}$$

If $\mathcal{I}$ satisfies every axiom and assertion of an ontology $\mathcal{K}$, $\mathcal{I}$ is called a *model* of $\mathcal{K}$, written $\mathcal{I} \vDash \mathcal{K}$. In turn, $\mathcal{K}$ is said *satisfiable* iff it has at least one model; otherwise, it is *unsatisfiable* or *inconsistent*.

Definition 2.6 (Logical Entailment) *Given an ontology $\mathcal{K}$ and an axiom α, α is called a logical entailment of $\mathcal{K}$, denoted $\mathcal{K} \vDash \alpha$, if α is satisfied in every model of $\mathcal{K}$.*

Definition 2.7 (Instance Checking) *Given an ontology $\mathcal{K}$, a DL concept C and an individual $a \in I$, instance checking is defined to test if $\mathcal{K} \vDash C(a)$ holds.*

Notice that, instance checking is considered the central reasoning service for information retrieval from ontology ABoxes [19], and more complex reasoning services, such as instance retrieval, can be realized based on this basic service. Instance checking can also be viewed as a procedure of individual "*classification*" that verifies if an individual can be classified into some defined DL concepts. An intuition to implement this instance checking service is to convert it into a concept subsumption test by using the so-called *most specific concept* (MSC) method.

Definition 2.8 (Most Specific Concept [20]) *Let $\mathcal{K} = (\mathcal{T}, \mathcal{A})$ be an ontology, and a be an individual in I. A concept C is called the most specific concept for a w.r.t. $\mathcal{A}$, written $\mathrm{MSC}(\mathcal{A}, a)$, if for every concept D that $\mathcal{K} \vDash D(a)$, $\mathcal{I} \vDash C \sqsubseteq D$.*

The MSC method turns the instance checking into a TBox reasoning problem. That is, once the most specific concept $\mathrm{MSC}(\mathcal{A}, a)$ of an individual a is known, to decide if $\mathcal{K} \vDash D(a)$ holds for an arbitrary concept D, it suffices to test if $\mathcal{T} \vDash \mathrm{MSC}(\mathcal{A}, a) \sqsubseteq D$ [10].

Ontology reasoning algorithm in current systems (e.g. Pellet, and HermiT, etc.) are based on (hyper) tableau algorithms [4] [6] [7] [21]. For details of a standard tableau algorithm for $\mathcal{SHIO}$, we refer readers to the work in [22].

3. Classification of Individuals

The MSC method for individual checking is based on the idea that, an individual can be classified into a given concept D, if and only if there exists a concept behind its ABox assertions subsumed by D [17] [18] [20]. Computation of the MSC for a given individual then demands converting its ABox assertions into a concept. This task can be easily accomplished if the individual possesses only concept assertions, by simply collapsing the involved concepts into a single term using the concept conjunction. When role assertions are involved, however, a more complex procedure is demanded, and the method we used here is called *rolling-up* [23], which is elaborated in the next section.

Using the MSC method for instance checking might eliminate the memory limitation for reasoning with large ABoxes, especially when the ABox $\mathcal{A}$ consists of data in great diversity and isolation. This is simply because each computed $\mathrm{MSC}(\mathcal{A},a)$ should comprise of only related information of the given individual, and makes the subsumption test (*i.e.* $\mathcal{T} \vDash \mathrm{MSC}(\mathcal{A},a) \sqsubseteq D$) as efficient as an ontology reasoning that explores only a (small) portion of $\mathcal{A}$.

However, as discussed in Section 1, due to the support of existential restrictions in DLs, great complexity for computation of MSC's may arise when role assertions are involved. Besides, due to the *completeness* that should be guaranteed by each $\mathrm{MSC}(\mathcal{A},a)$ (*i.e.* the MSC should be subsumed by any concept that the individual a belongs to.), the resulting MSC's may turn out to be a very large concept, whenever there is a great number of individuals in $\mathcal{A}$ connected to each other by role assertions. In the *worst* case, reasoning with a MSC may degenerate into a complete ABox reasoning that could be prohibitively expensive. For example, when $\mathrm{MSC}(\mathcal{A},a)$ preserves complete information of $\mathcal{A}$, its interpretation will form a tableau, the size of which can be in the same scale of $\mathcal{A}$.

3.1. The Call-by-Need Strategy

Since the larger than desired sizes of MSCs are usually caused by its completeness as discussed above, a possible optimization to the MSC method is thus to abandon the completeness that is required to deal with any query concepts, and to apply a "*call-by-need*" strategy. That is, for an arbitrary query concept D, instead of computing the MSC for each individual a, we compute a concept that is only *specific-enough* to determine if a can be classified into D. As suggested by its name, this revision to the original MSC method, instead of taking the complete information of individual a when computing the "MSC", will consider only the ABox assertions that are relevant to the current query concept.

A simple way to realize this strategy is to assign a fresh name A every time to a given (complex) query concept D by adding the axiom $A \equiv D$ to $\mathcal{T}$[1], and to concentrate only on ABox assertions that would (probably) classify an individual a into A w.r.t. $\mathcal{T}$. Consequently, this implementation requires an analysis of the ontology axioms/assertions, such that the possibility of each role assertion to affect individual classification (w.r.t. named concept in $\mathcal{T}$) can be figured out. Computation of a specific-enough concept should then concentrate on role assertions that are *not impossible*. We abuse the notation here to denote this specific-enough concept for individual a w.r.t. ABox $\mathcal{A}$, current query concept $\mathcal{Q}$, and named concepts in $\mathcal{T}$ as $\mathrm{MSC}_{\mathcal{T}}(\mathcal{A},\mathcal{Q},a)$, and we call the method that uses $\mathrm{MSC}_{\mathcal{T}}$ for instance checking the $\mathrm{MSC}_{\mathcal{T}}$ method.

Definition 3.1 *Let* $\mathcal{K}=(\mathcal{T},\mathcal{A})$ *be an ontology, a be an individual in $\mathcal{A}$, and $\mathcal{Q}$ a current query concept for individuals. A concept C is called a specific-enough concept for a w.r.t. named concepts in $\mathcal{T}$, $\mathcal{Q}$ and $\mathcal{A}$, written* $\mathrm{MSC}_{\mathcal{T}}(\mathcal{A},\mathcal{Q},a)$, *if* $\mathcal{K} \vDash \mathcal{Q}(a)$, $\mathcal{T} \vDash C \sqsubseteq \mathcal{Q}$.

Since in our procedure we will add the query concept $\mathcal{Q}$ into $\mathcal{T}$ as a named concept, we can simplify the notation $\mathrm{MSC}_{\mathcal{T}}(\mathcal{A},\mathcal{Q},a)$ as $\mathrm{MSC}_{\mathcal{T}}(\mathcal{A},a)$.

3.2. A Syntactic Premise

To decide whether a role assertion could affect classification of a given individual, a sufficient and necessary condition as stated previously is that, the concept behind this assertion conjuncted with other essential information of the individual should be subsumed by the given concept w.r.t. $\mathcal{T}$ [17] [18] [20]. Formally, for a role assertion $R(a,b)$ that makes individual a classified into a concept A, the above sufficient and necessary condition in $\mathcal{SHI}$ can be expressed as:

$$\mathcal{K} \vDash \exists R.B \sqcap A_0 \sqsubseteq A \tag{1}$$

where $b \in B$ is entailed by $\mathcal{K}$, and concept A_0 summarizes the rest of the information of a that is also

---

[1]Note that, to follow the simple-form concept restriction, multiple axioms may be added.

essential to this classification, with $A_0 \sqsubseteq A$.

As shown in [16], for subsumption (1) to hold when A is a named concept, there must exist some role restriction $\exists R'.C$ with $R \sqsubseteq R'$ in left-hand side of TBox axioms (see (2) and the following axiom equivalency) for concept definition; otherwise $\exists R.B$ is not comparable (w.r.t. subsumption) with other concepts (except T and its equivalents). This syntactic condition for the deduction of (1) is formally expressed in the following proposition.

Proposition 3.1 ([16]) *Let* $\mathcal{K} = (\mathcal{T}, \mathcal{A})$ *be a* $\mathcal{SHI}$ *ontology with simple-form concepts only,* $\exists R.B$, A_0 *and* A *be* $\mathcal{SHI}$ *concepts, where* A *is named. If*

$$\mathcal{K} \models \exists R.B \sqcap A_0 \sqsubseteq A$$

with $A_0 \not\sqsubseteq A$, there must exist some GCIs in $\mathcal{T}$ in the form of:

$$\exists R'.C_1 \rhd\lhd C_2 \sqsubseteq C_3 \tag{2}$$

where $R \sqsubseteq R'$ and $\rhd\lhd$ is a place holder for $\sqcup$ and $\sqcap$, C_i's are $\mathcal{SHI}$ concepts. Also note the following equivalence:

$$\exists R.C \sqsubseteq D \equiv \neg D \sqsubseteq \forall R.\neg C$$

$$\exists R.C \sqsubseteq D \equiv C \sqsubseteq \forall R^-.D$$

$$C_1 \sqcap C_2 \sqsubseteq D \equiv C_1 \sqsubseteq D \sqcup \neg C_2$$

This proposition is proven in [16]. It states in fact a syntactic premise in $\mathcal{SHI}$ for a role assertion to be essential for some individual classification. That is, if a role assertion $R(a,b)$ is essential for derivation of $A(a)$ for some named concept A, there must exist a related axiom in $\mathcal{T}$ in the form of (2) for $R \sqsubseteq R'$. We denote this syntactic premise for $R(a,b)$ to affect a's classification as SYN_COND. Using this condition, we can easily rule out role assertions that are definitely irrelevant to the query concept and will not be considered during the computation of a MSC_T.

4. Computation of MSC$_T$

In this section, we present the technique that computes a MSC_T for a given individual w.r.t. a given query. We assume the ABox considered here is consistent, since for any inconsistent ABox, the MSC_T is always the bottom concept $\bot$ [24]. Essentially, the task is to convert ABox assertions into a single concept for a given individual, using the concept conjunction and the so-called *rolling-up* technique. This rolling-up technique was introduced in [23] to convert conjunctive queries into concept terms, and was also used by [25] to transform datalog rules into DL axioms. We adapt this technique here to roll up ABox assertions into DL concepts.

4.1. The Rolling-Up Procedure

Converting concept assertions into a concept is straightforward by simply taking conjunction of the involved concepts. When role assertions are involved, the rolling-up technique can be used to transform assertions into a concept by eliminating individuals in them. For example, given the following assertions

$$\text{Male(Tom)}, \text{has Parent(Tom,Mary)}, \text{Lawyer(Mary)}, \tag{3}$$

transforming them for individual Tom using the rolling up and concept conjunction can generate a single concept assertion

$$(\text{Male} \sqcap \exists \text{has Parent.Lawyer})(\text{Tom})$$

Generalize the Information: The transformation here is for individual Tom, and if individual Mary is not explicitly indicated in the query, it should be sufficient to rewrite has Parent(Tom,Mary), Lawyer(Mary) into $\exists$has Parent.Lawyer(Tom), without loss of any information that is essential for query answering. Even if Mary is explicitly indicated in the query, we can still eliminate it by using a *representative* concept that stands for this particular individual in the given ABox [26]. For example, we can add an assertion $A_{\text{mary}}(\text{Mary})$ to the ABox, where A_{mary} is a new concept name and a representative concept for individual Mary. The above role assertions for Tom then can be transformed into concept $\exists$has Parent.$(\text{Lawyer} \sqcap A_{\text{mary}})(\text{Tom})(\text{Mary})$; and if the query is also rewritten using concept Mary, the *completeness* of the query answering can be guaranteed, as indicated by the following theorem [26].

Theorem 4.1 ([26]) *Let* $\mathcal{K} = (\mathcal{T}, \mathcal{A})$ *be a DL ontology,* a, b *be two individuals in* $\mathcal{A}$, R *a role, and* $C_1, \cdots, C_n$ *DL concepts. Given a representative concept name* A_b *for* b *not occurring in* $\mathcal{K}$:

$$\mathcal{K} \vDash R(a,b) \wedge C_1(b) \wedge \cdots \wedge C_n(b)$$

if and only if

$$\mathcal{K} \cup \{A_b(b)\} \vDash \exists R.(A_b \sqcap C_1 \sqcap \cdots \sqcap C_n)(a)$$

The rolling-up procedure here can be better understood by considering a *graph* induced by the role assertions to be rolled up, which is defined as follows:

Definition 4.1 *A set of ABox role assertions in* $\mathcal{SHI}$ *can be represented by a graph* $\mathcal{G}$, *in which there is a node* x *for each individual* x *in the assertions, and an edge between node* x *and* y *for each role assertion* $R(x,y)$.

Notice that, due to the support of inverse roles in $\mathcal{SHI}$, edges in $\mathcal{G}$ are not directed. A *role path* in the graph $\mathcal{G}$ is then defined as a set of roles corresponding to the set of edges (no duplicate allowed) leading from one node to another. For example, given assertions $R_1(x,y)$ and $R_2(x,y)$, the role path from x to z is $\{R_1, R_2^-\}$, and its reverse from z to x is $\{R_2, R_1^-\}$.

The rolling-up for a given individual x is then able to generate concepts by eliminating individuals in branches of the *tree-shaped* graph $\mathcal{G}$, starting from the leaf nodes and rolling up towards the root node indicated by x. Moreover, all the information of each individual being rolled up should be absorbed into a single concept by conjunction during the procedure. For example, if we have additional assertions

$$\text{has Sister}(\text{Mary,Ana}) \quad \text{and} \quad \text{Professor}(\text{Ana})$$

for Mary in (3), the rolling-up for Tom should then generate concept

$$\text{Male} \sqcap \text{has Parent.}(\text{Lawyer} \sqcap \text{has Sister.Professor})$$

Inverse Role: The support of inverse roles in $\mathcal{SHI}$ makes this rolling-up procedure bidirectional, thus, making it applicable to computing $\text{MSC}_\mathcal{T}$ for any individual in the ABox. For example, to compute a $\text{MSC}_\mathcal{T}$ for individual Mary in example (3), we simply treat this individual as the root, and roll up assertions from leaves to root to generate the concept

$$\text{Lawyer} \sqcap \text{has Parent}^-.\text{Male}$$

Transitive Role: In the rolling-up procedure, no particular care needs to be taken to deal with transitive roles, since any role assertions derived from transitive roles will be automatically preserved [26]. For example, given R a transitive role, $R(a,b)$, $R(b,c)$ two role assertions, and $B(b)$, $C(c)$ two concept assertions in the ABox, rolling-up these four assertions for individual a can generate assertion $\exists R.(B \sqcap \exists R.C)(a)$, from which together with the TBox axioms, we can still derive the fact that

$$\left(\exists R.(B \sqcap \exists R.C) \sqcap \exists R.C\right)(a)$$

Assertion Cycles: This rolling-up technique, however, may suffer information loss if the graph $\mathcal{G}$ contains cycles (*i.e.* a role path leading from one node to itself without duplicate graph edges). For example, given the following two assertions:

$$R_1(x,y) \quad \text{and} \quad R_2(x,y) \tag{4}$$

individuals x and y are related by two roles, and a cycle is thus induced in the corresponding graph. Rolling-up assertions for individual x using the method described above might generate concept $\exists R_1.\top \sqcap \exists R_2.\top$, and the fact that x is connected to the same individual y through different roles is lost. Consequently, this may compromise the resulting concept as a specific-enough concept for x to answer the current query. For example, let C be a query concept defined as:

$$\exists R_1.\exists R_2^-.\exists R_1.\top$$

It can be found out through ABox reasoning that individual x is an instance of C; while on the other hand, it is also not difficult to figure out that $\exists R_1.\top \sqcap \exists R_2.\top$ is not subsumed by C.

Multiple solutions to this problem have been proposed, such as an approximation developed by [27], and the use of cyclic concept definition with greatest fixpoint semantics [24] [28]. In this paper, we choose to use the *nominal* (e.g. $\{x\}$) to handle circles as suggested by [19] [20], which allows explicit indication of named individuals in a concept, hence, being able to indicate the joint node of a cycle. The above two assertions in (4) then can be transformed into a concept for individual x as either $\exists R_1.\{y\} \sqcap \exists R_2.\{y\}$ or $\{x\} \sqcap \exists R_1.\exists R_2^-.\{x\}$, each with the nominal used for a chosen joint node, and both preserve complete information of the cycle. In our approach, when rolling up a cycle in $\mathcal{G}$, we always treat the cycle as a single branch and generate concepts of the second style. That is, our procedure will treat a chosen joint node x as both the tail (*i.e.* leaf) and the head (*i.e.* root) of the branch. For clarity of the following presentation, we denote the tail as x^t and the head as x^h.

Based on the discussion so far, the transformation of assertions for a given individual now can be formalized as follows. Let x be a named individual, and γ be an ABox assertion for x. γ can be transformed into a concept C_γ for x:

$$
C_\gamma = \begin{cases}
C & \text{if } \gamma = C(x)\,\big|\,C(x^h) \\
\exists R.D & \text{if } \gamma = R(x,y), \text{ and } D(y) \\
\exists R^-.D & \text{if } \gamma = R(y,x), \text{ and } D(y) \\
\{x^h\} \sqcap \exists R.\{x^t\} & \text{if } \gamma = R(x^h,x^t) \\
\{x^h\} \sqcap \exists R.D & \text{if } \gamma = R(x^h,y), \text{ and } D(y) \\
\{x^h\} \sqcap \exists R^-.D & \text{if } \gamma = R(y,x^h), \text{ and } D(y) \\
\{x^t\} & \text{if } \gamma = R(x^t,y)\,\big|\,R(y,x^t)\,\big|\,C(x^t)
\end{cases}
$$

Notice that, concept D here is a obtained concept when rolling up branch(es) in $\mathcal{G}$ up to node y, and transforming any assertion of a cycle tail x^t always generates $\{x^t\}$, as complete information of x will be preserved when rolling up to the head x^h. Thereafter, given a set S of all assertions of individual x, $\text{MSC}_\mathcal{T}(\mathcal{A},x)$ can be obtained by rolling up all branches induced by role assertions in S and taking the conjunction of all obtained concepts. When S is empty, however, individual x in the ABox can only be interpreted as an element of the entire domain, and thus, the resulting concept is simply the top entity $\top$. Computation of a $\text{MSC}_\mathcal{T}(\mathcal{A},x)$ then can be formalized using the following equation:

$$
\text{MSC}_\mathcal{T}(\mathcal{A},x) = \begin{cases}
\top & \text{if } S = \varnothing \\
\sqcap_{\gamma \in S} C_\gamma & \text{if otherwise}
\end{cases}
$$

4.2. Branch Pruning

To apply the call-by-need strategy, the previously defined syntactic premise SYN_COND is employed, and a branch to be rolled up in graph $\mathcal{G}$ will be truncated at the point where the edge does not have SYN_COND satisfied. More precisely, if an assertion $R(x,y)$ in a branch does not have the corresponding SYN_COND satisfied, it will not affect any classification of individual x w.r.t. $\mathcal{T}$. Moreover, any effects of the following assertions down the branch will not be able to propagate through $R(x,y)$ to x, and thus should not be considered during the rolling-up of this branch.

This branch pruning technique could be a simple yet an efficient way to reduce complexity of a $\text{MSC}_\mathcal{T}$, especially for those practical ontologies, where many of the ABox individuals may have a huge number of role assertions and only a (small) portion of them have SYN_COND satisfied. For a simple example, consider an individual x in an ontology ABox with the following assertions:

$$
R_1(x,y_1), R_2(x,y_2), \cdots, R_n(x,y_n)
$$

where n could be a very large number and only R_1 has SYN_COND satisfied. Rolling up these assertions for individual x without the pruning will generate the concept

$$\exists R_1.C_1 \sqcap \exists R_2.C_2 \sqcap \cdots \sqcap \exists R_n.C_n$$

where $y_i \in C_i$. Using this concept for any instance checking of x could be expensive, as its interpretation might completely restore the tableau structure that is induced by these assertions. However, when the pruning is applied, the new MSC_T should be $\exists R_1.C_1$, the only role restriction that is possible to affect individual classification of x w.r.t. named concepts in T.

Going beyond such simple ontologies, this optimization technique may also work in complex ontologies, where most of the role assertions in ABox could have SYN_COND satisfied. For example, consider the following assertions

$$R_0\left(x_0, x_1\right), R_1\left(x_1, x_2\right), \cdots, R_n\left(x_n, x_{n+1}\right)$$

with all roles except R_2 having SYN_COND satisfied. Rolling up these assertions for individual x_0 will start from the leaf x_{n+1} up towards the root x_0, and generate the concept

$$\exists R_0.\exists R_1.\cdots.\exists R_n.C$$

where $x_{n+1} \in C$. However, with pruning applied, the rolling-up in this branch will start from x_2 instead of x_{n+1}, since $R_2\left(x_2, x_3\right)$ will not affect classification of individual x_2 w.r.t. T and the branch is truncated at this point.

Furthermore, with branch pruning, cycles should only be considered in the truncated graph, which may further simplify the computation of MSC_T's.

4.3. Further Optimization and Implementation

The branch pruning here is based on SYN_COND to rule out irrelevant assertions, which in fact can be further improved by developing a more rigorous premise for a role assertion to affect individual classification. For exposition, consider the following ontology $\mathcal{K}$:

$$\left(\{\exists R.C \sqsubseteq D\}, \ \{\neg D(a), R(a,b), \neg C(b)\}\right) \tag{5}$$

When computing $MSC_T\left(\mathcal{A}, a\right)_T\left(\mathcal{A}, a\right)$ using the proposed method, assertion $R(a,b)$ will be rolled up as the corresponding SYN_COND is satisfied. However, it is not difficult to see that, $R(a,b)$ here actually makes no contribution to a's classification, since individual b is in the complement of concept C, making a an instance of $\exists R.\neg C$. Besides, individual a has already been asserted as an instance of concept $\neg D$, and hence cannot be classified into D unless the ABox is inconsistent.

With these observations, a more rigorous premise based on SYN_COND can be derived. That is, to determine the possibility for $R(a,b)$ to affect classification of individual a, beyond checking in T the existence of any axiom in the form of

$$\exists R'.C_1 \rhd\lhd C_2 \sqsubseteq C_3$$

with $R \sqsubseteq R'$ and $\rhd\lhd$ a place holder for $\sqcup$ and $\sqcap$, we also check the following cases for any found axiom:

Case 1 If there is any concept B_0 in explicit concept assertions of individual b, such that $\mathcal{K} \vDash B_0 \sqsubseteq \neg C_1$,

Case 2 If there is any concept A_0 in explicit concept assertions of individual a, such that $\mathcal{K} \vDash A_0 \sqsubseteq \neg\left(C_3 \sqcup \neg C_2\right)^2$ or $\mathcal{K} \vDash A_0 \sqsubseteq \neg C_3$, respectively for $\rhd\lhd$ standing for $\sqcap$ or $\sqcup$.

If either one of the above cases happens, that particular $\exists R'.C_1$ in the left hand side of the axiom in fact makes no contribution to the inference of a's classification, unless the ABox is *inconsistent* where MSCs are always $\perp$ [24]. Thus, a revised condition requires not only the existence of a related axiom in the form of (2) but also with none of the above cases happening. We denote this condition as SYN_COND*, and use it to rule out assertions that are irrelevant to the current query.

This optimization is useful to prevent rolling-up of role assertions in an arbitrary direction on existence of related axioms in T. Instead, it limits the procedure to the direction that is desired by the original intention underlying the design of the given ontology. For example, in (5), the axiom $\exists R.C \sqsubseteq D$ specifies that, any individual having a R-neighbor in C is an instance of D and any individual having a R^--neighbor in $\neg D$

---

[2]Note the axiom equivalence $C_1 \sqcap C_2 \sqsubseteq D \equiv C_1 \sqsubseteq D \sqcup \neg C_2$.

is an instance of $\neg C$ [3]. However, if individual x is asserted to have a R-neighbor in $\neg C$ or a R^--neighbor in D, that role assertion should not be rolled-up for x just on existence of this axiom.

With all the insights discussed so far, an algorithm for computation of $\mathrm{MSC}_T(\mathcal{A}, a)$ is presented here as a *recursive* procedure, the steps of which are summarized in **Figure 2**.

Proposition 4.1 (Algorithm Correctness) *The algorithm presented in* **Figure 2** *computes a* $\mathrm{MSC}_T(\mathcal{A}, a)$ *for a given* $\mathcal{SHI}$ *ontology* $(T, \mathcal{A})$ *and an individual* x *in* $\mathcal{A}$.

Proof. We prove by induction.

Basis: For a leaf node x in $\mathcal{G}$, which has no other role assertions except those up the branches, rolling it up yields the conjunction of concepts in its concept assertions, which preserves sufficient information of the part of the branch being rolled so far. If x is the tail of a cycle, returning $\{x^t\}$ is sufficient, as other information of x will be gathered when the rolling-up comes to the head.

Inductive Step: Let x be a node in the middle of some branch(es) in $\mathcal{G}$. For every role assertion $R_i(x, y_i)$ of x down the branch, assume the procedure generates a concept D_i for rolling up to each node y_i, which preserves sufficient information (w.r.t. current query) of the part of branches being rolled up so far. Then, rolling up each $R_i(x, y_i)$ generates $\exists R.D_i$, and together with concept assertions of x, the concept conjunction preserves sufficient information of all branches being rolled up to x. If x is marked as a joint node of a cycle, $\{x^h\}$ is also in the conjunction, so that the circular path property can be preserved. If x is the root node, the conjunction is thus a $\mathrm{MSC}_T(\mathcal{A}, x)$ that preserves sufficient information of x w.r.t. current query.

This algorithm visit every relevant ABox assertion at most once, and it terminates after all related assertions are visited.

5. Related Work

The idea of most specific concept for instance checking was first discussed in [18], and later extensively studied by [17] [20] for the algorithms and the computational complexity. To deal with existential restrictions when computing the most specific concept, [24] [28] [29] discussed the use of cyclic concepts with greatest fixpoint semantics for preservation of information induced by the role assertions, and [27] also proposed an approximation for most specific concept in DLs with existential restrictions.

On the other hand, for efficient ABox reasoning and instance checking, various optimization techniques have been developed, including lazy unfolding, absorption, heuristic guided search, exploration of Horn clauses of DLs [4] [5] [22], model merging [2] and extended pseudo model merging technique [3] [30].

A common direction of these optimization techniques is to reduce the high degree of nondeterminism that is mainly introduced by GCIs in the TBox: given an GCI $C \sqsubseteq D$, it can be converted to a disjunction $C \sqcup \neg D$, for which a tableau algorithm will have to nondeterministically choose one of the disjuncts for tableau expansion, resulting in an exponential-time behavior of the tableau algorithm w.r.t. the data size. Absorption optimizations [22] [31] [32] were developed to reduce such nondeterminism by combining GCIs for unfoldable concepts, such that the effectiveness of lazy unfolding can be maximized. For example, axioms $A \sqsubseteq C$ and

1. In this recursive procedure, if x has already been visited before (cycle detected), mark x as the joint node and return $\{x^t\}$.

2. Obtain a set S of all explicit assertions in $\mathcal{A}$ of the given individual x, which have not been visited before.

3. For every role assertion $\gamma : R_i(x, y_i) \in S$ (respectively $R_i(y_i, x)$) that has SYN_COND* satisfied and has not been visited yet, invoke this procedure *recursively* to compute concept D_i for y_i. The rolling-up in this branch for x then yields $C_\gamma = \exists R_i.D_i$ (respectively $\exists R_i^-.D_i$).

4. For every concept assertion $\gamma : C_i(x) \in S$, $C_\gamma = C_i$.

5. Return $\mathrm{MSC}_T(\mathcal{A}, x)$ that equals to:

$$\begin{cases} \top & \text{if } S = \emptyset \\ \sqcap_{\gamma \in S} C_\gamma \sqcap \{x^h\} & \text{if } S \neq \emptyset, \text{ and } x \text{ is marked} \\ \sqcap_{\gamma \in S} C_\gamma & \text{if } \text{otherwise} \end{cases}$$

Figure 2. A recursive procedure for computation of $\mathrm{MSC}_T(\mathcal{A}, x)$.

---

[3]Note that $\exists R.C \sqsubseteq D$ is equivalent with $\exists R^-.\neg D \sqsubseteq \neg C$.

$A \sqsubseteq D$ can be combined into $A \sqsubseteq C \sqcap D$, where A is a named concept; then the inference engine can deduce $C \sqcap D(a)$ if the ABox contains $A(a)$. Notice however, this technique may allow only parts of TBox axioms to be absorbed, thus, may not be able to eliminate all sources of nondeterminism especially when ontologies are complex. Based on the absorption optimization, [33] proposed an approach for efficient ABox reasoning for $\mathcal{ALCIQ}$ that will convert ABox assertions into TBox axioms, apply a absorption technique on the TBox, and covert instance retrieval into concept satisfaction problems.

Another way to reduce nondeterminism is the exploration of Horn clauses in DLs, since there exist reasoning techniques for Horn clauses that can be deterministic [5] [34]. [5] takes advantage of this in their HermiT reasoner by preprocessing a DL ontology into DL-clauses and invoking the hyperresolution for the Horn clauses, avoiding unnecessary nondeterministic handling of Horn problems in existing DL tableau calculi.

For non-Horn DL, techniques such as model merging [2] and pseudo model merging [30] can be used to capture some deterministic information of named individuals. These techniques are based on the assumption of a consistent ABox and the observation that usually individuals are members of a small number of concepts. The (pseudo) model merging technique merges clash-free tableau models that are constructed by disjunction rules for a consistent ABox, and can figure out individuals that are obviously non-instance of a given concept. For example, if in one tableau model individual a belongs to concept C while in another a belongs to $\neg C$, it is then obvious that individual a cannot be deterministically inferred to be an instance of concept C, thus, eliminating the unnecessary instance checking for $C(a)$.

Another option for scalable ABox reasoning is the use of tractable DL languages. For example, the description logic EL and its extension EL^{++}, which allow existential restrictions and conjunction as introduced by [35] [36], possess intriguing algorithmic properties such that the satisfiability problem and implication in this DL language can be determined in polynomial time. Another notable example of lightweight DLs is the so-called *DL-LITE* family identified by [37], which is specifically tailored to capture basic DL properties and expressivity while still be able to achieve low computational complexity for both TBox and ABox reasoning. In [9] [38] they further identified that, for conjunctive queries that are FOL-reducible, answering them in ontologies of any DL-LITE logic enjoys a LOGSPACE data complexity.

Based on the above lightweight DLs, efficient DL reasoners are developed, such as OWLIM [39], ELK reasoner [40], and Oracle's native inference engine for RDF data sets [41].

[42] proposed an approximation technique for instance retrieval, which computes both lower bound and upper bound of an answer set of individuals for a given query concept. Their approach invokes an axiom rewriting procedure that converts an ontology in Horn DL into a datalog program, and then uses Oracle's native inference engine to derive the bounds for query answering.

Recently, techniques for partitioning or modularizing ABoxes into logically-independent fragments have been developed [15] [16]. These techniques partition ABoxes into logically-independent modules, such that each will preserve complete information of a given set of individuals, and thus can be reasoned independently w.r.t. the TBox and be able to take advantage of existing parallel-processing techniques.

6. Empirical Evaluation

We implemented the rolling-up procedures for computation of $MSC_\mathcal{T}$'s based on the OWL API[4], and evaluated the MSC method for instance checking and retrieving on a lab PC with Intel(R) Xeon(R) 3.07 GHz CPU, Windows 7, and 1.5 GB Java Heap. For the test suite, we have collected a set of well-known ontologies with large ABoxes:

1) LUBM(s) (LM) are benchmark ontologies generated using the tool provided by [43];

2) Arabidopsis thaliana (AT) and Caenorhabditis elegans (CE) are two biomedical ontologies[5], sharing a common TBox called *Biopax* that models biological pathways;

3) DBpedia[*] (DP) ontologies are *extended* from the original DBpedia ontology [44]: expressivity of their TBox is extended from $\mathcal{ALF}$ to $\mathcal{SHI}$ by adding complex roles and concepts defined on role restrictions; their ABoxes are obtained by random sampling on the original triple store.

Details of these ontologies can be found in **Table 1**, in terms of DL expressivity, number of atomic concepts (# Cpts), TBox axioms (# Axms), named individuals (# Ind.), and ABox assertions (# Ast.). Notice that, DL

---

[4]http://sourceforge.net/projects/owlapi
[5]http://www.reactome.org/download

Table 1. Information of tested ontologies.

Ontology	Expressivity	# Cpts.	# Axms.	# Ind.	# Ast.
LM1	$\mathcal{SHI}$	43	42	17,175	67,465
LM2	$\mathcal{SHI}$	43	42	78,579	319,714
AT	$\mathcal{SHI}$	59	344	42,695	117,405
CE	$\mathcal{SHI}$	59	344	37,162	105,238
DP1	$\mathcal{SHI}$	449	465	273,663	402,062
DP2	$\mathcal{SHI}$	449	465	298,103	419,505

expressivity of AT and CE is originally $\mathcal{SHIN}$, but in our experiments, number restrictions (*i.e.* $\mathcal{N}$) in their ontology TBox are removed.

6.1. Complexity of $MSC_{\mathcal{T}}$

Using the MSC (or $MSC_{\mathcal{T}}$) method, the original instance checking problem is converted to a subsumption test, the complexity of which could be computationally high w.r.t. both size of a TBox and size of the testing concepts [10]. Therefore, when evaluating the rolling-up procedure for computation of $MSC_{\mathcal{T}}$'s, one of the most important criteria is the size of each resultant $MSC_{\mathcal{T}}$, as it is the major factor to the time efficiency of a subsumption test, given a relatively static ontology TBox.

As we already know, one of the major source of complexity in ontology reasoning is the so-called "*and-branching*", which introduces new individuals in the tableau expansion through the $\exists$-rule, and affects the searching space of the reasoning algorithm as discussed in [10]. Thus, when evaluating sizes of computed $MSC_{\mathcal{T}}$'s, we measure both the level of nested quantifiers (*i.e.* quantification depth) and the number of conjuncts of each $MSC_{\mathcal{T}}$. For example, the concept

$$\exists R_1.C_1 \sqcap \exists R_2.\left(C_2 \sqcap \exists R_3.C_3\right)$$

has quantification depth 2 and number of conjuncts 2 (*i.e.* $\exists R_1.C_1$ and $\exists R_2.\left(C_2 \sqcap \exists R_3.C_3\right)$).

6.1.1. Experiment Setup

To evaluate and show efficacy of the proposed strategy and optimization, we have implemented the following three versions of the rolling-up method for comparison:

V1 The original rolling-up procedure adapted to ABox assertions without applying the call-by-need strategy, which computes the most specific concept w.r.t. $\mathcal{A}$ for a given individual;

V2 The rolling-up procedure with the proposed *call-by-need* strategy based on SYN_COND, which features the branch pruning as fully discussed in Section 4.2;

V3 The rolling-up procedure with the *call-by-need* strategy based on SYN_COND* discussed in Section 4.3.

We compute the $MSC_{\mathcal{T}}$ for each individual in every ontology using the three methods respectively, and report in **Table 2** and **Table 3** the maximum and the average of quantification depth and number of conjuncts of the concepts, respectively. We also demonstrate the running-time efficiency of the optimized rolling-up procedure by showing the average time spent on computation of a $MSC_{\mathcal{T}}$ for each individual in **Figure 3**.

6.1.2. Result Analysis

As we can see from **Table 2** and **Table 3**, the sizes of $MSC_{\mathcal{T}}$'s generated by V2 and V3 are significantly smaller than those generated by V1 (the original method), which are almost in the same scale of size of the corresponding ontology ABox. The large size of $MSC_{\mathcal{T}}$'s from V1 is caused by the fact that most individuals (greater than 99%) in each of these ontologies are connected together by role paths in the graph. The bulk of each $MSC_{\mathcal{T}}$ makes the original MSC method completely inefficient and unscalable for answering object queries, as a subsumption test based on these concepts would be prohibitively expensive as a complete ABox reasoning. Thus, the comparison here reflects the potential and the importance of our proposed optimizations in

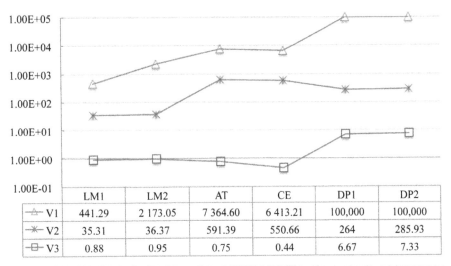

	LM1	LM2	AT	CE	DP1	DP2
V1	441.29	2 173.05	7 364.60	6 413.21	100,000	100,000
V2	35.31	36.37	591.39	550.66	264	285.93
V3	0.88	0.95	0.75	0.44	6.67	7.33

Figure 3. Average time (ms) on computation of a MSC_T. Timeout is set to be 100,000 ms.

Table 2. Quantification depth of MSC_T's from different rolling-up procedures.

	V1	V2	V3
Ontology	Max./Avg.	Max./Avg.	Max./Avg.
LM1	5103/4964.68	215/98.8	2/1.48
LM2	23,015/22654.01	239/103.59	2/1.51
AT	2605/2505.50	1008/407.97	8/3.02
CE	3653/3553.4	1106/437.18	8/2.76
DP1	3906/3070.80	50/2.98	4/1.13
DP2	3968/3865.60	58/2.94	5/1.12

Table 3. Number of conjuncts of MSC_T's from different rolling-up procedures.

	V1	V2	V3
LM1	104/31.34	8/3.58	4/1.56
LM2	203/64.71	8/3.78	4/1.59
AT	88/87.99	19/5.92	13/1.97
CE	52/50.70	16/6.25	17/1.94
DP1	33,591/26864.50	71/5.19	12/1.83
DP2	60,047/60011.60	64/3.95	12/1.79

this paper, which revive the MSC (*i.e.* MSC_T method as an efficient way for instance checking and object query answering.

The comparison between V2 and V3 demonstrates the efficacy of the optimization technique discussed in Section 4.3, which could prevent the rolling-up in arbitrary directions by providing a more rigorous precondition based on SYN_COND. This optimization could be useful in many practical ontologies, especially when their ABoxes contain "hot-spots" individuals that connect (tens of) thousands of individuals together and could cause the rolling-up to generate concepts with a prohibitive quantification depth.

In particular, in our previous study of modularization for ontology ABoxes [16], the biomedical ontologies (*i.e.* AT and CE) are found to be complex with many of their ontology roles (33 out of 55) used for concept definitions, and their ABoxes are hard to be modularized even with various optimization techniques applied [16]. However, in this paper, we found much simpler $MSC_{\mathcal{T}}$'s can also be achieved in these complex ontologies when the optimization (*i.e.* SYN_COND*) is applied. For example, the maximum quantification depths of computed $MSC_{\mathcal{T}}$'s in both AT and CE are decreased significantly from more than 1000 to less than 10. Nevertheless, it should also be noted that, effectiveness of this optimization may vary on different ontologies, depending on their different levels of complexity and different amount of explicit information in their ABoxes that can be explored for optimization.

6.2. Reasoning with $MSC_{\mathcal{T}}$

In this section, we will show the efficiency that can be achieved when using the computed $MSC_{\mathcal{T}}$ for instance checking and retrieving. We conduct the experiments on the collected ontologies, and measure the average reasoning time that is required when performing instance checking (for every ABox individual) and instance retrieval using the $MSC_{\mathcal{T}}$ method, respectively.

6.2.1. Experiment Setup

We will not compare our method with a particular optimization technique for ABox reasoning, such as lazy unfolding, absorption, or model merging, etc., since they have already been built into existing reasoners and it is usually hard to control reasoners to switch on or off a particular optimization technique. Additionally, the $MSC_{\mathcal{T}}$ method still relies on the reasoning services provided by the state-of-art reasoners. Nevertheless, we do compare the reasoning efficiency between the $MSC_{\mathcal{T}}$ method and a regular complete ABox reasoning using existing reasoners, but only to show the effectiveness of the proposed $MSC_{\mathcal{T}}$ method for efficient instance checking and data retrieving. Moreover, we also compare the $MSC_{\mathcal{T}}$ method with the ABox partitioning method (*modular reasoning*) developed in [16], as they are developed based on the similar principles and both allow parallel or distributed reasoning.

The $MSC_{\mathcal{T}}$'s here are computed using algorithm V3, and the ABox partitioning technique used is the most optimized one presented in [16]. For a regular complete ABox reasoning, the reasoners used are OWL DL reasoners, HermiT [5] and Pellet [6], each of which has its particular optimization techniques implemented for the reasoning algorithm. Both the $MSC_{\mathcal{T}}$ method and the modular reasoning are based on reasoner HermiT, and they are not parallelized but instead running in an arbitrary *sequential* order of $MSC_{\mathcal{T}}$'s or ABox partitions.

Queries: LUBM comes with 14 standard queries. For biomedical and DBpedia* ontologies respectively, queries listed in **Figure 4** are used.

Query on biomedical ontologies :

Q1 = Control $\sqcap$ $\forall$controlled.Catalysis $\sqcap$ $\forall$controller.PhysicalEntity

Q2 = Interaction $\sqcap$ $\forall$participant.PhysicalEntity

Q3 = Interaction $\sqcap$ $\exists$interactionType.$\top$ $\sqcap$ $\exists$participant.$\top$
       $\sqcap$ $\forall$participant.Gene $\sqcap$ $\exists$phenotype.$\top$

Q4 = PhysicalEntity $\sqcap$ $\forall$entityReference.DnaReference
       $\sqcap$ $\forall$memberPhysicalEntity.Dna

Q5 = PhysicalEntity $\sqcap$ $\exists$entityReference.SmallMoleculeReference
       $\sqcap$ $\exists$feature.BindingFeature $\sqcap$ $\exists$notfeature.BingdingFeature
       $\sqcap$ $\exists$memberPhysicalEntity.SmallMolecule

Query on DBpedia* ontologies :

Q1 = Person $\sqcap$ $\exists$nationality.(Country $\sqcap$ $\exists$officialLanguage.Engilish)

Q2 = Music $\sqcap$ $\exists$composer.MusicalArtist

Q3 = Person $\sqcap$ $\exists$child.Human $\sqcap$ $\exists$spouse.Person

Q4 = Event $\sqcap$ $\exists$commander.Person $\sqcap$$\exists$place.City

Q5 = Produce $\sqcap$ $\exists$manufacturer.(Organization $\sqcap$ $\exists$place.Country)

Figure 4. Queries for biomedical and DBpedia* ontologies.

For each test ontology, we run the reasoning for each of the given queries. We report the average reasoning time spent on instance checking (**Figure 5**) and instance retrieval (**Figure 6**), respectively. The reasoning time reported here does not include the time spent for resource initialization (*i.e.* ontology loading and reasoner initialization), since the initialization stage can be done offline for query answering. However, it is obvious that the MSC_T method should be more efficient, since it only requires to load an ontology TBox while a regular ABox reasoning requires to load an entire ontology (including large ABoxes). For reasoning with MSC_T's and ABox partitions, any updates during the query answering procedure (e.g. update the reasoner for different ABox partitions or different MSC_T's) is counted into the reasoning time.

Another point worth noting here is that, for answering object queries using either modular reasoning or the MSC_T method, the overhead (time for ABox modularization or computation of MSC_T's) should be taken into account. However, as shown in previous section and in [16], this overhead is negligible comparing with the efficiency gained on the reasoning, not to mention when these two methods get parallelized using existing frameworks such as MapReduce [45].

6.2.2. Result Analysis
As can be seen from the above two figures, using the MSC_T method, reasoning efficiency for both instance checking and instance retrieval in the testing ontologies has been improved significantly: 1) by more than three

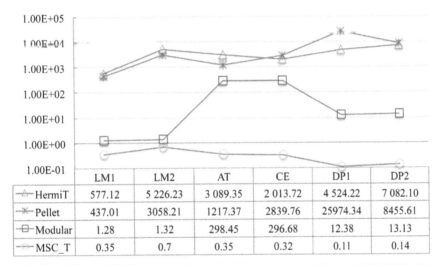

	LM1	LM2	AT	CE	DP1	DP2
HermiT	577.12	5 226.23	3 089.35	2 013.72	4 524.22	7 082.10
Pellet	437.01	3058.21	1217.37	2839.76	25974.34	8455.61
Modular	1.28	1.32	298.45	296.68	12.38	13.13
MSC_T	0.35	0.7	0.35	0.32	0.11	0.14

Figure 5. Average time (ms) on instance checking.

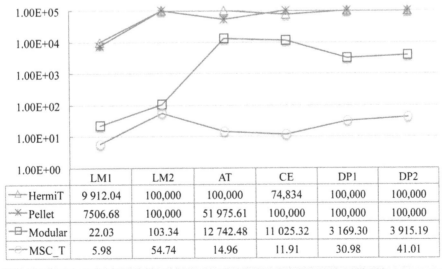

	LM1	LM2	AT	CE	DP1	DP2
HermiT	9 912.04	100,000	100,000	74,834	100,000	100,000
Pellet	7506.68	100,000	51 975.61	100,000	100,000	100,000
Modular	22.03	103.34	12 742.48	11 025.32	3 169.30	3 915.19
MSC_T	5.98	54.74	14.96	11.91	30.98	41.01

Figure 6. Average time(s) spent on instance retrieval. Timeout is set to be 100,000 s.

orders of magnitude when comparing with a complete reasoning; 2) and by about two orders of magnitude (except in LUBM1 and LUBM2) when comparing with the modular reasoning. For the latter, the improvement in LUBM1 and LUBM2 are not as significant as in others, which is because of the simplicity of these two ontologies that allows fine granularity of ABox partitions to be achieved [45].

On the other hand, using the $MSC_\mathcal{T}$ method in complex ontologies, such as AT and CE, the great improvement in reasoning efficiency comes from the reduction of searching space for reasoning algorithms, by branch pruning and also *concept absorption* during the computation of $MSC_\mathcal{T}$'s. For example, consider an individual x having the following n role assertions:

$$R(x, y_1), R(x, y_2), \cdots, R(x, y_n)$$

where $y_i \in D$ and n tends to be large in these practical ontologies. Rolling up these assertions may generate a set of $\exists R.D$'s, the conjunction of which is still $\exists R.D$. Thus, when using this concept for instance checking, the interpretation may generate only one R-neighbor of individual x instead of n.

6.3. Scalability Evaluation

Using the $MSC_\mathcal{T}$ method for query answering over large ontologies is intended for distributed (parallel) computing. However, even if it is executed sequentially in a single machine, linear scalability may still be achieved on large ontologies that are not extremely complex; and there are mainly two reasons for that: first, the computation of $MSC_\mathcal{T}$'s focuses on only the query-relevant assertions instead of the entire ABox; second, the obtained $MSC_\mathcal{T}$'s could be very simple, sizes of which could be significantly smaller than that of the ABoxes. We test the scalability of this method for query answering (sequentially executed) using the benchmark ontology LUBM, which models organization of universities with each university constituted about 17,000 related individuals. The result is show in **Figure 7**.

7. Conclusions and Outlook

In this paper, we proposed a revised MSC method for efficient instance checking. This method allows the ontology reasoning to explore only a much smaller subset of ABox data that is relevant to a given instance checking problem, thus being able to achieve great efficiency and to solve the limitation of current memory-based reasoning techniques. It can be particularly useful for answering object queries over those large *non-Horn* DL ontologies, where existing optimization techniques may fall short and answering object queries may demand thousands or even millions of instance checking tasks. Most importantly, due to the independence between $MSC_\mathcal{T}$'s, scalability for query answering over huge ontologies (e.g. in the setting of semantic webs) could also be achieved by parallelizing the computations.

Our technique currently works for logic $\mathcal{SHI}$, which is semi-expressive and is sufficient for many of the practical ontologies. However, the use of more expressive logic in modeling application domains requires more advanced technique for efficient data retrieving from ontology ABoxes. For the future work, we will investigate on how to extend the current technique to support $\mathcal{SHIN}$ or $\mathcal{SHIQ}$ that are featured with (qualified) number restrictions. We will concentrate on extending the rolling-up procedure to generate number restrictions, such as

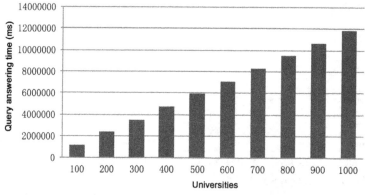

Figure 7. Scalability evaluation.

$\geq nR.\mathrm{T}$ or $\geq nR.C$, whenever there is a need. We will also have to take a particular care of the identical individual problem, where concepts and role assertions of an individual can be derived via individual equivalence.

Acknowledgements

This work is partly supported by grant # R44GM097851 from the National Institute of General Medical Sciences, part of the U.S. National Institutes of Health (NIH).

References

[1] Horrocks, I. (2008) Ontologies and the Semantic Web. *Communications of the ACM*, **51**, 58-67. http://dx.doi.org/10.1145/1409360.1409377

[2] Horrocks, I.R. (1997) Optimising Tableaux Decision Procedures for Description Logics. Ph.D. Dissertation, University of Manchester, Manchester.

[3] Haarslev, V. and Möller, R. (2008) On the Scalability of Description Logic Instance Retrieval. *Journal of Automated Reasoning*, **41**, 99-142. http://dx.doi.org/10.1007/s10817-008-9104-7

[4] Motik, B., Shearer, R. and Horrocks, I. (2007) Optimized Reasoning in Description Logics using Hypertableaux. *Proceedings of Conference on Automated Deduction* (*CADE*), **4603**, 67-83.

[5] Motik, B., Shearer, R. and Horrocks, I. (2009) Hypertableau Reasoning for Description Logics. *Journal of Artificial Intelligence Research*, **36**, 165-228.

[6] Sirin, E., Parsia, B., Grau, B.C., Kalyanpur, A. and Katz, Y. (2007) Pellet: A Practical Owl-Dl Reasoned. *Journal of Web Semantics*, **5**, 51-53. http://dx.doi.org/10.1016/j.websem.2007.03.004

[7] Haarslev, V. and Möller, R. (2001) RACER System Description. *Proceedings of the First International Joint Conference on Automated Reasoning*, Siena, June 2001, 701-705.

[8] Horrocks, I. (1998) Using an Expressive Description Logic: Fact or Fiction? *Proceedings of Knowledge Representation and Reasoning*, **98**, 636-645.

[9] Calvanese, D., De Giacomo, G., Lembo, D., Lenzerini, M. and Rosati, R. (2007) Tractable Reasoning and Efficient Query Answering in Description Logics: The DL-Lite Family. *Journal of Automated Reasoning*, **39**, 385-429. http://dx.doi.org/10.1007/s10817-007-9078-x

[10] Donini, F. (2007) The Description Logic Handbook: Theory, Implementation, and Applications. Cambridge University Press, Cambridge.

[11] Glimm, B., Horrocks, I., Lutz, C. and Sattler, U. (2008) Conjunctive Query Answering for the Description Logic. *Journal of Artificial Intelligence Research*, **31**, 157-204.

[12] Ortiz, M., Calvanese, D. and Eiter, T. (2008) Data Complexity of Query Answering in Expressive Description Logics via Tableaux. *Journal of Automated Reasoning*, **41**, 61-98. http://dx.doi.org/10.1007/s10817-008-9102-9

[13] Tobies, S. (2001) Complexity Results and Practical Algorithms for Logics in Knowledge Representation. Ph.D. Dissertation, RWTH Aachen, Aachen.

[14] Guo, Y. and Heflin, J. (2006) A Scalable Approach for Partitioning OWL Knowledge Bases. *International Workshop on Scalable Semantic Web Knowledge Base Systems* (*SSWS*), Geogia, November 2006, 636-641.

[15] Wandelt, S. and Möller, R. (2012) Towards ABox Modularization of Semi-Expressive Description Logics. *Applied Ontology*, **7**, 133-167.

[16] Xu, J., Shironoshita, P., Visser, U., John, N. and Kabuka, M. (2013) Extract ABox Modules for Efficient Ontology Querying. ArXiv e-Prints. arXiv: 1305.4859

[17] Donini, F., Lenzerini, M., Nardi, D. and Schaerf, A. (1994) Deduction in Concept Languages: From Subsumption to Instance Checking. *Journal of Logic and Computation*, **4**, 423-452. http://dx.doi.org/10.1093/logcom/4.4.423

[18] Nebel, B. (1990) Reasoning and Revision in Hybrid Representation Systems. Vol. 422, Springer-Verlag, Germany.

[19] Schaerf, A. (1994) Reasoning with Individuals in Concept Languages. *Data and Knowledge Engineering*, **13**, 141-176. http://dx.doi.org/10.1016/0169-023X(94)90002-7

[20] Donini, F. and Era, A. (1992) Most Specific Concepts for Knowledge Bases with Incomplete Information. *Proceedings of CIKM*, Baltimore, November 1992, 545-551.

[21] Tsarkov, D. and Horrocks, I. (2006) FaCT++ Description Logic Reasoner: System Description. *Proceedings of 3rd International Joint Conference on Automated Reasoning*, Seattle, 17-20 August 2006.

[22] Horrocks, I. and Sattler, U. (2007) A Tableau Decision Procedure for Mathcal SHOIQ. *Journal of Automated Reasoning*, **39**, 249-276. http://dx.doi.org/10.1007/s10817-007-9079-9

[23] Horrocks, I. and Tessaris, S. (2000) A Conjunctive Query Language for Description Logic Aboxes. *Proceedings of AAAI*, Austin, August 2000, 399-404.

[24] Baader, F. and Küsters, R. (1998) Computing the Least Common Subsumer and the Most Specific Concept in the Presence of Cyclic ALN-Concept Descriptions. In: Herzog, O. and Gunter, A., Eds., *KI-98: Advances in Artificial Intelligence*, Springer, Bremen, 129-140.

[25] Krötzsch, M., Rudolph, S. and Hitzler, P. (2008) Description Logic Rules. *European Conference on AI*, **178**, 80-84.

[26] Horrocks, I., Sattler, U. and Tobies, S. (2000) Reasoning with Individuals for the Description Logic SHIQ. *Proceedings of Automated Deduction (CADE)*, Pittsburgh, June 2000, 482-496.

[27] Küsters, R. and Molitor, R. (2001) Approximating Most Specific Concepts in Description Logics with Existential Restrictions. In: Baader, Franz, Brewka, Gerhard, Eiter and Thomas, Eds., *KI 2001: Advances in Artificial Intelligence*, Springer, Vienna, 33-47.

[28] Baader, F. (2003) Least Common Subsumers and Most Specific Concepts in a Description Logic with Existential Restrictions and Terminological Cycles. *International Joint Conference on Artificial Intelligence*, **3**, 319-324.

[29] Baader, F., Küsters, R. and Molitor, R. (1999) Computing Least Common Subsumers in Description Logics with Existential Restrictions. *International Joint Conference on Artificial Intelligence*, **99**, 96-101.

[30] Haarslev, V., Möller, R. and Turhan, A.Y. (2001) Exploiting Pseudo Models for TBox and ABox Reasoning in Expressive Description Logics. *International Joint Conference*, IJCAR 2001, Siena.

[31] Hudek, A.K. and Weddell, G. (2006) Binary Absorption in Tableaux-Based Reasoning for Description Logics. *Proceedings of the International Workshop on Description Logics (DL 2006)*, **189**, 86-96.

[32] Tsarkov, D. and Horrocks, I. (2004) Efficient Reasoning with Range and Domain Constraints. *Proceedings of the 2004 Description Logic Workshop (DL 2004)*, **104**, 41-50.

[33] Wu, J., Hudek, A.K., Toman, D. and Weddell, G.E. (2012) Assertion Absorption in Object Queries over Knowledge Bases. *International Conference on the Principles of Knowledge Representation and Reasoning*, Rome, June 2012.

[34] Grosof, B., Horrocks, I., Volz, R. and Decker, S. (2003) Description Logic Programs: Combining Logic Programs with Description Logic. *Proceedings of WWW*, Budapest, May 2003, 48-57.

[35] Baader, F., Brand, S. and Lutz, C. (2005) Pushing the EL Envelope. *Proceedings of IJCAI*, Edinburgh, August 2005, 364-369.

[36] Baader, F., Brandt, S. and Lutz, C. (2008) Pushing the EL Envelope Further. *Proceedings of the OWLED 2008 DC Workshop on OWL: Experiences and Directions*, Karlsruhe, October 2008.

[37] Calvanese, D., De Giacomo, G., Lembo, D., Lenzerini, M. and Rosati, R. (2005) DL-Lite: Tractable Description Logics for Ontologies. *Proceedings of AAAI*, **5**, 602-607.

[38] Calvanese, D., De Giacomo, G., Lembo, D., Lenzerini, M. and Rosati, R. (2006) Data Complexity of Query Answering in Description Logics. *Proceedings of Knowledge Representation and Reasoning (KR)*, **6**, 260-270.

[39] Bishop, B., Kiryakov, A., Ognyanoff, D., Peikov, I., Tashev, Z. and Velkov, R. (2011) OWLIM: A Family of Scalable Semantic Repositories. *Journal of Semantic Web*, **2**, 33-42.

[40] Kazakov, Y., Krötzsch, M. and Simančík, F. (2011) Concurrent Classification of EL Ontologies. *International Semantic Web Conference*, Bonn, October 2011, 305-320.

[41] Wu, Z., Eadon, G., Das, S., Chong, E.I., Kolovski, V., Annamalai, M. and Srinivasan, J. (2008) Implementing an Inference Engine for RDFS/OWL Constructs and User-Defined Rules in Oracle. *Proceedings of IEEE 24th International Conference on Data Engineering (ICDE)*, Cancun, April 2008, 1239-1248.

[42] Zhou, Y., Cuenca Grau, B., Horrocks, I., Wu, Z. and Banerjee, J. (2013) Making the Most of Your Triple Store: Query Answering in OWL 2 Using an RL Reasoner. *Proceedings of the 22nd International Conference on World Wide Web*, Rio, May 2013, 1569-1580.

[43] Guo, Y., Pan, Z. and Heflin, J. (2005) LUBM: A Benchmark for OWL Knowledge Base Systems. *Journal of Web Semantics*, **3**, 158-182. http://dx.doi.org/10.1016/j.websem.2005.06.005

[44] Auer, S., Bizer, C., Kobilarov, G., Lehmann, J., Cyganiak, R. and Ives, Z. (2007) DBpedia: A Nucleus for a Web of Open Data. *Proceedings of ISWC*, Busan, November 2007, 722-735.

[45] Dean, J. and Ghemawat, S. (2008) MapReduce: Simplified Data Processing on Large Clusters. *Communications of the ACM*, **51**, 107-113. http://dx.doi.org/10.1145/1327452.1327492

18

Motivation Learning in Mind Model CAM

Zhongzhi Shi[1*], Gang Ma[1,2], Xi Yang[1], Chengxiang Lu[1,3]

[1]Key Laboratory of Intelligent Information Processing, Institute of Computing Technology, Chinese Academy of Sciences, Beijing, China
[2]University of Chinese Academy of Sciences, Beijing, China
[3]School of Information Science and Engineering, Qufu Normal University, Rizhao, China
Email: *shizz@ics.ict.ac.cn

Academic Editor: Shifei Ding, China University of Mining and Technology, China

Abstract

Motivation learning aims to create abstract motivations and related goals. It is one of the high-level cognitive functions in Consciousness And Memory model (CAM). This paper proposes a new motivation learning algorithm which allows an agent to create motivations or goals based on introspective process. The simulation of cyborg rat maze search shows that the motivation learning algorithm can adapt agents' behavior in response to dynamic environment.

Keywords

Motivation Learning, Motivation Processing, Consciousness and Memory Model, Cyborg Rat

1. Introduction

Learning is one high-level cognitive function in Consciousness And Memory model (CAM) [1]. Through learning, humans, animals and some machines acquire new, or modify and reinforce existing knowledge, behaviors, skills, values, or preferences. Learning produces changes in the systems and the changes are relatively permanent.

Human learning may occur as part of education, personal development, schooling, or training. It may be goal-oriented and may be aided by motivation. Motivation is defined by psychologists as an internal process that activates, guides, and maintains behavior over time. Mook [2] defined motivation as "the cause of action" briefly. Maslow [3] proposed hierarchy of needs which was one of the unified motivation theories. Since it introduced to the public, the Maslow's theory has a significant impact on every aspect in people's life. Various attempts have

---

*Corresponding author.

been made to either classify or synthesize the large body of research related to motivation. Green *et al.* [4] categorized motivation theories as physiological, behavioral or social. Mook [2] took the view that motivation theories are behaviorist, mediationist or biological. Merrick [5] argued that the theories of motivation can be classified into 4 categories: biological theories, cognitive theories, social theories and combined motivation theories.

Motivation learning is based on a self-organizing system of emerging internal motivations and goal creation. The motivation learning mechanism creates higher level motivations and sets goals based on dominating primitive and abstract event signals. It can be treated as a meta-learning technique in which a motivation process provides a learning algorithm with a motivation signal that focuses on learning. The role of the motivation process is to use general, event-independent concepts to generate a motivation signal to stimulate the learning of event oriented behaviors. Intrinsic motivations that trigger curiosity based learning can be compared to the exploratory stage in reinforcement learning. In reinforcement learning, a machine occasionally explores the state-action space, rather than performing an optimal action in the task of maximizing its rewards [6]. However, without proper control of these explorations, a machine may not develop its abilities or even develop a destructive behavior [7]. Intrinsic motivations can also select actions that yield a maximum rate of reduction of the prediction error, which improves learning when the machine tries to improve one kind of activity.

Berlyne [8] defined curiosity as a form of motivation that promoted exploratory behavior to learn more about a source of uncertainty, such as a novel stimulus, with the goal of acquiring sufficient knowledge to reduce the uncertainty. Schmidhuber implemented curious agents using neural controllers and reinforcement learning with intrinsic rewards generated in response to an agent improving its model of the world [9]. In fact, most of curiosities are caused by novelty. Novelty detection is a useful technology to find curiosity. Novelty detection is the identification of new or unknown data or signal that a learning system is not aware of during training [10] [11].

In CAM we use introspection learning to find novelty and interestingness. By checking and caring about knowledge processing and reasoning method of intelligence system itself and finding out problems from failure or poor efficiency, introspection learning forms its own learning goal and then improves the method to solve problems [12]. Introspective reasoning has a long history in artificial intelligence, psychology, and cognitive science [13].

In early 1980s, introspective reasoning was implemented as planning within the meta-knowledge layer. SOAR [14] employed a form of introspective reasoning by learning meta-rules which described how to apply rules about domain tasks and acquire knowledge. SOAR's meta-rules were created by chunking together existing rules and learning is triggered by sub-optimal problem-solving results rather than failures. Birnbaum *et al.* proposed the use of self-models within case-based reasoning [15]. Cox and Ram proposed a set of general approaches to introspective reasoning and learning, automatically selecting the appropriate learning algorithms when reasoning failures arise [16]. They defined a taxonomy of causes of reasoning failures and proposed a taxonomy of learning goals that is used for analyzing the traces of reasoning failures and responding to them. Leake *et al.* pointed out that in introspective learning approaches, a system exploited explicit representations of its own organization and desired behavior to determine when, what, and how to learn in order to improve its own reasoning [17].

Attention is the behavioral and cognitive process of selectively concentrating on one aspect of the environment while ignoring other things. Eriksen *et al.* developed a spotlight model for selective attention [18]. The attention focus is an area that extracts information from the visual scene with a high-resolution, the geometric center of which being where visual attention is directed. In this paper we will adopt maximal interestingness as the spotlight to pay more attention.

In this paper, a motivation learning algorithm will be proposed and applied to cyborg rat maze search by agent simulation. The motivation learning algorithm is different from reinforcement learning and supervised learning since it does not need global world model and training examples.

The remainder of this paper is organized as follows. Section 2 outlines the motivation processing. Section 3 describes the motivation learning algorithm. Section 4 shows that the motivation learning algorithm will be applied to cyborg rat maze search by agent simulation. Finally, the conclusions of this paper are drawn and future works are pointed out.

2. Motivation Processing

Consciousness And Memory model (CAM) is a general framework for developing brain-like intelligent machines. The architecture of CAM is depicted in **Figure 1**. We propose the architecture for exploring how human

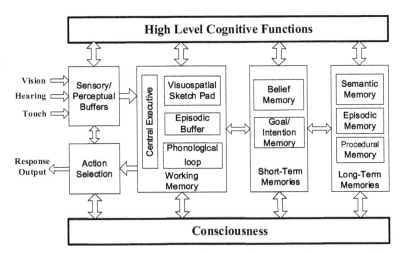

Figure 1. Architecture of CAM.

mind work and study hierarchical memories and consciousness. For consciousness the primary focus is on global workspace theory, motivation model, attention, and the executive control system of the mind in CAM. The consciousness is modeled by a finite state machine. The state of the finite state machine corresponds to the human's mental state.

Hierarchical memories contain working memory, short-term memory, and long-term memory. Working memory provides temporary storage and manipulation for language comprehension, reasoning, problem solving, reading, planning, learning and abstraction. The working memory involves four subcomponents: central executive, visuospatial sketch pad, phonological loop and episodic buffer. The central executive is the core in working memory. It drives and coordinates other subcomponents in working memory to accomplish cognitive tasks. The visuospatial sketch pad holds the visual information about what the cognitive system has seen. The phonological loop deals with the sound or phonological information. The episodic buffer stores the linking information across domains to form integrated units of visual, spatial, and verbal information with time sequencing, such as the memory of a story or a movie scene. The episodic buffer is also assumed to have links to long-term memory and semantic meaning [19].

Short-term memory systems are associated with the process of encoding. In CAM model, short-term memory stores agent's beliefs, goals and intention contents which are changed rapidly in response to environmental conditions and agent's agenda.

Long-term memory is considered to be relatively permanent. It is associated with the processes of storage and retrieval of information from memory. According to the stored contents type, long-term memory is divided semantic, episodic and procedural memory. Semantic memory stores general facts which are represented as ontology. Ontology specifies a conceptualization of a domain in terms of concepts, attributes, and relations in the domain. The concepts provide model entities of interest in the domain. They are typically organized into a taxonomy tree where each node represents a concept and each concept is a specialization of its parent. Each concept in the taxonomy is associated with a set of instances. By the taxonomy's definition, the instances of a concept are also instances of an ancestor concept. Each concept is associated with a set of attributes. In CAM, dynamic description logic (DDL) is used to describe ontology.

Cognitive cycle is a basic procedure of mental activities in cognitive level. Human cognition consists of cascading cycles of recurring brain events. In mind model CAM we propose the cognitive cycle shown in **Figure 2** [20]. The CAM cognitive cycle depicts as three phases: Perception-Motivation-Action Composition. Perception phase is the process of attaining awareness of the environment by sensory input. Using the incoming percept and the residual contents of working memory as cues, local associations are automatically retrieved from transient episodic memory and declarative memory. Motivation phase focuses on learners' beliefs, expectations, and needs for order and understanding. Action composition will compose a group of actions through action selection, planning to reach the end goal.

The motivation processing is shown in **Figure 3** and consists of 7 modules: environment, internal context, motivation, motivation base, goal, action selection, and action composition [21]. Their main functions are

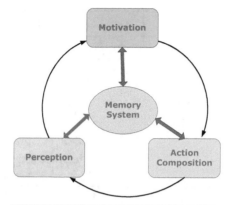

Figure 2. Cognitive cycle in CAM.

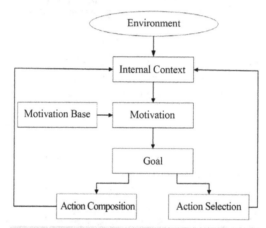

Figure 3. Motivation processing.

explained as follows.

1) ***Environment*** provides the external information through sensory devices or other agents.

2) ***Internal context*** represents the homeostatic internal state of the agent and evolves according to the effects of actions.

3) ***Motivation*** is an abstraction corresponding to tendency to behave in particular ways according to environmental information. Motivations set goals for the agent in order to satisfy internal context.

4) ***Motivation base*** contains a set of motivations and motivation knowledge with defined format.

5) ***Goal*** is a desired result for a person or an organization. It is used to define a sequence of actions to reach specific goals.

6) ***Action selection*** is used to perform motivated action that can satisfy one or several motivations.

7) ***Action composition*** is the process of constructing a complex composite action from atomic actions to achieve a specific task.

The action composition is composed of overlapping hierarchical decision loops running in parallel. The number of motivations is not limited. Action composition of the most activated node is not carried out at each cycle, as in a classical hierarchy, but only at the end in the action layer, as in a free flow hierarchy. In the end, the selected action is activated.

3. Motivation Learning

In CAM, motivation learning needs a mechanism for creating abstract motivations and related goals. Once implemented, such a mechanism manages motivations, as well as selects and supervises execution of goals. Motivations emerge from interaction with the environment, and at any given stage of development, their operation is influenced by competing event and attention switching signals.

The learning process for motivations needs to obtain the sensory states by observing, then the sensed states are transformed mutually by the events. Where to find novelty to motivate an agent's interestingness will play an important role. Once the interestingness is stimulated, the agent's attention may be selected and focused on one aspect of the environment. Therefore, it will be necessary to define observations, events, novelty, interestingness and attention before describing the motivation learning algorithm.

3.1. Observations

An observation is essentially a combination of sensations from the sensed state. For an agent to function efficiently in complex environments, it may be necessary to select only a subset of these combinations as observations.

Observation function is a subset to map the sensed state $S_{(t)}$ to a set of observations $O_{S(t)}$.

Definition 1: *Observation Functions*

Observation functions define the combinations of sensations from the sensed state that will motivate further reasoning. Observations containing fewer sensations affect an agent's attention focus by making it possible for the agent to restrict its attention to a subset of the state space. Where, a typical observation function can be given as:

$$O_{S(t)} = \left\{ \left(o_{1(t)}, o_{2(t)}, \cdots, o_{L(t)}, \cdots \right) \middle| o_{L(t)} = s_{L(t)} \left(\forall L \right) \right\}$$

The equation defines observation function $O_{S(t)}$ in each observation which focuses on every element of the sensed state at time t.

3.2. Events

Events are introduced to model the transitions between sensed states. Events are computed using difference functions and event functions that control the level of attention focus on the transition. Events are represented in terms of the difference between two sensed states. The difference between two sensed states, $S_{(t')} = \left(s_{1(t')}, s_{2(t')}, \cdots, s_{L(t')}, \cdots \right)$ and $S_{(t)} = \left(s_{1(t)}, s_{2(t)}, \cdots, s_{L(t)}, \cdots \right)$ where $t' < t$ as a vector of difference variables is calculated using a difference function Δ which is defined as follows.

Definition 2: *Difference Function*

A difference function Δ assigns a value to the deference between two sensations $S_{L(t)}$ and $S_{L(t')}$ in the sensed states $S_{(t)}$ and $S_{(t')}$ as follows:

$$\Delta \left(s_{L(t)}, s_{L(t')} \right) = \begin{cases} s_{L(t)}, & \text{if } \neg \exists s_{L(t')}; \\ s_{L(t')}, & \text{if } \neg \exists s_{L(t)}; \\ s_{L(t)} - s_{L(t')}, & \text{if } s_{L(t)} - s_{L(t')} \neq 0; \\ 0, & \text{otherwise.} \end{cases}$$

Difference function offers the information about the change between successive sensations and calculates the magnitude of the change.

Definition 3: *Event Function*

Event functions define which combinations of difference variables an agent recognizes as events, each of which contains only one non-zero difference variable. Event function can be defined as following formula:

$$E_{S(t)} = \left\{ E_{L(t)} = \left(e_{1(t)}, e_{2(t)}, \cdots, e_{L(t)}, \cdots \right) \middle| e_{e(t)} \right\}$$

where,

$$e_{e(t)} = \begin{cases} \Delta \left(s_{e(t)}, s_{e(t')} \right), & \text{if } e = L \\ 0, & \text{otherwise} \end{cases}$$

Events may be of varying length or even empty, depending on the number of sensations to change.

3.3. Novelty

Detecting novel events is an important ability of any signal classification scheme. Given the fact that we can never train a machine learning system on all possible object classes whose data is likely to be encountered by the system, it becomes important to differentiate between known and unknown object information during testing. It has been realized in practice by several studies that the novelty detection is an extremely challenging task. Novelty is a useful motivator in some environments. In complex, dynamic environments, there is often a possibility of random observations or events as a result of either the environment dynamics or sensor noise. Saunders and Gero [22] developed computational models of curiosity and interest based on novelty. They used sigmoid functions to represent positive reward for the discovery of novel stimuli and negative reward for the discovery of highly novel stimuli. The resulting computational models of novelty and interest are used in a range of applications.

Novelty detection identifies new or unknown data or signal that a machine learning system is not aware of during training [11]. Novelty detection is one of the fundamental requirements of a good classification or identification system since sometimes the test data contains information about objects that were not known at the time of training the model. Berlyne [8] defined perceptual novelty is in relation to perceptions, while epistemic novelty is in relation to knowledge. Based on a fixed set of training samples from a fixed number of categories, novelty detection is a binary decision task to determine for each test sample whether it belongs to one of the known categories or not.

Novelty detection determines the novelty of a situation. Novelty detection is considered as a meta-level conceptual process because the concept of novelty is based upon the concepts built by other conceptual processes categorizing the situation.

Definition 4: *Novelty Detection Function*

The novelty detection function, N, takes the conceptual state of the agent, $c \in C$, and compares it with memories of previous experiences, $m \in M$, constructed by long-term memory to produce a novelty state, $n \in N$:

$$N : C \times M \to N$$

Novelty can be detected by introspective search comparing the current conceptual state of an agent with memories of previous experiences.

3.4. Interestingness

Interestingness is defined as novelty and surprise. It depends on the observer's current knowledge and computational abilities. Interestingness can be either objective or subjective: objective interestingness uses relationships found entirely within the object considered interesting, while subjective interestingness compares properties of the object with beliefs of a user to determine interest. The interestingness of a situation is a measure of the importance of the situation with respect to an agent's existing knowledge; interesting situations are neither too similar nor too different from ones previously experienced.

Definition 5: *Interestingness Function*

The interestingness function determines a value for the interestingness of a situation, $i \in I$, basing on the novelty detected, $n \in N$:

$$I : N \to I$$

3.5. Attention

Attention is the behavioral and cognitive process of selectively concentrating on one aspect of the environment while ignoring other things. After we get the interestingness function we can select certain event. There are two selection strategies: threshold selection mechanism (TSM) and proportion selection mechanism (PSM) [23].

TSM is a threshold filtering algorithm. Assume that we have a threshold, T. If the interestingness value is larger than T the event is chosen to build a motivation; on the contrary, if the value is smaller than T the event is omitted.

PSM is a bottleneck filtering algorithm. The number of the input stimuli, which can be processed by the brain, is restricted to a maximal one.

Definition 6: *Attention Selection*

Attention is a complex cognitive function which is essential for human behavior. Attention is a selection process for an external (sound, image, smell...) or internal (thoughts) event which has to be maintained at a certain level of awareness. The selective or focused attention selects the information that should be processed in priority, according to relevance in the situation at hand or needs in a given context. Selective attention enables you to focus on an item while mentally identifying and distinguishing the non-relevant information. In CAM we adopt maximal interestingness strategy to select attentions to create a motivation.

3.6. Motivation Learning Algorithm

Motivation learning creates internal representations of observed sensory inputs and links them to learned actions that are useful for its operation. If the result of the machine's action is not relevant to its current goal, no intentional learning takes place. This screening of what to learn is very useful since it protects machine's memory from storing unimportant observations, even though they are not predictable by the machine and may be of sufficient interest for novelty-based learning. Novelty-based learning still can take place in such a system when the system is not triggered by other motivations. However, it will play a secondary role in goal-oriented learning.

The following describes basic steps of novelty-based motivation learning and goal creation algorithm in CAM.

Motivation learning algorithm

1) Observe $O_{S(t)}$ from $S_{(t)}$ using the observation function
2) Subtract $S_{(t)} - S_{(t')}$ using the difference function
3) Compose $E_{S(t)}$ using the event function
4) Look for $N_{(t)}$ using introspective search
5) Repeat (for each $N_{i(t)} \in N_{(t)}$)
6) Repeat (for each $I_{j(t)} \in I_{(t)}$)
7) Attention $= \max I_{j(t)}$
8) Create a *Motivation* by *Attention*.

The algorithm involves collaboration of CAM processing within central executive, reward and consciousness processing blocks, episodic and semantic memory, and interaction with sensory and motor pathways. The central executive block in working memory is spread between several functional units without clear boundaries or a single triggering mechanism. It is responsible for coordination and selective control of other units. This block interacts with other units for performing its tasks. Its tasks include cognitive perception, attention, motivation, goal creation and goal selection, thoughts, planning, learning, supervision and motor control, etc. The central executive directs cognitive aspects of machine control and learning experiences but its operation is influenced by competing signals representing motivations, desires, and attention switching coming from short-term memory. In CAM, short-term memory looks like BDI structure with memory and reasoning functions. Semantic memory stores previous experiences represented as ontology. Introspective search can perform novelty detection to discover novel events.

4. Application for Cyborg Rat Maze Search

One outstanding feature of motivational system is that it can enhance the automatic level and improve system quality. Here we apply the motivation system to cyborg rat maze search.

Using rat sensitivity to ultraviolet (UV) flash, mixed perception of the robot directly extracted from rat visual cortex of rat brain signals, decoding the rat visual perception of their own results and visual recognition and machine intelligent integration, and finally can be used for large Mouse robot autonomous navigation.

To get the flash visual stimuli related neural information, we select the visual nerve pathways in rats which contain the most abundant of the primary visual cortex of visual information as an experimental brain region. By embedding 16 channels filaments in the rat visual cortex area recording electrodes, nerve signal acquisition using professional equipment, access to the rat visual cortex nerve signals. Freely moving rats with recording elec-

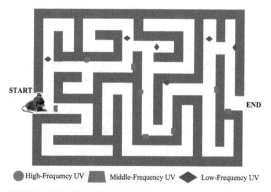

Figure 4. Pattern of maze.

trodes are placed in the stimulus act which has a flash tank, record neural signals, experimental environment under different conditions of darkness and bright selection of two states, high and low to stimulate multiple source selection stimuli. It was found that the particular characteristics of the flash frequency stimulation can elicit specific release in rat brain neurons; the group established a multi-channel spectrum-related characteristics and decoding model to achieve a UV flash nerve signals with specific resolution.

In the maze search task, the machine will give certain maze clues message alert information via electrical stimulation to robot rat, so that the machine can be aware of information in the biological brain, making decisions for its maze search. **Figure 4** shows a pattern of maze.

We define 3 kinds of actions for maze search: go ahead, turn left, and turn right, which correspond to high frequency, middle frequency and lower frequency UV flash respectively. Cyborg rat sends a signal to agent when cyborg rat gets a high UV flash and agent creates motivation which causes cyborg rat to go ahead.

We have developed a multi-agent simulation platform MAGER. One agent plays the role of cyborg rat and receives UV flash from outside. Agent performs motivation learning to decide the moving direction after get the UV flash signal.

5. Conclusions

Motivation learning creates abstract motivations and related goals. It is one of the high-level cognitive functions in CAM. This paper presents a new motivation learning algorithm which allows an agent to create motivations or goals based on introspective process. The simulation of cyborg rat maze search shows that the motivation learning algorithm can adapt agents' behavior in response to dynamic environment.

Motivation learning is an important topic for collaboration work of brain machine integration. We will continue research on meta-cognition for introspective process to improve the motivation learning algorithm's efficiency.

Acknowledgements

This work is supported by the National Program on Key Basic Research Project (973) (No. 2013CB329502), National Natural Science Foundation of China (No. 61035003, 61202212), National Science and Technology Support Program (2012BA107B02).

References

[1] Shi, Z.Z., Wang, X.F., Chen, L.M. and Zhang, Z.X. (2010) A Mind Model CAM—Consciousness and Memory Model. *Proceedings of 7th International Conference on Cognitive Science*, Beijing, 17-20 August 2010, 226-227.

[2] Mook, D.G. (1987) Motivation: The Organization of Action. W. W. Norton and Company, Inc., New York.

[3] Maslow, A.H. (1943) A Theory of Human Motivation. *Psychological Review*, **50**, 370-396.
     http://dx.doi.org/10.1037/h0054346

[4] Green, R.G., Beatty, W.W. and Arkin, R.M. (1984) Human Motivation: Physiological, Behavioral and Social Approaches. Allyn and Bacon, Inc., Boston.

[5] Merrick, K. (2007) Modelling Motivation for Experience-Based Attention Focus in Reinforcement Learning. Ph.D. Thesis, The University of Sydney, Sydney.

[6]   Starzyk, J.A. (2012) Motivated Learning for Computational Intelligence. In: Information Resources Management Association, Ed., *Machine Learning*: *Concepts, Methodologies, Tools and Applications* (3 *Volumes*), IGI Global, Hershey, 120-146.

[7]   Oudeyer, P.-Y., Kaplan, F. and Hafner, V. (2007) Intrinsic Motivation Systems for Autonomous Mental Development. *IEEE Transactions on Evolutionary Computation*, **11**, 265-286. http://dx.doi.org/10.1109/TEVC.2006.890271

[8]   Berlyne, D.E. (1960) Conflict, Arousal and Curiosity. McGraw-Hill, New York. http://dx.doi.org/10.1037/11164-000

[9]   Schmidhuber, J. (1991) Curious Model—Building Control Systems. *Proceedings of the International Joint Conference on Neural Networks*, Singapore City, 18-21 November 1991, 1458-1463.

[10] Markou, M. and Singh, S. (2003) Novelty Detection: A Review—Part 1: Statistical Approaches. *Signal Processing*, **83**, 2481-2497. http://dx.doi.org/10.1016/j.sigpro.2003.07.018

[11] Markou, M. and Singh, S. (2003) Novelty Detection: A Review—Part 2: Neural Network Based Approaches. *Signal Processing*, **83**, 2499-2521. http://dx.doi.org/10.1016/j.sigpro.2003.07.019

[12] Shi, Z.Z. (2011) Intelligence Science. World Scientific, Singapore City.

[13] Cox, M. (2005) Metacognition in Computation: A Selected Research Review. *Artificial Intelligence*, **169**, 104-141. http://dx.doi.org/10.1016/j.artint.2005.10.009

[14] Laird, J.E., Newell, A. and Rosenbloom, P.S. (1987) SOAR: An Architecture for General Intelligence. *Artificial Intelligence*, **33**, 1-64. http://dx.doi.org/10.1016/0004-3702(87)90050-6

[15] Birnbaum, L., Collins, G., Brand, M., Freed, M., Krulwich, B. and Pryor, L. (1991) A Model-Based Approach to the Construction of Adaptive Case-Based Planning Systems. *Proceedings of the DARPA Case-Based Reasoning Workshop*, Morgan Kaufmann, San Mateo, 215-224.

[16] Cox, M.T. and Ram, A. (1999) Introspective Multistrategy Learning: On the Construction of Learning Strategies. *Artificial Intelligence*, **112**, 1-55. http://dx.doi.org/10.1016/S0004-3702(99)00047-8

[17] Leake, D.B. and Wilson, M. (2008) Extending Introspective Learning from Self-Models. In: Cox, M.T. and Raja, A., Eds., *Metareasoning*: *Thinking about Thinking*, AAAI Press, Palo Alto, 143-146.

[18] Eriksen, C. and St James, J. (1986) Visual Attention within and around the Field of Focal Attention: A Zoom Lens Model. *Perception & Psychophysics*, **40**, 225-240. http://dx.doi.org/10.3758/BF03211502

[19] Baddeley, A. (2000) The Episodic Buffer: A New Component of Working Memory? *Trends in Cognitive Sciences*, **4**, 417-423. http://dx.doi.org/10.1016/S1364-6613(00)01538-2

[20] Shi, Z.Z., Wang, X.F. and Yue, J.P. (2011) Cognitive Cycle in Mind Model CAM. *International Journal of Intelligence Science*, **1**, 25-34. http://dx.doi.org/10.4236/ijis.2011.12004

[21] Shi, Z.Z., Zhang, J.H., Yue, J.P. and Qi, B.Y. (2013) A Motivational System for Mind Model CAM. *AAAI Symposium on Integrated Cognition*, Virginia, 15-17 November 2013, 79-86.

[22] Saunders, R. and Gero, J.S. (2002) Curious Agents and Situated Design Evaluations. In: Gero, J.S. and Brazier, F.M.T., Eds., *Agents in Design*, Key Centre of Design Computing and Cognition, University of Sydney, Sydney, 133-149.

[23] Li, Q.Y., Shi, J. and Shi, Z.Z. (2005) A Model of Attention-Guided Visual Sparse Coding. *Proceedings of IEEE International Conference on Cognitive Informatics*, Irvine, 8-10 August 2005, 120-125.

Permissions

List of Contributors

Mohamed Shenify and Fokrul Alom Mazarbhuiya
College of Computer Science, Albaha University, Albaha, Saudi Arabia

M. Shenify and F. A. Mazarbhuiya
College of Computer Science and IT, Albaha University, Albaha, Saudi Arabia

Necmettin Firat Ozkan and Emin Kahya
Department of Industrial Engineering, Eskisehir Osmangazi University, Eskisehir, Turkey

Ron Cottam and Roger Vounckx
The Living Systems Project, Department of Electronics and Informatics, Vrije Universiteit Brussel (VUB), Brussels, Belgium

Willy Ranson
IMEC vzw, Leuven, Belgium

Qiang Xu, Zhengquan Xu and Tao Wang
State Key Laboratory of Information Engineering in Surveying, Mapping and Remote Sensing, Wuhan University, Wuhan, China

Juyang Weng
Department of Computer Science and Engineering, Michigan State University, East Lansing, MI, USA
School of Computer Science and Engineering, Fudan University, Shanghai, China

Tielin Zhang, Yi Zeng and Bo Xu
Institute of Automation, Chinese Academy of Sciences, Beijing, China

Tielin Zhang
University of Chinese Academy of Sciences, Beijing, China

Ning Ning, Wei He, Li Pan and Kiruthika Ramanathan
Data Storage Institute, Agency for Science, Technology and Research, Singapore

Luping Shi and Guoqi Li
Department of Precision Instrument, Tsinghua University, Beijing, China
Center for Brain-Inspired Computing Research (CBICR), Tsinghua University, Beijing, China

Kejie Huang and Rong Zhao
Singapore University of Technology and Design, Dover, Singapore

Edna Márquez, Jesús Savage and Ron Leder
Facultad de Ingeniería, Universidad Nacional Autónoma de México, México D.F., México

Jaime Berumen and Ana Espinosa
Unidad de Medicina Genómica, Hospital General de México, México D.F., México

Christian Lemaitre
Departamento de Ciencias de la Comunicación, Universidad Autónoma Metropolitana, México D.F., México

Ana Lilia Laureano-Cruces
Departamento de Sistemas, Universidad Autónoma Metropolitana, México D.F., México

Alfredo Weitzenfeld
Department of Computer Science and Engineering, University of South Florida, Tampa, FL, USA

Kun Yue, Mujin Wei and Weiyi Liu
Department of Computer Science and Engineering, School of Information Science and Engineering, Yunnan University, Kunming, China

Feng Wang
Yunnan Computer Technology Application Key Lab, Kunming University of Science and Technology, Kunming, China

Zilong Xu, Kaifu Yang and Yongjie Li
Key Laboratory for Neuroinformation of Ministry of Education, School of Life Science and Technology, University of Electronic Science and Technology of China, Chengdu, China

Jun Miao
Key Laboratory of Intelligent Information Processing of Chinese Academy of Sciences(CAS), Institute of Computing Technology, CAS, Beijing, China

Lijuan Duan
Beijing Key Laboratory of Trusted Computing, Beijing Key Laboratory on Integration and Analysis of Large-Scale Stream Data, College of Computer Science and Technology, Beijing University of Technology, Beijing, China
National Engineering Laboratory for Critical Technologies of Information Security Classified Protection, Beijing, China

David M. W. Powers
School of Computer Science, Engineering & Maths, Flinders University of South Australia, Adelaide, South Australia

Jili Gu
Beijing Samsung Telecom R&D Center, Beijing, China

Laiyun Qing
University of Chinese Academy of Sciences, Beijing, China

Jose Israel Figueroa-Angulo and Jesus Savage
Biorobotics Laboratory, Universidad Nacional Autonoma de Mexico, Mexico City, Mexico

Ernesto Bribiesca
Computer Science Department, Universidad Nacional Autonoma de Mexico, Mexico City, Mexico

Ron Leder and Boris Escalante
Electrical Engineer Department, Universidad Nacional Autonoma de Mexico, Mexico City, Mexico

Luis Enrique Sucar
Computer Science Department, Instituto Nacional de Astrofisica, Optica y Electronica, Puebla, Mexico

Anne T. Galante
Department of Computing Systems, SUNY Farmingdale State College, Farmingdale, USA

Wenfang Cheng and Jie Zhang
Polar Research Institute of China, Shanghai, China
Key Laboratory for Polar Science, State Oceanic Administration, Shanghai, China

Qing'e Wu
School of Computer Science, Fudan University, Shanghai, China
College of Electric and Information Engineering, Zhengzhou University of Light Industry, Zhengzhou, China

Xiao Cheng
College of Global Change and Earth System Science, Beijing Normal University, Beijing, China

Zhuanling Song
The First Institute of Oceanography, SOA, Qingdao, China

Zhiwu Chen and Qing E. Wu
College of Electric and Information Engineering, Zhengzhou University of Light Industry, Zhengzhou, China

Qing E. Wu and Weidong Yang
School of Computer Science, Fudan University, Shanghai, China

Jia Xu, Patrick Shironoshita, Nigel John and Mansur Kabuka
Department of Electrical and Computer Engineering, University of Miami, Coral Gables, USA

Ubbo Visser
Department of Computer Science, University of Miami, Coral Gables, USA

Zhongzhi Shi, Gang Ma, Xi Yang and Chengxiang Lu
Key Laboratory of Intelligent Information Processing, Institute of Computing Technology, Chinese Academy of Sciences, Beijing, China

Gang Ma
University of Chinese Academy of Sciences, Beijing, China

Chengxiang Lu
School of Information Science and Engineering, Qufu Normal University, Rizhao, China